Four-Hole Br.
Red Bank
Sullivan's Fy.
Walterborough
Parker's Fy.
Horseshoe Br.
Ashepoo R.
CHARLESTON
Rantowles Br.
St. Andrews Ch.
Adams Run
Church Br.
Rugby's Br.
Legareville
Blue House
Ashepoo Fy.
Willstown
Combahee Fy.
Garden's Corners
Port Royal Fy.
Rockville
Edisto Island
Prampton's Inlet
Bay Pt.
Bird I.
ST HELENA SOUND
Egg Bank
Port Royal I.
St. Helena I.
Fripps Inlet
Pritchards Inlet
Ft. Beauregard
PORT ROYAL ENT.
Ft. Walker
Hilton Hd.
Spring I.
Bull I.
Braddock's Pt.
Bloody Pt.
ANTIC OCEAN

WANDERING TO GLORY

WANDERING TO GLORY

Confederate Veterans Remember Evans' Brigade

Edited by

DEWITT BOYD STONE JR.

UNIVERSITY OF SOUTH CAROLINA PRESS

Published in Columbia, South Carolina, by the
University of South Carolina Press

Manufactured in the United States of America

06 05 04 03 02 5 4 3 2 1

Library of Congress Cataloging-in-Publication Data

Wandering to glory : Confederate veterans remember Evans' Brigade / edited by DeWitt Boyd Stone, Jr.
p. cm.
Includes bibliographical references and index.
ISBN 1-57003-433-8 (cloth : alk. paper)
1. Confederate States of America. Army. Evans' Brigade. 2. Evans, Nathan George, 1824–1868. 3. United States—History—Civil War, 1861–1865—Regimental histories. 4. South Carolina—History—Civil War, 1861–1865—Regimental histories. 5. United States—History—Civil War, 1861–1865—Personal narratives. 6. South Carolina—History—Civil War, 1861–1865—Personal narratives. 7. Veterans—South Carolina—Biography. 8. Soldiers—South Carolina—Diaries. 9. Soldiers—South Carolina—Correspondence.
I. Stone, Dewitt Boyd.
E577.4 .W36 2001
973.7'457—dc21 2001006914

Endsheets: Map of coastal South Carolina (*Atlas to Accompany the Official Records*, Plate CXLIV). Map of North Carolina and South Carolina (*Campaigns of the American Civil War: Atlas*, Plate 5).

This book is dedicated to the memory of my great-grandfather,
First Lieutenant John Francis Stone,
Company D, Eighteenth Regiment,
Evans' Brigade,
who enlisted December 4, 1861,
was captured at the Battle of the Crater, and
was paroled on June 14, 1865, from Fort Delaware Prison.

Contents

Illustrations

PREFACE

Evans' Brigade included the Seventeenth, Eighteenth, Twenty-second, Twenty-third, and Twenty-sixth Regiments of South Carolina Volunteers, the infantry regiment of the Holcombe Legion, and also the Macbeth Artillery. It involved over eighty-three hundred men during the course of its existence; however, almost nothing has been written about this unit or its colorful commander. At the end of the war most of the survivors went home to scratch out a living from the ground, and those who were literate had little time for writing. Brigadier General Nathan George Evans was not able to write his own memoirs, because he was ill at the war's end and he died in 1868. Brigadier Generals William S. Walker, Stephen Elliott Jr., and William H. Wallace led the brigade during the final year of the war, but none of them wrote their memoirs. It is my purpose to weave together the accounts of the veterans, along with selected items from the letters and diaries of the soldiers, and a few items from military records and established reference works, in order to portray the history of Evans' Brigade of South Carolinians from the viewpoint of the men who served.

A word about available sources is in order: The process of writing the book, *Wandering to Glory: Confederate Veterans Remember Evans' Brigade*, has occupied my spare time for the better part of ten years because there is so very little primary source material available.

Around the turn of the century, reunions of Confederate veterans became popular events, and a number of the men of Evans' Brigade put pen to paper to record the histories of their units and their own experiences in the war. Many of these accounts were printed in booklet form by local job printing shops for distribution to other survivors and family members, or published in local newspapers. The accounts of Captain William H. Edwards (Company A of the Seventeenth South Carolina Volunteers), Rev. Albert Allison James (chaplain of the Eighteenth South Carolina Volunteers), Captain John Floyd and the Committee on History of the Darlington Rifles (Company I of the Eighteenth South Carolina Volunteers), Rev. Silas Pinckney Holbrook Elwell (Twenty-third South Carolina Volunteers), Private George R. Jones (Company I of the Twenty-third South Carolina Volunteers), Private Welborn J.

Andrews (Company K of the Twenty-third South Carolina Volunteers), Lieutenant Colonel Joshua Hilary Hudson (Twenty-sixth South Carolina Volunteers), Captain B. Lewis Beaty (Company K of the Twenty-sixth South Carolina Volunteers), and Lieutenant H. F. Scaife (Macbeth Artillery) are located in various historical depositories across South Carolina. They are somewhat difficult to find, and a complete copy of one account, John Floyd's *History of the Darlington Rifles*, was rediscovered only recently. Three other personal accounts—those of William G. Stevenson, John Forrest Robertson, and William Porcher DuBose— are located in archives in other states.

The stories of these veterans contain rich descriptions of how the men followed their local leaders to war, how they fought the monotony of training and camp life, how they chased the Yankees through the swamps as they defended the South Carolina coast, how they joined the Army of Northern Virginia and lost two of their regimental commanders (one a former governor) at Second Manassas, and how many of the men "went AWOL" for a few days to visit their homes as they traveled to Mississippi to reinforce Vicksburg. Their accounts of the Battle of the Crater give a detailed view of this intense and important Confederate victory, which some historians say prolonged the war by a year. Four of the writers (DuBose, Elwell, Andrews, and Hudson) were wounded and/or captured in various campaigns, and their personal stories are included in some detail because they give interesting insights into Civil War medical care and prison life. Although General Evans' continuing difficulties with his peers and superiors is noted, he is not the major theme of this work.

The fact that these accounts are written from the perspective of the soldiers, rather than from the perspective of the generals, makes them particularly interesting reading today. Captain Edwards put it very well when he wrote, "The glory of war is very different in theory than in practice." It is to be assumed that the veterans put the best face on the activities of their units, the courage of their compatriots, and the gallantry of their leaders; a number of tall tales must certainly be included. Each account is incomplete, because the writer focuses upon those events that were of particular interest to himself, his company, or his regiment. Taken together, however, the veterans' accounts furnish a fairly complete story of the activities of the brigade from its formation in Charleston in July 1862 to its surrender at Appomattox in April 1865.

Diaries and letters to family and friends provide a more accurate portrayal of events than recollections that were written twenty to thirty years later for public, rather than private, audiences. However, only a small number of the letters and diaries written by the men of Evans' Brigade are preserved in public archives. By an approximate calculation—taking the literacy rate (perhaps

75 percent) and attrition (each regiment shrank from about one thousand men in early 1862 to about one hundred at Appomattox) into account, and assuming that each literate soldier wrote six letters home each month—we can estimate that the men of the six regiments probably wrote more than sixty-five thousand letters home during the three and one-half years that these regiments existed. I was, however, able to find only about five hundred letters written by about forty-five different men. It would have been very useful to have a larger number of personal letters and diaries. They might have even changed the image of Nathan George "Shanks" Evans, the unit's colorful commander for most of the war.

All information in chapters 2 through 16—except for my remarks, which are printed in bold type—is taken from the sources indicated in the bibliography. The accounts and letters have been edited very sparingly, primarily to correct typesetting errors, to omit passages that are not relevant, or to improve punctuation. Particularly interesting and important passages have been quoted unchanged, and this is indicated by the use of quotation marks; otherwise no attempt has been made to document the exact wording of the original sources. I have chosen the most interesting accounts of each event for inclusion and have arranged these accounts in chronological order. Excerpts from the accounts of the veterans are not footnoted, because most of these accounts do not have numbered pages. Each writer is identified at the beginning of each passage, using the highest military rank achieved while serving with the brigade.

My approach has been to construct a story framework based upon the veterans' accounts and then to find every possible letter, diary, or military report in order to verify the accuracy and completeness of the veterans' accounts. I seek to reach battlefield visitors, Civil War enthusiasts, and persons interested in state, local, and family history. My goal is to provide an interesting account —a "good read" for the general reader. I hope that this goal has been achieved.

ACKNOWLEDGMENTS

I wish to thank the following for their assistance: Alexander Moore of the University of South Carolina Press, who provided guidance and encouragement to a novice author. Tracy Power of the South Carolina Department of Archives and History, who provided very good advice from the viewpoint of an accomplished Civil War historian.

Allen Stokes and Beth Bilderback of the South Caroliniana Library at the University of South Carolina, for their professional assistance on many occasions.

Jane Yates at The Citadel Archives, Annie Armour at the University of the South Archives, and Phillip Stone at the Wofford College Archives. Special Collections staff members at Auburn University, Clemson University, Duke University, the Medical University of South Carolina, and the University of North Carolina (both at Chapel Hill and at Charlotte).

John Bigham of the South Carolina Confederate Relic Room, Chris Calkins of the Petersburg National Battlefield Park, Mike Cavanaugh of the Civil War Library and Museum, and John Coski of the Museum of the Confederacy.

Debbie Roland of the Calhoun County Museum, Horace Rudisill of the Darlington County Historical Society, Hurley Badders of the Pendleton District Historical Society, Allan Charles of the Union County Museum, and Samuel Thomas of the York District Historical Society.

William L. Kinney Jr. and Gray Bostick of the *Marlboro Herald-Advocate*.

Judy Bainbridge of Furman University, for helpful discussions regarding McCollough, DuBose, Stevens, and other nineteenth-century leaders in the Episcopal Church in South Carolina; Earl Hess of Lincoln Memorial University; Roger Grant, Ernest M. "Whitey" Lander Jr., Len McCall, and Tom Parks of Clemson University, and Sam Davis of Lander University, for helpful discussions about writing and history.

Descendants of veterans of Evans' Brigade: Harold S. Boozer of Sumter, South Carolina, Charles D. Cox of Huntsville, Alabama, David Felder Huffman of St. Matthews, South Carolina, Carlos and Cynthia Moseley of Spartanburg, South Carolina, Celeste Phillips of Charleston, South Carolina,

Edward D. Sloan of Greenville, South Carolina, and Laura N. Vardell of Charleston, South Carolina.

Carlanna Hendrick, who shared her research notes on the Evans family, and Mike Wadsworth of First Corps Books, who found obscure books as required.

Colleagues at Clemson University: Jo Ann Koonce, who converted the original veterans' accounts to typescript, and Carl Helms, who skillfully edited many of the digital images.

Most of all, my wife, Carolyn Varner Stone, whose Varner ancestors from the Spartanburg District fought alongside mine, and whose patience during this writing has already exceeded the length of the war.

DeWitt Boyd Stone Jr.

Introduction

Brigadier General Nathan George Evans, the brigade's leader throughout most of the war, was brave, intelligent, and decisive, but he could also be difficult and arrogant. His tactical military skills were considerable, but his interpersonal skills were minimal. He was much too fond of liquor and was always accompanied by his Prussian orderly, who bore on his back the famous "barrelita" containing a gallon of whiskey.

Evans became a hero early in the war when he led a "demi-brigade" of South Carolina and Louisiana troops with great skill at First Manassas. He literally saved the day for Beauregard, who wrote in his official report, "It is fit that I should in this way commend to notice the dauntless conduct and imperturbable coolness of Colonel Evans . . ." A few months later he led a brigade of Mississippi and Virginia troops to victory at Ball's Bluff near Leesburg, Virginia, and the resulting public acclaim led Governor Pickens to ask that Brigadier General "Shanks" Evans be returned to South Carolina to assist in the defense of his native state. For a few months Evans commanded coastal defense districts just south of Charleston. He was then placed in command of a newly formed brigade that included South Carolina's Seventeenth, Eighteenth, Twenty-second, and Twenty-third Regiments, the Macbeth Light Artillery, and the infantry companies of the Holcombe Legion. (The Twenty-sixth Regiment of South Carolina Volunteers would be added to Evans' Brigade in 1863.) The brigade's first assignment was to the Army of Northern Virginia.

Since this was an independent brigade and not permanently assigned to a particular army, it traveled very widely, fighting at Second Manassas, South Mountain, Sharpsburg, Kinston, Jackson, Charleston, Petersburg, and Five Forks, and its extensive travels soon gave it the nickname "The Tramp Brigade." In the late spring of 1864 its wanderings brought it to the trenches around Petersburg, Virginia. Specifically, the brigade occupied Elliott's Salient, under which Federal troops from the Pennsylvania coalfields were preparing a tunnel filled with explosives. When this mine was detonated at 4:44 A.M. on July 30, 1864, hundreds of the men of the brigade went to glory, and the remainder found themselves in one of the most glorious and furious battles of the war—the Battle of the Crater. After the war, the brigade's veterans would claim that they, not Mahone's Virginians, "saved the day" at this important battle. Many historians feel that a Federal victory at the Battle of the Crater would have shortened the war by a year.

Following the Battle of the Crater, the brigade spent eight miserable months in the trenches at Petersburg. It fought at Five Forks on April 1, 1865, and then retreated with Lee's army to the surrender at Appomatox.

WANDERING TO GLORY

1

Nathan George "Shanks" Evans

> Goodbye, Shanks, I suppose that they will make you a general.
>
> Robert E. Lee

The South Carolina brigade that is the subject of this book was officially Evans' Brigade from its organization on July 17, 1862, until May 28, 1864. Brigadier General Nathan George Evans was its leader from its formation until he was injured in a buggy accident in Charleston on April 16, 1864.

Nathan George Evans was from a large and prominent old South Carolina family.[1] His great-great-grandfather, John Evans, came from Wales and England to Delaware in the early eighteenth century, and John's son, Nathaniel Evans, migrated to the Pee Dee region of South Carolina in the 1730s. Nathaniel's grandson, Thomas Evans (1790–1845), first engaged in the mercantile business and was later a cotton planter. He held local office, served in the state senate, and was a presidential elector for James Madison and again for Andrew Jackson. He and his wife, Jane Beverly Daniel, had thirteen children. This relatively prosperous family educated its children well, and the ten who survived to adulthood included two graduates of The Citadel Academy,[2] two graduates from medical school, and one each from William and Mary, the South Carolina College (now the University of South Carolina), the United States Military Academy, and the United States Naval Academy. In addition, two sons "read law" and were admitted to the bar.

Nathan George Evans, the fourth child of Thomas and Jane Evans, was born in 1824. He was educated at Marion Academy and then attended Randolph-Macon College. Upon receiving an appointment to the United States Military Academy from John C. Calhoun, who was a friend of his father, he continued his studies there. A fellow student, John C. Tidball, recalled Evans: "Well do I remember the orating of one N. George Evans, a wimble-jointed youth from South Carolina, a typical scion of his sunny clime, who from his knock-kneedness was dubbed 'Shanks' Evans. With his vehemence he downed every adversary and ever sought among his more silent companions new fields in which to press his conquests."[3]

Shanks graduated thirty-sixth of thirty-eight cadets in the class of 1848.[4] His first military assignment was to the First Dragoons, which was active in Indian fighting on the western frontier. Indian fighting seemed to suit Shanks' character very well, and in early 1855 he was one of the officers handpicked by Secretary of War Jefferson Davis for the new Second Cavalry. This unit was organized at Louisville, Kentucky, and then at Jefferson Barracks, Missouri, under Colonel Albert S. Johnston and Lieutenant Colonel Robert E. Lee. From late 1855 until 1861, the unit was stationed in Texas, with frequent forays into the Comanche Nation territory to the north. Historians of the cavalry during this period portray Shanks as a popular but fiery member of this unit.[5] Copies of a number of very friendly and personal letters from Robert E. Lee to "Captain N. G. Evans" survive from this period.[6] All of these sources report Evans' fondness for whiskey.

The Comanches, in addition to raiding the white settlers, preyed upon neighboring tribes. In one such incident in October 1858, Shanks killed two Comanche Indians in hand-to-hand combat in the Battle of Wichita Village. In recognition of his valor, the General Assembly of South Carolina awarded him a "handsome sword."[7]

In 1860, Nathan George Evans married Ann Victoria Gary of Cokesbury, South Carolina. Her family also extended back to the colonial period in South Carolina. Her father, Thomas Reeder Gary, was a physician and planter who served as a member of the General Assembly and also as a director of the Columbia and Greenville Railroad. Thomas and his wife, Mary Porter Gary, had ten children. Two of their four daughters married men who would become Confederate officers, and all six sons served as officers during the war. One son, Martin Witherspoon Gary, claimed the rank of major general.[8]

In February 1861, upon receiving the news of South Carolina's secession, Nathan George Evans resigned his commission in the United States Army. Robert E. Lee told him as he left Texas, "Goodbye, Shanks, I suppose that they will make you a general."[9] Leaving his post in Texas, Evans traveled to Montgomery, Alabama, where the Confederate Congress was in session, and sought an appointment in the Confederate forces. An appointment was not forthcoming. Evans then proceeded to South Carolina, where he obtained an appointment as major in the South Carolina Army. During the bombardment of Fort Sumter, he served as adjutant general on the staff of Brigadier General Richard G. M. Dunovant, commander of the South Carolina forces, who later reported that he was pleased with Evans' performance.

Finally, in early May 1861, the Confederate War Department, after many requests from Evans and letters of support from Dunovant and Beauregard, appointed him as a captain of cavalry. On May 20 he was promoted to major and ordered to Virginia.[10] There Beauregard gave him the assignment of

Captain Nathan George Evans, U.S.A.
(courtesy of Virginia Historical Society)

Major Evans, C.S.A. (at left) and others inspecting Fort Sumter
(*Atlas to Accompany the Official Records*, Plate CXXI, no. 4)

taking the Fourth South Carolina Regiment to reinforce the Confederate defenses at Leesburg. A few weeks later Evans brought the Fourth South Carolina Regiment back to Manassas, and Wheat's Louisiana Battalion, a small squadron of cavalry, and two smoothbore cannons, were added to his command to form a "demi-brigade."

Shanks Evans and his "demi-brigade" were among the heroes of the First Battle of Manassas, the first major battle of the war.[11] General P. G. T. Beauregard's battle plan called for the forces of his right flank to make the main attack toward Centreville. Evans and his troops were placed at the extreme left end of the Confederate line and ordered to defend the Stone Bridge, which carried the Warrenton Turnpike over Bull Run Creek. Evans hid his troops and artillery in the woods overlooking the creek and the bridge. He placed skirmishers in front of his line, so he was not surprised by the Federals when they began firing across the creek near the Stone Bridge at daybreak on July 21, 1861. Evans' troops patiently received the enemy's fire while holding their own in order to conceal their location and the small size of their unusual unit. After an hour of this, it seemed to Evans that Federal General Robert C. Schenck and his Ohio troops did not intend to cross Bull Run Creek but were simply holding him in position. Then one of Evans' cavalry pickets from the left flank brought word that other Federal units were moving to ford the creek upstream at Sudley's Ford to turn the left end of the Confederate line. At the same moment, Evans received a message from Edward Porter Alexander, stationed in a nearby signal tower: "Look out for your left. You are flanked."[12] Leaving two cannons and four companies of the Fourth South Carolina Regiment to defend the bridge, Evans quickly swung his remaining troops to the left and placed them on Matthews Hill, overlooking the road from Sudley's Ford. Again he hid his troops in the woods and awaited the Federals. Shortly after 9 A.M. two full brigades of Yankee troops appeared. Evans' demi-brigade of fewer than two thousand men held them off, alternately defending and attacking for nearly an hour. Beauregard said in his official report that "Evans and his men had maintained their stand with an almost matchless tenacity." Additional Federal troops arrived, and General Barnard Bee and Colonel Francis Bartow brought up additional troops to reinforce Evans' unit. By mid-morning, approximately twenty-eight hundred Confederates were desperately holding off nearly thirteen thousand Federal troops.

By 10:30, Beauregard had finally become aware that the enemy had the initiative. He realized that the battle would be fought on his left, and he abandoned his original plan to have the right wing of his line attack Centreville. Unfortunately, by then Evans, Bartow, and Bee were being overwhelmed and driven back from Mathews Hill across the Warrenton Turnpike to Henry Hill. Again, from Beauregard's official report: "For an hour did these stout-hearted men of the blended command . . . breast an unremitting bullet-storm, animated surely by something more than the ordinary courage of even the bravest men under fire." By late morning, the Hampton Legion of South Carolinians had arrived to assist at the left end of the Confederate line, and additional help was on the way. By noon, however, General Irvin McDowell's Federal line was sufficiently reinforced to begin what he assumed would be a final and victorious assault on Henry Hill. It was now that General Thomas J. Jackson arrived with his brigade of Virginians. Bee consulted with him and then went to lead the Fourth Alabama Regiment, which had lost all of its officers, back into the battle. As he rallied his men, Bee spoke those words—the exact quote has been debated ever since—which gave "Stonewall" Jackson his famous nickname. The hard fighting continued until late in the afternoon, when additional reinforcements led by Jubal Early and Kirby Smith secured the Confederate victory. Evans' small unit of approximately thirteen hundred men lost twenty men who were killed and 129 who were wounded, but his competent field leadership and their willingness to fight had probably saved the Confederates from defeat. Beauregard reported: "It is fit that I should in this way commend to notice the dauntless conduct and imperturbable coolness of Colonel Evans."[13] General Bee was killed in this battle, and Evans would later name his third child Bernard Bee Evans in his honor.

Two months later James Pelot, a South Carolina soldier who served in another unit and who evidently knew the Evans family, wrote the following to his sister in Cokesbury, South Carolina. Pelot refers to Nathan George Evans' mother, who had been killed in an accident, and then gives an interesting view of the character of "General" Nathan George Evans:

> I am very sorry to hear of the death of Mrs. Evans. She was an excellent lady and bid fair to live many years longer. That reminds me of the General . . . On the matter of whiskey, our officers are exceedingly strict, and justly so. Our Colonel will not allow a drop to come into camp if he can prevent it. The men have all bound themselves to him not to bring it in without the consent of their Captains, and consequently we have the soberest regiment in the service . . . General Evans is not so particular on the subject. When he was retreating from this point to Bull Run a day or two before the battle, he urged his men to pack up fast (for the Yankees were in sight) and told them to burn their trunks and all such heavy trash, "but," says he, "if you have any light baggage, such as barrels of whiskey or so, throw it into the wagons and get away from here" . . . He told me that there was no use for other Generals to brag about what they did in that battle—that he inaugurated that fight, he and General Bee fought it through, and he and Bee whipped the fight before any reinforcements came; and that all the reinforcements had to do was to make the Yankees run the faster . . . Another remark he made, though highly irreverent, was certainly true and more modest. He said that "the fight was really won by God Almighty and a few private gentlemen."
>
> Now don't let the people in Cokesbury hear these things, for his folks would accuse me of lying. But to tell the truth, if Nathan is the bravest and best General in the C.S. if not the world, he is at the same time about the best drinker, the most eloquent swearer (I should say voluble) and the most magnificent bragger I ever saw. Still I would rather be under him than this Jones of ours, who is not only a coward but a fool in the bargain.[14]

Following the First Battle of Manassas, Evans was temporarily promoted to colonel and given command of the Seventh Brigade in Beauregard's First Corps. This brigade consisted of the Thirteenth, Seventeenth, and Eighteenth Mississippi Infantry, the Eighth Virginia Infantry, three companies of Virginia cavalry, and the First Company Richmond Howitzers. Again, General Beauregard placed Shanks Evans' troops at the extreme left flank of his army, this time with orders to keep watch on the fords and ferries of the Potomac River between Point of Rocks, Maryland, and Edward's Ferry.

Federal troops under General Charles P. Stone had the same task on the Maryland shore. About two miles east of Leesburg, Evans' men constructed a small earthworks that he called Fort Evans and utilized as his headquarters. From mid-August until mid-October, Evans' and Stone's forces watched each other across the Potomac. Sometimes the opposing pickets became so neighborly that they would converse across the river and even declare a local truce in order to wade over to talk and swap food and other items. Stone's commander, George McClellan, was being criticized for his inaction, and the phrase "all quiet along the Potomac" become a joke at his expense in Washington. A Federal spy told General McClellan that Evans commanded twenty-seven thousand men in the Leesburg area, and he worried that the Confederates might attack across the river and move on toward Baltimore. To counter this threat, McClellan sent George McCall's division to occupy Dranesville, about twelve miles southeast of Leesburg, and suggested to General Stone: "Perhaps a slight demonstration on your part would have the effect to move them." On October 20, 1861, Stone sent Willis Gorman's brigade to make a demonstration at Edward's Ferry near Leesburg, and late that night he sent a small scouting force under Captain Chase Philbrick across the river at Ball's Bluff. Hoping to confuse Evans with these diversions, Stone planned to turn the enemy's left flank by moving a larger force across the Potomac River at Smart's Mill Ford, where the river was shallow enough so that a crossing would not require boats.

From this point onward, the Federals made a series of blunders. First, Evans was able to discount the threat from McCall because the Confederates captured a courier carrying dispatches from McCall to Meade. Second, Philbrick's scouts reported spotting the "tents of an enemy camp," which later proved to be haystacks at a distance. General Stone reacted to Philbrick's report by ferrying four hundred men across the Potomac River at Ball's Bluff, where the river was fairly deep and swift, to attack the "camp." Colonel Charles Devens left Colonel William R. Lee and two companies at the bluff and proceeded to the Confederate "camp" at daybreak. He discovered Philbrick's error, sent a report back to Stone, and hid his men in the woods to await reinforcements. Unfortunately for him, the Federal crossing had not gone unnoticed. Devens' troops were soon under attack by Company K of the Seventeenth Mississippi Regiment, and they retreated back to join Colonel Lee at Ball's Bluff. The third Federal blunder was General Stone's decision to send reinforcements across the Potomac at Ball's Bluff via small boats, rather than using the shallow ford a short distance upriver at Smart's Mill, where a large number of soldiers could have quickly waded across.

In contrast to Stone, Shanks Evans managed his resources skillfully. In many ways he faced the same general enemy strategy that he faced at First

Manassas. He rebuffed a Federal thrust at Edward's Ferry and maintained a defense there while redeploying some of the troops from his right at Burnt Bridge on the Leesburg Turnpike to assist on his left at Ball's Bluff. There his Mississippi troops held the higher ground, and they trapped Devens' troops and a large reinforcing force under Colonel Baker—a sitting United States senator who unfortunately had little military experience. The river effectively blocked any Federal retreat. By late evening the bluff was in Confederate hands, although a few Federal soldiers still remained uncaptured along the riverbank. On the next day, October 22, 1861, the Thirteenth Mississippi Regiment applied pressure to the Federal troops that had made a crossing at Edward's Ferry, and they withdrew to the Maryland shore. Overall, the Confederate losses (killed, wounded, captured, and missing) at the Battle of Ball's Bluff were 155 of 1,709, and the Federal losses were 921 of 1,720 infantry participating.[15]

Although there were conflicting reports of his role in leading his troops at Ball's Bluff,[16] Evans was praised by the Confederate Congress, the secretary of war, and the state of South Carolina. He was promoted to brigadier general and placed in command of the Fourth Brigade at Leesburg, Virginia, under General Edmund Kirby Smith's Fourth Division.

Meanwhile, Federal naval forces were preparing to attack South Carolina. General P. G. T. Beauregard had been in charge of strengthening the coastal defenses since early spring, but when the fall came he lost his principal labor force as the planters recalled their slaves to harvest the rice crop. Much remained to be done. On November 5, upon receiving word that a Federal invasion fleet of fifteen men-of-war and thirty-six transports carrying over twelve thousand troops was approaching Port Royal Sound, Jefferson Davis created the new military Department of South Carolina, Georgia, and Florida and sent General Robert E. Lee to command it. The sound was the first major harbor north of the Savannah River, and the surrounding area included Hilton Head Island and the town of Beaufort. Lincoln's advisors felt that this would be a good base of operations for blockading Confederate shipping and for the siege of Charleston. Lee arrived on November 7 just as the Federal fleet was subduing Fort Walker and Fort Beauregard and occupying that area. There was panic in Charleston. After the fall of Port Royal, many of the sea islands soon fell into Federal hands, and Lee focused his attention upon defending the vital Charleston and Savannah Railroad.[17]

Gov. Francis W. Pickens of South Carolina now asked Jefferson Davis for the transfer of General Evans so that he might assist in the defense of his home state. Davis wrote to the governor on November 29 that "Generals Evans and Pemberton will be sent to General Lee immediately." Some of Evans' troops and associates were sorry to see him go, but some criticized

Brigadier General Nathan George Evans, C.S.A.
(courtesy of Oakley Park Historic Home, Edgefield, S.C.)

his drinking and general cussedness.[18] On December 18, Evans reported to General Lee in South Carolina. He was given command of the Third Military District of South Carolina, located just south of the city of Charleston between the Stono and Ashepoo Rivers. Troops initially assigned to the Third Military District were the Sixteenth (Colonel Elford's) and the Seventeenth (Colonel Means') Regiments and the Third Battalion of South Carolina Volunteers. On December 24 Lee reported: "General Ripley writes that Elford's and Means' regiments are poorly armed and equipped and at present ineffective, and that the organization of the troops thrown forward on

James Island is so brittle that he fears that it will break."[19] These were newly formed units that were still in South Carolina, rather than Confederate, service.

Two months later, Lee wrote to Evans regarding his general strategy for defending the coast and the need for cooperation among the different military districts: "It will be impossible to find sufficient troops to garrison the whole line of the coast and all that can be done is to ascertain the points of attack, concentrate the troops in the district to meet the advance of the enemy, and if unable to drive him, to hold him in check until reinforcements can be forwarded from other districts."[20]

Meanwhile, the regiments which would be assigned to Evans' Brigade were being recruited and trained. Some of them would soon serve under Evans in the coastal defense effort. The flaws in Evans' character would become increasingly evident.

2

ORGANIZING AND TRAINING THE BRIGADE

> The glory of war is very different in theory than in practice.
>
> William H. Edwards

This was a war in which brothers, cousins, and neighbors from a particular community or district went off to war together, and the companies of Evans' Brigade represented at least twenty-five of the thirty South Carolina districts which existed in 1861.[1] Because the veterans' accounts were written at the turn of the century, some thirty to forty years after the war, the writers often refer to men or companies from particular "counties." To be precise, however, there were no counties in South Carolina until the new Constitution of 1868 changed the designation of each political subdivision from "district" to "county."

The basic organizational unit of the Confederate army was the company of approximately one hundred men. A prominent man in a community would call for volunteers to form a company, and they would usually elect him as their captain. Ten such companies made a regiment, which would be commanded by a colonel. Four to six regiments, with the addition of a cavalry unit and an artillery unit (all usually from the same state) constituted a brigade, commanded by a brigadier general. Early in the war, an entire regiment might be formed of companies from the same district. However, by 1862 a South Carolina regiment would be assembled in Columbia or Charleston by combining companies that had arrived at the training camp from a number of different districts. Three of the regiments of Evans' Brigade—the Seventeenth, Eighteenth, and Twenty-second—were formed by combining companies from communities across the state.

The formation of a company of men from Yorkville was described by Samuel Lowry, who began by introducing himself.[2] Samuel and his neighbors would become Company F of the Seventeenth Regiment:

The Company to which I belonged was called The Carolina Rifles, commanded at that time by my uncle, Captain William B. Wilson, and having also in command First Lieutenant J. W. Avery (another uncle of mine), and Second Lieutenants D. J. Logan and R. H. Whisonant. Our company consisted of 100 men from the York District, all as stout and hardy a set of men as ever left the peaceful firesides of home to meet the foul oppressor. I had joined lacking two months of my 17th year, having obtained the consent of my parents, after worrying them and begging them, and having two uncles in the company. My company left Yorkville on the 27th day of November, 1861, and proceeded from there by railroad to the Camp of Instruction at Columbia, on the College Grounds.

We proceeded to the Camp College Green at Columbia, South Carolina, where we remained for a week drilling. I had been for two years a pupil at the Kings Mountain Military Academy, and being well-drilled I was kept busily employed in assisting to drill the Company. This being our first camping ground and this being then something new, we had our fun sitting around the camp fires, cracking jokes, and telling tales.

After staying here a week we moved out of Columbia to Camp Hampton, five miles distant, on the plantation of the now celebrated Brigadier General Wade Hampton. We encamped on an open field which was formerly a race course. We set up camp in the rain, which was then pouring down in torrents, and got a thorough wetting. We soon pitched our tents, and building some cheerful fires, we soon got dry and comfortable. While staying at this, one of our most pleasing camps, I spent my time most agreeably, playing our camp games and living on boxes from home filled with substantial food such as meat and bread which we cooked on our camp fires and ate with unusual appetites.

I may as well here name my mess-mates and the faithful servants who attended us through all our hardships. My mess-mates were the Captain and three Lieutenants, also W. H. Moore, and W. B. Byers. Captain Wilson's servant and head cook was named Dick, Lieutenant Avery's servant was named Noah, a stoutly built Mulatto, full of fun and as faithful as the day is long. My boy was called Horace; he was about 40 years of age, and one of the best and most faithful negroes, who I later had the misfortune to lose to a disease contracted in camp. So you see, we were well waited on. These boys added a great deal to our amusement by telling their wonderful tales, and singing songs around the camp fires at night.

To return to my story. The spot on which we were encamped was bordered on one side by large ponds, known as the Hampton Ponds. In these ponds, I sometimes went duck hunting, finding plenty of the feathered tribe but they were extremely wild. One day, having better luck than usual, I succeeded in killing two very large Dock O Mallards, from which we had a royal feast prepared by the skillful hands of our cooks. My uncle and I went several times to hunt them, sometimes with success. I fished some in these ponds, but it was too late in the year and consequently I failed to catch any.

While at this camp we spent our time mostly drilling and performing the duties of camp. It was here also that our Regiment was organized, officers elected, etc.

The combining of ten companies from various districts to form the Seventeenth Regiment of South Carolina Volunteers was described in 1906 by William H. Edwards of Chester, South Carolina.[3] He had been the captain of Company A, and he wrote a history of the regiment at the request of the daughter of Colonel McMaster:

Some of the companies composing the regiment gathered at Camp Hampton, in the City of Columbia, about the middle of November 1861. We first organized a battalion and elected [former Governor] J. H. Means, Lieutenant-Colonel, and F. W. McMaster, Major, with the understanding that as soon as we could secure the requisite companies to form a regiment, Means was to be Colonel and McMaster to be Lieutenant Colonel. In a few days the necessary number of companies had joined us, the two above-named officers were promoted, and Julius Mills of Chester County was named Major. The companies were as follows: Company A, Captain J. R. Culp, of Chester County; Company B, Captain Preston Coleman, of Fairfield County; Company C, Captain John A. Witherspoon, of York County; Company D, Captain James Beaty, of Chester County; Company E, Captain Thomas Meacham, of York County; Company F [the Carolina Rifles described above by Samuel Lowry], Captain W. B. Wilson, of York County; Company G, Captain James Sanders, of Barnwell County; Company H, Captain Rice, of Barnwell County; Company I, Captain Caskey, of Lancaster County; Company K, Captain Lucian Sadler, of York County. The companies of the regiment were mustered into service by General Preston, of the Confederate War Department. However, the regiment was mustered in as State Troops, the men having volunteered for twelve months' service.

In 1888, in an address to the Survivors of Fairfield County, Colonel Edward McCrady Jr. gave this character sketch of the colonel of this regiment:[4]

"Governor Means . . . had constantly advocated secession. But when it came he was an elderly man, beyond the age even of reserve duty. With his age, too, his physique had become such as to unfit him for the field. The dignity of his position as an ex-governor of the State would seem to have excused him had his age and physical condition fitted him for active service. His family, too, were fully represented in the army. All these conditions might well have persuaded him that the proper sphere of action was at home where, by

John Hugh Means
(courtesy of United States Army Military History Institute, Fitzhugh McMaster Collection)

his countenance, he might have encouraged his people in their adversities and by his wisdom have aided them in their necessities. So he might have reasoned, if indeed he had felt himself called upon to reason at all, why he, a man advanced in life, should not go into the field. But so he did not reason. He reasoned on the contrary, thus: I have been advocating secession all my life; by my conduct I have done much to bring it about; now it has come, age or not, I will myself go with them and share the dangers to which the boys have been brought by my advice."

Captain Edwards recalled how his regiment was outfitted with weapons and uniforms in Charleston:

About the middle of December the regiment was sent to Charleston and went into camp on the south side of the Ashley River bridge. There the men were armed with old British muskets that had been changed from the old flintlock to percussion locks. Eight of the companies were armed with these antiquated guns, but the right and left companies, A and E, were given new English made Enfield rifles that had been run into Charleston through the blockade. No better guns than these were used in either army during the war, and these companies carried and used them to the end of the struggle. There we also drew our uniforms, gray jackets and black pants, with blue stripes up the outside seams of the pants. I will always remember how proud the boys of Company A were with their new guns and uniforms. By the way, these were the only uniforms the men ever received during the war. They were good clothes and lasted about a year, and after they were worn out the men wore whatever kind and color of clothes they could get, except blue or black. Most of us despise a blue uniform until this day.

We named this, our first camping place, "Camp Lee." For the information of the young generation of South Carolinians, I will say that General R. E. Lee was then in command of the defenses of the South Carolina and Georgia seacoasts. It is a matter of history that some of the prominent citizens of this territory petitioned President Davis to send to this department a better general. He replied that he did not have a better one, and in his judgment there was not a better one in the United States. So much for that.

Early in the previous November, the day before a Federal flotilla captured Port Royal and Hilton Head, President Davis had sent Lee to strengthen the coastal defenses between Charleston and Savannah. Governor Pickens was critical of the choice of commanders because of Lee's recent defeats in West Virginia, but Davis informed Pickens that he had full confidence in Lee. Less than four months later, on March 2, 1862, President Davis would ask General Lee to come to Richmond to be his principal military advisor.[5]

Captain Edwards continued his account:

While in this camp the measles broke out among the men, resulting in many fatalities in the regiment. Company A lost eight fine young men from the effects of this disease from Christmas, 1861, to March, 1862. It was at this camp that Colonel Means first took command of the regiment, the Lieutenant Colonel having had charge of it up to that time. Dr. William Wylie was commissioned Surgeon, and R. H. Jordan, Assistant Surgeon of the regiment, both of Chester County. We remained at Camp Lee until about the 1st of February, 1862, when we were moved to John's Island, and were camped on John's and Wadmalaw Islands doing camp and picket duty and drilling.

The glory of war is very different in theory than in practice, and many changes took place in the personnel of the commissioned officers. By this time the war cloud had thickened and was growing darker, and the new-born courage of some men was on the wane. They were looking back with a longing desire towards the ease and comforts of home life with Catie and the baby.

The men had enlisted initially as state troops and for a twelve-month period, but in April 1862 the Confederate Congress passed the two conscription acts

that called every able-bodied white male between eighteen and thirty-five into Confederate service for three years or for the duration of the war. These acts allowed the older men to resign and also provided for the men to elect their officers. As Captain Edwards noted, the latter proved to be a mixed blessing:[6]

On the 22nd day of May, 1862, on John's Island, the regiment was reorganized for Confederate service. Colonel J. H. Means and Lieutenant Colonel F. W. McMaster were re-elected. Stark Means, who left the army in Virginia and who was a son of the Colonel, defeated Julius Mills, of Chester, for Major. Up to this time Stark Means had not been a member of the Seventeenth Regiment. Mills was a strict disciplinarian and a fine drill officer, but the men did not like to be under him as a drill officer, and they were afraid he might become Colonel of the regiment, as they knew he would require them to chalk the line. I had been Orderly Sergeant and was now elected First Lieutenant; John Waters was re-elected Second Lieutenant, and Joseph Nunnery was elected Brevet Second Lieutenant. John R. Culp was re-elected Captain of Company A from Chester County. Culp, being the senior captain of the regiment was given the letter A and the right of the regiment. Preston Coleman was re-elected Captain of Company B from Fairfield County. John A. Witherspoon was re-elected Captain of Company C from York County. James Beaty was re-elected Captain of Company D from Chester County. J. C. Holley was elected Captain of Company E from York County, Dr. Meacham retiring from the service. J. W. Avery was elected Captain of Company F from York County, W. B. Wilson retiring from the service. William Dickinson was elected Captain of Company G, Captain Sanders retiring from the service. H. M. Ray was elected Captain of Company H, Captain Rice retiring. Both of these last named companies were from Barnwell County. James Steele was elected Captain of Company I from Lancaster County, Captain Caskey retiring. E. A. Crawford was elected Captain of Company K from York County, Captain Lucian Sadler retiring. I will not attempt to give the names of the Lieutenants of the companies after so many years, for while I remember them all and also their names, I would now get mixed as to their rank. Some of their names, however, will figure in this narrative—some of them as Captains and some in other positions. James W. Connor, formerly Brevet Second Lieutenant of Company A, from Chester, was appointed Adjutant; Isaac Means, Quartermaster; and Walter B. Metts, Commissary.

In early June the Yankees became troublesome about Legareville on John's Island, and captured a couple of Confederate soldiers who were on picket. Our regiment was ordered on the Island and remained there several days. On the march towards Legareville a small body of cavalry was retreating at full speed, being chased by a superior force of Yankee cavalry. A small squad of our men who were in front passed the Seventeenth Regiment (some of the companies of which had fallen out of the road, some on the right and some on the left), and shouted, "The Yanks are just behind us." Our men construed this to mean that no more of our cavalry was in their rear. This was not the case for there was another squad of our cavalry behind them that had not been so precipitate in their flight. The Seventeenth Regiment at that time were not veteran soldiers and were very eager to shoot Yankees, and were so sure they now had the opportunity that they opened fire on this last squad of about two dozen of our own cavalry men and killed several of them and mortally wounded two or three others. Lieutenant W. G. Stevenson, who afterwards became Captain of Company D, was badly wounded in this unfortunate affair. The Yankee cavalry had halted and gone back, and before the regiment could march to Legareville these enterprising and heroic warriors had taken shipping and left the Island.

It was either at the return to camp from this march or some other march about this time when the regiment had formed in line (which was done before breaking ranks), when Captain Holley, of York, fell dead, of heart failure.[7] He never spoke or breathed after he struck the ground. He was a fine officer and an educated Christian gentleman. E. R. Mills then became the captain of Company E. We returned to Rantowles and remained a few days, and while there James F. Buist, of Barnwell, was appointed Chaplain of the regiment. He served in that capacity until after the Second Battle of Manassas, when he retired. He was then quite a young man, but was a splendid preacher, and a consecrated Christian man. In later life he became a man of great prominence and usefulness in the Barnwell Association. Up to that time the Seventeenth Regiment had been without a Chaplain, but not altogether without religious services. We often had song and prayer services, conducted by Christian men of the different companies. Captain Witherspoon held prayer meetings in his own company, and we were first attracted to James F. Buist by hearing him conducting religious exercises in the companies from Barnwell. These Barnwell companies were remarkable for the large number of Christian men among them, the majority of them being members of the Baptist Church, and they were not ashamed to let people know they were Christians, but gloried in their religion. The first captain of Company G was a Baptist preacher, and was at least forty-five years old. He was of sterling integrity and great force of character. R. W. Sanders, who was for many years pastor at Chester, was his nephew.

The regiment was then moved a few miles further down the railroad, towards Adams Run. While at this camp we took two trips to Pocotaligo, both times trying to get a fight with some roving bands of our Northern cousins, whose disposition to meddle with other people's property and to appropriate the same to their own use would bring them out into the country on marauding expeditions. Their instinct of self-preservation was wonderfully operative in giving us leg bail. We had five or six regiments, besides several companies of cavalry and several batteries of artillery. Some six or eight thousand men were hungry for a fight with these uninvited visitors to our shore, but in every instance they acted upon the principle that prudence is the better part of valor. At another time three regiments of the brigade were thrown across the river after night on Jehossee Island and camped for an hour or two in Governor Aiken's negro village. Soon, however, a courier came with orders for us to return. I guess if we had hunted diligently for it we could have got the long hoped for fight by remaining on the Island, as we learned afterwards that the Yankees had a strong force on the Island and occupied a splendid position to withstand an attack, but we had no artillery, and no way to take it with us. In coming back the tide was down and the boat could not get near the shore, the gang planks were sunk in the mud, and many of us would miss the planks and get stuck thigh deep in the nasty slimy salt water slush. My oh my, but we had a dandy time that night. To compensate us for the loss of sleep, a hard march and getting stuck in the mud, our thoughtful, tender-hearted[8] General N. G. Evans had sent us down a barrel of whisky, which was issued in water buckets with tin cups to drink it out of. I recollect singing that night:

Gie him strong drink until he wink,
That's sinkin in despair.
In liquor gude to fire his blude,
When prest wi grief and care;
Then let him bouse in deep carouse
In bumpers flowing o'er,
Till he forgets his loves and debts
And minds his griefs no more.

Many years after the war, Private Dock Owen of the Holcombe Legion wrote of the soldiers' fondness for whiskey in his book, *Campfire Stories:*[9]

We had two men in our company that never drank, John Pinson and Jesse Lomax. Two of the boys caught on and after they got their share come back with a cup each and told Captain Smith these men were broke down and wanted theirs. He told me to let them have it. Captain Smith was getting gentlemanly groggy. The boys saw a chance to lay in a supply, and when we were busy would call for Pinson and Lomax's ration. Finally Captain Smith said "Durn Pinson and Lomax. I have sent whiskey enough to Company F to kill a mule and they still want more." The boys had half a gallon each.

Peter Fayssoux Stevens
(courtesy of The Citadel Archives and Museum)

The process of forming the Twenty-third and Twenty-sixth Regiments of South Carolina Volunteers differed from the more common process of combining companies from scattered districts as outlined above. Each of these units was first organized as a battalion (having fewer than the ten companies required to constitute a regiment) for coastal defense—the future Twenty-third for the defense of the coast near Charleston and the future Twenty-sixth for the defense of the coast of the Pee Dee region of South Carolina. In each of these two units, most of the companies came from a regional grouping of districts.

James H. Trapier, South Carolina's chief of ordnance who had helped to construct the defenses of Charleston harbor, wrote on July 6, 1861, to C. G. Memminger, a South Carolinian who was C.S.A. Secretary of the Treasury: "I cannot but in the strongest terms express my approval for the project originated by Colonel L. M. Hatch for organizing a corps (say 200 men) whose duty it shall be to keep a watch upon the movements of the enemy hovering upon the coast and give speedy notice to our different outposts, and thence

to Head Quarters should he appear in larger force at any time or make any demonstrations toward effecting a landing—whether upon any of the islands, or through the creeks, upon the Main . . ."[10] He goes on to say that mounted scouts were not useful when the enemy is at sea but that Hatch planned for his men to scout using boats and oars. Four companies were soon organized, and the unit became known as "Hatch's Coastal Rangers." This unit eventually grew to become the Twenty-third Regiment of South Carolina Volunteers.

Corporal John Forrest Robertson later recalled the organization of Hatch's Battalion:[11]

I enlisted for the war in Company A, "Bee Rifles," Hatch's Battalion, which was made up of Companies A, B, C, and D and which did service on James Island. Colonel Hatch, when getting together his battalion, advertised in the Charleston papers: "Parents do not fear putting your boys in my charge. They will be morally, mentally, and physically brought up." I can not say much about our advance in morals and mind, but plenty of strenuous work we had to do, rowing boats, etc.

While stationed on James Island, each company was required to perform out-post duty on Folly island, watching the enemy's fleet off Charleston Bar, and to prevent if possible the landing of troops. When the attempt to obstruct Charleston Bar with stone-laden vessels was made by the Yankees—that fact being unknown to us—Company A happened to be on Folly Island. I was one of the squad detailed for duty at the beach on that eventful night. When we reached the beach, from indications that we saw, a supposed large fire burning on the beach, we concluded that the enemy was certainly making a landing. We surely were about to have our first taste of war. The whole company was immediately called to arms, war paint put on, and all hands made ready to meet the onslaught of the enemy, if on investigation by two of the officers said enemy did not appear too numerous. In that event a signal resembling the screech of an owl was to be given. Two of the boys that were with the beach patrol came rushing in, declaring as a fact that the Yanks were landing on the beach in surf boats. Oh, how we wished to hear the signal. As the island was inhabited by many species of that bird, we did not have to wait very long. Quickly did we beat a retreat to the back beach, taking our places in the boats and awaiting orders to pull for the friendly shore of James Island.

The whole scare turned out to be a false alarm. There was no enemy on the island, and the supposed fire on the beach was a calcium light on one of the vessels to aid the enemy in their devilish work, attempting to block up Charleston's entrance with old vessels' stone-laden hulls.

In the spring of 1862 . . . companies from the interior of the state were added to the Battalion, making up the Twenty-third Regiment of South

Carolina Volunteers with H. L. Benbow, colonel; John Roberts, lieutenant colonel; J. M. Whilden, major; Dr. Michel, surgeon; and Reverend John L. Girardeau, chaplain.

The formation of Smith's Battalion was described in 1903 by Judge Joshua Hilary Hudson of Bennettsville.[12] This unit evolved into the Twenty-sixth Regiment, and Hudson became its lieutenant colonel:

In the fall of 1861, General W. W. Harlee of Marion, Brigadier of the State Militia, at the request of prominent citizens and with the sanction of Governor Pickens, undertook to raise a force for the defense of that part of the State watered by the Great Pee Dee River and its tributaries. Volunteers were called for, and an encampment located at Centenary Campground, in the present county of Marion. A considerable force of infantry, with a fair complement of cavalry and artillery, was here collected and organized into companies, battalions, and regiments; and the whole styled the Pee Dee Legion.

In the winter of 1861–62 these troops were moved from Centenary and concentrated at and near Georgetown, S.C. A battalion of seven companies, under the command of Lieutenant Colonel Nesbitt, was stationed at Camp Lookout, on the Waccamaw Neck. On his staff were Dr. L. C. Hasell, surgeon, Captain Wright, commissary, and Major Thomas Holmes, quartermaster. Having organized his legion, General Harlee promptly tendered his service and legion to President Davis. But being Lieutenant Governor of the State, a member of the Executive Council and also of the State Convention, he was urged by President Davis and also by the civil authorities of the State to continue in civil service, where he had already proved himself indispensable. To this advice he yielded, although his taste and inclination were in the military line. Early in 1862 the troops composing the Pee Dee Legion were, under act of Congress and at the call of the President, mustered into Confederate service as volunteers for one year, not as a legion under their favorite brigadier general, W. W. Harlee, but as distinct commands destined for wide separation and varied experience. Under the reorganization thus rendered necessary, Captain Alexander D. Smith, of Marlboro, was chosen Lieutenant Colonel of the Battalion of seven companies commanded as State troops by Lieutenant Colonel Nesbitt. Captain R. D. F. Rollins, of Darlington, was chosen Major; Joshua H. Hudson, a private in the company of J. A. W. Thomas, 21st S.C.V., was appointed Adjutant; Dr. Louis C. Hasell, surgeon, and Samuel J. Townsend, of Marlboro, quartermaster. Thus reorganized, the battalion was mustered into Confederate Service for one year at Camp Lookout, Waccamaw Neck, in March, 1862. We were then ordered to Charleston, and there placed in camp at Magnolia Cemetery.

The Act of Congress called the Conscript Act was enacted in April or early May of 1862. By this act, all soldiers between the ages of eighteen and thirty-five years already in service for a shorter period were required to be mustered in for the whole period of the war, and all within the prescribed age not in service were called in. Under this Act our battalion stationed at Magnolia was reorganized and a reelection of officers resulted in the choice of A. D. Smith, lieutenant colonel, and J. H. Hudson, major; Dr. Louis C. Hasell was appointed surgeon; John A. McRae, quartermaster; Benjamin F. Miller, a lieutenant of a Chesterfield company, adjutant; and F. W. Emanuel, of Marlboro, sergeant-major.

In 1886, an officer writing under the pen name "VIDI" (probably Lieutenant H. F. Scaife of Union) wrote a series of articles about the Macbeth Light Artillery for his local newspaper. He gave this account of its organization:[13]

The happy thought of raising an Artillery Company and naming it in honor of one of Union's most popular sons, was a stroke of policy that led to the organization of the Macbeth Light Artillery. The company, however, was not made up exclusively of men from Union County. Spartanburg, Laurens, and Chester each contributed handsomely to its organization, and Camden and Charleston were both represented. However, all the commissioned and most of the non-commissioned officers were taken from Gadberry's old company [which had served out its six-month tour of duty in Gregg's First South Carolina Regiment]. With a complete organization, we quietly left Union on the 12th of November, 1861, and on the evening of the same day went into South Carolina's Camp of Instruction at Lightwood Knot Springs, seven miles north of Columbia on the Charlotte and Columbia Railroad. We found several newly-organized regiments already there, and interspersed among them were men from Gregg's old command who, with cadets from the Citadel, were busy preparing these raw troops for "a place in the picture near the flashing of the guns." At first we had no cannon, and our drilling was confined exclusively to the infantry tactics. In the course of time, we received a brace of superannuated guns, worth just as much, however, for learning the details of artillery drill as if they had been brand new pieces out of the molds with the latest improvements. We maneuvered around with these ancient-looking guns, the commands now ringing in our ears—"load by detail," "load, one, two, three, four, sponge," and "men to the front," and "men to the rear" until the drill became as monotonous as a protracted summer drought is to a croaking farmer. We ought to have been proficient soldiers in the details of artillery tactics, for in addition to the one duty of drilling day in and day out, our camp was situated in the midst of a barren waste of glaring white sand, and there was nothing of interest, so far as I never knew, in the surrounding country to divert us from our military duty.

We were the last troops ordered from Lightwood Knot Springs, and when the order came for us to go to Charleston, the welkin was made to ring with acclamations of joy. On arriving at Charleston, the company went into camp at Half Moon Battery in the northeastern suburbs of the city and overlooking the confluence of the Cooper River. Our surroundings were vastly improved, and we enjoyed some of the spice of life. Variety was added to our diet, books and daily newspapers to our scanty reading matter, and some whole-soul patriotic citizens living contiguous to Half Moon Battery shared with us their noble hospitality. The kindness and consideration shown us by the Nowell and Manigault families will ever remain, like an oasis in the desert, fresh in the memory of the officers of the Macbeth Light Artillery. The change from the sand hills north of Columbia to Charleston, where attractions were numerous and whiskey and sweethearts convenient, was of such a demoralizing tendency that a more rigid discipline became necessary. However, I have never seen a discipline so exacting or sentinels so vigilant that a man thirsty for a drink—or that which is more laudable, to see his sweetheart—that the drink was not found and the sweetheart not seen . . .

A short time after going into this camp we were furnished with a battery of six guns, and Lieutenant Starks W. Porter was immediately dispatched to upper South Carolina to buy horses for it. He returned in a few weeks with a choice lot of horses . . . Drilling with horses was more exciting and interesting than the detail and practice of firing stationary guns. Our drilling was more animated and we were enthusiastic over the changes for awhile. The inconvenience of going a mile to the race course for the purpose of drilling made it necessary to move our camp there. Then our drills were much more frequent and much longer . . . One afternoon, General Ripley, commander of the post, and several other officers put in an appearance to witness our drill. Our proficiency drew from them words of commendation, which was to us, in a measure, some justification of the good opinion we had of the Macbeth Light Artillery.

A final word about the organization of Confederate military units: One of the units of Evans' Brigade was the Holcombe Legion. A legion was a "small army," usually consisting of infantry, cavalry, and artillery units. Most often a legion would be organized, financed, and led by a single person—for example, the Hampton Legion led by Colonel Wade Hampton, the wealthy South Carolina planter. Hampton trained his legion at Hampton's Race Course on his family's land, a few miles outside of Columbia. A number of the regiments of Evans' Brigade were later trained at "Camp Hampton."

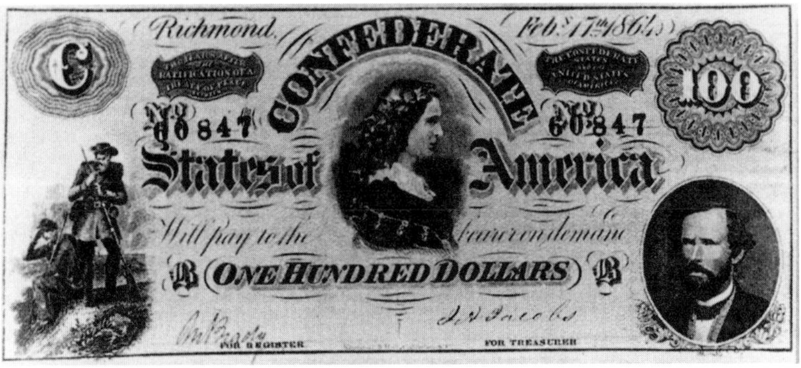

Lucy Holcombe Pickens' likeness on a Confederate $100 bill
(courtesy of South Caroliniana Library)

The Holcombe Legion was organized by Peter Fayssoux Stevens, who had been the superintendent of The Citadel Academy of the South Carolina Military Academy. In October 1861, he had resigned from The Citadel to enter the ministry, and he had been ordained and assigned to Trinity Parish at Black Oak in the Charleston District. Soon afterward, the enemy took Port Royal, and the invasion of the state seemed imminent. Stevens offered his services to Gov. Francis W. Pickens, who authorized him to raise a legion of infantry, cavalry, and artillery. The governor's wife, Mrs. Lucy Holcombe Pickens, was present when the governor asked Stevens what name should be given to the legion. Mr. Stevens replied, bowing toward Mrs. Pickens, "The Holcombe Legion." Both the governor and his wife smiled and accepted the name.[14] Lucy Pickens may have personally assisted in raising funds and in publicizing the recruiting effort for the Holcombe Legion. She designed the unit's flag, which featured the palmetto, the crescent, and the motto, "It is for the brave to die, but not to surrender." She placed the star of Texas, her native state, on the reverse.[15]

The Holcombe Legion included an infantry regiment and a cavalry battalion, but the authorized artillery unit was never added.[16] Six of the ten companies of infantry were raised in the Spartanburg District, at least partly through the efforts of Rev. John DeWitt McCollough, who was a personal friend of the governor and his wife. McCollough became the legion's first chaplain. The Holcombe Legion assisted in the defense of Charleston until the summer of 1862, when it was assigned to Evans' Brigade. Soon after the brigade reached Richmond the legion's cavalry battalion was separated and assigned to the defense of the city. The infantry and cavalry forces of the Holcombe Legion never served together again.[17]

Pvt. Dock Owen later paid tribute to the legion's namesake:[18]

I was present on the stand at Adams Run when Mrs. Pickens presented the large blue silk banner to the Legion. Our Colonel P. F. Stevens introduced her, and she made a fine talk. There was an entire brigade to hear her. The officers escorted her about the camp, where we were cooking our dinner of beef and corn bread, she taking a keen interest in our fare, our tents, and how we slept. Seven companies marched to the station to see her off, fired an infantry salute, and gave her many cheers. God bless her, we all loved her.

By the late spring of 1862, all of the regiments that would soon comprise Evans' Brigade (with the exception of the Twenty-sixth, which was still a battalion) had been formed and were serving in the Charleston area. The Seventeenth and the Holcombe Legion were serving in the military district commanded by Evans, and he was receiving mixed reviews from his men.[19] **The Eighteenth, Twenty-second, and Twenty-third were in the next district to the north, which included Charleston.**

At this time, early in the war, Federal forces occupied Port Royal, sixty miles southwest of Charleston, and the sea islands from Hilton Head Island to John's Island. James Island, the only remaining island between John's Island and Charleston harbor, was now threatened. If the enemy could take James Island and occupy it in force, it could shell Charleston from less than one mile away and could control the harbor.[20] **The defenses of James Island were relatively new and relatively weak, and since January the Confederates had been building additional fortifications there. Perhaps the strongest fortification was an earthwork known as the Tower Battery, which had been proposed and begun by Colonel Hatch near the small settlement of Secessionville** [21]**. (The name apparently had nothing to do with the state's secession, as the settlement was established years before as a fishing retreat where the young men "seceded" from their local plantation families during the summers.)**

Lieutenant Colonel Hudson described the situation at Secessionville:

Later in May, 1862, the Federals began landing troops on James Island with a view of approaching the city of Charleston from that direction. Smith's Battalion was ordered to Secessionville, an important point on James Island, defended by a battery and short line of earthworks across the narrow tongue of land by which it was approached from the coast side. This battery was small and crude, and mounted with one long rifled cannon, one Columbiad, and one mortar.[22] It was manned by two companies of Lamar's Artillery supported by Smith's Battalion and the Seventh Battalion of Infantry, under command of Lieutenant Colonel P. C. Gaillard of Charleston. The two units were in camp at Secessionville, two hundred to three hundred yards to the rear. For several weeks these infantry commands of Gaillard and Smith did vigilant picket duty by day and night in the direction of the Legare and Grimball residences, where the Federals were posted in force, whilst other troops watched and skirmished with the enemy on other parts of the Island.

On the 10th of June there occurred in sight of us on the margin of the woods next to Grimball's a spirited engagement between a Georgia regiment and the Federals, but with no decisive result except to ascertain that a strong force lay on the banks of the Stono River at Grimball's. One company of Smith's Battalion was absent at Mount Pleasant on detached duty, but a working party of two companies of the 22nd S.C.V. were sent over shortly before June 16, 1862, and stationed with Colonel Lamar's Artillery in the earthworks.[23]

Having established a strong land battery about a mile in our front and to the left, the enemy unmasked about the 14th of June and commenced shelling Secessionville.[24] On Sunday, the 15th, all the guns of this battery opened upon the works at Secessionville, and throughout the day the battery and the exposed camp of infantry were subjected to an incessant cannonade, but with nominal loss. At night the firing ceased and the harassed Confederates sank to rest, little dreaming of the bloody conflict of the coming morn.

Brigadier General Johnson Hagood of South Carolina wrote in his memoirs:[25]

At 4 A.M. they had advanced upon that work with, according to their own account, two brigades of infantry and three companies of artillery, numbering in all 3337 men under the command of General I. I. Stevens. Moving swiftly and noiselessly upon the picket, they succeeded in capturing some of them and the rest fled without firing a gun. The gallant Lamar had been superintending all night the operations of a working party, and exhausted had fallen asleep on the parapet. Aroused by the sentinel over the guns, he discovered the enemy at the heels of his picket, not fifty yards from him. With no time to give an order, he pulled the lanyard of a Columbiad, ready shotted with grape, and as the deadly missiles tore their way through the approaching column, the bellowing thunder aroused the garrison to the bloody work before them.

Lieutenant Colonel Hudson continued his account of the conflict:

The gallant Lamar with his artillerists, the two companies of the 22nd S.C.V., and the picket guard of the Seventh and Ninth Battalions, heroically met the first onset of the enemy with a withering fire of grape, canister, and small arms, and held them in check until the battalions of Smith and Gaillard could rush to their assistance, which was done in a surprisingly short time. The enemy were then repeatedly repulsed with great slaughter, many being slain on the parapet and at the cannon's mouth.

Baffled in this direct assault, General Benham attempted to capture our works by a flank movement, and to accomplish this dispatched General Williams with a strong force to strike our lines on the right. Fortunately, a marsh on this flank covered us so that he could not approach nearer than one hundred yards of us, nevertheless, a destructive fire was poured into us from a position at short range, completely enfilading our battery and lines. The infantry at once moved from and out of the lines, and facing the foe, returned the fire across the marsh. At this juncture the Louisiana Battalion, commanded by Lieutenant Colonel McHenry, crossed the long bridge leading to Secessionville at the double-quick, and speedily aligning themselves along the marsh confronting Williams, opened upon his forces a fire so deadly as soon to put him to flight. This event was also hastened by the appearance of other troops under the command of Generals Hagood and Evans, which in turn threatened him in the flank and rear. Williams command suffered severely, and with difficulty escaped capture.

The battle of Seccessionville was a fierce and bloody struggle, and the conduct of all of the Confederate troops in this (to most of them) their first encounter with the enemy, was highly creditable.[26] The gallant Lamar was severely wounded in the neck, but kept his post until the victory was won. He died shortly afterwards in the city of Charleston from the effects of the wound, aggravated by fever.[27] The Federals soon thereafter evacuated the island, and during the remainder of our stay nothing noteworthy occurred, our time being occupied in training the soldiers and picketing the island.

Cpl. D. W. McLaurin, one of the color-bearers of the Twenty-third Regiment, later gave this account of the battlefield ministry of Chaplain John L. Girardeau:[28]

On the morning of June 16, 1862, I, with others of my command, was detailed to act as one of a bodyguard and as a courier for General N. G. Evans, in command of our troops in defense of James Island. Immediately after the repulse of the enemy, General Evans rode into the earthworks in order to make arrangements to meet a second assault, momentarily expected.

As we approached the rear of the work, the first thing that attracted my attention was a large number—fifty or more—of mortally wounded and dying Federal soldiers, who had been collected and placed in the excavation behind the magazine. In the midst of these, on his knees, was Dr. Girardeau offering up an earnest and eloquent prayer for these dying soldiers, so lately the enemies of all he loved. I was so moved I forgot war and the dangers incident thereto. In view of the fact that Dr. Girardeau was an ardent, if not bitter, advocate of Southern rights, this triumph of Christian virtue over human nature, this absolute forgiveness according to dying and no longer active enemies, emphasized his God-like soul and brings out in radiant light the benediction of this true disciple of the Master.

The Confederate victory at Secessionville, followed by the construction of additional forts and batteries on James Island, secured Charleston from Federal attack by land until early in 1865.

Although some of the various regiments had been involved together in the defense of Charleston for a number of months, they did not constitute a formal brigade until, on July 17, 1862, General Evans received the following order from General Pemberton: "You will proceed at once to Richmond, Virginia, in command of Means' Regiment, Seventeenth South Carolina Volunteers, Holcombe Legion,[29] Benbow's Twenty-third Regiment South Carolina Volunteers, Gadberry's Eighteenth Regiment South Carolina Volunteers, Leake's Virginia Battery, Boyce's South Carolina Battery.[30] A portion of your troops will move via Charlotte, N.C." In mid-August Goodlett's Twenty-second Regiment of South Carolina Volunteers would join Evans' Brigade at Gordonsville, Virginia.[31]

Captain Edwards of Company A of the Seventeenth Regiment described the brigade's departure from South Carolina:

About the middle of July the whole brigade was ordered to Virginia, which was glad news to the majority of us, for we were tired of sandflies, fleas and mosquitoes,[32] and prancing up and down the seacoast after a cowardly gang of thieving scoundrels who always ran away before we could get near enough to get a shot at them. On the 19th of July the Seventeenth Regiment received orders to prepare rations and get ready to move on the 21st. At that time every company in the regiment had a wagon and a team of good mules, and when we moved from one camp to another it required two or three trips with each company wagon to move our tents, cooking utensils and camp furniture. We were very rich in those days, and never knew what it was to be hungry. We turned over our wagons and teams to the Quartermasters Department at Charleston and never saw them again.

We broke camp on the 21st and were sent by rail to Charleston and thence by the Northeastern Railroad to Wilmington, N.C., thence on to Richmond, where we arrived on the 24th of July, 1862. Captain Culp got permission to go by home, which left me in command of the company. The Seventeenth and Eighteenth South Carolina Volunteers were sent by Wilmington to prevent the Fairfield, York and Chester men from stopping at home. Other regiments, whose people lived in the Pee Dee section of the State, were sent by Columbia, Chester and Charlotte. It was a dog mean trick. Scores upon scores of Chester and York County women were at the stations with baskets of provisions and clothing for their husbands, sons and brothers, only to learn that we had gone the other route and they would not get to see us. My wife and a married sister of mine had driven through the country twenty miles to Chester to meet us and to bring us something nice to eat. They knew neither my brother-in-law nor I could leave the regiment, for we were both officers. When these good women found out that the Seventeenth Regiment had gone the other way, they distributed their provisions to the soldiers of the other regiments that came by that route. My wife has often told me that on that day she was both sorry and glad—sorrowful and disappointed because she had not seen me, but glad to see how those hungry soldiers enjoyed the good victuals prepared for their own loved ones who were not there to get it. These Confederate women were pure gold. These little incidents are small matters, but they are part of the history of the Seventeenth South Carolina Regiment. Some of the women who came to those railroad towns that day, seizing this opportunity to look into the faces of their loved ones once more, went away sad-hearted and never saw them again.

At this time, in the summer of 1862, Smith's Ninth Battalion took up some of the defensive positions that had just been vacated by Evans' Brigade as it left for Virginia. Additional companies would soon arrive to allow Smith's Battalion to become reorganized as the Twenty-sixth Regiment of South Carolina Volunteers.

Lieutenant Colonel Hudson, one of the officers of the regiment, recalled its formation:

About the last of August we were ordered to report to Brigadier General Hagood at Adams Run, and were by him stationed at Church Flats, about three miles from Rantowles Station, on the Charleston and Savannah Railroad. Whilst in camp at Church Flats, in the fall of 1862, the battalion of Major S. D. M. Byrd, composed of three companies and stationed at McClellanville, was consolidated with Smith's Battalion of seven companies, and thus was formed the 26th Regiment S.C.V. Here we remained in camp, doing picket duty and keeping watch over the movements of the enemy's vessels on the coast, until the spring of 1863.

Lieutenant Colonel A. D. Smith was promoted to the office of Colonel, and Major J. H. Hudson to the office of Lieutenant Colonel, it being a regulation of the army that upon the consolidation of two commands, the officer of the larger will be promoted over one of equal rank in the smaller. Captain C. D. Rowell, of Marion, being the senior captain, was promoted to the office of major upon the resignation of Major Byrd.[33] Captain T. E. Dudley was appointed commissary, being at that time on duty as a private in Virginia in the 8th S.C.V.

The Twenty-sixth Regiment remained in the area south of Charleston for the next year, defending the city, the coast, and the Charleston and Savannah Railroad. One of the soldiers, D. J. Blanton, related this humorous story in a letter to his family on November 16, 1862:

". . . the eaving that I got back to campe there came 2 two fine lades from Charleston as I thought riding in a two Horse Carage and a negro a driving of them and tha inquired for heade quarters and tha were invited in and it paste on very well but to my grait supris when we came to find thim out tha were Strumpets that had the inshorance to come thar to make money but some time after night tha were routed by some of the comanding oficers and tha Wente away as quick as tha could and the Drum a beating and the Boys yeling and such a fus you niver did here in all youre life you ought to have been here to heare me laff and we Just Drummed the things out of Campe and was glad"

The Twenty-sixth Regiment would be added to Evans' Brigade the following summer as it traveled from Charleston to participate in the Mississippi Campaign.

3

Skirmishes in Northern Virginia

> I have the Sharpe's rifle and the cavalry sabre of one of them to this day, keeping them as a trophy of the first Yankee killed by the Seventeenth Regiment.
>
> William H. Edwards

When Lee arrived in Richmond in March 1862, he found considerable political turmoil and a city hard at work to furnish the supplies of war to the Confederate troops. By early April, General George B. McClellan's Federal forces began landing at Fort Monroe at the end of the Virginia peninsula between the York and James Rivers, threatening Richmond from the southeast. As the Confederate defenders under General Joseph E. Johnston withdrew towards Richmond, another Federal force under General Irvin McDowell occupied Fredericksburg and seemed to threaten Richmond from the north. When Johnston was wounded in the Battle of Fair Oaks on May 31, Lee was placed in command of the Army of Northern Virginia, and a few weeks later, he successfully defended Richmond in the Seven Days Battles (June 25–July 1, 1862). These engagements were fought a few miles east of Richmond at a number of sites along the Chickahominy River and, as the enemy retreated to the southeast, at Frayser's Farm and Malvern Hill.[1] Following this series of hard battles around Richmond, Lee sought, in the words of Douglas Southall Freeman, to "rest, refit, reinforce, and reorganize the Army of Northern Virginia."[2] Drayton's and Evans' Brigades were sent from Charleston to reinforce Lee's army.

Lieutenant Lowry of Company F of the Seventeenth Regiment described their arrival in Richmond:

We were one week on the road without the occurrence of anything worth mentioning. It was near ten o'clock at night when we reached Richmond. We were formed into lines in the streets and marched directly through them, saluted by deafening cheers of the populace. The ladies looked timidly from their windows, and waved handkerchiefs and night-caps in abundance. We marched out to the race course, two miles from the city and encamped there that night without tents. Although it was raining a little, we soon got to abhor tents and would take the open air from long usage. We remained here several days, spending our time visiting the city, the theater, and the different curiosities that Richmond affords. My father came to see me here but stayed only two days and left at the same time that we got orders to move. In obedience to the order we moved seven miles from Richmond to the neighborhood of Laurel Hill.

Captain Edwards gave an account of the music at "Camp Mary":

The command remained in Richmond until the 28th of July, when we were marched on the Darbytown road, seven miles from the city, and went into camp. Colonel Means named this place "Camp Mary," in honor of Mrs. F. W. McMaster. The weather was very warm and the men had a hard time throwing up breastworks and drilling every day.

I will here relate an amusing incident that happened at "Camp Mary." There was a fine brass band, composed of splendid trained musicians from Chester, that belonged to the Sixth South Carolina Volunteers. The regiments that went into service in April, 1861, reorganized in April, 1862, as they had volunteered for only one year. At that time the Seventeenth Regiment was on the coast of South Carolina and had an ex-Governor of the State for Colonel, and this band being at that time a free lance group, tendered their services to Colonel Means. I and other men from Chester who knew the efficiency of this band begged Colonel Means to accept them. But he obstinately refused, saying he intended to train a band of his own. I told him that good material of that kind was scarce and it would take a long time to train raw material to creditable efficiency. This tender was made about the middle of January, 1862, with the understanding that they would come to us as soon as their time was out in Virginia. The Colonel absolutely and flatly refused the offer. He then went to work and detailed his men and sent to Charleston and got an old German, about a third rate musician, to teach them.[3] He was a cross old coon, but they hammered away with a poor set of instruments and got so they could play a half-dozen simple pieces that would have sounded fairly well at a negro picnic, but the band was a standing joke in the regiment. Jenkins' Brigade was camped not far from "Camp Mary," and as soon as we had gotten well settled their band came over and serenaded us. It was a magnificent band, and rendered some fine pieces of music. Colonel Means never came out of his tent; the old man was sore. Colonel McMaster tried to get him to go out and give them a speech of thanks, but he told Colonel McMaster to go himself, that he was not in the humor. So, Colonel McMaster came out and made them a nice little speech, thanked them for the entertainment, praised them for their proficiency, and told them they were an honor to the State and county and a source of great pleasure and enjoyment to the soldiers of the Confederate army. Our band when we got into the Army of Northern Virginia threw up the sponge and until the end of the war we were satisfied with Moorhouse and his kettle drum to beat reveille, tattoo and the long-roll. Colonel Means knew many things, but he knew but little of instrumental music, and the time, labor and talent necessary to proficiency in band music. Colonel McMaster enjoyed many a hearty laugh at my remarks in regard to the music ground out by the Seventeenth Regiment Band. We remained at "Camp Mary" and in that vicinity until about the 10th or 12th of August.

Lieutenant Lowry recorded an encounter near Malvern Hill:

While in camp at Laurel Hill our pickets below Malvern Hill reported the Yankees advancing, and we were marched out to meet them and oppose their further progress. The Yankees, after driving in our pickets, stopped at Malvern Hill and established themselves there, which was about seven miles from our encampment. General Longstreet determined to take the hill and for that purpose we, Evans' Brigade, were sent forward to drive in the enemy's pickets. We left camp in battle trim with three days' rations, and marched within two miles of Malvern Hill. We then deployed at two paces apart and advanced on the Yankee pickets. We marched these two miles through the thickest kind of black-jack oak woods, but the Yankee pickets, getting wind of us, fled leaving guns, ammunition, knapsacks, and everything to us. We could not remove any of this as we were still advancing on the enemy. After getting through the woods we came upon an old open field with the woods of Malvern Hill on the other side. Just as we got on the edge of the wood, it being then about dusk, our cavalryman guide spied a Yankee come galloping across the field. He deliberately got off his horse, took aim through a crack in the fence, and fired, but his gun misfired and the Yankee wheeled and rode away. The fellow belonged to the enemy's picket and not knowing that they had been driven in, thought his own men had fired at him by mistake and he rode back up the road to us. Our guide rode out in the road to meet him, and when he came up, familiarly addressed him. After holding some conversation with him, he asked the Yankee if he ever saw a Rebel. The Yankee answered, "no," and our guide then burst out in a horse-laugh, and clapping the fellow on the shoulder said, "Well, old buck, you see one now. You belong to me. Come along with me or I'll spile your bacon."

In 1911, Rev. William Porcher DuBose, then emeritus dean and professor of theology at the University of the South, recalled that he had been involved in this incident:[4]

The Federal forces were not yet entirely withdrawn from the neighborhood of Malvern Hill, near which we were encamped, and we had one or two slight brushes with them.[5] R. Y. Dwight and myself were riding some distance from the camp. Neither of us had any arms. As we rode down the road, we saw crossing the field in front of us a heavily armed cavalryman. It was too late to determine his uniform. As he reached the road we met face to face in the dark. He inquired of us if we could tell him where such and such Yankee regiment was. Of course I didn't know, but I replied that he would find it just along that road that he was going. As he turned his back on us, Dwight clapped his hand on the Yankee's shoulder and said, "You are my prisoner, sir." The man, thoroughly surprised, surrendered his carbine, pistol, sword, and self. I would have just gone on, for it was a thoroughly reckless thing to do, but Dwight did the right thing. As I had not yet secured a substitute for Archie, his horse also came in very handy.

Colonel Stevens of the Holcombe Legion was apparently the final beneficiary. He wrote to his mother on August 10:

I am now riding a captured horse, a good walker but an indifferent animal. My Adjutant and private secretary captured him and his rider.

Captain Edwards witnessed the shooting of two Yankee soldiers by his regiment:

A few days prior to the 12th our brigade was sent on a reconnoitering expedition down in the neighborhood of Malvern Hill. The object was to ascertain if the Federal army was moving. We lay on our arms all night and could hear the rumbling of their wagons and artillery from dark till day. About dusk that evening Company A killed two Yankee cavalrymen—the first Yankee soldiers killed by the Seventeenth Regiment. Our company was sent out two or three hundred yards in advance of the regiment as videttes. We were marching by flank down a public road, and were inside a field. There was an old fence grown up in bushes and brambles that somewhat hid us from view. A batch of cavalry came riding up the road and in the dusk of the evening it was difficult to recognize the uniforms, and Captain Culp was not sure they were not Confederates, and called out, "Who goes there?" and their leader replied, "Who goes there?" His voice settled his identity, and Culp quickly commanded, "Company into line," and the Yankees began wheeling their horses round. About the time a dozen of our men got into line they saw the Yankees were getting away, and they did not wait for any other command, but began to fire into them, and killed two men and two horses that were left lying in the road. These men were killed by the few men that first began to fire. Before all the company could get into line the Yankees were gone, for they were on good horses, and they used all the speed that spurs could get up. I have the Sharpe's rifle and the cavalry sabre of one of them to this day, keeping them as a trophy of the first Yankee killed by the Seventeenth Regiment. This was the first time that we had ever got in rifle range of one of them.

Welborn J. Andrews gathered eight of his compatriots together in Sumter in 1909 to assist him in writing a history of Company K of the Twenty-third Regiment S.C.V.[6] He gave this account of the brigade's next activities:

We were ordered to Malvern Hill to assist General Longstreet in his attack on the Yankees holding the hill. Reaching a spring of good water near noon (soldiers dote on good water) we rested several hours. That afternoon the Twenty-third Regiment formed in line of battle; right half-wheeled and halted. General Evans approached, and after the usual salutation, commanded Colonel Benbow (of the Twenty-third Regiment) to deploy as skirmishers, advance through a piece of woods in our front and drive the Yankees out. Just before the left wing of the regiment had winged into line, we left two men behind. Near the edge of the woods we crossed a low rail fence, and deployed as skirmishers as ordered. Before we were through the woods the right wing of the regiment (the flag or center company being the dividing line between the right and the left) became separated from the left and was in a sure-enough skirmish. Several of Company K got lost and turned up in a Mississippi regiment next morning. The flag company (Captain Seabrook), Company K, and the rest of the left wing, found no enemy in their front. We halted, and a detail was sent forward. On their return, they reported no enemy between us and the public road in front. After a rest, Edgar Murden, the senior captain, ordered our return to the spring we had left. We tried to do this, but being unfamiliar with our surroundings, we lost our bearings and were forced to remain in the woods during the remainder of the night. After sun-rise we left our impromptu couches (oak leaves for beds and oak limbs for pillows) and hastened to the temporary spring camp, no worse for sleeping in the woods. Towards noon we took the line of march for Taylor's farm, and on reaching it, occupied our old camping ground. We soon settled down as was our custom.[7]

In late June 1862, as Lee was defending Richmond, Lincoln chose John Pope to lead the newly formed Army of Virginia. Pope placed his fifty-one thousand troops on a line extending north and west from Fredericksburg to Culpeper to Sperryville. On July 13, Lee dispatched Jackson with fourteen thousand men to Gordonsville to contain Pope, and soon thereafter Jackson defeated Pope's Second Corps at the Battle of Cedar Mountain. Lee then determined to move most of his army to join Jackson in order to push northward before McClellan could bring his forces from the peninsula to join

Pope. On August 13, Lee ordered Longstreet to move ten brigades, including Evans' Brigade, from Richmond to Gordonsville via the Virginia Central Railroad. Goodlett's Twenty-second Regiment of South Carolina Volunteers was added to Evans' Brigade at Gordonsville.[8] Lee followed his troops to Gordonsville by train on August 15.[9]

Private Andrews remembered the brigade's hasty departure:

We were suddenly aroused one day out of our lethargy by the order to leave. Five days' rations were issued to each man, and two hours given to cook and be ready for departure. Every available utensil was brought into use. Flat rocks were heated on which to bake bread. He was the lucky one who secured a piece of flour-barrel head to place wheat dough on and lean it before the fire. Even ramrods were brought into use, and the famous ramrod bread was the result. The process was, viz., pull out the dough into a long strip, and wind it around the ramrod as a climbing, clinging vine encircles a bush or tree; then one end of the ramrod was stuck into the ground in a reclining or oblique position before he fire. It was necessary to turn the ramrod around during the baking that the bread may be evenly cooked brown. That all may understand our rations, I will state them in full: Beef—good, bad, and indifferent; occasionally a little bacon instead; flour and salt (coffee played out); sometimes a hard tack (a cake of flour and water minus salt and soda).

On the way to Manassas
(courtesy of Library of Congress)

While preparations for departure were being made, the orderlies (first sergeants) were busy bringing up the sick to the regimental surgeon. The sick list was very large, and many were sent to the hospitals in Richmond. Details were made to bring ammunition to the companies from the ordnance wagons, sufficient in quantity to distribute fifty rounds to each man.

The Twenty-third Regiment marched to Richmond. As soon as the dilatory authorities saw fit to get together a train of platform cars, we jumped aboard. As we journeyed along, cinders from the engine fell upon us in profusion.

In 1902, Rev. Albert Allison James, a Presbyterian minister who had been the chaplain of the Eighteenth Regiment, related this story about the coming death of Colonel Gadberry:[10]

As we were traveling by train to Gordonsville, several officers from South Carolina accompanied us, among them Colonel Means, Colonel Marshall, and Colonel Moore. Colonel Gadberry remarked that he had a presentiment that he would be killed in the first battle he got into, and asked Colonel Marshall what he should do. Marshall replied: "Do your duty and trust in your God." This remark was made by Colonel Gadberry, not because he was wanting in courage or to shirk duty, for he deserves to be ranked with a Hobson or a Dewey. When Beast Butler issued his infamous order in New Orleans, characterizing the ladies of that city as "common street walkers," he consulted with some of his friends as to the propriety of his making his way into New Orleans and shooting Butler down on sight and sacrificing his own life in vindication of the honor of the women of the South. He was anxious to put his purpose into execution, but was persuaded by his friends not to undertake it. There was not a braver man in the Confederate service than Colonel James M. Gadberry. He no doubt had, in some way unknown to mortals, been apprised of the fate that awaited him.

Private Andrews continued his account:

We landed in Gordonsville, Virginia, and there we first glimpsed General Jackson's men. Their uniforms looked like the men had been wallowing on the clay hills while wet, the clay adhering and drying. They were of medium height, their faces bronzed.

From Gordonsville we marched to Martin's Cross-roads and camped in a delightful oak grove. We were daily drilled both morning and afternoon for several hours at a time in the space of a week. One mid-afternoon the drill was speedily stopped; we were marched into camp and dismissed after receiving marching orders. Twenty-five additional rounds of ammunition were procured and distributed. The regiment left after sunset enroute for Manassas. There were quite a number of small streams crossing the road we traveled

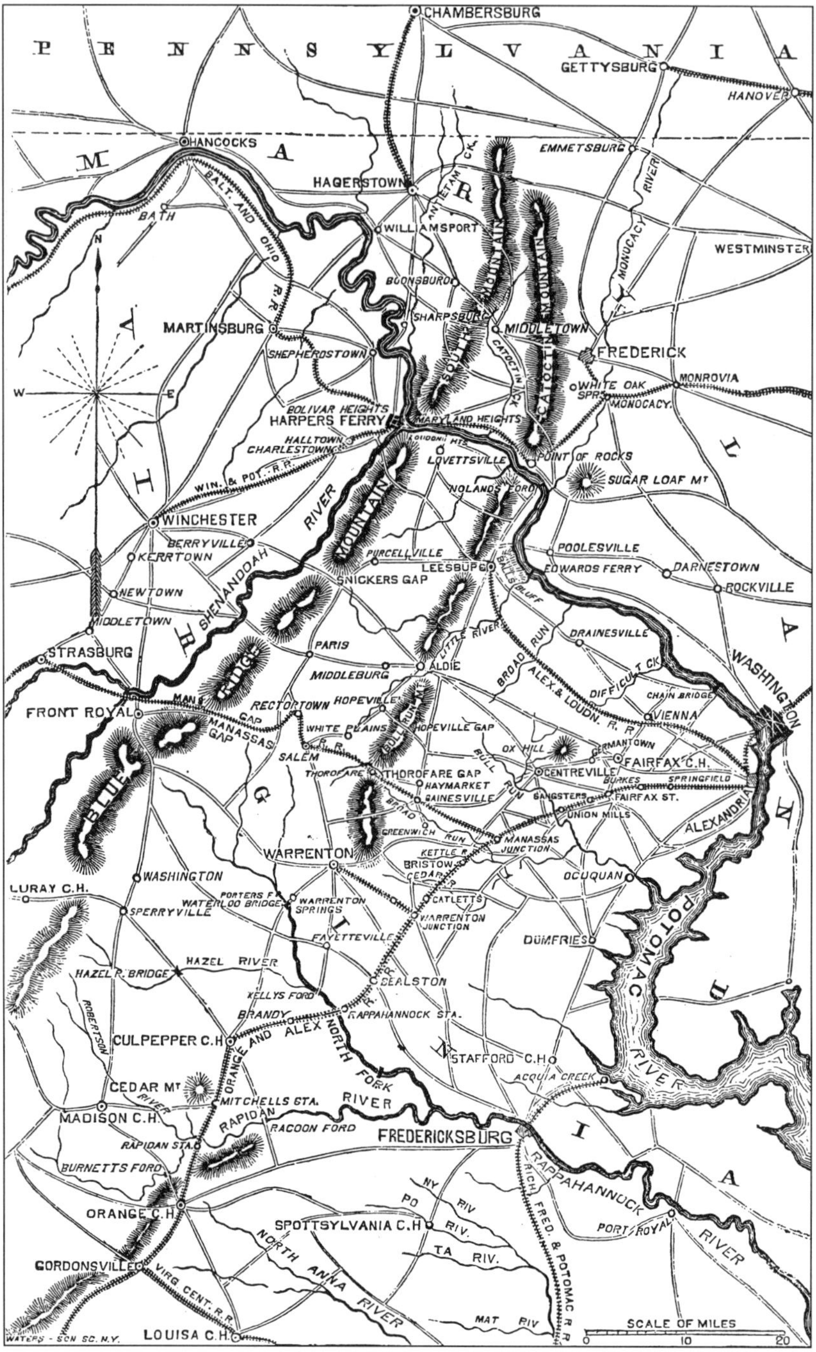

Map of the campaign in Virginia
(*Harper's Magazine*, August 1862)

and, being unaccustomed to wading, we were harassed no little. The narrow crossing admitted only single file, it necessarily consumed much time and frequently a delay of half an hour was thus occasioned. After a while we became restless, the streams were passed, yet no quick advance. Some of us concluded that the right of the regiment was gone. By permission, several of Company K went about a company's length beyond the flag company, and peering into the darkness (it was a dark night) neither saw nor heard anyone. On their return they reported and stated their belief that the right wing was far ahead. Striking double-quick we (Company K) were soon far on our way. When we tired, we came down to quick-step, alternating for hours.

Just before daybreak a handful of soldiers from Company K, the rest having given out on this our first forced march, came up to the right wing of the regiment. Chickens were crowing for the day when we halted, worn out. We fell at roadside and were soon fast asleep, our heads pillowed on rocks. We slept soundly until the sun was shining on us. Those of Company K who gave out in the night, put in an appearance next morning. Our resting place was about three miles from the Rapidan River.

Lee had hoped to fight Pope on August 20, after assembling his troops and allowing them one day of rest. However, at midday on the nineteenth, Lee learned that the enemy was retreating across the Rappahannock, and he began to move his troops across the Rapidan shortly after midnight on the twentieth in order to pursue Pope.[11]

Private Andrews described their advance:

We remained there until 10 A.M., fell into line and advanced. At the river, bodies of soldiers were plainly seen on the hills beyond. We waded the shallow stream then hurried some hundreds of yards to the right, and halted, remaining in line of battle two or more hours awaiting the enemy. The beaming rays of the sun at noon on an August day were severe. Some almost fainted from the excessive heat. A detail of men (Joe Lewis and others) were sent for water. As the enemy did not advance against us, we leisurely advanced towards the Rappahannock River. We came to a residence on a hillside and spent the night near the enclosure. Next morning we were ordered to leave all our baggage, over which a guard was placed. Some hesitated about leaving all their luggage, but we were told that we would return that night and get everything. While we were absent, our belongings were sent to Brandy Station and stored away. Yankee cavalry, on a raid, went there and burnt them. Picture yourself a body of men forced to wear the same clothing day after day, week after week, and month after month, without change, trodding daily along dusty roads, at times sloppy, the rain wetting and the sun drying them, and this will give you some idea of our condition and looks.

Captain William G. Vardell, quartermaster of the Twenty-third Regiment, wrote in a letter to his wife from Culpeper, Virginia, on August 24, 1862:[12]

Before reaching the place just below here (Brandy) a road diverges to the right and onto this the other day our brigade was led by a spy, who came with forged letters from General Longstreet, as a guide. We advanced some miles and discovered our mistake and situation only when the enemy commenced shelling. The guide was forthwith seized (as he was before suspected, not being able to answer some questions that had been put to him, and which had he been who he professed he would have been able to answer) and examined. Satisfied of his being a spy, he was then and there hung. He was set upon a horse, and they gave the horse a cut and there ended his traitorous life. He was a Virginian—I hope not one of direct descent. I am afraid that the Virginians are rather bitter against the South Carolinians, as they regard them as the whole and sole cause of all their misery and suffering—this is simply sinful and absurd; they chose to follow us, we certainly did not force it.

Captain Edwards recalled the spy's conviction and execution:

On the evening of the 22d, near Kelly's Ford, a spy was captured, who had on gray clothes over his Yankee uniform. He had killed a Confederate courier and captured his dispatches.[13] He fell into the hands of General N. G. Evans, who tried him by what in army parlance is called a drumhead court-martial. General Evans ordered Captain J. R. Culp, of Company A, of the Seventeenth Regiment, who was in command of our brigade rear guard, to hang him. It was very unpleasant orders for Captain Culp, but fortunately for him before he had time to carry out the order a batch of cavalry came up and begged for the pleasure of giving the gentlemen their assistance in performing the tight rope act. Captain Culp readily granted the request, and they accepted the duty and took him a little distance from the road and hung him to a pine limb. I was in a short distance of the hanging, but did not go to see it.

Private Dock Owen of the Holcombe Legion recalled how soldiers survived on meager rations:

The soldier's life was a hard life. Think for a moment; one pint of flour for one day's ration, meat—beef and bacon—just what we could get. When on a march we would cook up three day's rations, and on various occasions we have cooked three day's rations and eat it all in one day and depend on buying, begging, or stealing for the other two days. I passed over three days without a morsel to eat, except green apples. In our mess there were five of us and we were fortunate in foraging. The night before the Rappahannock artillery fight we went into camp late at night and two of my messmates captured six of the oldest hens in Virginia. We started them to cooking about three o'clock in the morning and boiled them until sunrise. We were counting on a feast, when to our horror the command, "Fall in, fall in, fall in men, fix bayonets." Gee buck anthony, we had to leave the chickens in the pot. We had to leave them and charge a battery. We took the battery, and the enemy withdrew to the opposite bank of the river and kept us under a galling cannon fire for three and a half hours. We lost nine men killed. After we buried the dead and left the field, we marched about three miles, struck camp, and sent a delegation of two to see if the hens were still in the pot. They reported hens and pot had gone (we stole the wash pot), but they brought back five more chickens, some green corn, and they had grabbed a fine chance of potatoes. We skinned the chickens, cooked, and eat until late in the night. We all five of us went to sleep eating.

On the August 21, Lee ordered Longstreet to take a position in front of the enemy in the vicinity of the Orange and Alexandria Railroad bridge across the Rappahannock River in order to mask the movements of Jackson, who was moving up the river. Early on the twenty-third Longstreet directed the Washington Artillery and other units to drive back the enemy force that had crossed to the south bank of the river near the railroad bridge.

Captain Edwards described the conflict by the river:

Marching on up the river we reached Stephensburg and camped that night near Rappahannock Station (where the railroad crosses the Rappahannock River). On the morning of the 23rd the brigade, or a large portion of it, acted as the supporting column to the Washington Artillery and other batteries which engaged in a heavy artillery duel with the enemy's artillery on the opposite side of the Rappahannock. This took place where the railroad crosses the river. This artillery battle lasted from early in the morning until late in the evening. Our troops were somewhat protected by the crest of a hill near the river, but the brigade lost ninety men killed and wounded, and we did not fire a gun except the accidental discharge of a rifle that killed W. L. Jones, of Company A, the first man in the company killed in battle. This engagement was to fool Pope and make him believe that General Lee intended to force the crossing of his army at that point, and attract his attention from General Jackson, who was rapidly moving his corps towards other fords far above this point. We remained at that point, at the camp where we lay the night of 23rd, and buried our dead and sent back the sick and wounded.[14]

According to VIDI, the Macbeth Artillery did not play a major role in this artillery duel. Evans ordered the unit to "a position that was not tenable," and enemy fire quickly drove them from it. Later in the battle the unit did participate in shelling the enemy battery that had fired upon them.[15]

Lieutenant Lowry gave this account of the engagement:

We arrived [on August 22] in the neighborhood of the Rappahannock, and here the enemy seemed determined to make a stand and dispute the passage of the river. We had now been about twenty days on the march continually. The enemy now drew up his artillery on this side of the river, and threw his pontoon bridges across to facilitate his retreat. The next morning at dawn, General Evans formed his Brigade in battle order and advanced on the enemy's batteries. We marched over several wheat fields, and being supported by a Detachment of the celebrated Washington Artillery from New Orleans, we pressed forward into range of the enemy's cannon. The Washington Artillery got to the top of the hill and opened the ball, and then commenced one of the fiercest artillery duels ever fought.[16] We were about 100 yards behind the Washington Artillery and in full range of the enemy's guns. The shells fell around us as thick as hail, and the air above our heads was fairly rent with the shrieks of the cannon balls and the shells bursting, ricocheting, and whizzing amongst us. The roar of seventy-five pieces at once was truly dreadful, but strange to say, we had lost few men so far.[17] However, we were lying exposed to every shot, and General Evans seeing this, rode up to us and swore he would take the enemy battery. He ordered the Holcombe Legion to charge it, and we were to follow next. We had an open field to

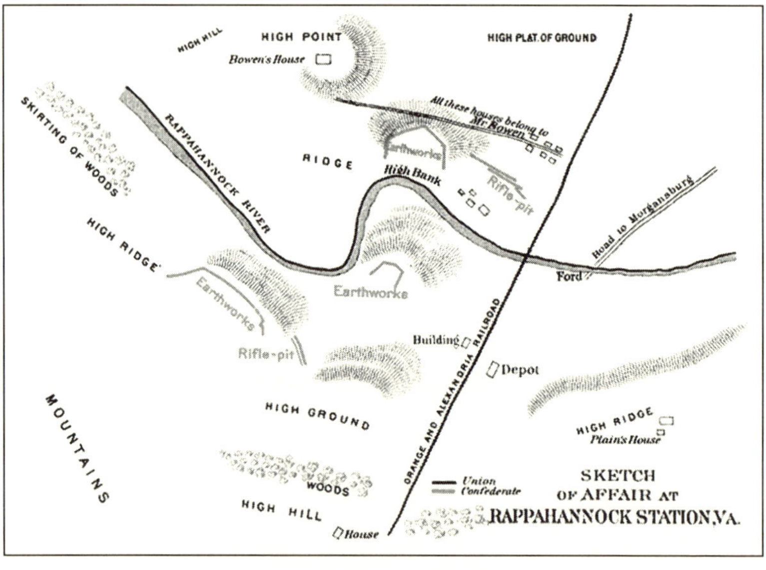

Rappahannock Station
(*Atlas to Accompany the Official Records*, Plate CV, no. 3)[18]

cross and the enemy seeing this, directed their fire at us and rained grape, canister, shrapnel, and shells on us. Men were falling thick, but we charged up the hill shouting like demons. But lo! The enemy had fled, crossed the river, taken up his bridges, and established his battery on a hill on the other side of the river. Now, out of our reach, they poured their fire into us. We were ordered to lie down on the side of the hill, and there we lay for eight hours beneath a scorching sun, partially shielded by the hill from the enemy's fire which flew over us like rain. The enemy at last found our whereabouts, and moving their batteries, raked the side of the hill we were lying on, killing and wounding several at the first discharge. We shifted around to the other side of the hill and laid there awhile, when General Evans came up and ordered us to retreat to a piece of woods a short distance back. We were again compelled to cross this old field, and in view of the full fire of the Yankees, but we reached the woods with slight loss. Here we remained until night, and the enemy ceased firing and resumed their retreat. We advanced to the hill we had driven the Yankee battery from and found several dead Yankees and a quantity of commissary. After this severe shelling and having buried our dead and cared for our wounded, we resumed the pursuit of the Yankees. Our Regiment was particularly fortunate in this instance. While the Holcombe Legion lost about sixty in killed and wounded, we only had about six.[19]

Many years later, Colonel Stevens wrote in his autobiography this account of the role of the Holcombe Legion in this fight:

Our first fight was at the Rappahannock. The enemy were on our side of the river on a hill from which they were firing on us with artillery . . . I was ordered to attack the hill. My command was in fine condition. I was under General Evans in his brigade. I had sent a scout down to examine the ground and he had just reported to me, when I was ordered to attack the hill. The General was by me, and naturally I asked him how I should proceed. His reply was to "go ahead and do the best I could" or something of that sort. It nettled me, and I immediately moved according to my judgement based on the report of my scout. There was a stream which I had to cross before I could reach the hill, and I was in column of companies with my flank toward the hill. The General sent an aide galloping after me to say that I would have my men cut all to pieces. My reply was very improper: "Tell him to mind his own business. When I asked his advice he had none to give." As I struck the stream the shelling opened on me and one shot (as the General feared) did great damage, killing my color bearer and one or two others. But I was right. By my maneuver, tho' exposed for a time, I crossed the stream with unbroken ranks and immediately wheeled into line facing the hill. I could see our troops advancing from another direction, the artillery had ceased firing. I supposed the hill was full of infantry and as I got near enough I ordered the charge. With a yell we swept to the top, but no enemy. From a prisoner afterwards taken it was learned that the march of my command was taken for that of regulars, and they had concluded that it was best to evacuate before the charge. We halted in the wood of the hill, most of the command behind a stone fence. The enemy had crossed the Rappahannock and were safe on the other side. They now opened on us with artillery, and unfortunately several of my men were killed while lying down . . . By order of General Evans, I threw out a line of skirmishers who went down to the edge of the river and our own artillery opening about the same time, the enemy were driven from the river in retreat. What forces opposed us I do not know.

Shanks may have visited his "barrelita" a few times during the artillery fight. General G. Moxley Sorrel, then on Longstreet's staff, related in his memoirs that after the Federals had burned the railroad bridge, Shanks ordered G. T. Anderson to take his Georgia brigade across the river and silence a particular enemy battery. When Anderson protested that there was no bridge across the swollen river, Evans said to cross anyway.[20] Sorrel intervened and related that "Anderson's indignation at the impossibility of the order was highly amusing."[21] Adjutant DuBose later said that he was riding with Colonel Means on the day after the battle and overheard him muttering, "A bombing, bungling, blustering day," in reference to Evans' leadership at Rappahannock Station.[22]

Captain Vardell's letter of August 24 lamented the carnage and destruction brought on by the war:

Whilst the battle was going on of course I had but little to do, and so arranging my business as to have everything ready to move at a word and further to let me know at once should any order be received, I determined to go down to the hospital and help and that is how I came there. I was afraid my courage would fail me as I somewhat anticipated the sights that would meet my eyes and try my nerves. I was more shocked than I even expected, still I found my help needed, offered, and accepted and shortly, though sick at heart to see the suffering around me, worked on until the battle ceased a little before sunset . . . Mr. Girardeau was also at the hospital assisting both by word and deed. One has but to visit the Field Hospital to realize the horrors of war. As I looked around and saw the mangled forms, I could not but ask: "Is it possible that civilized human beings cannot settle a question without recourse to this? Does this test truth; does this insure justice? God grant that this be soon ended in accordance with his will."

Just look out of my tent door and what meets the eye? Far out and beyond there runs the undulating tops of the Blue Ridge, enveloped in that peculiar blue mist always seen there. They look so peaceful and calm, dreamy like. My eye comes down and beautifully the country slopes into hill and vale. My eye travels on and downward and now it rests on the scene immediately before me. An entrance to a mansion, with beautiful shade trees and walks (now trampled and cut up by the passing to and fro of wagons) shows care and taste to have been here. But now, wagons and soldiers occupy the ground, mules and horses under the trees feeding, here and there camp fires burning, shutters and doors lying about—some half burnt. There stands the mansion—a most heavy sight to behold, porch broken down, door open. You walk in—filth from top to bottom. Enter the room—there stands a sofa, here and there a few old-fashioned chairs (no doubt the remains of some prized family set), bureaus with the drawers out, wardrobes laid on the floor and men asleep on them. Everything bespeaks sad ruin. You pass through the back door and there you see the remains of a neat paling fence surrounding a garden. You enter and everything there shares the general ruin. It is one of the saddest sights to witness scenes such as these in passing through the country. Just as I looked out there caught my eye in the yard one of those old-fashioned oak bottomed rocking chairs, and I thought perhaps how many happy naps the ancestry of those once domiciled here may have taken in that chair.

Captain Edwards marched with the troops toward Thoroughfare Gap:

On the morning of the 24th Longstreet's Corps took up the march again for the purpose of crossing higher up the river. All day long we could see the columns of Pope's army moving in a parallel direction. We reached Jefferson late in the afternoon. I have but a vague recollection of the place as I was sick and very tired. On the afternoon of the 26th the whole corps crossed the Rappahannock. I think the ford we crossed at was called Hinson's Ford, but my recollection is hazy in regard to the local names of places. We camped that night at a place I think called Orleans. On the night of the 27th we came to a place called White Plains. On the 28th we marched about thirty miles, passing through the little town called Salem, and reached the Thoroughfare Gap, where the railroad crosses the mountain. We found the enemy in possession of the mountain gap. Two brigades were sent off a considerable distance to the left. They clambered up the mountain and formed a line and took the Yankee force on the flank and cleared the gap.

Private Andrews recalled the search for food for hungry soldiers:

Rations were two days behind, and many had nothing to eat and no prospects of food for the day, so far as we knew. Colonel Benbow sent orders to each captain to detail men to go into an adjoining cornfield and pick mutton corn

Longstreet's march through Thoroughfare Gap
(*Battles and Leaders of the Civil War*, vol. 2)

for their men. The corn was gathered, brought, and distributed. The orderly of Company K counted out nine ears of corn to each man. The Colonel further said that if the corn was not sufficient to go into a large apple orchard nearby and fill themselves with green apples. Soon the orchard was reached and some ate immoderately and paid the penalty. Ben Weeks (one of the best foragers in Company K) learned that corn-bread and fried bacon could be had near our halting place (corn bread was a great rarity then). The orderly went with Ben Weeks. We found others there seeking same. We secured each a corn-cake and fried bacon. We enjoyed that treat—we were hungry for it.

Taking up our line of march we went to Manassas [actually Thoroughfare] Gap, and our rations (poor beef and hard tack) arrived during the afternoon, Thursday, August 28, 1862. We bivouacked for the night, but the noise of the tramp of horses aroused us from our sleep. We were soon under arms, looking for an enemy. It proved to be only the breaking loose of horses belonging to mounted officers. Quiet being restored, we resumed our rest.

General J. B. Hood, commanding his Texas brigade, gave this more detailed and interesting account of the midnight ramble:[23]

Amid the stillness and darkness which reigned in the encampment, some of the officers, who had dismounted upon the summit of the hillock, kicked over an empty barrel which had been used by the cavalrymen as a receptacle for forage, and it came rolling and bounding down the slope over the bushes, toward the Texans who were in a sound sleep. Just at this moment a favorite animal of one of the regiments, "the old gray mare," loaded with kettles, tin cups, and frying pans dashed up the hill from the forest below with a rattling noise. Some one gave the alarm, crying out with a loud voice "Look out!" and the brave men who had fought so nobly at Cold Harbor sprang to their feet, deserted their colors and guns, and ran down the slope and over a well-constructed fence, which was soon leveled to the ground. They had continued their flight several hundred yards before they awoke sufficiently to recover their wits, and boldly marched back, convulsed with laughter.

Private Andrews remembered finding a source of fresh water:

When day approached we saw a large iron pipe emptying water into a railroad tank (the railroad ran through the gap). We tried the water and found it excellent. Casting the eye upward we soon saw the spring about 50 or 60 feet upon the side of a mountain spur. General Longstreet had driven the Yankees from that position the day before. On our forward route, bodies of unburied Yankees were seen on the roadside. The Twenty-third Regiment proceeded for several hours and rested.

Soon Evans' new brigade would take part in the Second Battle of Manassas. General Evans had been there before.

4

Second Manassas and the Maryland Campaign

> More South Carolina blood was spilled in this battle than in any other battle of the war.
>
> William H. Edwards

If Federal general John Pope had chosen to send a small force to defend Thoroughfare Gap, he might have been successful in delaying Longstreet's arrival at Manassas. It would have been a great advantage to Pope if his main army could have attacked Stonewall Jackson's troops before Longstreet and Lee could arrive with reinforcements; however, Pope did not know where Jackson was. Conversely, Jackson had good information regarding the enemy's whereabouts and ambushed Pope's army at Brawner's Woods near Groveton on August 28.[1] After this fight the Federal forces retreated, and Jackson chose to move his line to the good defensive position afforded by the unfinished railroad line about a mile northwest of the site of the First Battle of Manassas. The battle resumed early in the morning of August 29, and by eight o'clock Jackson was having difficulty in holding his position.[2]

Evans' Independent Brigade was among the first units of Longstreet's Corps to arrive to assist Jackson. As they arrived, units of Longstreet's Corps were placed along and to the south of the Warrenton Turnpike, extending and defending the right end of Jackson's line. Lee was inclined to move immediately against Pope's left flank, but Longstreet asked for time to scout the topography and the enemy's positions, and Lee agreed. Longstreet's scouts discovered a large Federal force (later determined to be that of Fitz-John Porter) about a mile east of the extreme left end of Pope's line, making an attack most unwise.[3] Evans' Brigade spent the afternoon resting and listening to the sounds of the violent battle to their left as Pope attacked Gregg's South Carolina Brigade and Thomas' Georgia Brigade in the center of Jackson's line along the unfinished railroad.[4] At sundown on the twenty-ninth Longstreet sent Hood's Brigade to attack the Federal line, with Evans' Brigade following closely behind and other brigades nearby in support. This

"Twilight Clash" was for the purpose of testing the strength and position of Federal forces in preparation for the attack that Lee planned for the following morning.[5]

Many years after the war, Captain John Floyd and a few survivors of Company I of the Eighteenth Regiment wrote a history of their unit, which was known as the Darlington Rifles.[6] They gave this account of the early part of this battle:

On the morning of the 29th day of August, we passed through Thoroughfare Gap, and appeared on the field of Manassas just in time to save Jackson's army from destruction. Our division arrived upon the field at about 3 o'clock, and was formed in line of battle in a piece of woods, as a reserve to support the troops in our front. Heavy fighting continued in our front all day and to our right and left for miles. About sundown we were ordered to charge and moved forward at the double-quick. We passed out of the woods in line of battle into an open field and soon came contact with the enemy, and after exchanging a few rounds with them, again charged and drove them for half a mile or more. We then halted, and when the lines were corrected, we found that in the charge our brigade and General Law's brigade, by some means or other, had separated, leaving a space of some forty yards between them. A Federal squadron of cavalry noticed this open space and dashed through to our rear. It being in the night, we really did not know who they were, but upon investigation it was found that they were Federals. General Law then wheeled our right regiment half back and the left regiment of his brigade half back, forming them into the shape of a V with the lower end cut off, then coming to where I and several others of his old Darlington friends were, said: "Boys, that Yankee squadron of cavalry will come back again directly and I have set a trap for them; they can't get out anywhere else and after they blunder around awhile they will come back to the place where they came in, hoping that they have not been observed." While we were talking the squadron came dashing back, and General Law hastened back to see that his orders were carried out. Just as the Federals were passing through the two regiments placed by General Law, every man fired upon them and the whole squadron was literally annihilated. I don't think that a single horse or man went out alive.

Brigadier General Evander Law of Alabama knew that a part of Evans' Brigade was spread across the Warrenton Turnpike immediately behind his and Hood's brigades. Private Andrews told the story from the viewpoint of the Twenty-third Regiment:

Soon the sound of horsemen in front, advancing in our direction, caused Colonel Benbow to order fix bayonets, the front rank to kneel and, at the command fire, the front rank to fire and the rear rank to reserve fire. The men, however, in the excitement of the moment, forgot and guns were fired promiscuously almost in the faces of the adversaries, they were so near. Not one in our front reached our line . . . As soon as their horses could be checked, they wheeled about and left. Many guns were fired at them in their retreat.

Lieutenant Lowry offered his view of events with the Seventeenth Regiment:

We kept steadily on and waded a deep creek, until we came in view of General Law's Brigade of Alabamians. Here we halted in a corn field and remained half the night, wringing wet and shivering with cold. About midnight a rumor reached us that the enemy were trying to get into our rear and General Evans ordered us back to the farm house where we spent the remainder of the night. All night long the pickets kept up a constant firing, indicating that the enemy still confronted us. We all knew that the following day would be an eventful one for some of us, aye, a fatal one. The 30th of August dawned and ushered in a glorious day for our young Confederacy. As the day dawned, cannon after cannon boomed forth their iron hail, and the increased firing showed plainly the fierceness of the battle. Regiment after regiment advanced to the contest.

Early on July 30 the Macbeth Artillery was apparently stationed near Stephen D. Lee's artillery on the Brawner Heights. From here they could fire on the left flank of Porter's troops as they attacked Jackson across the unfinished railway cut. VIDI of the Macbeth Artillery gave this account:[7]

Longstreet, acting on the impulse of the moment and with the discretion of an experienced officer, hurried twelve guns into position and in less than ten minutes broke the furious onslaught of the charging Federals. While we were standing on our gun and caisson carriages, watching with intense interest and great admiration the heroic effort of Jackson's men to beat back the ever increasing numbers of the Federal soldiers, a courier was seen emerging from a piece of woodland to the right and well in front of Jackson's line, urging his horse towards us with all the speed that the urgency of the occasion could impel him. In answer to the message, we moved forward at a sweeping gallop and took our position on the crest of a hill to the left of the pike, and well in Jackson's right front. Within three minutes after we received our order we were in position hurling shot and shell into the double columns of the Federal soldiers sweeping down in tremendous odds against Jackson's struggling heroes. The enemy were approaching Jackson's position by a left oblique march, for the purpose of turning Jackson's right flank. The move exposed their left flank to an enfilade fire from our guns . . . only an occasional shell and ball fell among us—most of them passing over our heads. We fired therefore with deliberation, but rapidly and with great accuracy. Luckily, the first shell struck the head of the Federal column and bursted just right. The number of seconds [the fuse was] cut ran down the line as a gauge for the cutting of others, and thus it happened, from the very beginning, that we fired into the advancing columns of the enemy without guessing at distance or shooting at random. We cut them down like grass. A soldier who had a commanding view from the woods said, "I never saw such splendid shooting. Each fire seemed to lift the Federals off the ground."

Private Andrews noted that some Yankee uniforms made vibrant targets:

About 2 P.M. Saturday, August 30, 1862, with General Evans commanding our Division and Colonel Stevens our Brigade, Hood's Brigade was sent to skirmish in our front. They met Yankee zouaves dressed in red. Hood's men wore dark-green uniforms. The red furnished a bright, shining mark at which to shoot, and, judging from the number of red-clad bodies left on the ground, their slaughter must have been great. We advanced over the same ground soon after, hence our knowledge of the skirmish.

Lieutenant Lowry reported the great casualties of this battle:

We lay for over half the day listening and watching the contest, and still no orders for us to advance. But at length the order came. General Evans ordered us to advance, and the whole brigade started forward in as pretty a line as they had ever formed on dress parade. We advanced first across a little open space, or small strip of an old field, and on entering the woods on the other side the shells came flying over us in close proximity. General Evans ordered us to lie down until the shells passed over us. As I lay down a shell came whizzing over me about a foot above my head and fell right at my heels, but fortunately it did not explode. We got up then and charged forward in a good line, through the woods, over the dead and wounded men, shouting like demons. After passing through the woods we entered a thicket of cedars, and here the enemy sent their great shots in perfect hurricanes, crushing and maiming man after man.

Grape, canister, and shrapnel fairly rattled amid the trees. Here we lost very heavily; the man by my side was killed dead on the spot. Our gallant Colonel Means fell pierced with a ball through the breast while gallantly cheering us on. It seemed strange how a man could escape, still we pressed resolutely on. Upon clearing the woods at Mrs. Chinn's house we came in full sight of the enemy drawn up in good line and showering their leaden missiles upon us. The red uniforms of Colonel Duryea's New York Zouaves were shining prominently in their ranks. With a shout that sounded loud above the cannons' roar we charged forward on the run, firing and loading

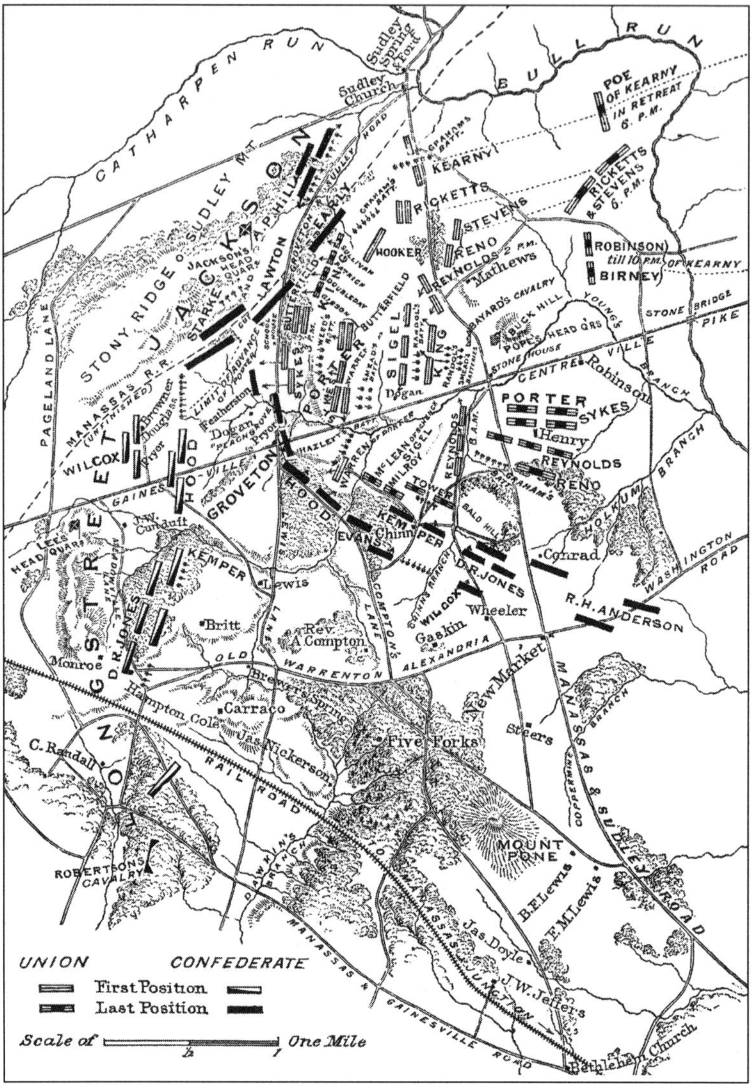

First and last positions in the fighting of August 30th
(*Battles and Leaders of the Civil War*, vol. 2)

as fast as possible. The Yankees did not wait to lock bayonets with us, but turned precipitately, still keeping up a desultory fire. While giving our whole attention to the fleeing foe, a regiment of Yankees suddenly drew up in line a few yards from us on our left, and poured in a destructive fire. And now my turn came, for it was here while busy loading my rifle, that a ball from the enemy came through my thigh. My first thought was to look at it, but there was so much blood on my leg that I could not distinguish the wound. The balls continued to fly around me, knocking up the dirt all around me, and I was in eminent danger of getting another one. I got up and found I could walk a little and hobbled about five steps back and lay down. The battle continued with unabated fury. Grape shells, shot, and Minié balls were plowing the air around me, and at that time I was suffering acute pain from my leg. My leg seemed to be numb all over, with a dull kind of pain throbbing through it. Several other wounded were lying near me. It was while lying here that someone came and lay down beside me saying, "We are friends now, even if we have been enemies." I did not understand him, in fact I did not take any notice of him, but I saw that he had on a Yankee uniform, which a great many of our men wore, and I supposed him one of our men. I lay still sometime without speaking to him, examining my leg, but having finished I asked him to what regiment he belonged. He replied, "I belong to the 24th Ohio." You are a Yankee then, says I. "Yes," he replied, "but I am tired of this damned war and won't fight anymore." I told him I would not trust a Yankee no further than I could see and demanded his gun, which he complacently delivered, remarking, "It is loaded." I turned him over to our soldiers on their return. I lay there where I was wounded until the battle ended, which was about a half hour after I got wounded. The Yankees were thoroughly whipped. It seemed that the field at Manassas was peculiarly unfortunate for them. As the retreating foe disappeared in the distance I got up on my legs again and commenced to hobble along. I found myself very weak and stiff, just able to limp along, but I assure you it afforded me infinite satisfaction as I knew when I could walk that my leg was not broken. I hobbled up to Mrs. Chinn's house about one hundred yards from where I was wounded, and there I fortunately met one from our company, William Clark, who kindly assisted me, bound up my leg and gave his blanket and oil cloth to me. I will never forget this kindness.

Private Andrews told of his regiment's advance:

We followed Hood's Brigade, but had not gone over fifty yards before Colonel Benbow was wounded. He called to Major Whilden to take charge of the regiment, but just then Lieutenant-Colonel Roberts came up and commanded. In our advance Colonel Stevens rode in front of the Twenty-third Regiment.[8] As Colonel Stevens saw the flash of the enemy's cannon, he immediately gave the command, "Lie down!" The men had scarcely fallen down ere the grape and canister whizzed over their heads. Then, "Up! Forward, March" was given in a clear ringing voice. These alternate commands were repeated until we reached the opposite side of the woods.

We found a very high rail fence with stake and rider in our immediate front, enclosing an open field. This we scaled, right half-wheeled, and marched up a hill. Just as we were descending the opposite side, Anderson Mills was shot in the thigh. The orderly sergeant, J. Grier White, was shot in the fullness just below the curvature of the ribs. The ball came from the left, cut its way through vest, pants, and drawers, both coming and going and passed on, leaving its mark about five inches above the navel and making him unconscious for some time. He had fallen forward and was thought to be killed, according to the memory of our captain, D. R. McCallum. We continued to advance. After going about one-half mile we charged and captured the enemy's battery which was trying to prevent our advancement. The Confederates pressed forward; the Yankees continued to retreat. Hood's Brigade, after skirmishing, flanked to our right and came to our assistance after our line had passed a house on a hill, where many of our wounded were afterwards carried. We were hard pressed, and to avoid a galling artillery fire, Colonel Stevens ordered a flank movement to the right, down a hill. Then it was that Hood's Brigade came up. After that, the Yankees did not even halt to return our fire but steadily and rapidly retired. Three of Company K were killed and nineteen wounded.

Captain McCallum spent nearly the whole night looking over the battlefield for the wounded of Company K, using a torch-light to enable him to identify them. Private Nichols assisted him in the search.[9]

Captain Edwards of the Seventeenth Regiment recorded how Colonel Gadberry's premonition of his own death was realized:

The battle was opened about 4 P.M. by the Confederates advancing on Pope's lines. The fighting was fierce and continuous from about 4:30 until after sundown, when Pope's lines were all completely shattered and driven off the field. About 6 o'clock, Evans' Brigade was thrown against one of the strongest points in the Federal lines. It was on a hill covered with field batteries, supported by two heavy lines of infantry. They succeeded in breaking the Federal lines, but it was a fearful sacrifice. Colonels Means and Gadberry were both killed (Gadberry killed and Means mortally wounded). Many other field and line officers were killed and wounded. In a number of the companies of the Seventeenth Regiment not an officer was left unhurt, and at least 75 percent of the men were either killed or wounded. More South Carolina blood was spilled in this battle than in any other battle of the war.[10] Colonel Means lived until Monday about 2 P.M. His body was buried in a churchyard in the little town of Haymarket and the following winter it was brought home and buried at Buckhead, and the grave is still unmarked.

The Charleston Mercury newspaper published on September 9, 1862, Colonel Goodlett's September 1 account of the death of Colonel Means: "Colonel Means, of the 17th Regiment, S.C.V., died this morning of a wound

received in the battle of Manassas, on the 30th August. He fell in the thickest of the fight, gallantly leading his regiment in a charge. The wound was severe, and as his valiant comrades pressed on he said: 'Push on! my boys; push on!' Governor Means was beloved by all of Evans' brigade, and his regiment feels as if they had lost a father." Means' death resulted in the promotion of FitzWilliam McMaster to colonel of the Seventeenth Regiment.

Private George R. Jones of Company I of the Twenty-third Regiment recalled:

The next day was Sunday, and Sunday it was to all appearances, for it was as calm and peaceful as any Sabbath could be. Had it not been for the shocking evidence of war all around us, one would have supposed there was no blighting curse of war in our land. Several of us repaired to the battlefield, and I will say here that one who has never been on a battlefield or visited one, need never want to do so, for they will behold a sight that is simply awful. On reaching the battlefield we went over it and witnessed the terrible consequences of war 'till the heart became sick.

In this particular part of the battlefield I visited, I am satisfied the Federals' loss was at least five to three of the Confederates'. The loss on the part of the Federals as admitted on the part of the authorities of the United States was never correct, for they have always tried to convey the impression that the loss of the Confederates in this battle was as heavy or heavier than theirs, which was not the case, for they were soundly whipped and got many men killed and wounded besides prisoners. It was reported at the time that the Confederates captured nine thousand prisoners or more. The loss on the part of the Confederates I do not remember as officially reported. The official report of the 23rd I very well remember: four hundred and forty-one men engaged, and one hundred and fifty-seven killed and wounded. A great many, of course, were but slightly wounded. The readers can very well imagine how thick shot and shell flew around the 23rd on that occasion.

This, I think, is sufficient to relate about this memorable battle, so I will turn from the battlefield and relate a little incident connected with this affair that was very amusing at the time. It appears that General Pope imagined during some part of the day's battle that he was gaining the day and the Confederates would soon be in full flight before his victorious army, and while enjoying this delusive expectation, he telegraphed to Washington that Lee was retreating to the mountains and that a great Union victory was being achieved by the grand Union army; also saying that anyone wishing to visit the battlefield to view the Rebel dead could do so with safety. On reception of this telegram, about sixty citizens of Washington set out to visit the battlefield and see all these gratifying sights. But disappointed they were. Before they were aware of it, they were safe within the lines of the Confederates, and

Pope was, with his defeated and flying troops, making for the north bank of the Potomac River by way of Centerville. The mortification and chagrin of these nicely dressed citizens was as great to themselves as it was amusing to the Confederates. They abused Pope at a high rate and called him everything but a man of unquestioned veracity and a good general . . . After teasing them a good deal in different ways, they were marched to the rear, and after a day or two released and sent through the lines under a flag of truce back to Washington, a wiser set at least than when they left.

Adjutant DuBose noted the losses suffered by the Holcombe Legion:

The victory was a great one; but it was a bloody one, one of the bloodiest of the war. Of our own St. John's connection, Henry Stevens, who was acting aide to Colonel Stevens, was killed, and Major Palmer was mortally wounded. The Holcombe Legion was practically destroyed as a regiment; when we gathered up the remains there were about a hundred men. I was commanded to reorganize it and to do the best possible with it in the campaign to follow. I organized the men into three companies and had hardly enough officers to man them.

No time was lost after the battle. General Lee followed the retreating Federals some little distance toward Washington and then turned up the

Lee's army crossing into Maryland
(*Harper's Magazine*, September, 1862)

Potomac as far as Leesburg.[11] We entered the town some time after dark. We had been through, of course, an awful experience and had been marching, I with my clothes literally shot off my back and my wound not dressed. As I passed through the little town of Leesburg in this condition suddenly the sound of a piano came to me and I saw a little ahead of us quite an illumination. I rode up on the pavement and in the dark looked in. There were a number of our officers, beautifully dressed, and a number of ladies—a scene so utterly out of keeping with all we had known this past month, that it was indelibly impressed upon my mind. By the side of the young lady at the piano and with his back to me was one officer whose appearance seemed somewhat familiar. As he turned I recognized Colonel Frank Gaillard, who had been through all the battles of the days before but in a very different part from the Holcombe Legion. He looked very fresh and gay. These little touches of home scenes, right in the midst of war, of which I have a number in my mind, are painted there for always. Next morning we crossed the Potomac and began the first Maryland invasion.

Following his victory at Second Manassas, Lee invaded the Union for the first time. Public morale in the North was low, and Lee hoped that another victory, this time on Union soil, would result in a negotiated peace. Longstreet's Corps crossed the Potomac near Ball's Bluff, the site of Evans' famous victory a year earlier. Felix Gregory DeFontaine, the field correspondent for the Charleston Daily Courier who wrote under the pen name "PERSONNE," recorded the words of an old Maryland gentleman who was watching the troops' crossing at White's Ford:[12]

"Goodness gracious, look at the Seceshes. (This, I may remark, is the unpoetic name by which we are generally known) . . . I've been to shows and circuses and theaters and all them things, but I never seen such a sight'n all my life. Why you've got soldiers enough to whip all creation; but look yere, won't these fellers hurt us Marylanders? I'm a little afeared that when they get to ranging around the country, they'll interfere with my family, and do something wrong. To tell the truth, I don't care to leave my farmhouse."

PERSONNE noted that this old gentleman then returned to his home and had his family prepare a meal for a dozen soldiers, reluctantly charging them twenty-five cents each and accepting Confederate money. Many other local families did likewise. However, as the Confederate troops pressed on into Maryland, the percentage of sympathizers declined. PERSONNE estimated it at fifty percent at Frederick, Maryland, an important railroad and trade center that was used by the Federals as a camp of instruction, a general depot for the army, and a general hospital for the sick and wounded.

Adjutant DuBose recalled tending to some of the sick and injured in the days after the battle:

Our men, the survivors of the battle, were very much knocked up in many ways and sickness and ailments began to break out among them. We had no doctors—all had been left behind on the battle field. I rode up one day, as we passed through a little village, and asked them what medicine they had that might be of use. I got some half-dozen little bottles, very small, of pain-killer, and with these I played doctor for a week or two.

Our first stop was in Frederick City, where we spent a very short time. From there we marched on in the direction of Hagerstown, passing through the beautiful Boonsboro Gap, over South Mountain.

Longstreet's Corps was sent to Hagerstown to guard against the arrival of Federal troops from Pennsylvania. DuBose continued:

Arriving in Hagerstown for the first time, we settled down for a good rest. Here the sickness became more apparent among the men for want of proper food and other causes. I was in despair. When I heard that in a neighboring regiment the first surgeon, Dr. Dick Mickel, had come up from the rear I lost no time in bringing him to do what he could for the men. He came and diagnosed a number of cases, delivering a sort of lecture upon the symptoms as he did so and showing the indications of typhoid fever. Of course that made the matter a great deal worse. After going the rounds, he turned and very pleasantly bade me a good evening. When I said to him, "Well, doctor, what are you going to do about it?" he said, "Nothing. There is not a remedy at hand or in reach." Everything was left behind with the wounded.

We had the promise of a delightful rest at Hagerstown. I had the opportunity of a bath in a nice mountain stream and at last a little change of apparel. But on the second or third morning, we were hastily put under arms and hurried back to Boonsboro Gap [at South Mountain].

Near the end of the Second Battle of Manassas, General Hood's troops had captured a number of new Federal ambulances. Evans, claiming to outrank him, ordered Hood to give the ambulances to his Carolina troops. Hood refused, and Evans had him arrested. Lee ordered Hood to remain with his brigade but did not restore him to command. At the beginning of the Battle of South Mountain, Lee needed Hood's leadership and asked him to "merely say that you regret this occurrence." This Hood refused to do. Finally, in desperation, Lee suspended Hood's arrest until the conclusion of that battle. This was one of many disputes that Evans would have with fellow officers.

Chaplain James of the Eighteenth Regiment recalled the brigade's march to South Mountain:

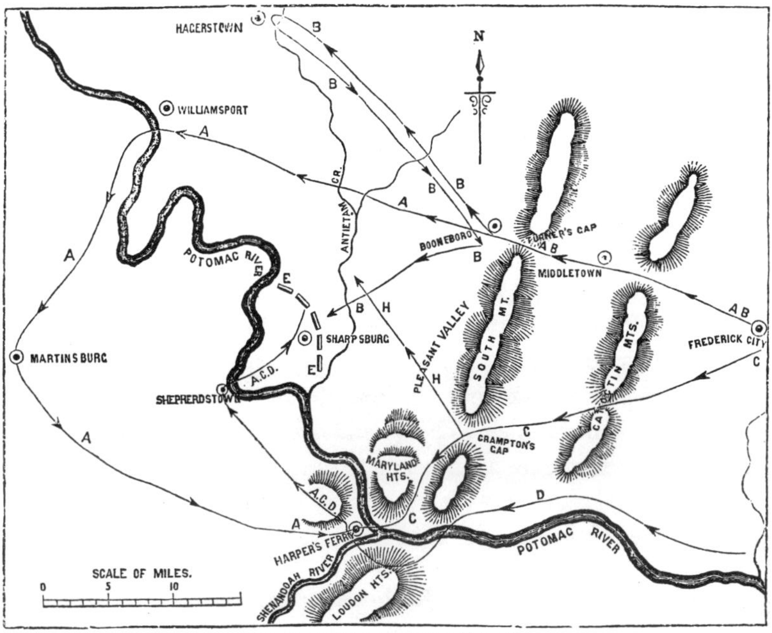

MOVEMENTS FROM SEPTEMBER 10 TO 17.

A, A. Jackson's March from Frederick to Sharpsburg.
B, B. Longstreet's " " "
C, C. McLaws and Anderson's " "
D, D. Walker's March from the Monocacy to Sharpsburg.
E, E. Confederate Position at Antietam.
H. H. Franklin's March from Pleasant Valley to the Antietam.

Franklin followed the same route as McLaws from Frederick to Pleasant Valley; the remainder of the Union army that of Longstreet from Frederick to Boonesboro', and thence to the Antietam. The arrows show the direction of the march. Where two or more letters come together, it indicates that the several bodies followed the same route.

(*Harper's Magazine*, September, 1862)

General D. H. Hill had been left in the pass in South Mountain for its defense, while Jackson had turned towards the Potomac in order to capture the garrison at Harper's Ferry, which he succeeded in taking with eleven thousand prisoners. General Hill, being hard pressed at South Mountain, sent a dispatch for Longstreet's command at Hagerstown to join him. We arrived on Sunday about 4 o'clock P.M. and ascended the mountain under a furious cannonading from the enemy, and were engaged until after dark.

Adjutant DuBose described the role of the Holcombe Legion:

The march was a heavy and trying one upon the men in their physical condition. The object was to arrest the splendid army of General McClellan in its passage across South Mountain, until General Lee could unite his army to meet them as he did a day or two later at Sharpsburg. One corps of the army under General Stonewall Jackson was engaged at the time in the capture of the garrison of some eighteen thousand men at Harper's Ferry. This he accomplished just in time for the two corps, Longstreet's and Jackson's, to unite at the Battle of Sharpsburg. In the meantime to meet, and as expected, to overwhelm our little army of thirty or forty thousand men, McClellan had reorganized a splendid new army of eighty thousand men or more. It was this army that we were sent to Boonsboro Gap to detain or delay as long as possible, until General Lee could combine his two corps.

We arrived in the gap early in the afternoon of the fourteenth of September of 1862, and the several commands were stationed on the heights, north and south of the gap, at the various points of passage. Our brigade was immediately sent to the top of a height on the northern side. It was quite a steep climb to the top of the mountain as we ascended it, and on the top there was a tolerably large plateau bounded on the eastern edge by a line of rocky cliffs. Behind this cliff the line was formed and our small command, the Holcombe Legion, was deployed in front as skirmishers. We had barely got into position when the enemy's heavy and overlapping line appeared slowly climbing up. It was only a question of time, a matter of <u>retarding</u> their progress, and by dark we had been forced back into the gap below. But it was too late for the enemy to make any further advance that night.

Captain Floyd of the Eighteenth Regiment was wounded:

When we arrived we heard heavy firing on South Mountain and were ordered to that point. We went up the mountain to the place where the battle was raging and went into action at double quick. "On right, by file, into line," the men firing as soon as they got into line. We had just about gotten our brigade into line of battle when Rhodes' Brigade on our left gave way, exposing our flank to a heavy fire from the enemy and we, too, had to fall back. Sergeant Waters, who was carrying the regimental colors, was wounded. J. O. Wilson, of Company I, caught the colors as they were falling and carried them through the battle and also through the battle of Sharpsburg with the greatest gallantry. I was wounded in the head. Five privates were wounded and two captured.

According to Private Andrews, the Confederates were heavily outnumbered in this battle:

The fight was a most unequal combat; the enemy had five full lines of battle, while we had only one and that stretched far out. They could have easily surrounded and captured our force, but failed to realize it. We were forced back to the top of the mountain and had to retreat.

Adjutant DuBose described his harrowing nighttime scouting expedition:

I have now to raise a personal adventure which altered for a long time my own relation to the further course of the war. The march, as I have said, from Hagerstown had been a forced one, the ascent of the mountain a hard and steep one, and the short engagement an exhausting experience, to say the least. By the time we found ourselves back in the turnpike in the gap, it was quite dark and the men were so overcome with fatigue and sleep that they dropped by the roadside and settled themselves for the night. I had barely resigned myself to this situation when I received orders to pick the soundest and ablest men of my command and to return in the direction from which we had just been driven and to extend the picket line on the mountain side to the left.

I selected, I suppose, some thirty or forty men, but found some difficulty in the dense forest of the mountain-side in discovering the picket-line which I was to extend. However, I did so, and proceeded to place my men singly at intervals of ten or fifteen steps as far as they would go. When this was done, I selected a spot just in the middle and rear of my line, spread my oilcloth, and was just pondering whether it was safe to lie down for fear of falling asleep. Then Robert Rutledge, my own sergeant-major appeared on the scene with the instructions that General Lee was under the impression that the mountain in front of us had been abandoned by the enemy and that I was to advance with my men cautiously as far as the scene of our recent engagement and ascertain the facts of the case. I don't suppose that physically I or my men could ever have been more unfit for such an enterprise after all that we had been through. But I hastily called my men together into the center, gave them instructions as to our orders, and commanded them to move as noiselessly as possible through the virgin forest to the top of the mountain.

Before starting I said to Robert Rutledge, who at the time was serving on the brigade staff and who was an intimate personal friend, "Your coat is lighter than mine. Let's exchange." I also borrowed his pistol, as I carried no arms except my sword. I then paced myself at the center of the line with the men on both sides to "dress" the center, and we began the ascent.

In spite of the effort to be as silent and secret as possible while moving so swiftly, we were subject to so many false alarms and necessarily made so much noise through the bushes, that we endangered our own discovery before we could discover the enemy. When we reached the last and steepest ascent, I put my men into convenient position and climbed myself to the plateau, intending to listen and make what observations I could before bringing them up. When I got to the top, the silence of the night was so profound that I thought it impossible that there could be a body of men in the small space of the plateau which I was to reconnoitre. Moving on quietly toward the edge, or cliff, behind which we had fought, I convinced myself more and more that there could be nothing there besides the primeval and natural environment. Then I became conscious of what was to me a strange experience. Sleepiness or fatigue had vanished utterly. I never moved more easily or lightly on my feet, and I was aware of an almost unnatural elation and exaltation.

There at last I was on the very battlefield of the afternoon before, surrounded by the bodies of those who had fallen and actually searching for them to assure myself that I had arrived at the proper point, and yet I felt not one trace of loneliness or superstition. As I was about to return it came to my mind that to make doubly sure I should take a further turn around the plateau. Every step made me more confident of my utter loneliness and I remember distinctly what was passing through my mind. I was framing the report I would send up of my reconnaissance to headquarters. I was also thinking what an unexpectedly good scout I was, moving so easily and rapidly and lightly, when suddenly the word "Halt!" sounded in my ears.

I stopped immediately, wondering whether it was the voice of the enemy or one of my own men in search of me. I could see one or two figures not more than twenty steps in front of me, but I could not distinguish the uniform. Robert Rutledge's cloak was a civilian's with a cape falling over the arms with slits in the sides of the body for armholes. My arms were within the slits, holding the pistol. I quietly cocked it and slowly moved to the figures before me, which were between me and my own men. They made no movement as I approached and I hoped very strongly still that they really were my men. As I approached to within a very few feet, my immediate antagonist and myself simultaneously recognized each other as enemies. As he jerked up his gun, I was near enough to ward it off with one hand and with the other attempted to draw my pistol from within the cloak. In the necessary scuffle, the cocked pistol discharged itself prematurely. At once, thinking himself shot, the man dropped his gun and with a loud yell precipitated himself upon me. Instantly the woods were alive. My effort then was simply to get away. In the scuffle that ensued, I several times nearly did so, but my antagonist was a much larger and stronger man than I was, and I finally had to surrender.

I was confronted in a few moments with the officer in command and a crowd of others. Being asked who I was and what I was doing there, I told him that I was a Confederate Adjutant and that I was on a scout; that it had been reported that the mountain top had been abandoned and I had been sent to ascertain the fact. "Abandoned!" he said, and then proceeded to tell me who and what were there.

My immediate captor was brought up and questioned. He said he was on post just without the lines, that I had come upon him not from the front but from the rear (I had walked around them), that I had walked upon him and when halted had answered with a shot. He persisted in saying that I had shot him. One thing the officer asked me to explain. It seems that in the scuffle, I suppose in order to keep off those that surrounded me, I had twice shouted "Charge!" I was asked to explain that, if I was as I said, alone. My reply was that I supposed it was to gain time to get away. It had detained them actually.

They then began to notice my cloak, which was suspiciously near to blue and raised the question of my being a spy. In this and in many other ways my situation was getting rather ticklish. They were evidently angry and expressed themselves so at the rude disturbance. The commanding officer was distinctly disagreeable. In the midst of this, I was relieved by the intervention of a young staff officer who, in a very timely way, made himself my advocate and smoothed things over. When I was asked where I was from and replied "Charleston, South Carolina," this young officer in a very kindly and friendly way said that he had met friends from Charleston in Paris and gave quite a pleasant turn to things.

Then the commanding officer said: "Well, we haven't beds of down, but we'd better get down to our beds." At that word, I surrendered to my exhaustion and fatigue. I literally dropped in my tracks and knew nothing further.

After his capture, DuBose was taken to Fort Delaware Prison, where he resided for about one month until paroled and sent to Richmond. After another month in Richmond awaiting exchange, he rejoined the Holcombe Legion in Wilmington, North Carolina. His experiences as a prisoner are related in the next chapter.

Chaplain James told of a surprising battlefield injury:

In this battle we had several killed and wounded. Lieutenant Campbell of Company H was shot in the eye with a Minié ball, coming out behind his ear on the opposite side of his head. He was left for dead, as we fell back that night to Sharpsburg. Two days afterwards he was found on the battlefield still breathing by some persons living in the neighborhood.

Samuel Campbell was treated in a hospital in Middletown, Maryland, where he wrote this letter with the assistance of a Union soldier:[13]

3rd Regiment
New York Volunteers
Headquarters, Camp
Middletown Hospital, Md. Oct. 10th 1862

Dear Wife;

I will try to write you a few lines this morning. I am getting along first best, but it will be a long time before I can get so as to go unless someone comes after me. I want you to send either Peter McCallum or someone after me as soon as you can. Be sure and do it as soon as possible. I am paroled and can come home as soon as possible as I can get well enough. Bring plenty of money with you. I want to see you very much.

For Samuel L. Campbell
By Jeremiah C. Foster

Chaplain James continued the story of Campbell's recovery:

They carried him to their home and nursed him for six months and then conveyed him to Richmond, where he met with a friend who brought him on to Rock Hill in South Carolina. From there he was taken by a friend to his home ten miles distant. He was completely blind and could not see the face of his wife, but when she saw him she rushed forward to his embrace and fell prostrate on the ground. He was entirely blind and resided at Clover, in York County, South Carolina [where he was thereafter known as "Blind Sam" by his neighbors]. He raised a large family, supporting them by pumping water at the railroad tank. He died in 1898.

In the Battle of South Mountain, Evans' Brigade was in support of Rodes' Alabama Brigade late in the afternoon when George Meade's division of Federal troops attempted to flank the left end of the Confederate line. Rodes' Brigade was a part of the division of Lieutenant General Daniel H. Hill, who said in his account of the battle, "His supports [Evans' Brigade] fought gallantly and saved him from being entirely surrounded, but they got on the ground too late to effect anything else. Evans' Brigade under Stevens had been wasted by two campaigns and was small when it left Hagerstown that morning, and many had fallen out on the hot and dusty forced march . . . the brigade must have been about 550 strong."[14] Hill estimated that Rodes' and Stevens' men were outnumbered by about three to one.

Colonel Stevens' wife received a letter from him that was written just after the Battle of South Mountain. She quoted from it in a letter to his mother: "His legion numbering 50 men—the entire brigade 275!"

Captain Floyd recalled the next battle against an overwhelming number of enemy soldiers:

On the morning of the 16th of September we formed line of battle between the town of Sharpsburg and Antietam Creek, a little to the left of the center, and when the battle commenced were holding that position. The battle raged for hours. The right had been assaulted many times and the enemy repulsed; the left and center had been assaulted, with like results. The left was again assaulted, this time with 30,000 men under Joe Hooker and General Mansfield. Stonewall Jackson was holding that position with only 6,000 men, a portion of his command having not yet arrived. Though the world never saw 6,000 braver men, human endurance was unable to withstand the terrible onslaught of those 30,000 Federals, and old Stonewall, with his brave men, were being pushed back. The left wing of Lee's army was being crushed, but at this juncture, when everything seemed to be lost, old Stonewall Jackson in person wheeled Hood's three brigades to the left from the left centre and with them charged Hooker's and Mansfield's 30,000 men, causing them to waver and finally to break, at the same time ordering his own 6,000 men to charge. We drove the enemy from our lines and re-established them. In this charge Lieutenant A. H. Woods, commanding Company I, was killed and six men of the company were wounded. We returned to our position in the left center just in time to repel a charge of the enemy and remained there through the two day's fighting, though charged again by overwhelming numbers. The remainder of Jackson's command arrived some hours afterwards, and our left was secure.

Captain Edwards noted Stonewall Jackson's role in the Confederate effort at Sharpsburg:

On the 16th and 17th of September occurred the memorable battle of Sharpsburg, in which the Seventeenth Regiment, together with what was left of Evans' Brigade, took an active part and lost heavily in proportion to the number present. Longstreet's Corps had been fighting the enemy all day until the evening of the 16th, when Jackson's Corps arrived from Harper's Ferry. I heard men say they were present when Jackson rode up to General Lee on the field at Sharpsburg and heard what was passed between them. Jackson saluted Lee, and said: "The Lord has given us another victory." Lee replied: "In behalf of the Confederacy, I thank you and your brave troops." Jackson then said: "Where do you want my troops on the line?" Lee replied: "On the left, and I expect you will have to fight for position." Jackson said: "Very well," and touched his hat, rode off and put his troops in rapid motion, and before very long could be heard the roar of his artillery and the steady rattle of his musketry. Very soon the enemy was pressed back and the integrity of Lee's lines restored. The fighting ceased on the evening of the 17th, after two days of awful strife. Lee remained upon the field all day of the 18th, but there was no fighting. This battle has always been regarded as a draw game or what the school boys call a "dog fall." The Federal army had done the attacking and it was a plain case that they had got enough and were tired of the job.

Evans' Brigade was at the left (north) end of Longstreet's line and near the center of the Confederate line. The Twenty-second, Eighteenth, and Twenty-third Regiments and the Macbeth Artillery were just north of the Boonsboro Pike. About one-half mile in front of and slightly to the left of these units was the soon-to-be infamous "Bloody Lane," defended by the right (south) end of Jackson's line. Facing the Bloody Lane were a number of Federal artillery units, including that of Captain John C. Tidball, Evans' West Point classmate.[15] The Seventeenth Regiment and the Holcombe Legion were placed on the south side of the Boonsboro Pike. For the most part, Evans' small brigade,

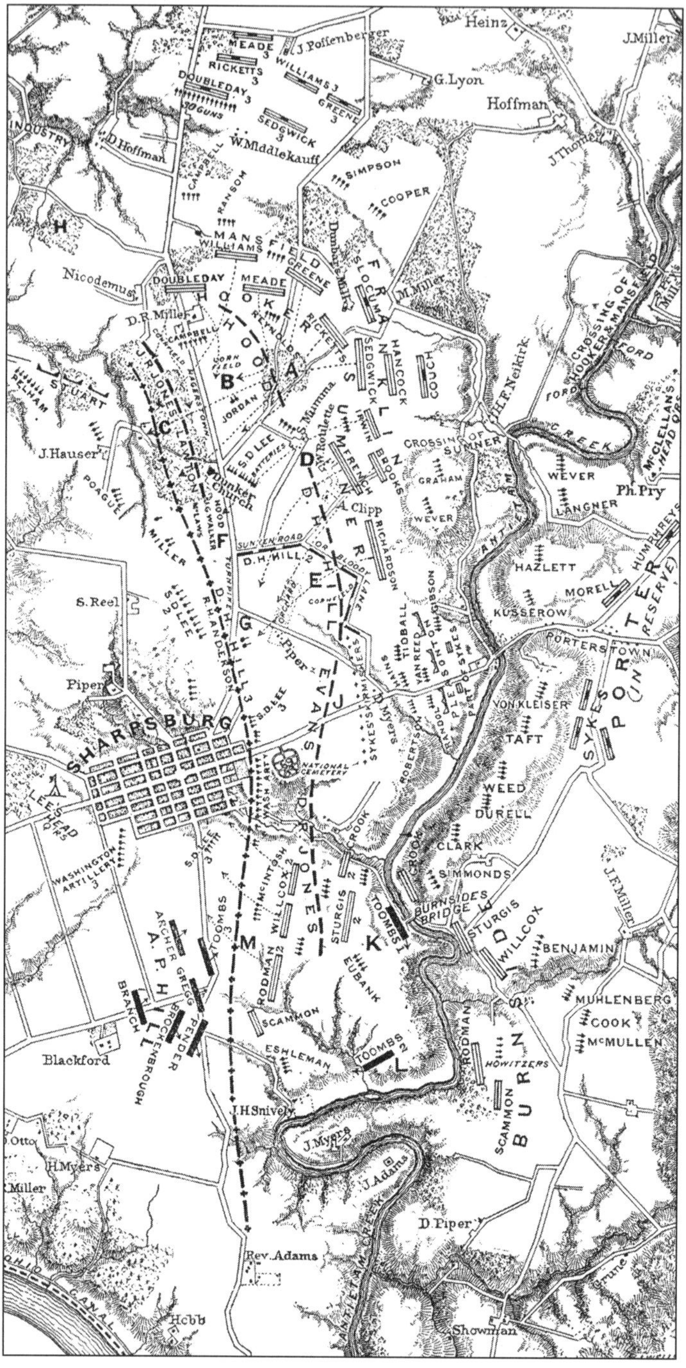

The Battle of Sharpsburg
(*Battles and Leaders of the Civil War*, vol. 2)

numbering only about 120 men, served to defend the road and to provide infantry support for the Macbeth and Washington Artillery units.[16]

PERSONNE described the battle as follows:[17]

The position occupied by the brigade of General Evans . . . was near the center of the line, and to the left of the Turnpike, which runs through the town and crosses the battle field. Owing to the severe repulse of the brigade at Boonsboro Gap, it by no means presented its full numbers, and the deficit was made up by a body of stragglers whom the General had captured and forced into his ranks. On the right of his command, Colonel Stevens with his Holcombe Legion was detailed to act as skirmishers, and on the left was Boyce's Battery of South Carolina. Altogether the little force numbered less than six hundred men. Against these the enemy advanced two brigades, seeking to turn our right flank. The Legion, however, met them and falling back, united with the main body in repelling the attack. Our position favored us, and after a sharp conflict we succeeded in driving the Federals fully five hundred yards through a cornfield and back upon their main supports . . .

Boyce's Battery behaved with great gallantry on the occasion, and twice shot down the colors of the approaching columns. At one time the enemy advanced within four hundred yards, when the artillery suddenly turned upon them with grape and canister, which opened great gaps in their lines, disorganized their troops, and drove them back. A second and third time they met with the same reception, and it was only when Captain Boyce found that he had no support within several hundred yards that he fell back and took a new position further to the right. Here, later in the day, he opened again upon the Federals, and held his ground until the termination of the battle . . . The losses of the battery were two killed, fifteen wounded, and fifteen horses. Most of the casualties in the artillery during the day were occasioned by Federal sharpshooters, who were posted in the treetops and behind stone fences where, with their long range guns and telescopic sights they picked off our officers, men, and horses with almost unerring aim . . . Another loss that falls heavily upon his associates, was the mortal wounding of young Fauquier Trezevant, of Columbia. One of his brothers had been previously wounded, and another killed, and, mere lad though he was—being only 17 years of age—he came to Virginia, hoping to be able to avenge these double injuries. Being a young man of great intelligence, General Evans at once adopted him as his private secretary, and through all the various engagements in which he was engaged, Trezevant was ever to be found close by the General's side. During the battle, Evans being in a very exposed position where the balls were whizzing around him, he told the lad several times to "Go back to the wagons —get out of this fire." "No, General," was the reply of the spirited boy; "I don't want to go back—I want to see the fight, and be by your side." A few moments afterwards he was struck in the leg by a shell. Borne at once from the field, he received immediate surgical attention, and was then carried to the house of a worthy clergyman in Shepardstown, where, according to the last intelligence, his wound had been pronounced mortal. He was a student of the South Carolina College, and there are few young men whose loss will be more deeply deplored . . .[18]

VIDI reported the activities of the Macbeth Artillery:[19]

We usually hauled our baggage in our caissons and in the limber chests of our guns. On the morning of the first fight, when one of our caissons was blown up, a bundle of blankets was sent heavenwards. Ike Ison, who fell just when the explosion took place, rose just as the blankets, under the force of gravity, were returning. In the confusion of the disaster he cried out: "Boys, they are shooting blankets at us!"

Suffering from nausea and paroxysm of pain from the blow-up, I took advantage of a calm in the storm of battle and retired from the field. As I passed along the streets in the western surburbs of Sharpsburg I saw . . . General Lee, almost alone on the crest of a high hill just beyond, with his glasses to his eyes, intently watching his center that had already been broken, without the slightest apparent indication of alarm. The Macbeth had advanced and planted her guns in the gap and was maintaining her position with distinguished gallantry, wholly unconscious that the eyes of our great chief were watching her actions, or that so much depended upon the hero's efforts. I doubt very much if there was another command that fought "from early morn to dewey eve" without relief. Reserves generally do the relieving, but it so happened that when it came the Macbeth's time to be relieved there was no reserve. For every soldier in Lee's army had already smelt the smoke of battle that day.

We had one gun disabled before we reached our first position and lost another between the first and second positions. Hence it is that the Macbeth is referred to in the official reports as a battery of four guns A section of the Washington Light Artillery received distinguished mention in connection with the saving of our center. It fought well and merited all the official notice it received, but the Macbeth was in front of it and nearer to the enemy, and was there after the section referred to had left the field

Lee noted the "well-directed fire of . . . Captain Boyce's South Carolina battery" in his report of the battle.[20] VIDI continued his account:

As McClellan failed to accept Lee's offer of battle on the 18th, our army was ordered to cross the Potomac that night. The Macbeth reached the river before twilight, and there we remained until dawn the next morning. The infantry began to enter the river as we drove up, and as the ford was deep the crossing was slow. As we neared the southern bank of the Potomac, an exhausted horse in a battery to our front fell. He was too weak to pull out of the water. General Lee, riding out of the river just then, watched the ineffectual efforts to put the feeble animal on its feet and said: "Every minute is worth an hour to us. Roll him out of the way." The horse went into the river, and Lee and his men moved on.

Captain Edwards described a welcome period of rest near Winchester, Virginia:

On the night of the 18th General Lee moved his army toward the Potomac, crossed it successfully and by the 20th had his army encamped around Winchester, Va. Our brigade remained in camp at Winchester from the 20th of September until the 12th of November. It was remarkable how rapidly they recuperated in health, morale and numbers.[21] We got fat beef from the Shenandoah Valley, and the men enjoyed it hugely, as the campaign in Maryland had been a succession of rapid marches with but little time for cooking food. Hardtack and bacon, and none too plenty of that, had been the usual bill of fare.

About the latter part of October, I saw the whole of the Army of Northern Virginia pass in review before General Lee and his corps commanders. It was a grand sight to behold, and one that a soldier of that historic army will never forget.

On October 8, 1862, while the brigade was encamped near Winchester, Colonel Peter Fayssoux Stevens decided that he had volunteered to serve in the defense of his home state, not in order to fight in Virginia and Maryland, and he resigned to return to the ministry. A few days later, General Evans wrote his official report of the campaign, observing that since July 30 his brigade had lost 1,024 of its twenty-two hundred men in battle.[22]

5

THE FIGHTING ALMOST ENDS FOR ADJUTANT DUBOSE

I found that I had been numbered among the dead . . . he took me around to a reading room and there I read an account of my death and a brief obituary . . .

William Porcher DuBose

We briefly interrupt the story of the brigade to relate the experiences of William Porcher DuBose after his capture at South Mountain. His story illustrates the treatment of captured officers (he was at that time the adjutant of the Holcombe Legion) and the conditions at Fort Delaware Prison, which was located on an island in the Delaware River.[1] He also described the custom, practiced early in the war by both sides, of paroling a prisoner on his honor not to rejoin the fighting until exchanged for an enemy prisoner.[2]

Adjutant DuBose told the story of his capture, imprisonment, and parole:

The next morning I opened my eyes to the light of day, though very early day, and saw two soldiers politely sitting at my head and feet, waiting for me to take out my sleep. I arose and looked around. The mountain was indeed abandoned; no one was there but we three. The Yankee officer—and the army—had marched off hours before and must have been approaching the next day's battlefield at Sharpsburg. My two guards, both of them Irishmen, I think, were as deferential as valets. They had orders to keep me and to convey me to an adjacent camp. On our way we passed just over the battlefield, which I had searched in the night for dead bodies. There they were plain enough in the morning. As I passed by a certain one of them, outside of his haversack, lay a nicely folded *clean* cotton handkerchief. I stooped down and picked it up with the remark, "Poor fellow, he'll have no further use for it, and it will come in quite handy for me." My two companions were quite shocked at my venturing to appropriate anything belonging to the dead. They had that Roman Catholic superstitious feeling.

William Porcher DuBose
(courtesy of University of the South)

The camp to which I was consigned was a small one, composed apparently of college or schoolboys, left behind there by the main army for just such uses, I suppose. They were very friendly, but very patriotic. When they asked me if I didn't know that Lee would be annihilated, I didn't answer at all to their liking and they got right provoked.

In the course of the morning, I found myself in the charge of a single officer, a cabinet-maker from Michigan. We soon came to an understanding and I let him feel that I would respect his confidences. He was practically putting me on my parole and allowing me apparently complete liberty. In this way he and I stood in the gap and saw McClellan's army march by. It was perfectly marvelous how, after the disastrous conclusion of Pope's campaign just two weeks before, McClellan could have organized and furnished such an apparently thoroughly supplied new army. I saw McClellan himself ride into the small cleared space of the gap at the head of a thousand splendidly mounted and equipped body-guard. As command after command, interspersed with artillery, marched through, my heart sank lower and lower. I thought of Lee's thirty thousand ragged, hungry, and in great part, sick men waiting to receive these eighty thousand well and strong. But when again and again my friend would say, "What do you think now?" I could only answer, "Wait and see."

After the army had passed, my Michigan friend and myself went scouting along for something to eat. We went into a little hut by the wayside and were served with a very simple repast of bacon and cornbread. I ought to have been ravenous, but somehow I was disappointed to find that I couldn't eat. When it had been suggested to me that we go on this foraging expedition, I had remarked, "You know, my money doesn't go far." "Oh," he said, "that doesn't matter." Now when we had finished it made me open my eyes to see that man take out dimes and nickels to pay for it. It had been long since we had dealt with anything less than dollars.

We could hear in the gap the thunder of Sharpsburg. The Yankees during and after the battle had very little to say. It was impossible for me to get the slightest intelligence of the result, then or afterwards, as long as I was in their hands. But it was very evident that it had been nothing for them to boast of. As a matter of fact, after two days at Sharpsburg, where General Lee held his own to the last, he quietly withdrew and crossed the Potomac, as was said at that time, without the loss of a skillet.

To return to myself. As the Federal troops retired in the direction of Frederick City, I was transferred to a cavalry command where I found myself one of a dozen captured officers. As was always my experience, so long as we were treated individually and personally there was nothing to complain of in our treatment at the hands of the enemy.[3] The cavalry commander informed us very courteously that he could not do much for us in the way of food, because he had none himself.

At Frederick City we twelve officers were placed in a quite small room and the news of our being there quickly reached a number of Southern sympathizers. We were really just about famished and our friends, who brought us at first only little delicacies, began to hurry up more substantial viands. After settling our physical condition, we managed to have a little fun. Among the twelve of us there was a captain and one or two of his lieutenants. The captain, though thoroughly southern in his sentiments, was, as I found out later, a Yankee. We all noticed a tendency to absorb everything for himself, and some of us concocted a scheme of a court martial. They appointed me Judge Advocate and seated me upon a chair to conduct the meeting. The culprit brought before me was our Yankee friend, whose crime was as follows: Someone had called up from the courtyard outside our room to ask for the return of the bucket in which someone had sent us some fine grapes. None of us had heard of the grapes, and when they were finally discovered it was proved that they had been hidden away in a corner by our captain for private consumption. The evidence thoroughly convicted him and a penalty was imposed. Such little bits of fun sometimes lightened up the very hardest corners of our wartime experience.

From Frederick City we were transported to Baltimore, through the streets of which city we were marched in a drizzling rain with the most pathetic indications on every side of the deepest interest and sympathy. We went by boat up the Chesapeake Bay to the little canal that connects the Chesapeake to Delaware Bay, at the extremity of which we came to Fort Delaware.

I might as well give here a little experience, which I found it harder to deal with, I believe, than any in the war. Up to this time, with the help always of a devoted servant, I had been able to keep myself clean and free from the very worst form of dirt, specifically *live dirt*. Keeping up my habit on the boat, I kept myself aloof from contact with the mass of infected men. But we were all night on the boat and I was physically weak and fatigued. When it came to the last, the whole space of the deck was covered with sleeping men, and *then* I discovered that it was impossible for me to stand on my feet all night long. The only square inch of uncovered space on the deck was small. At the battle-field of Manassas, I had spent one night practically on a rail in the mud, and on this occasion I had to squeeze myself onto a narrow space between sleeping men. I knew the consequences, but had no choice. The first few days at Fort Delaware, I did all that I could to master the situation and make the most out of my stay in prison, however *little* that most might be. I had not as yet a change of underclothing and to my horror on the third or fourth day, I found myself inhabited in spite of everything I could do to prevent it. I have to confess that the strongest religious principles I could summon to my help were inadequate to this occasion. I could not reconcile myself to it.

Fort Delaware was built around a very large court or parade ground. The whole length of the space between the interior court and the exterior river was occupied by a very long, wide room in which the officer prisoners were incarcerated, amounting to at least some seventy-five of us. On our first entrance to this room, at a time when I was hoping to make the most of things, I secured a couple of empty boxes in which shoes had been sent from Baltimore. I put these end to end to make a couch and put a blanket over them. The entire length on both sides of the room was occupied by one continuous bunk intended for the common bunk of us all. The two deep windows overlooking the river were arranged for lavatory purposes with running water on each side of each seat. On the end of the room overlooking the inner court, there were also two windows and between these I placed my two boxes so that I had a bed of my own. Every morning, even in the crowd, I could take something of a half-bath before the window-seat. Here I was exposed to observation and attracted much attention. When my back was exposed, my undressed and still somewhat fresh wound of several weeks became visible. As I stooped forward the wound had the appearance of having gone straight through my backbone, and occasioned much comment and surprise.

Boxes of shoes and clothing came in from Baltimore, but as the crowd increased, there developed a competition and scrambling that was very distasteful, and repulsive even, to some of us, even to our refusing to take part in it. Any body of men thrown promiscuously together without organization or law of any kind is liable to degenerate, on the part of some, into a very offensive selfishness. Here my Yankee captain of Frederick City memory showed his hand again. One of the twelve who had roomed together at Frederick asked me if I'd got a pair of shoes. I told him no, that I could not take part in such scrambling. He then said, "Captain ______ has two pairs and I am going to get one pair from him." So he took the occasion to call attention to the fact publicly that I had no shoes and Captain ______ had two pairs. The proof of the fact was so clear that the shoes were produced and I was provided for.

Among those same twelve who had been thrown together at Frederick was a Captain Grimes, brother of General Grimes of North Carolina and a member of his staff. When we were first thrown together before we got to Frederick, I introduced myself to him and asked him if he was any relation to the Misses Grimes, the two ladies with whom I had ridden during the summer of 1860 from Abbeville to Hot Springs and back. He said he was their brother. I was very much drawn by his manliness and gentleness and unselfishness in all our experiences together.

I found several other friends in the prison. Among my University of Virginia friends and contemporaries there were a very great many in the ordnance department of the army. General Gorgas, who was the very efficient head of the Confederate Ordnance Department, very early made all of the appointments to it subject to a very rigid examination. There were no greater adepts in the art of being examined than the University of Virginia graduates, and soon all of the appointments began to fall into their hands. Owing to my long residence at the University, I had often said that I had never found myself out of the reach of some University friend. I thought I had done so, as I entered the door of that prison, but at once two men grasped my hands, one from Charlottesville and one from Portsmouth, Virginia. Very early I had another friend from the Ordnance Department, Captain F. W. Dawson, a young English boy who had come over with Captain Pegram in, I believe, the very first boat that ran the blockade into Richmond. He was later the very distinguished editor of the *Charleston News and Courier.*

My only disagreeable experience at Fort Delaware had been when I was summoned up before the commandant, as a number of others were, and asked to give information about the Confederate Army and affairs generally. An effort was made to extort this information, but in one way or another, I think that we all succeeded in not contributing much of the information desired.

Then I had a very remarkable experience in prison. The very day after we arrived we were informed that there would be a service on the inside of the fort the next day and that we would be allowed to attend. I went. The services were conducted by Dr. Benjamin Franklin and Dr. J. W. Tustin. A day or two afterward, Dr. Tustin appeared in the entrance to our quarters in company with an officer. The officer said in a loud voice, "Are there any Charlestonians present in this room?" I was standing near, and when there was no reply, I remarked, "I'm practically a Charlestonian although I do not live there. Can I be of service?" Dr. Tustin at once stepped forward and introduced himself to me. It had been some years then since I had been in Charleston and he informed me that he had been for a considerable time the pastor of the Huguenot Church in Charleston. I should note that the bulk of the Low Country Huguenots had entered the English Church even in Colonial times. There was, however, some years before the war, a little revival of the old Huguenot feeling and of a small Huguenot congregation. The pastor of the Huguenot church was generally a Presbyterian but had to use the Huguenot ritual. This time, however, the pastor had been a Baptist, the Rev. Mr. Tustin. Mr. Tustin had been very acceptable to the Huguenot congregation, but for reasons which will be apparent as we go on, had resigned his charge, had gone north, and had been ordained in the Episcopal Church. That was the reason he resigned. In the fort, he spoke with much feeling of his Charleston charge and showed me a very handsome watch that had been given him at the time of his resignation. My brief acquaintance with Dr. Tustin was very interesting to me at the time, but in the subsequent terrible experiences of the war made no very deep impression upon me. I was to hear of him later, however.[4]

About this time rumors began to circulate of our probable exchange or parole, and there was some kind of a vessel that was to take us to Richmond for that purpose. As I have said before, I had made myself tolerably comfortable and for a while tolerably satisfied, with my two boxes and with a book or two. But after hearing this rumor, I have to confess that I completely lost control of my philosophy or religion and spent most of my time gazing up the river to see the boat that was to take us away. After much hope deferred the boats actually came, and we embarked upon my first sea voyage—around to Richmond.

After a voyage of a day or two we arrived at Aiken's Landing on the James River, some miles below Richmond. On the route the vessels were separated

The steamer *New York* at Aiken's Landing
(courtesy of Library of Congress)

and that reason was assigned for the lack of food on our boat. We had nothing for several days but dry hardtack. After a little while it became almost impossible to swallow this, and our appetites revolted against it. In consequence, we arrived at Aiken's Landing practically starved. Our Confederate commissioner, Ould, who should have been there to receive us, failed to make his appearance for twenty-four hours after our arrival and our famine grew apace. Some neighbors in the vicinity sent some provisions but being not yet paroled we were allowed to go off the boat only in detachments. By the time I got out, all the platters had literally been licked clean. I'm ashamed to confess that I was reduced to the extremity of getting my hardtack down by running it round the crevices of the empty pans to get a slight taste of the bacon. After returning to the vessel, one of my prisoner friends said confidently that, if we could raise a little silver, he had found his way to the kitchen on the boat and we might get something. I fortunately had a little change. My friend soon appeared with a small pot of coffee and a few potatoes. Somehow, I did not care much for the potatoes, but that cup of coffee was one of the incidents of my life. I remember telling Bishop Davis soon afterwards that I could now appreciate the feeling of a drunkard. If I had been at the cannon's mouth, I could not have withheld that cup from my lips. You may understand, therefore, a happy incident which occurred upon the belated arrival of Commissioner Ould.

It was a rather gloomy outlook. We were eight miles from Richmond and had no conception of how we were to get there. As I walked down the gangway of the boat, I must have been a sorry looking object. I still had the old coat on, that had been torn from my back when I was captured. As I stepped on the land and was making my way through the small crowd that had collected, I suddenly heard at my elbow a loud laugh which carried me back instantly a number of years to my old University of Virginia days. Standing in easy touch of me was a splendid looking officer in a fine artillery captain's uniform, and the face was the face of Sam Preston.

Captain Preston was an officer of the heavy artillery stationed on the banks of the Potomac for the protection of Richmond. His camp was a very short distance off and I was promptly conveyed there. Fortunately it was supper-time and the camp arrangements were luxurious to my eyes. Perhaps to my salvation, there wasn't enough on the table, but what was there was of the very best Virginia cooking and was quite enough to keep me alive and to raise my spirits somewhat. I must have been in appearance quite a contrast to the really elegantly attired men who resided there and who could accumulate not only comforts, but elegancies. There was a little damper to my spirits when at bedtime Captain Preston showed me into a nice tent with a nice cot and clean sheets with a blanket spread over it. I tried hard to decline the indulgence but there was no arguing with him so I had to make up my own mind what to do about it. I had absolutely no clothing except what was on my back, and that had been there for a long time. I determined not to put my clothing or myself on that bed. However, at last I arranged it in this wise: I took a sheet and covered the entire bunk so that the edges would fall down to the ground and slept *on* it and not *under* it. In this way I could make up my bed in the morning with assurance that I left no unseemly remembrances behind me. The next day Sam Preston arranged for me to get into the city. I made my way at once to what had been and was still a real Richmond home to me, the home of the Dudley's. It was a home not to me only, but to all of my South Carolina friends who had been at the University of Virginia with me, the Haskells especially. Here I quickly effaced all traces of my recent experiences.

The paroled prisoners had orders to remain in Richmond and to report from time to time at a parole camp until they could be exchanged. I could not have had a home that was more of a home to me than the one I was in, and in this respect I was as fortunate as it was possible to be.

On my first arrival in Richmond I went to the old Exchange Hotel, which was a sort of a center of things in the city. There I came upon my cousin and almost brother, Captain C. S. Dwight of the Engineer Corps. From him I had the first intimation of what somehow or other had not occurred to me. I found that I had been numbered among the dead; the circumstances were these: On the midnight of my capture my men, waiting and expecting my return as they reported, heard a sudden shot and then a loud cry. The cry, as I have reported before, was not from me but from my antagonist. There then followed, they said, a long silence. Drawing the natural conclusion, after waiting a sufficient time, they returned to the gap and found the army gone. They followed on and regained connection with it at Sharpsburg. Colonel Stevens, commanding our brigade, assumed as everyone else did, that I was killed. Soon after he resigned his office, took orders in the church, and having a son born about that time he named him after me. He felt in some way responsible for my death because it was he who had sent me on my midnight reconnaissance.

To return to Richmond! Captain Dwight instantly hurried me off to announce my resurrection elsewhere. A friend of our family, Miss Victoria Murden, had been a month or two in Richmond, one of her objects being to ascertain the fate of myself and my cousin, Moultrie Dwight. Moultrie Dwight had been easily discovered. He had a serious injury, not a wound, while running over those rocks at Harper's Ferry and had fallen into the hands of the enemy. But he had the good fortune to be taken in by friends in Baltimore and was living like a prince there while we were pining away in prison. Miss Victoria was staying with the Richardsons, just across the street from Capitol Square. As we crossed the square from below and approached a long walk just opposite the Richardson's and within the square, we saw three persons, Mr. and Mrs. Richardson and Miss Victoria, sauntering up and down the walk in the beautiful moonlight. They turned as they reached the walk and we approached them from the rear. Captain Dwight touched Miss Victoria and she turned and saw me in the moonlight. She had finally given up hope of finding me alive, and her surprise completely overcame her. She had kept in communication with my home, and from her I learned what was going on there.

The next day while walking in the street I met an old Citadel man, Sam Depass. He spoke to me cordially and finally said, "How is your brother?"

I asked, "Which brother?"

"Your brother William."

"I am my brother William myself."

"You aren't. He's dead."

"I don't think so."

"Yes, he is. I can prove it to you."

So he took me around to a reading room and there I read an account of my death and a brief notice of myself written by Mr. Richard Yeadon of Charleston.

As required, I went around to the parole camp to report. The officer was in a nicely prepared tent, and behind the table and prepared to receive my record, sat a young officer. He looked up and said, "Your name, sir."

"DuBose, William Porcher."

He dropped his pen and stood up a minute. "DuBose," he said, "I'm a DuBose, myself." The different branches of the DuBose family had been so effectively separated in different parts of the state, that they had lost track of each other's existence. The war threw us together on many occasions. I found the name scattered right widely over the South. This young man was from Washington, Georgia, and was of a large connection of which the most prominent member at that time was Mrs. Robert Toombs.

Our exchange was delayed for a long time and we were kept waiting in Richmond for it to take place. During my stay I had some few adventures. The city was right full at that time of refugees from Baltimore, the least desirable class of which was the Baltimore plugs, who made the streets quite unsafe at night. Walking home one night with Captain Dwight along a deserted street, we encountered three men coming from the opposite direction. As we met, I passed quite safely on one side and suddenly heard a scuffle behind me. It seemed that one of these men had tried to push Captain Dwight off the pavement. It led to quite an active collision. As I turned suddenly around with both hands and head full of other things, I encountered a blow which brought me to the earth sprawling. As I rose, I saw the men in the distance making off and Captain Dwight standing with a handkerchief to his nose, trying to save his new uniform. His remark was, "Well, I gave better than I got."

The Chief Surgeon of the Confederacy was Dr. Edwin Gaillard, a connection of ours. I called on him one day and in the course of the conversation he asked why I didn't go home. I told him that there was an order against it; we were to remain there until exchanged. He said, "Why don't you get a sick leave?" I told him, "Because I am not sick." He said, "Yes, you are, and I'll make you out a furlough." which he proceeded to do. In fact, I *had* been very severely used up by my experience, and I suppose he truly could call me a sick man. At any rate, he did, and I went home.

I ought to have stated before that during the long period of the bombardment of Charleston, all citizens were expelled from the city and many found refuge in all the upcountry towns.[5] The Peronneaus removed to Anderson, and my sisters had long wished to have them pay them a visit. It was so arranged that Sue and Nannie Peronneau would be at my home near Winnsboro during my furlough. In this way several weeks were spent at Roseland, very delightfully to us all.

I remember one day especially of the most perfect Indian summer I ever saw—so perfect that I always define Indian summer by my recollection of it—a day which Nannie and myself spent in the woods just in front of Roseland, and in which I had never seen quite so much beauty before. We strolled about, then found a nice delightful place in the sun and enjoyed ourselves and each other.

I was exchanged and rejoined my command, finding it stationed in the vicinity of Wilmington, North Carolina.

Unfortunately for DuBose, he rejoined Evans' Brigade just in time to participate in the Battle of Kinston.

6

The Battle of Kinston

> . . . though General Evans has once surrendered to a crinoline skirt, the breeches do not walk the earth or fly the air before which he will bow in homage as a captive.
>
> Felix Gregory DeFontaine

As soon as North Carolina left the Union, it began to make preparations to defend its coast. Federal excursions inland from coastal waterways could threaten the state's ports as well as the Wilmington and Weldon Railroad, a main connector from Richmond to Charleston. To prevent this, forts were constructed at the Oregon, Ocracoke, and Hatteras inlets. Privateers operated from these defended waters to prey upon Union shipping until a Union force under General Butler attacked and captured the two forts at the Hatteras inlet in late August 1861. The Confederates then abandoned their forts at the Oregon and Ocracoke inlets without a fight. These were welcome Federal victories, coming as they did just after the Federal defeat at First Manassas.[1] In February 1862, an expedition under General Burnside captured Roanoke Island, occupied Elizabeth City and Edenton, burned the town of Winton, blocked the Dismal Swamp Canal to Norfolk, and destroyed the Confederate navy in the area. His troops proceeded up the Neuse River and captured New Bern in mid-March. In early July, Burnside was ordered to advance on Goldsboro, an extremely important Confederate railroad junction point. This order was countermanded three days later when Burnside was ordered to bring seven thousand troops to the aid of General McClellan in the Peninsular Campaign near Richmond.[2] General Foster was left in charge of the Department of North Carolina with nine thousand troops, too few to press the Federal attack further inland. For the next few months, the opposing forces carried out small raids against each other. On November 5, Federal troops advanced to within a few miles of Tarboro, but the sounds of numerous train whistles from the town convinced General Foster that Confederate reinforcements were steadily arriving, and he retreated back to New Bern.[3] Among the reinforcements was Evans' Brigade.[4]

VIDI of the Macbeth Artillery reported on the diversion of Evans' Brigade to North Carolina:[5]

When McClellan marched southward about the last of October, with Fredericksburg as his objective point, Lee at once broke up his camp in the vicinity of Winchester and threw his army between Richmond and the Federal host, halting at Culpeper long enough to discern McClellan's plans and then moving on and confronting him at Fredericksburg. Lee left his camps near Winchester on 31st October, and bivouacked that night on the banks of that most beautiful of streams, both in name and surroundings—the Shenandoah.

The morning of the first of November was bright and frosty, and brave men who had marched unblanched in the face of a perfect storm of whistling bullets on a score of hard-fought battle fields, trembled as they approached the chilly waters of the Shenandoah. There was no time for debating on the manner of crossing. They moved into the water with a shivering whoop and pulled for the other side in a style that did not remind a looker-on of troops making time. The artillery men, seated on their caissons above the water, enjoyed the scene more than did the infantry, because they saw more that was laughable. Lee's army bivouacked that night at Front Royal. . . . Leaving Front Royal on the morning of the 2nd November, we camped that night at a little town by the name of Washington, situated in the midst of the surrounding mountains. On the night of the 3rd, we bivouacked near Culpeper; on the 4th in a chestnut grove in the vicinity of Culpeper; and on the 5th at the Court House. From this place Evans' Brigade, to which the Macbeth was nominally attached, was ordered to North Carolina.[6] The hardships through which the men had passed during the campaigns through Virginia and Maryland made them quite willing to go towards home, and the order to go to North Carolina was a source of much rejoicing. Rations were cooked and our guns were soon packed on open flats. The accommodation for the men was on a par with that made for the guns. They were crowded on the same open flats, and the guns and caissons and the blankets spread over them were our only protection from the weather. It was night when we left Culpeper. Snow was already falling, and our suffering from cold was intense. We spent most of the night at Gordonsville, without fires.

Private Jones of the Twenty-third Regiment recalled that the infantry did not fare much better:

When the 23rd left Culpeper, we had to ride on platform cars, which was by no means comfortable. About half way between Culpeper and Gordonsville we were caught in a heavy snow storm and being so much exposed, we suffered very much from the intense and bitter cold. Our torture in this biting cold, as it may be truthfully called, was prolonged and increased by the locomotive drawing the train of cars becoming in some way out of fix, which caused a delay of several hours. We tried to make fires, but with very poor success; everything being wet and everything in shape of fuel scarce. After a long time of bamming, hammering, and twisting, the old iron horse was pronounced better, and after a good feed of wood and fire and a good supply of water, we started again on our way to Gordonsville. We were in the snow for several days, for the snow had fallen to the depth of seven or eight inches on the level.

Corporal John Forrest Robertson of the Twenty-third Regiment recalled the train ride to Richmond:

From Culpepper we were transported to Richmond on cars; the train was made up of three or four box cars, the balance open platform cars. Soon after the train got underway, snow commenced to fall rather lively. In the box cars we were so crowded we could not stretch our limbs, but what difference—we were Confederate soldiers and anything ought to be good enough for us. Before reaching our destination I took a look out ahead from the box car I was in. The sight met my eyes of open platform cars loaded with half-fed soldiers, many with scant clothing and shoeless, and all covered with snow. Upon arriving in Richmond, I filled up with apple-jack and took the middle of the streets through the snow in bare feet—no fires for me as I did not feel the want of them. Everybody was willing to treat Mars Robert's boys with as much and as often as they desired. There our Brigade was ordered to Petersburg. We marched to the depot to take the cars for that place and found the transportation that was awaiting us in little better shape that what we had just left. The open platform cars had rough board seats without backs and furnished with cushions of snow. Attached to this train was one passenger coach; being with the first crowd, I with others filled up said coach. I enjoyed its comfort immensely, the first of that class I had been in since the war started. My railroad travelling up to that time had been in box cars, on top of box cars, and on open platform cars. After a while, into this passenger coach walks the General and his aids. He ordered the men to vacate saying that this car had been set apart for himself and his staff. Silence for the time reigned all around, and no vacating was done. The treatment that we had just passed through, after a campaign of hard fighting and an ordeal of privations and suffering which no words in the English language can describe, had exhausted our patience and sent discipline to the winds. He dared not to use violence. After a minute or so, one of the soldiers remarked: "General, we tried the snow last night. I guess you will have to try it tonight—we boys are going to stay right in this car." I do not know how the General got to Petersburg; he did not travel in the car that he claimed was set apart for him.

VIDI continued his account of the Macbeth Artillery:

On the night of the 8th we remained on the cars at Petersburg, Virginia, and on the 9th at Weldon, North Carolina. It was generally believed that we were on our way to Wilmington, but after leaving Weldon we were switched off on a branch road and ran down to Tarboro. This beautiful little town on the banks of the Tar River was in the midst of one of the prettiest farming countries I ever saw. This lovely little place is associated in my mind with fine apples and kind people. The water of the Tar River is as black as tar, hence its name. We crossed to the southern side of the river and remained in camp there four days. That was long enough to convince General Evans that Tarboro was not a place of strategic importance and not likely to be invaded by the enemy. On the morning of the 15th we repacked our guns on the cars, ran up to the Wilmington and Weldon railroad, thence to Goldsboro, and from thence down to Kinston on the Newberne railroad. Kinston is situated on the eastern side of the Neuse River in what seemed to be a low marshy country. North of the town was a beautiful grove, and the land was more elevated. As Tarboro was remembered for its good apples, so Kinston is remembered most of all as abounding in large sweet potatoes and big fat opossums.

The river was crossed by a bridge one mile south of the town. Two roads led from the bridge on the western side—one leaving the river at right angles, and the other running down it and on to Newberne. In about one-half of a mile from the bridge the river bends sharply to the left; at this point a road leaving the Newberne road ran down the river for a mile to some breastworks at the mouth of South Creek; then leaving the river at right angles ran back to the Newberne road about three miles from Kinston. The confluence of these two roads was known as Wise's Fort. It was in an old field at this place that the Macbeth, after having bivouacked for a few days in a beautiful grove on Washington Hill north of Kinston, was camping when the enemy advanced from Newberne.

Private Andrews of the Seventeenth Regiment noted the soldiers' recurrent quest for food and drink:

Passing through the town, we took the road toward Newbern and encamped five miles beyond Kinston at a country church. The people living near were kind enough to let us have vegetables, which we craved, having been without them for quite a while. Some men had scurvy in consequence. Some of the regiment found apple jack near the camp. When freely imbibed the apple jack (so said) made the best of friends not only quarrel but desire to kill each other.

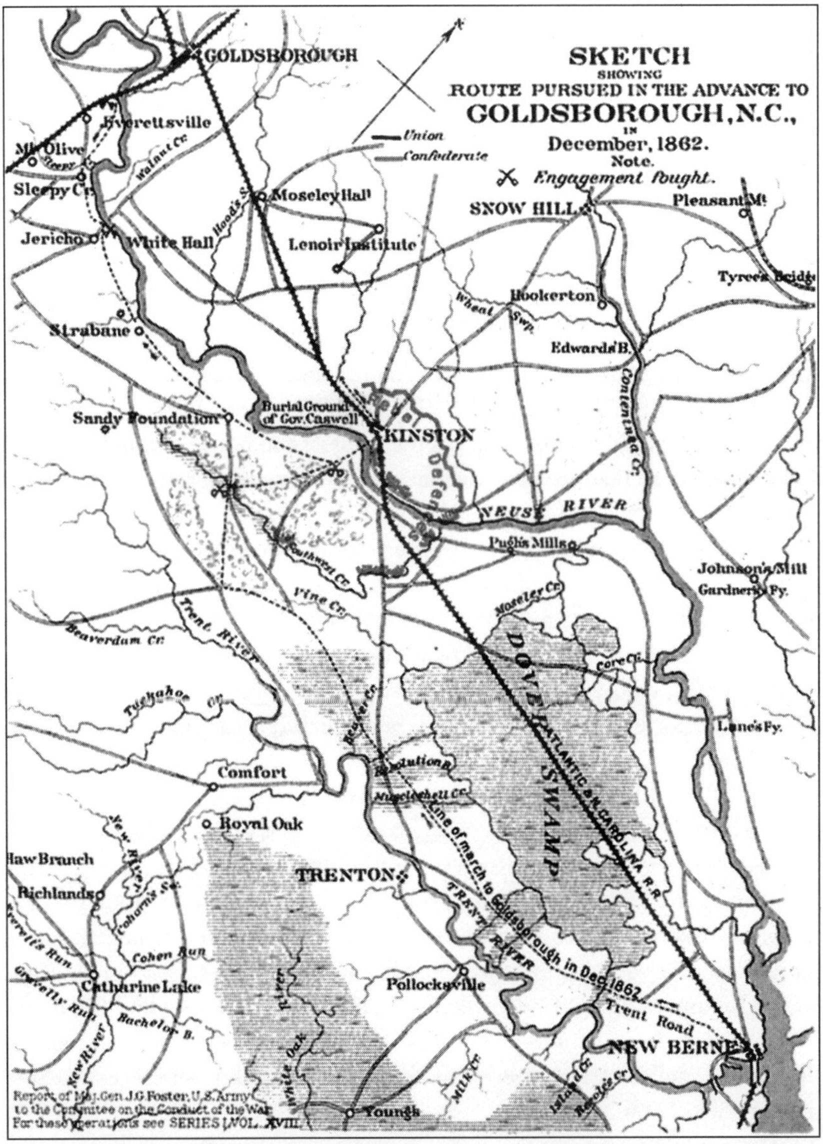

Foster's route from Newbern to Goldsboro
(*Atlas to Accompany the Official Records*, Plate XCI, no. 3)

Captain Edwards marched to Kinston with the Seventeenth Regiment:

On the 12th of December Companies A and E were sent out on picket on the main road leading to Newbern. We went down the road until we were four or five miles away from the regiment. We found at the point where we intended to remain for the night, a company of raw Confederate cavalry. Captain Mills and I formed our companies in line of battle in the edge of the woods so as to command the road and intended to lie on our arms, for we expected to have to use them at any minute. About an hour before sunset Colonel McMaster sent a courier on horseback with orders for us to bring our companies back to the regiment as quick as possible. The cavalry was in a house with their horses picketed around it. They had placed a vidette about a quarter of a mile down the road. Before we left there Mills and I begged the officer in command to bring his men out of the house and mount them and hold them in readiness for an attack. He did not seem to be at all uneasy, and said his videttes would give him timely notice. But, alas, his over confidence and the lack of knowledge of the rules of war proved his undoing. At dusk the Yankee cavalry captured his videttes, surrounded the house and captured the whole layout, men and horses. When we got to camp, the tents were all struck and the regiment ready to move, which we proceeded to do in short order, falling behind Falling Creek.

On the morning of the 13th, the Seventeenth Regiment was marched towards Kinston. On the way four companies were detached and sent, in command of Major J. R. Culp, to guard a bridge on Falling Creek on another road leading into the town, while the other six companies, under Colonel McMaster, marched down the New Road some four or five miles from Kinston. We had with us the Holcombe Legion, Boyce's Battery and the Sixty-first North Carolina Regiment. We skirmished with the enemy all evening, holding them in check as our numbers were too few to take the aggressive. The Eighteenth Regiment was at Greenville, N.C., and the Twenty-second Regiment was posted to defend another road leading into the town.[7] We finally, late in the evening, fell back on the edge of a piece of timber bordering on a swamp through which the public road passed. It was the first time the Sixty-first North Carolina Regiment had been under fire, and they behaved very badly. Late in the evening Company A and Company F, of the Seventeenth Regiment, were sent on four or five hundred yards in advance of the line as skirmishers. Captain J. W. Avery placed his company behind a fence on the left of the road, and I formed Company A behind a fence on the right of the road, and waited the approach of the enemy. Soon a batch of about a dozen Yankee cavalrymen came riding up the road in fine style. When we first saw them coming Captain Avery and I agreed to let them ride up to us and capture them and had ordered the men not to fire on them, but the vidette who had been placed some twenty steps in advance of the companies in a fence corner in the lane did not fancy the arrangement, that they might shoot him before the capture could take place, consequently when they got within about one hundred yards of his post he fired on them. But just before he fired we heard the leader say to his men: "Keep a sharp look out, and keep your guns in your hands." Just then our vidette fired on them and they began to pull their horses round. We then ordered our companies to fire, and as well as I could see through the smoke the whole batch, men and horses, went down. We could then hear the command all along the line of battle of infantry giving the command forward. We did not, however, wait the near approach of these gentlemen, knowing that we were not about to fight a whole army corps. We fell back and formed on the regiment. Night was then approaching and this Yankee line of battle marched up in sight of us. Their artillery exchanged a few rounds with Captain Boyce, when they stacked arms, built up camp fires and went to cooking supper.

We lay there and watched them until about 9 P.M., when we quietly withdrew to the opposite side of the swamp and camped near a church building which stood on a sandy knoll nearby. We were cold and hungry and in crossing the little creek which ran through the swamp we had gotten wet and muddy. We were ordered to build no fires. About 11 o'clock I went to Colonel McMaster and told him the men were freezing and we must have some fire. His reply was that if we built fires the Yankees would be likely to shell us. My reply was that death by a shell would be much easier than to slowly freeze to death. He then told me to say to the men to build very small fires. We did so, and it was not many minutes until we had good hot fires. The Yankees did not shell us. We had acted so saucily all day that General Foster had no idea that we were so few in number. We had some troops on all the roads, and Major Culp had made a gallant stand and held his position until it was no longer necessary to defend that road, as the Twenty-second South Carolina Regiment had fallen back and given the enemy the parallel road.

Major General G. W. Smith, then at Petersburg, informed the War Department on December 13 that "Evans has been fighting in advance of Kinston all day, principally artillery. We were retiring slowly, and at night the enemy were near the bridge at Kinston. Evans calls for reinforcements. One regiment started from here at 8 o'clock and one more will start at 6 o'clock in the morning from this place and one from the Blackwater." On December 15, Smith reported his own arrival at Goldsboro at 3 P.M. to take command.[8]

VIDI gave this account of the events of December 13:[9]

The enemy were in full force at Newberne, and it was believed that an advance was contemplated. For some purpose Evans, with the 18th South

Carolina Regiment commanded by Colonel, now Judge, Wallace had gone over to Greenville, North Carolina, and Colonel Goodlett, being the ranking officer, was left in command at Kinston. Lieutenant Jeter and I called on Colonel Goodlett [of the Twenty-second Regiment], and as was usual among soldiers the conversation turned on the campaigns through which we had recently passed. In referring to the affair at Graveyard Hill [at Rappahannock Station], where we had had a bitter experience, he said: "I thought Evans' Brigade was unnecessarily exposed there and I asked Colonels Gadberry and Means if they were going to remain there. They said, 'until we get orders to leave.' I took it on myself to march my regiment out, and I intend to act on my judgement whenever I think I am unnecessarily exposed." I could not but think how inefficient must be an army where each sub-officer was to determine for himself the proper time to leave the battlefield. It was this independent action on the part of Colonel Goodlett a few days afterwards that converted what ought to have been a glorious victory into shameful defeat.

We were not pleased with the drift of things, and our anxiety on the morning of the 13th was greatly increased as the booming of cannon on the upper road convinced us that our position had been flanked and the enemy already nearer the bridge than was the position occupied by the Macbeth. As the day wore on, the firing was perceptibly nearer to the bridge. It was quite evident that the enemy were cautiously feeling their way towards Kinston. It looked as though Goodlett had either forgotten or did not need us. Evans reached the field from Greenville just before night and, finding the enemy advancing less than a mile from the bridge, led the Twenty-second South

The Battle of Kinston
(*Harper's Magazine*, December, 1862)

Carolina Regiment in a charge that forced them back and checked them for the evening. He then selected his ground and made a disposition of his troops for a fight the next day. The Macbeth was at once ordered up to the bridge. The timely arrival of Evans was all that saved us from capture.

Stretching out from the bridge westward and southward for more than a fourth of a mile was an open field, save for a cluster of old-field pines on top of a little hill some three hundred yards from and directly in front of the bridge. Beyond this field was a dense forest in the shape of a half-moon, with its concave towards our position. Along the edge of this forest, Evans formed his line of battle—the Twenty-second on the river to our left and a battalion of North Carolina Conscripts on an impassable swamp to our right. Our position was a good one. The enemy could not flank us on either wing, and we had enough men to fill up the line from the swamp on our right to the river on our left. The guns of the Macbeth were placed in position at the end of the bridge on the east side of the river. Small breastworks were thrown up in front of our guns. I believe it was done by our own men during the night of the 13th for their own protection. Just back of our guns was a marsh more than one hundred yards wide which was almost an unbroken sheet of water at that time. It was through this marsh that I made my escape after the bridge was fired.

Before sunrise on the morning of the 14th, as the train ran into Kinston the whistle blew, soldiers yelled, and the drums were beat at a fearful rate. It sounded as if a large part of Lee's army had been sent to reinforce us. Directly the noisy fellows came into sight. It was a "tempest in a tea-kettle"—a regular game of bluff. It was only a 'battalion' of about one hundred and fifty North Carolina Conscripts. Following just in the rear of this command came General Evans.

When the fight began, General Evans was with us at the west end of the bridge. A soldier came running out of the fight and on being asked what was the matter said "My gun is bent." Evans took it from him and after looking at it for a moment said "You put this gun between two trees and bent it on purpose to get out of the fight." He gave him another gun, and the poor fellow was marched back into the fight.

On reaching our position, addressing Captain Boyce, he said that the enemy had twenty-two thousand men and that he had only twenty-two hundred, that he might be forced to retreat across the river, and in that event he wanted the bridge burnt, and that he would entrust that to him: "Appoint an officer and two men to make the necessary preparation." Such language from the commander on the eve of battle was not inspiring—eleven to one . . . It was a poor way to encourage troops. The burning of a bridge between the fire of two armies was a distinction that no one was likely to covet. Captain

Boyce evidently appreciated the danger, and the order to burn the bridge was given to the writer with an apology. He said Lieutenant Munro had been seriously wounded and had just returned to the company, and that he did not think it right to impose that duty on him. "I want you to pick two men and burn the bridge, if it becomes necessary." Without special reference to the courage of the men, I took the two first I came to—John McCrady and Joe Bennett, both of Spartanburg. We at once began our preparation by scattering cotton along the sides of the bridge from end to end. On the cotton we piled old rails, planks, and other such combustible material as we could find. This combination of combustibles was made more so by being thoroughly saturated with turpentine. We then prepared faggots of fat pine and made a fire at the west end of the bridge from which to light our torches at the opportune moment.

Captain Edwards reported from the Seventeenth Regiment:

On the morning of the 14th our line of battle was formed on the edge of the swamp on each side of the church and on each side of the public road. Companies A and C, of the Seventeenth Regiment, were again sent out as skirmishers. We re-crossed the swamp and waited the enemy on the edge of a large stubble field, taking a position behind a rail fence. It was not long until the enemy appeared in line of battle in our front, slowly advancing. According to arrangement agreed upon by Captain Avery and myself, when they approached within rifle range we fired a volley into them and quietly fell back across the swamp and united with the regiment. About that time Major Culp rejoined us with his four companies. The Holcombe Legion was on our right, and Boyce's Battery and four North Carolina guns were posted on the edge of the public road.

Adjutant DuBose rallied his men for a fight in the early morning hours:

I was in command of the Holcombe Legion and as morning began to approach, the command, worn out and unnerved by the long waiting, was naturally in a rather demoralized condition. I believe that it is acknowledged that life is at its lowest ebb at three or four o'clock in the morning. Certainly ours was that morning, when all of a sudden there was a rapid discharge of musketry in our immediate front. In a few moments our own outposts began to run in. If ever a panic might have been justified, it might have been that morning at that hour. To help it on and almost produce it, I received the command to fall back and take up a better position about fifty yards behind where we were in line, where the slope of the ground was more favorable to us. Such a command at that critical moment was an awful blunder. The enemy were coming on and our men had been suddenly awakened and surprised. A panic practically began, and I have never in my life had to work harder than in taking up that new position and bringing the men up to the point of meeting the enemy. The moment, however, that they got into action everything was instantly restored and they were as cool in possession of themselves as possible. As I walked up and down the lines producing this effect, a Minié ball, fired from a distance of not more than a hundred yards, entered my side. Fortunately, the ball had scraped a part of itself off on the slope just in front of us and then passed through a half-dozen thick folds of clothing. As it was, it touched at least two mortal spots without actually penetrating. I had no feeling, and I was suddenly hurried away on a stretcher to the rear. As we passed over the bridge we came up to General Evans, who commanded the operations. The general stopped the stretcher and asked who it was. When he discovered, he said, "Ah, poor fellow, poor fellow!"—and drew out a flask of whiskey.

DuBose did not say whether Evans took a drink or offered him a drink.

Shortly after this battle, PERSONNE reported upon Evans' use of his "barrelita":[10]

I have heard it said that his orderly carries with him, whenever he follows his chief, a small two-quart cask of liquor, from which the general draws his rations. This is true; but there is something more touchingly true of that little cask, still. A badly wounded man, be he friend or foe, has never passed it by without a draft upon its contents. Three times at the battle of Manassas, and several times at Sharpsburg, was it emptied and refilled, and then emptied again among the feeble ones who lay bleeding on the ground, the General himself dismounting, and on bended knee applying the grateful relief to the parched lips. "A drop for me General, if you have got it," moaned poor Colonel Means, and in a moment more he was lifted into life again, and so strengthened that he could be carried from the field. Captain Seabrook, too, lay dying there, with the brains gushing from his forehead. And again the flask was made to perform its charitable work in bathing the pale face and moistening the lips of the sufferer.

Captain Edwards contemplated the irony of the battle fought on a Sunday morning:

The Yankee advance was greatly obstructed by the swamp, and their fire upon our lines was very heavy and continuous, but fortunately for us they could not see our position and they were firing above us all the time. I remember only one in the regiment who was hit while the regiment remained at that point, which was several hours. Rice Mullinax, of Company A, was shot in the head and instantly killed. It was about 10 A.M. when this heavy fire opened upon our lines, about the usual time when country congregations begin to assemble for worship. This was a handsome little white church [Harriet's Chapel] and it was Sunday morning. There was a large congregation present at the church, not to worship God, but intent upon destroying each other's fellowman, made in God's image. Oh what a cruel thing is war! As I lay there and listened to the Yankee bullets rattling upon the walls of that church and saw the weather-boarding perforated like a pepper box, I felt and thought of the injunction contained in the decalogue, "Remember the Sabbath day to keep it holy." Those Yankee scamps were making that building mighty holey. This engagement was on Sunday, December 14th. We held our position until about midday, when we were ordered back across the bridge. The Seventeenth, Twenty-third and Twenty-second Regiments crossed the river with the artillery. The Holcombe Legion failed, by some means, to get the order and remained fighting until after the bridge was fired and many of them swam the river and quite a number of them were captured.

Private W. Henry Sullivan of the Holcombe Legion described the battle in his December 27 letter to Lalla Pelot:

We were marched across the bridge about a half mile and drawn up in line of battle. The Legion was drawn up across the main road to the bridge. There were two or three regiments in a piece of woods to our right and the same number to our left though at a little distance and concealed from our view. At ten o'clock our skirmishers were driven in and the Yankee line soon made its appearance. The cannon opened and the sharp rattle of small arms began. We were within seventy five yards of each other and the balls flew thick and fast. It was a time to try the soul—the balls whizzing past and men falling around. The man next to me on the left was shot. I thought we would all be killed. We held them in check for four hours and a half. At last, it seemed, the Yankees got too strong for our left and they retreated across the bridge. Of this, however, we knew nothing at the time. No orders were sent to the center or right. We were fighting away when we were startled by cannon balls in our rear coming from the river. This was our *own artillery* across the bridge firing upon us. Captain Boyce of the artillery states that he was ordered to fire by General Evans, who thought we were Yankees. At this time too he ordered the bridge to be set on fire thinking we had all got across. In the meantime, not knowing what to make of the fire from our rear, Captain Ziegler ordered a retreat. We fell back in good order 'till we came in sight of the bridge, when to our amazement we saw it in flames. Every man then broke ranks and rushed to the bridge. A North Carolina regiment on our right started at the same time and we reached the bridge together. It was an awful scene. I reached the bridge and tried to rush across. I could feel my hair singe as I passed through the fire. About the middle of the bridge, the man ahead of me stumbled and fell. I fell over him, and the men, unable to resist the pressure from behind, were piled on me. I never came so near being mashed to death and suffocated in my life. I thought my time had come and that I had passed through the balls only to perish miserably on that burning bridge, but at last I dragged myself out and tottered across the bridge.

VIDI also described the retreat:[11]

Already the firing in front was incessant, and balls and shell from the Federal guns were falling about the bridge. About this time the Twenty-third South Carolina Regiment fell back to the bridge. Captain Solon Durham, a North Carolinian who married a South Carolina girl at the beginning of the war, was in command of it. He made a patriotic appeal to his men telling them not to soil the reputation of South Carolina and then led them back into the fight. I was interested in the men remaining in the front, as I knew that there would be no necessity for burning the bridge as long as the troops held their position. My hope gave way when, in a short time after the Twenty-third had marched back into the fight, I saw Colonel Goodlett leading his regiment towards the bridge. His regiment had scarcely come under the fire of the enemy. The firing was mostly to our right center, but he had imagined his command in great danger and deliberately marched it out of the fight. General Evans saw him, and Captain Corrie of his staff came dashing across the bridge and said "Colonel Goodlett, General Evans orders you back to your position." Colonel Goodlett replied that "Evans is drunk. I will not obey the order." and led his regiment across the bridge.[12] He was immediately put under arrest and afterwards cashiered. A courier was then sent with orders for the other regiments to cross the river. The order was only given to the 17th and 23rd South Carolina Regiments. They crossed without any pressing on the part of the enemy. A member of the Holcombe Legion who was retreating without orders refused to go back and let the Legion know that the other members of the brigade had already crossed the river. Joe Bennett volunteered to go, but just then the Legion came into sight. On reaching the cluster of pines on top of the hill already mentioned, it about-faced and began to fire into the advancing Federals again. By this time the enemy had discovered that we had not troops on the left, and debouching from the woods, made a rush for the bridge. McCrady, thinking that the Legion would be cut off, ran, firing the lower side of the bridge from the end to end as he went.

Seeing that the race for the bridge, between the Federals and the Legion, would be close, I told Bennett to save himself, that there was no necessity for the lives of both of us to be exposed, and that I would fire the upper side of the bridge if the Legion got over in time. When Bennett reached the center of the bridge, he could not resist the temptation to fire the upper side. The flames on both sides of the bridge now swept heavenwards and being mutually attacked swept from side to side. Fearing that the lint, cotton, and turpentine would rapidly convey the fire from the center to the end of the bridge, thus cutting off the retreat of the Legion, I tried to extinguish the fire on the upper side. The members of the Legion were dashing through the flames, and the Federals were firing a storm of bullets across the bridge.

The fire was not extending as fast as I expected. Concluding that nothing more could be done, I ran over and sheltered myself behind the works that had been thrown up for the protection of the Macbeth. These were unfortunate works, for many of the Legion stopped behind them and were captured. When the enemy reached the bridge, the guns of the Macbeth that had been moved several hundred yards up the river opened up on them with slaughtering effect. It is true that some of the North Carolina battalion were wounded by our own shot. The North Carolina battalion being on our extreme right and not receiving orders to fall back, was cut off and most of the men were captured. The Macbeth retreated after firing a few rounds. I could now hear the Federal officers just across the river seventy-five yards from me ordering their troops to push off the fire and cross the river.

When I reached Kinston, our troops were all gone. I saw Evans, with his staff near the depot. A Federal officer, under a flag of truce, rode up and demanded the surrender of his command. Evans replied that as soon as the women and children got out of the way he would show General Foster the kind of surrender he would make. He only wanted time to get away.

PERSONNE gave this account of the Federal demand for surrender:[13]

Officer: "I understand, sir, (bowing) that some of your troops have indicated a wish to surrender, and I have been detached to receive the surrender, by General Foster. I presume, sir, that you are General Evans?"

General Evans: "I am—who are you, sir?"

Officer: (With a supercilious air) "I am Colonel Potter, sir, of the 1st North Carolina Volunteers, and attached to the staff of General Foster."

General Evans: "I am not aware, sir, that any of my troops desire to surrender, nor do I believe there is a South Carolinian under my command who has any intention of doing so. Give my compliments to General Foster, and tell him that he knows General Evans too well to suppose that he will ever surrender."

Colonel Potter: "Then you intend to renew the battle?"

General Evans: "Yes sir—to fight now and here!"

Colonel Potter: "Do you mean to begin at once, sir, or do you wish time to remove your wounded?"

General Evans: "Well, sir, you may say to General Foster that if he will give me an hour and a half to remove the women and children from the town I shall then be ready for him."

The North Carolina Yankee then made a wave of the hand which he doubtless intended as a polite mode of saying farewell, but which a bystander remarked to me as much resembled the fall of a pump handle as anything else, and accompanied by his brother officer and courier, turned and rode off. His manner was anything but that of a gentleman, while that of General Evans was all that a proper regard for courtesy could demand.

The most ridiculous part of the affair is that the flag of truce was a pair of white drawers, which flopped about on a bayonet in a decided state of looseness, and excited the risibilities of the spectators to a pitch of rebellious cachinations. Whether the Yankees intended it as an insult, or whether it was an inferential admission that it was a *drawn* game, I have no means of knowing, but one thing is certain, though General Evans has once surrendered to a crinoline skirt, the breeches do not walk the earth or fly the air before which he will bow in homage as a captive.

Evans' Brigade and its associated North Carolina units retreated from Kinston along the north side of the Neuse River towards Greensboro, and they camped that night at Falling Creek. On December 15, Foster's troops abandoned Kinston and proceeded westward along the south side of the Neuse River. They threatened a crossing at White Hall to cover their main advance towards Goldsboro. Evans sent troops under Brigadier General B. H. Robertson (mostly North Carolina troops, but including a few hundred dismounted cavalry from Evans' Brigade) who burned the White Hall bridge to prevent the Federals from crossing. The battle at White Hall consisted mainly of rifle and heavy artillery fire across the river for two hours on the evening of the fifteenth and a longer exchange on the morning of the sixteenth. That same morning, Major General Samuel G. French arrived at nearby Moseley Hall and took command of Confederate forces in the area from Brigadier General Evans.[14]

Captain Edwards blamed the poor showing against Foster's troops on ineffective leadership:

We camped near Goldsboro and marched through the town on the morning of the 17th towards the railroad bridge. We had by that time at Goldsboro seven or eight thousand men, with General Gustavus Smith in command. But, strange to say, the day was frittered away and Foster was allowed to burn the railroad bridge and march away under cover of the night and return to Newbern unmolested. We were told afterwards that General Smith's excuse to the War Department was that he had troops enough to give Foster battle, but had no transportation. We had our feet and a good county public road bridge and it was a shame and a scandal to Southern arms to allow a gang like Foster's army of twelve thousand men to get away without a standup fight. We did not need any more men to have given him a good licking. All we needed was a skillful, plucky general. We heard no more of Gustavus Smith to the end of the war.[15] Foster let no dirt stick to his feet until he got back to Newbern. His campaign resulted in stopping traffic on the railroad three or four days. The imbecility on our side was more than equaled by him and it was significant that we heard no more of him from that day to this.

Many incidents of that fight and our retreat and march to Goldsboro still linger fresh in my memory. The consensus of opinion among the officers and men of the brigade was that while our force was entirely inadequate to contend with the overwhelming numbers of General Foster's army, our troops were not skillfully handled. To burn the railroad bridge and tear up the railroad at Goldsboro, so as to destroy connection between Wilmington, N.C., and Petersburg and Richmond, Va., was the object of Foster's march. We could have retired from Kinston on the night of the 13th without the loss of a man, burned the bridge over the Neuse river, and could have beat Foster to Goldsboro by twenty-four hours.

Evans' Brigade was outnumbered by about five to one in the battles around Kinston. Nevertheless, it was important that they engage the enemy in order to delay the Federal march to Goldsboro until Confederate reinforcements could arrive to defend the railroad bridge there.[16]

Later, Captain Edwards related this story of an unusual fight between two regiments of the brigade:

Our brigade was sent back to Kinston, where we remained from the 20th of December until after Christmas. While there we had the heaviest snowstorm I ever saw. The next day after the storm, the snow being over a foot deep, the Twenty-third Regiment marched over to the camp of the Seventeenth Regiment in line of battle with flags flying, halted and sent in a flag of truce demanding surrender or battle. Lieutenant Colonel Culp being in command of the Seventeenth, informed the courier that the Seventeenth had never surrendered and was ready for battle. In a very few minutes the regiment was in line of battle and the two regiments met in deadly conflict, the weapons being snowballs. This was one of the hottest contested engagements these two regiments were ever in, notwithstanding it was fought with chilled weapons. The victory was won by the Seventeenth Regiment driving the Twenty-third off the field and driving them back three-quarters of a mile to their own quarters.[17] We fared better in the way of rations at Kinston than we ever did anywhere else during the war. We could get port, sweet potatoes, chickens, ducks and turkeys. We all got fat on the good fare.

I will mention as part of the history of the Seventeenth South Carolina Volunteers the trouble between Colonel McMaster and General N. G. Evans. It all arose from the fact that after the affair at Kinston, N.C., nearly all the officers of the brigade signed and sent to the War Department a petition to be transferred to some other command. He blamed Colonel McMaster for being the head and leader of the movement and trumped up charges that had no foundation, in fact false from beginning to end. General Evans had the Colonel arrested and court-martialed, the trial taking place at Wilmington, North Carolina, in the early months of 1863, in which Colonel McMaster proved to the entire satisfaction of the court and every officer and soldier in the brigade that the charges were false, and were the result of spite and hatred.[18]

Except for the miscommunication at the bridge, the brigade acquitted itself well in the Battle of Kinston. However, many of the officers were critical of Evans' leadership and many accused him of drinking during this battle and during the fight at Goldsboro.[19] A petition was prepared by Colonel McMaster and signed by the four regimental commanders, as well as thirty-four of the forty company commanders of the Seventeenth, Twenty-second, and Twenty-third Regiments and the Holcombe Legion, requesting a transfer from General Evans' command.[20] General Evans responded by bringing charges of "misconduct before the enemy" against Colonel McMaster and Captain Bancroft. McMaster was acquitted on all charges but one (for which he received a simple reprimand); no record of Bancroft's trial has been found.[21] Colonel Goodlett of the Twenty-second charged Evans with drunkenness, incompetence, unbecoming conduct, and cowardice. Evans was tried only on the drunkenness charge and was acquitted.[22] Of all of the officers arrested and court-martialed after the Battle of Kinston only Goodlett, who was arrested by Evans for cowardice, was convicted.[23]

Captain Edwards recalled tedious weeks spent in Wilmington during these trials:

Some time in February or early in March the brigade was moved to Wilmington, N.C. While there, several of the members of the Seventeenth Regiment, and also of the other regiments of the brigade, had the smallpox, but none of the cases proved fatal. We remained at Wilmington, N.C., until April 25th, 1863. During our stay around Wilmington nothing transpired but the monotonous and irksome duties of camp life. Companies A and F, of the Seventeenth Regiment, were detailed of provost duty in the city, which was under martial law. I was in command of the city for five or six weeks prior to our leaving for Charleston. Wilmington at that time had in it many tough citizens, both men and women, and our experience with them was often unpleasant.

Lieutenant J. Warren Pursley of Company G of the Eighteenth Regiment described a review of the troops in a letter to his sister on March 15, 1863:

"Jane we had one of the bigest reviews yesterday that I have ever saw since we have been in service the Brigade met and was drilled and Reviewed by Gen. Whiting Gen. Whiting drilled our Regt him self but he did not give us verry much praise he said we knowed how to drille but did not try."[24]

Private Jones of the Twenty-third Regiment found the time spent near Wilmington much more pleasant:[25]

Wilmington was a port in which the Confederates received a good deal in the way of guns, blankets, shoes, etc. through blockade runners from European powers. For this as well as many other reasons, it had to be guarded and closely watched.

On reaching Wilmington, the brigade was ordered to locate a camp about fourteen miles north-east of Wilmington, on the road leading from Wilmington to New Bern. After reaching this place, we received our tents, or a part of them. The tents had been left in Virginia when we left on the march for Manassas, and had never caught up with us 'till this time. Now things began to be a little more agreeable than for months. Duty was not very hard; camp and picket duty was about all. Active military operations had about ceased in every quarter, and the troops on both sides were enjoying "winter quarters." We had to do picket duty now by regiments, only leaving a few at camp to take care of things, or, as some of the boys used to jestingly remark, "keep house." It was about nine miles from camp to our point of picket duty. The distance was great and, having to foot it, we would stay two or three weeks at a time. At this place there were several salt works, and it was a place on the coast called Topsail Sound. These salt works had to be guarded in order to keep the Federals from landing in barges and destroying them. Salt was scarce and of great value.

At Topsail Sound we enjoyed the duty very much. Between this point and the ocean were several creeks winding about through the marsh. About two miles distant was an island where many would go to shoot ducks and to have sport generally. We could reach this island through the creeks. At the salt works there were several boats. These boats we would take and make the trip to and from the island. This island was not very large nor a very small one; as the fellow says, it was "betwixt and between." This island was on the ocean, and near the shore on the ocean side and in the creeks running in its rear were the duck haunts. On reaching the island we would divide and go in several directions, and in the course of a short while one would suppose that war had broken loose on the island. We had no guns, only our smooth bore muskets, and our shots consisted of ounce musket balls, and that being the case, there were not many ducks killed, but a great deal of powder and ball thrown away, and no doubt many ducks had their lives scared nearly out of them. We could use but one charge at a time in our muskets, and it took mighty good shooting to kill a duck with one of them unless accidental. To have used double charges to have more killing power in the shape of balls would have been dangerous, for there was as much danger in one of those old Confederate muskets overloaded behind as there was before it. About now times were bully with us; too much so to last long. It was not long before we had to bid farewell to this kind of fun and move again.

Dock Owen of the Holcombe Legion gave a less flattering description of the area:

It was the poorest country I ever saw. Potatoes, goobers, and rice were the principal products. The farmers owned vast quantities of slaves, stingy and close; they would not sell or give us a thing. What we got from them we had to steal. We did not have much to do; we were there to guard the Sound, as it was expected the Yankees would land there.

On April 17, 1863, Beauregard reported to the War Department that Evans (whose South Carolina brigade was in Wilmington) and Clingman (whose North Carolina brigade was in Charleston) desired to exchange places. Evans felt that this would allow him to recruit new men for his regiments. The War Department directed that Evans' Brigade be swapped for Cooke's North Carolina Brigade, then in Charleston.[26] Many of the men assumed that this swap meant that the brigade would stay in Charleston for some length of time, but they were mistaken.[27]

Captain Edwards recorded the details of the brigade's travels to South Carolina:

The brigade left Wilmington by the Northeastern Railroad on the 25th of April, 1863, and reached Charleston on the evening of the 26th. We camped at the Four Mile House until the 28th, when we marched into and through the city, crossing the Ashley River on the long bridge, bivouacked near the Charleston & Savannah Railroad until April 30th, then marched five miles and camped near the railroad until the 4th of May, when we broke camp and marched to Secessionville, on James Island. The Twenty-fourth South Carolina Volunteers were leaving Secessionville for the Western army and the Seventeenth was sent to take their place. On the 9th of May the Seventeenth South Carolina Volunteers and some other regiments of our brigade, together with the Twentieth South Carolina Volunteers, known in our brigade from that time to the end of the war as the "Pound Cake" Regiment, were ordered to John's Island, the Yankees having landed and were occupying

Legareville.[28] We marched out some five or six miles to the depot at St. Andrew's and got on the train and got to Rantowles Station about 10 A.M. of May 10th. We had left camp at Secessionville at midnight of the 9th, consequently had slept none. We immediately took up the line of march for our destination, the Seventeenth Regiment in the van and the "Pound Cake" Regiment in the rear of the brigade. We marched by the way of Church Flats, crossed the Stono River on a bridge that the men of the Seventeenth Regiment helped to build in the early summer of 1862, and marched by old "Camp Pillow," a camp occupied by the Seventeenth Regiment for several months in the spring of 1862.

I will pause here to remark that around this old camp lingered the memory of many important incidents and events connected with the history of the Seventeenth Regiment. It was at this camp the companies and regiment was drilled and converted from raw troops into well drilled and disciplined soldiers. It was at this camp that we lost, by sickness and death, quite a number of valuable men. It was from this camp the regiment went forth on the expedition that resulted, by an unfortunate mistake, in the killing and wounding of a number of our own soldiers. It was at this camp that Captain Holley dropped dead on the return from a march. It was at this camp the regiment reorganized for Confederate service, by which reorganization the writer of these reminiscences was promoted from Orderly Sergeant to First Lieutenant of Company A, Seventeenth South Carolina Volunteers. But to our tale.

We continued our long and weary march until late in the evening. We got near to where we expected to exchange warm greetings with our Northern visitors, but I guess they had heard of the rapid approach of the committee on entertainment, and were so discouraged as to refuse to receive us. This was a long weary march, the day was hot and the sand deep, and the men had not slept for thirty-six hours. Alas, for the "Pound Cake" Regiment, as this was their first experience of a long forced march. By the way, I will tell here how they got the name. When we got off the train at Rantowles this regiment had preceded us and was in line at the station. As it was a strange regiment to our brigade and was a fine looking, well clad body of men our fellows would naturally ask them, what regiment is this? Their reply was, the "Pound Cake" Regiment. On this march the Twentieth Regiment marched in the rear and we did not see much of them going, but on the return march, on the 11th of May, they marched in front and from 10 A.M. until 3 P.M. we would pass them in groups of from two to twenty lying under the bushes on the road side, exhausted. Our men had got a good night's sleep and marched in solid ranks and when we got back to the railroad not a single man of Company A was missing. As our men would march past these groups of exhausted men they would call out to them, "Pound Cake is mighty poor grub to march on, better try hard tack and bacon." And at Rantowles there were so few of the Twentieth in ranks that the officers of our brigade had to restrain the men from howling the inquiry, "I wonder where is our Pound Cake Regiment." The humor and exuberance of spirits of the seasoned disciplined Confederate soldier is one of the unique things connected with the memory of the Confederate army. We got back to Secessionville about 10 P.M. on the 11th of May, footsore and weary, and found the news that the brigade had been ordered to Jackson, Mississippi, to join General Joseph E. Johnston's army.[29]

Private William L. Faulkner of Company I of the Seventeenth Regiment wrote to his wife on May 12:[30]

There is great dissatisfaction in the regiment this morning. There is no fairness in it to keep some men lying about here all the time at their ease and make some do all the marching and fighting. Some troops have been stationed here for 12 months and done nothing. Reason would say that they should go, but they stick to the old rule, "whip the pulling horse." One thing I am certain of—we will live out our days some place. This is a very pretty place and if I have to remain in the war I would prefer staying here to any place that I have seen since I came into service. It is quite warm in the day time and quite cool at night.

We are ordered to be ready to go to Vicksburg, Missisippi. We expect to start today sometime. It may be that the great Battle of Armageddon will be fought there, no one knows. God's ways are not our ways, for if I had my way I would never go there now, no place else but home that desired place I am afraid I will never see. I want you my dear to train up our children and servants in the way that they should go and teach them to remember the Sabbath day and never allow them to take the name of their Creator in vain.

Private Jones was also disappointed to leave the Charleston area:

We reached Charleston about the 1st of May, and remained a few days around and near that city. Companies I and F were now detached from the regiment and sent to points on the Stono River. The point Company F was sent to I do not now remember. Company I was sent to John's Island Ferry to a battery of heavy artillery. The battery was know as Battery Palmer, not far from the Charleston and Savannah Railroad, about nine miles from Charleston . . . On reaching Battery Palmer, Company I was quartered in a large and roomy building that had been abandoned by its owner. The time of abandonment we could not tell. There was one thing about it we could very correctly tell, and that was we enjoyed it mighty well, for we had not been used to tabernacling in such a comfortable building as this one. Here again we began to think that we were in clover, and would have been glad to have terminated the war at John's Island Ferry and Battery Palmer. We know we were very well satisfied and were willing to stay 'till the end of the war at this place if left to our will. But we did not stay long before we heard some disagreeable news.

We heard that General Joseph E. Johnston was in Mississippi, and was trying to collect an army to go to the rescue of the besieged troops at Vicksburg. This news did not disturb us very much, for we were too well fixed to let it disturb us, and we consoled ourselves with the belief that the report would only be a "flash in the pan." Our duty was not hard here. We were very well fed, and to add to our pleasure the depot was close, and with the permission of our officers, we could jump aboard the train and roll in and out of Charleston as big as anybody else. Who would not be a soldier at John's Island Ferry! About the last of May hostilities had begun at every point, and we began to realize that our fine times were in a fair way of being things of the past. We felt that our next move would back to Virginia or to Mississippi, but which we could not tell. We had not long to wait for the order. It was to report to General J. E. Johnston at Jackson, Mississippi.

The order to proceed to Mississippi came just two weeks after Evans' Brigade returned from North Carolina. General Evans had wanted to keep his brigade in South Carolina for at least a few months in order that he might recruit additional men for his regiments. He and his men did not want to go to Mississippi. Captain William G. Vardell, the acting brigade quartermaster (detailed from the Twenty-third Regiment), wrote a letter to his wife from Charleston on May 10, 1863, in which he confided that he and Evans had "agreed to the want of wisdom in the order & he, Gen'l Beauregard, and Ripley have all protested against it, but I fear this will not avail anything & if it does not, then we will move away very quickly." At the end of his letter he repeats, "I hope that we will not have to go—I pray not—God willing." His next letter was posted from Montgomery, Alabama, on May 27, en route to Mississippi.

7

THE MISSISSIPPI CAMPAIGN

> . . . they determined to show the red tape department that the private soldiers were not hirelings fighting for money or glory and that they had some rights and feelings that should be respected.
>
> William H. Edwards

A major objective of the Federal forces in the west was to gain control of the Mississippi River, and they attacked from both the north and south. On April 7, 1862, Pope captured Island No. 10 below Cairo, Illinois.[1] Admiral Farragut and General Butler took New Orleans on May 1 and then proceeded up the river to secure Baton Rouge and Natchez in early May.[2] Memphis fell on June 6.[3] This left Port Hudson (a few miles north of Baton Rouge), Grand Gulf, and Vicksburg as the only impediments to Federal control of the entire Mississippi River. All three would fall to Federal forces by July 4.

Both Grant and Sherman had moved their forces from western Tennessee toward Vicksburg during the final days of 1862, and Sherman had attacked the city without success on December 29. During the early days of 1863, Confederate general John Pemberton was pressured southward by Grant along the Yazoo River system toward Vicksburg, where General Carter Stevenson had been fortifying the city and the bluffs overlooking the river. In late April, Grant brought his army around Vicksburg by moving west of the Mississippi River and re-crossing south of the city. He captured the city of Jackson, driving General Johnston's troops toward the northeast. Grant then abandoned Jackson and laid siege to Vicksburg from the east.[4]

On May 2, 1863, Richmond telegraphed Beauregard to send eight thousand to ten thousand men to General Pemberton's relief. Beauregard sent from Charleston the brigades of States Rights Gist and W. H. T. Walker and two small batteries, a total of about five thousand men. On May 9, Richmond asked that additional troops be sent. Beauregard responded that he must keep five thousand troops to defend the Charleston and Savannah Railroad. The Confederate secretary of war, James A. Seddon, replied that he should

keep five thousand troops and "send the rest." On May 12, Beauregard added the Twenty-sixth Regiment of South Carolina Volunteers to Evans' unit and sent the enlarged brigade to Mississippi.[5] The Twenty-sixth would remain with the brigade for the remainder of the war.

The veterans' accounts of the eight-day trip from Charleston to Jackson give a graphic description of the state of the railroads of the Confederacy. The railroads of South Carolina, Georgia, and Mississippi spaced their rails five feet apart, but the Montgomery and West Point Railroad in Alabama used the modern 4-foot-8½-inch gauge, so the troops had to change trains at these two points. In many cities, each railroad had its own station, often some distance from the station of the next needed railroad, so that troops traveling thorough had to march from one station to the other. There was no railroad between Montgomery and Selma, so the troops were carried by steamboat on the Alabama River. Also, the Tombigbee River had not been bridged, so steamboats connected the railroads at this place.

William C. Nesbit of Company I of the Seventeenth Regiment described the trip in a letter to his wife on June 6:[6]

We were eight days on the road. Nancy, it's a long road, it's 900 miles from Fort Mill. I will name the different places we had to change cars. We got to Columbia about daylight Saturday morning. We left there at six in the evening. We changed at Branchville, got to Augusta at 12 o'clock on Sunday, left there at 6 got to Atlanta at 6 next morning. We did change at Atlanta. We ran through to West Point and from there to Montgomery. There we took a steamboat. We sailed down the Alabama River 110 miles to a place called Selma. There we took the cars again to a place called Demopolis. There we took to the water again. Sailed about 5 miles down the Tombigbee River, landed at a place called McDowell's landing. There we took the cars again to run to Meridian, from there to Jackson.

Private Jones described an accident involving one railway car:

Things went all right in every way 'till we crossed the Tombigbee River. Between this river and Meridian we had an accident. The commissary car, by the breaking of its coupling in some way, jumped the track and rolled down an embankment some ten or twelve feet high and, striking the ground at the base of the embankment, broke in half. There were three men in the car, but luckily none of them were killed. One was seriously, one painfully, and one only slightly hurt. The one seriously hurt never fully recovered from the effects of the accident. He was ever after a cripple 'till his death which occurred about three years after the end of the war. The one painfully hurt recovered after awhile, and is still living, and I have no doubt has never forgotten and never will forget this accident. The account of the one in the car who was slightly hurt and went down the embankment in the car, was very amusing, and he used to enjoy relating the circumstance. He would tell that he was in the car, and when the car struck the ground at the base of the embankment, the commissary stores were tumbled about promiscuously. In the tumbling of things he tumbled down on the floor of the car, and a barrel of hard tack (soldier's bread) rolled on and over his head. He said when he heard the hard tack breaking and mashing in the barrel, he was certain that "the jig was up" with him . . . he thought that all the bones in his head were mashed to atoms. As soon as he could recover from his fright, he said he made a thorough examination of his knowledge box all by himself. In feeling the top and mashing the sides of his head, he was satisfied that the revolution of the barrel had not seriously interfered with the arrangements of nature, and that his head was still level and even, and would continue to be a sound and whole head if he did not get a Yankee bullet through it when he got down to . . . Vicksburg. After this accident the rest of the passage was made without any further hindrance, and the 23rd reached Jackson in due time.

Rev. Silas Pinckney Holbrook Elwell wrote in 1895 of his service as the color-bearer of the Twenty-third Regiment of Evans' Brigade during the Mississippi Campaign:[7]

Not being with my 23rd SC Regiment, at the time the order was received, I was left behind, and, taking advantage of the situation, I went by home (where I had not been for some time) for a few days. As my order and transportation were not limited, I could do this with safety.

On the 13th day of June I sadly left my home to join my regiment in Mississippi. Eight days of uneventful travel, save the scenes of parting at many railroad stations of mother and sons, wives and husbands, brothers and sisters, amid tears and prayers: "Be good, be brave, read your Bible, and don't neglect to pray; if you never get back, meet me in heaven." These constantly recurring events kept the heart sick, and the thoughts of home and dear ones displaced all others. It was somewhat a relief when I reached the end of the journey and found my regiment encamped in the suburbs of the city of Jackson. The Captain of Company I, to which I was then attached, seemed somewhat angered at my delay, and said that I had been reported to him as transferred from the office in Charleston two weeks before. He demanded to know the cause of my delay. I told him I had been home, that my transfer papers were directed to the Colonel, and that if he would accompany me to the Colonel's headquarters the whole matter would be explained. This he did, and when I presented my transfer to the Colonel, he saw that by an oversight on the part of the officers at Charleston no date had been fixed for my arrival in Mississippi. He then said: "I am very much obliged to you for coming at all."

Captain Edwards recounted how many of the men of the brigade took unauthorized leave:

The brigade left Charleston on May the 16th. The Seventeenth Regiment crossed the Ashley River in a ferryboat in the time of a heavy rainstorm and left by rail. It was the first and I am glad to say it was the last time that the soldiers of the brigade manifested a spirit of insubordination. Many of them left the train at Branchville and at other points on the railroad and went home. When the Seventeenth was sent from South Carolina to Virginia in 1862, it was sent via Wilmington, N.C., while hundreds of the women of Fairfield, Chester, and York were at the stations to see their husbands and sons. This showed a lack of confidence in the loyalty and patriotism in the soldiers, and they never forgave it. Now they were being sent seven hundred miles from home, and they determined to show the red tape department that the private soldiers were not hirelings fighting for money or glory and that they had some rights and feelings that should be respected. When General Evans got to Jackson and found half the men absent it dawned upon him that there were entirely too many of them for punishment and that conciliatory measures would be the better part of wisdom. He issued an order, through the newspapers of South Carolina, to all of the soldiers of the brigade to report to Captain McCready of the Holcombe Legion in Columbia, S.C., on or before the 30th of May, and that transportation would be furnished them and no further notice would be taken of their absence. This gave them three or four days longer than they intended to take, and thus ended the episode.[8]

Adjutant DuBose found time to get married before reporting to Mississippi:

In the spring our brigade was ordered to Mississippi to attempt the relief of Vicksburg, just then beginning to be besieged by General Sherman. In the transference, I procured a furlough of about two weeks and set my wedding date for the 30th day of April. My intended's family, the Peronneau's, were occupying at this time some offices, which they had converted into living-rooms in the over-crowded town of Anderson. In one of them we were married by the Rev. John E. Elliott under conditions of great privation at the time. The wedding was very greatly indebted to the family of Judge Whitner, whose two daughters, Misses Tallulah and Toccoa, had been unspeakably kind to the Peronneaus as refugees. They really made the wedding, so far as decoration and what little there was of luxury, went. Within the two weeks, we paid a visit to Greenville where we visited some other refugees, the Lowdnes, Miss Malvina Murdon, and Julia McCord. After this short and momentous digression, I rejoined my command in Mississippi.

William G. Vardell
(courtesy of Laura N. Vardell)

Captain Vardell wrote to his wife on June 6 and 15:

Our Brigade is increasing every day and numbers now over 3000 men, and the men who absented themselves without leave are fast returning. The officers will be dealt with very severely, so it is said. At present we are living very nicely and have vegetables and plenty of milk. By we, I mean General Evans and his staff and myself, for I board with them by the General's invitation at the same house at $2.50 per day, about as cheap as I can live in camp. . . . We all board with Mrs. Moody, who is very kind and offers to do anything she can for us. I have my tent very comfortably fixed with a board floor. My table is on one side, covered with my shawl and looking very nicely. There is a little shelf for my brush and wash basin, a bucket of water under the table, trunk in one corner, cot in the other, and a stool by the side of my cot. I look so genteel that the staff threatened to court martial me for being so comfortable and aristocratic and called the General down to see.

Private Andrews of the Twenty-third Regiment reported that life was less comfortable among the soldiers:

While at Jackson we camped on the Pearl River for several days. We put up forks, driving the lower ends into the ground to make them firm. We placed poles in the forks and floored across them. This made our couch from one to two feet high. A tent fly or oilcloth made the covering. Some, having neither, stripped off elm bark and stretched the bark over theirs. A heavy rain would cause the river to rise and overflow our camp four or six inches in depth. Our drinking water was from the river.

VIDI reported that the Macbeth Light Artillery received new guns:[9]

The artillery companies were placed under Major Graves, General Breckenridge's Chief of Artillery, for equipping and getting ready for the campaign then being inaugurated for the relief of Vicksburg . . . It was through him that our old guns were exchanged for a battery of new pieces—six beautiful Napoleon guns[10]—and many of our exhausted horses turned over to the Quartermaster and good horses given to us in the place of them.

The beginning of the Mississippi Campaign for Evans' Brigade was interrupted by the receipt of the report of the court-martial of Colonel McMaster, which had been held the previous April in Goldsboro, North Carolina. The court found that "this prosecution was not undertaken with the spirit and for the purpose of promoting the good of the service," and it declined to take any action. When the court published its findings, Evans had the following order read to the brigade:[11]

Headquarters Evans' Brigade Camp near Jackson, Miss. June 18th, 1863
General Orders, No. 60

The Brig. Gen. commanding announces to his command the acquittal of Colonel F. W. McMaster, 17th Reg. S.C.V., by a General Court Martial, of charges of a very grave nature, which the Brigadier General Commanding deemed it his duty to prefer. The Court seems to have been moved more by sympathy for the accused, than by a sense of moral obligation, or the interest of the service.

The interpretation by the Court of mutinous conduct, is certainly anomalous, and without precedent. It is to be hoped that the finding of the Court in the second charge, will remind Colonel McMaster of his duty as a soldier. Colonel McMaster, 17th S.C.V., will resume his sword and return to duty.

By command of BRIG. GENERAL EVANS

Evans' General Order No. 60 infuriated Colonel McMaster, who would later write a twenty-six-page booklet, *Colonel McMaster's Rejoinder to Brig. Gen. Evans*, and have it published and distributed.

Soon afterwards, Captain Vardell attended an inspiring outdoor church service with Evans:[12]

Sunday morning, June 21st—a day long to be remembered by me—I went to hear Mr. Girardeau preach. General Evans went with me. We arrived in camp and found a large assemblage; the scene was striking. Picture a ridge covered with trees and at one end of the ridge under a large tree a large table lay decently covered with a white napkin, the emblem of our Savior's love. On either side of the ridge a ravine and ridge and upon these groups of men and officers sitting on the earth. Mr. Girardeau rises and gives out his hymn, and all rise and sing. He reads from God's word, and he prays with fervour and eloquence. His text "He was a man of sorrows and acquainted with grief." What an impressive discourse, so feelingly and earnestly delivered, and then to look around and see the intent audience and to remember how careless they once were, it made one's heart melt with thankfulness. . . . How impressive the whole service was I cannot adequately convey to you—how with but a rude table, no exalted arch, no columns, no decorative architecture, no splendidly appointed pews, nothing but earth beneath, a clouded sky above, God's people stand in His own first temple and worship Him with joy. . . . General Evans was very much pleased, but I fear only temporarily, his heart I fear not touched; still I have had for a long time the strange impression that he is to be a changed man through God's mercy—I hope my impression will be confirmed.

However, in another letter written to his wife five days later, Captain Vardell would report that the brigade was on the move and that Evans was feuding with General Johnston's staff over the distribution of some ambulances.[13] Vardell described Evans as "hard headed and selfish" and was also critical of his staff. "General Evans has not about him one man of cool temperament or well-balanced mind. Had he tried he could scarcely have brought together a more useless set of men for his purpose." Some of Vardell's later letters continued this theme.

Private Elwell described the difficult march toward the Big Black River:

A few days of rest in camp, and we set out on our memorable and eventful march to the Big Black River. Our route was not directly towards Vicksburg, but almost North from Jackson. It lay along a thickly-settled country of fine farming lands with very little forest. The weather was intensely hot, and very dry. Water was exceedingly scarce. There were very few creeks or branches, and these were the sources of our supply, for there were only two wells that I now remember, and we had no access to private cisterns. The sufferings of the soldiers on that march cannot be described. The want of water and the suffocation from dust can better be imagined. At Livingston we found a few springs, and we camped for a week until we could obtain supplies or rations, which had become very scarce. Some days we had only a few hardtack biscuits in the shape of soda crackers, which were thin but too hard to bite and often required to be soaked in water to render mastication possible. We had no tents, but found plenty of shade in the day, as our camping place was in a thickly wooded belt of country that lay between the public road and a branch formed by the flow from the springs. At night the earth was our bed and the heavens our covering. Many were stricken with fever and other complaints which considerably reduced our effective force. A drought had long prevailed, and the branches and creeks, with but a few exceptions, had dried up. Vegetation was dying; the crops were failing and the reservoirs which had been dug out and cemented to hold water for the cattle were nearly all dry. In some of them there was a little muddy water, in the bottom of which tadpoles were to be found, and even for this we were sometimes very thankful. We left Livingston and her clear, cool springs to find no more along the line of our wearisome march. Here we changed our course, turning in the direction of Brownville, and from thence to the Big Black. We marched along dusty lanes separating large cornfields, now and then passing through a belt of woods which afforded a little shade but no water. I have frequently seen men who chanced to have some water in their canteens measuring it out to their suffering companions by the teaspoonful, merely to dampen their dry and paining throats. For this purpose also sassafras leaves and even oak leaves were eaten when they could be obtained.

Changing our course again we marched down the Big Black, carefully approaching the rear of Grant's army. We came to a large pond—I think a mill-pond—there we tarried two days resting and refreshing ourselves. It was Sunday, and Dr. Girardeau, the Chaplain of the regiment, preached to us and administered the sacrament as we sat among the bushes and trees that belted the pond. Here we spent a part of the 4th of July, expecting on the morning of the fifth to attack Grant's rear while Pemberton engaged his front. After nightfall on the fourth we resumed our march. It was understood in the ranks that we were to march down as near as safety would permit and form our line of battle before daylight should expose our approach. Our long march and much suffering had awakened our anger and inspired us with courage, and we felt that we were ready for the fray.

While Grant was negotiating the surrender of Vicksburg, he maintained telegraphic communications with Sherman. It had been agreed that at the moment Vicksburg surrendered, Sherman would turn away from the siege and attack Johnston and pursue him to Jackson.[14]

Private Elwell continued his account:

About midnight, however, we were halted, and turning our course in the direction of Clinton, we were placed under a forced march. Orders came that the Captains would be held responsible for their men and no private would be allowed even to go to the doctor without being guarded by a sergeant or corporal. It was then we learned that Pemberton had surrendered and that General Sherman, with an army of thirty thousand, was pursuing us.

On the first day of our retreat back to Jackson, at about 10 o'clock, I found myself completely overcome with heat. We were in the middle of a long lane with large corn fields on each side shutting off the air, the sun seemed to shine with unusual strength and the dust was almost suffocating. There grew in this lane a lone hickory tree. As I came near the tree everything seemed obscured from sight, and it appeared as if darkness had set in at midday. I said to the Captain, at whose side I was walking: "I can go no further." He said: "You know the orders; you must keep up." I told him I preferred to die here and dropped down under the tree. Soon the rear guard came on, and commanded me to rise; this I refused to do, for I felt that I could not. They had orders to take me upon their bayonets, if necessary, but they thought me in a dying condition and left me there. They had left me only a few minutes when, to secure a more comfortable position, I moved father around the tree and nearer to the fence. I then discovered a small hole near the root of the tree, and looking down into it, I saw water. I suppose it had collected there during the rain the night before. Loosing from my belt a half pint cup, I secured a sufficiency for my immediate need. Oh! how refreshing it was! I felt relieved in a moment. What a Providence! I would have died without this relief. I was soon sufficiently refreshed to arise and follow on.

The first day's march was very severe, the weather intensely hot and dry. A light shower of rain about nightfall relieved us very much. We camped in a belt of woods near Clinton. Our camping meant only to halt and lay down on the wet leaves which was cooling to our heated and fatigued bodies. Early the next morning we began a harder march than that of the day before. On reaching the suburbs of Clinton we discovered near the road a spring which seemed to be a large and bold one. Here we halted and a detail was made to fill from the springs the canteens of the company. I was one of the party detailed and taking as many canteens as I could manage went to the spring but had long to wait, for many others performing like service were ahead of me. When I at last was permitted to fill my canteens and returned to the road the company had marched on. I never overtook them all day. This I think saved my life, as I had water while many died for want of it.

Lieutenant J. W. Pursley of the Eighteenth Regiment described the water shortage in a letter to his sister on July 28:

We got no water at all, only out of ponds. The people have to dam up the hollows to make ponds to water their stock, but we ditched all of them we could to let the water out to keep the yankees from getting water. Some that could not be drained off, we drove in old cows and hogs and killed them in there to make the water bad.

Private Elwell caught up with his company at the Pearl River:

Shortly after dark I reached Jackson, but knew not where the company had camped. I started along one of the streets leading toward the Pearl River. A very heavy threatening cloud was rising and the city was in darkness. I could see only by the flashes of lightning which were rapid and attended with sharp and loud peals of thunder. Large drops of rain began to fall. I turned into a yard and entered the piazza of a new house built near the street. I suppose my foot-fall must have awakened the occupants, for a stern sonorous voice from within demanded "who is that?" I replied as pleasantly as possible, "a tired soldier just come in here to escape the rain." Then in a stentorian voice which indicated anger, he said, "get out of there." I replied "I will not." "Then I'll see if I can't make you do it." and I heard a heavy step upon the floor as if alighting out of bed and a gentle female voice said, "Oh, I'd let him alone." I forced a cartridge into my gun, which I think he heard, for he hesitated at the door and did not hasten to open it. I spoke calmly but very decidedly, "I want only shelter out of this rain (for it was then raining very hard). I do not mean to harm you or anything you have, but I do not intend to be driven out in this rain, and you or I one will die if you attempt it." He returned to his bed and I spent the night in the piazza sleeping soundly with a canteen for a pillow. I think I have never seen a harder rain than fell that night. I reached the camp early the next morning. Most of the company had arrived ahead of me and were resting on the banks of Pearl River. A day's rest on the banks of the river was indeed refreshing after such a severe and trying march, in which many lost their lives from heat, fatigue, and thirst.

Adjutant DuBose noted the destruction of private property:

We made a very hurried return to Jackson. A few days before, when we had marched out of Jackson in the direction of Vicksburg, I had ridden in to Battle Hill, the residence of Bishop Green, and spoken to him on the porch. I knew his daughters well, through Bishop Davis, but the Bishop I had never seen before. The Bishop offered us, he said, the coolest water in Mississippi from a cistern, which had just been put in and of which he was very proud. I suppose this was in anticipation of the thirst to which we were to be subjected on our march to and from Vicksburg. On the return to Jackson, I rode in again to Battle Hill. The next day it was burned, after the Bishop's fine library had been ruthlessly scattered over the face of the earth.

We hastily occupied the lines in front of the city. My command was stationed in the extensive grounds of Judge Sharkey. There was sharp-shooting at various parts along the line to the right and left of us for several days, but not just at our place. All around, though, the cannonading was going on, and we got the impression that Sharkey's house was immune because he was known to have been a Union man. At any rate, the house was not struck. As we lay on our arms, I made my way into the house and finally into his splendid library. I had had little chance for that sort of reading, and I thought I would take the opportunity of enjoying the luxury of it. My hands accidentally fell on a little book, the autobiographical recollections of the painter Leslie. It was charmingly written. I lay flat on my back in the house with the cannon bursting and roaring in the distance, I don't know that I ever enjoyed a little relaxation more.

After a day or two, our army continued to retreat. As I left the library and having heard of the fate of Bishop Green's house and library, I supposed a similar fate would befall this one upon our departure. After a slight debate with my conscience, I put the book in my pocket and finished it elsewhere. Some years afterwards, when I met Bishop Green at Sewanee, I took the book to him and asked him to return it to Judge Sharkey. Bishop Green refused, but he said he'd tell Judge Sharkey and he knew he would want me to keep it for the association. A few years after that again, I was in London and made a point of studying the two paintings there by Leslie in the National Gallery.

Colonel Benbow of the Twenty-third Regiment prevailed upon General French to pressure Evans to give Vardell back the Twenty-third Regiment on June 30. Evans took this occasion to express his "high gratification at the manner in which Captain Vardell has performed his arduous duties." The ever-religious Vardell wrote to his wife on July 5:

I am afraid the General's rupture with Colonel Benbow will keep him from coming to our camp to hear Mr. Girardeau. I hope not—I mentioned the other day . . . to Mr. Girardeau, my impression that General Evans was uneasy in his mind as to his future. He told me he thought so too, but was afraid that, surrounded as he was by such influences as are now about him, and his habits so fixed, that there was but little hope for him. General Evans is so uncertain in his temperament, too.

Private Elwell readied for battle on July 8:

On the seventh of July we spent the day in doctoring our feet and bathing our weary bodies in the south Pearl River. Sweet and refreshing was the sleep on that night as we lay among the roots of the trees, pillowing our heads against the trees or on pieces of wood that we could find lying loosely around.

At day-break on the 8th we were called into line by the beating of the long drum roll, and hurriedly marched to the opposite side of the city, where the line of battle was formed shortly after sunrise. We expected to enter at once into an engagement with a strong force of the enemy outnumbering us three to one. Many earnest prayers were offered up to the Divine Creator replete with promises to abandon all evil practices and perform all Christian duties. The way was strewn with cards, and gambling was denounced as a sin. Many vows were made never again to engage in drinking, gambling or swearing. These vows and pledges, as on former similar occasions, were designed only to be binding until the battle was over.

Our position was in the center of the line of battle, near the Clinton road. The line was crescent-shaped, receding on each wing to touch the river as the terminating points. On the right was Loring's division extending along beside the asylum until it touched French's division which held the center and Breckenridge's division which held the left wing. The trees and underbrush had been cut away to make an open space for the coming encounter. A brisk firing in our front, and the return of our pickets indicated the approach of the enemy. A temporary breastwork of earth afforded us some protection from their charge. Behind this we waited in constant expectancy of their onset.

While in this state of expectancy, with a brisk cannonading going on and our guns in hand, and watching the return of our skirmish line pressed by the enemy's advance, a rather singular incident occurred. A tall and graceful lady ran hurriedly through our lines and along the Clinton road as if going to the Federal lines. About midway between the lines there stood a small cottage. Into this she entered, and in a few moments came out again. Her position was an exceedingly dangerous one, as our skirmish line had passed the cottage and left her without our protection. She, however, came safely back to our line unhurt, but almost breathless. A Colonel standing near the spot at which she entered the line, asked why she exposed herself to such danger. Holding up before him a small, but beautifully-bound Bible, she said: "Sir, my mother gave me this Bible just three weeks ago on her death-bed, and I would rather have died in an attempt to secure it than that an enemy should have destroyed my mother's last gift."

No decided effort was made during the day to break our lines, but a heavy cannonading was kept up all day by the Federals, and their sharp-shooters did us much harm by occasionally killing and wounding our men along the line. Their whereabouts were hard to discover, as they were shooting from the tops of trees in a belt of wood that bordered the clearing just in our front. To the right, in front of our position, was the residence of Bishop Green, and beside his dwelling there were a number of small houses, all enclosed in a hedge of thorn bushes and vines. These served as forts for the Federal sharpshooters, from which they were annoying us very much. It was dangerous for a man to show his head above our breastworks. Throughout the day, or a part of it, they continued their work effectively. Quite a number of our men had been killed by them. General French, the commander of our division, ordered these houses fired. This could be effected only by a charge, which was made and the order executed by the Holcombe Legion.

VIDI related a slightly different story:[15]

The Federal sharpshooters became so annoying that the 26th South Carolina Regiment was ordered out to drive them away. This was a new regiment that had been added to Evans' Brigade when it left Charleston for the West. It had seen no active service and its ranks were full, numbering perhaps more than all the other regiments in the brigade put together. They wore good clothes and marched under a new banner that had neither been soiled or riddled by bullets. In appearance, the other troops contrasted most unfavorably by the side of this new regiment. The veteran regiments wore not only dirty, but ragged, clothes . . . Just as the 26th Regiment was ordered out to drive off the pickets in our front, Major Graves, with all of Breckenridge's staff rode up in the rear of our guns. The regiment went over the breastworks in a perfect line and in superb style. All eyes, for a quarter of a mile on either side of their position in the breastworks, were concentrated on them. They were observed by all observers as they cleared the works. So grand was their martial bearing that Major Graves exclaimed: "There go my Palmettoes!" How these words made my State Pride leap. Imagine what a fall it had when, all of a sudden, without the slightest cause as far as I could see, the men were thrown into a panic and came helter-skelter, pell mell, back to the works. The Holcombe Legion, dirty, ragged, and about one-fourth as many, then went out, chased the Federal pickets away and held the ground until after nightfall.

Private Elwell described the battle:

Picketing and scouting at night and fighting through the day continued for eight days. A futile attempt to turn the right wing of our line and a vigorous charge on Breckinridge's division on our left, in which the enemy was repulsed with a heavy loss, marked our principal infantry engagements.

Corporal Robertson remembered visiting with his Yankee enemies:

Having been repulsed in their assault on our left, they asked for a one-hour truce to bury their dead. There were no trees on the field where the skirmish lines were but plenty of stumps. My position was behind a stump and in front was my enemy at not a very great distance. We had been trying all morning to put an end to each other's existence. After the truce was on, this chap coming from behind his hiding place called out to me "Johnnie meet me half way." Not having orders to the contrary I complied. It was the signal for the

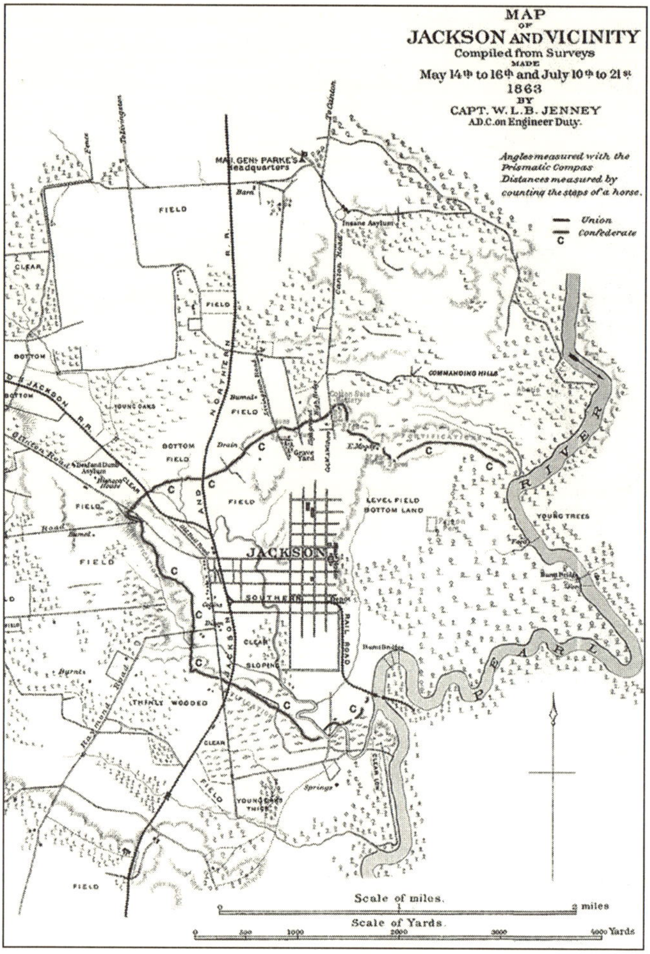

Jackson and vicinity
(*Atlas to Accompany the Official Records*, Plate XXXVII, no. 2)

gathering from both sides of thirty or more. At the say-so of one of the Yanks to smoke the pipe of peace, we proceeded filling pipes with each others tobacco. One Yank remarked that "Here we are perfectly friendly with each other and one hour from now we will be trying our best to kill one another. Is this not a strange war?" I replied that our fight was to drive the invaders from our homes and firesides. An Irish Yank butted in saying "Bedad, we are fighting for the stars and stripes." I told that individual that he was after dollars and cents. One fellow wanted to know how many troops we had in Jackson. I invited him to come with me and I would show him around and he could see for himself. He declined the invitation, saying some other day would suit him better. We quizzed each other and swapped lies. One said to me "Johnnie, I guess you believe as much of my news as I believe of yours so we are square." At the end of the hour "Rats to your holes" was sung out and to our holes we went.

Private Elwell continued:

The center was continually stormed with shell. Our position enabled them to reach us from both sides as well as in front and they tried for several days to drive us from our position with shot and shell. We did not return the fire, but kept our guns cool, expecting that they would make some desperate effort with their infantry to pierce our center. This expected movement on their part was delayed for some days, but came as expected. They amassed themselves in a strong line and made an effort to pierce our center. A large gully running almost parallel with our line, about twenty paces in our front, was much to our advantage. One of our large guns, managed by a true and trusted gunner and well supplied with grape and canister, commanded this gully. Here the work of death was fearful. The grape and canister sweeping down the gully, played havoc with their lines. They were repulsed and never again attempted a charge. They kept us under a storm of shell during the remaining days of the siege.

Elwell was wounded on July 13, and his treatment in Confederate and Federal hospitals is related in the next chapter. Captain Edwards, VIDI, and Private Andrews related the remaining activities of Evans' Brigade in the Mississippi Campaign.

Captain Edwards recalled the move from Jackson to Brandon:

Johnston's whole army remained at Jackson nine days, holding Grant at bay, and was ready to give him all the fighting he wanted, but it seems he was not hungry for a square standup fight with Johnston choosing the ground to fight on. On July 16th there were repeated charges made on our lines, but the enemy were repulsed every time. During the night of the 16th, General Johnston evacuated the lines at Jackson and moved out by the way of Brandon, and marched his army to Forest Station. Companies A and I, of the Seventeenth Regiment, had been left on picket duty at Jackson with a large number of troops from other commands. These all got out of the city and across the river safely and rejoined their commands at Brandon.

VIDI reported how Johnston "stole away in the night":[16]

Johnston's army was in no condition to withstand a siege, neither was he strong enough to go out and attack the Federals. Johnston decided to give up Jackson as soon as he was satisfied that the enemy would not assault our works. During the six days that the troops were in the trenches, they were supplied with barrels of water hauled by wagon at night from the Pearl River. Two nights previous to the one during which we left Jackson, Johnston kept wagons running all night, for the purpose of quieting any suspicion the rumbling of our wagons might awaken when we began to retreat. And the wagons did seem unusually loud these two nights. They must have been old wagons, gotten up for the purpose and run without oiling. The night the army left, we were ordered to muffle our guns and roll them from the breastworks by hand. We made much less noise that night than any of the nights during the siege. The enemy did not expect us, and it was late the next day before they knew we had gone.

General Rains, the inventor of sub terra shells and torpedoes, was sent to Jackson with the hope of making his new weapon of warfare very destructive to the enemy. I heard him imagining one day the terrible fate that awaited the Federals, when they passed over these explosives. When we crossed the Pearl River on our retreat, guards were stationed at different places where he had buried some of these weapons, to turn our troops out of the road so as to prevent the destruction of our own men. If they ever harmed any one of the enemy, I never heard of it.

Private Andrews gave a different report on the effectiveness of the mines:

General Johnston planted percussion cap bombs on every road leading from Jackson to his line of retreat, spiking with rat-tail files all of the siege guns that he could not carry away. It is a known fact that in attempting to follow General Johnston the enemy suffered much by the bursting of shells. Turn as they would, a bomb was there ready to blow up either wagon or artillery, when a wheel would strike it. They picked their way as best they could through the woods to avoid the demons in the road.

On August 2 General Joseph E. Johnston received the following order:[17] "Send Evans' Brigade, without delay, to Savannah, Ga., retaining the artillery and horses for the present." Captain Edwards recounted the move:

We all supposed that General Johnston's motive for retreating to Forest Station was to draw Grant further from his base. He knew Grant was a fighting man, and ambitious to make a reputation, and he expected that Grant would follow. However, Grant saw through Johnston's tactics and could not or would not follow him, and it was well for him he did not. Brandon is twelve miles from Jackson. On the 18th of July we marched fifteen miles, the last three miles in a drenching rain, and went into camp. On the 20th of July we marched fourteen miles and camped. That night Major Pagan bought a field of green corn, and the men of the brigade had a high old time cooking and eating roasting ears. We remained there until the 23rd of July, when we moved five or six miles and camped on a stream known as Beaverdam Creek. This is a running stream (uncommon in Mississippi), and there were also some good springs of water. The land in that neighborhood is poor and rolling. We remained there until the 4th of August, when the brigade marched to Forest Station, drew rations of fresh beef and corn meal, and the men went to cooking it. About the time the beef got to boiling and the corn dough in the skillets got hot, the train rolled up and the Seventeenth Regiment was ordered to get aboard. The men kicked over the pots, emptied out the hot raw beef, turned over the skillets, emptied out the hot dough and put their cooking utensils on the train, and we left there with nothing to eat. Our destination was Savannah, Georgia. That is the last sight our brigade ever had of the Western army.

That evening we got to Meridian, Mississippi, very hungry but with nothing to eat. Fortunately, there was a car load of bacon standing on a side track. There was a small crack in the box car and it was very easy, with an ax, to make the crack larger, and then men put their bayonets on their guns and would stick them in the sides of bacon and turn them up edgewise and then get them out through the crack. Company A had bacon for a week after we arrived at Savannah. I guess the bacon belonged to the Confederacy, and so did the soldiers.

We had been in Mississippi a little over two months. These two months had been big with important events for Southern arms. Vicksburg had fallen, cutting off all the Confederacy lying west of the Mississippi River, and the disastrous Battle of Gettysburg had been fought. At 7 o'clock A.M., on August 5th, we left Meridian and went by the way of Demopolis to Selma, then down the Alabama River to Montgomery, and then by railway through Georgia to Savannah. On the way from Meridian to McDowell's Landing, Major Dye of Company D, Seventeenth South Carolina Volunteers, got knocked off a platform car by dirt from a landslide and rolled under the train and was killed. He was a young man of sterling character and a gallant soldier from Chester County. We carried his body with us and buried him in Montgomery, Alabama. We arrived in Savannah at 10 A.M. of August 9th, 1863, and lay there all that day and night. The soldiers were allowed to ramble through the parks at will. Many of them went down to the canal and took a swim and a bath, which they needed very much. They got their skin clean, but their clothes were still dirty. On the 10th of August we left Savannah and marched down the Skidaway shell road ten miles and went into camp in a body of woods near Skidaway River and remained there sixteen days and had quite an easy time and got a good rest. We called this place "Camp Johnson." We left there August 26th and marched to Savannah and got there in the evening in a drenching rain. The men were tired and in low spirits, but quite a number of them soon found a remedy, and poured the spirits down to raise the spirits up, and in a short time many of them were as gay as larks and did not know they were wet. We left there by railroad some time in the night and got to Charleston at 9 A.M. on the 27th.

Private Faulkner of the Seventeenth Regiment wrote from Savannah of the poor condition and low morale of the brigade:[18]

We received orders last Monday evening to be ready to move [from Mississippi]. You ought to have heard the shouting of the mess. General Evans, immediately after he received orders, came riding along past the camp of our Brigade; the men cheered him dreadfully as he passed by.

I find that a goodly number of people about Montgomery think the South is pretty much whipped, but for my part I cannot say. The Yanks "has got the betterest of us" here of late but it may be that God will be for us yet. One thing that I am certain of—if we are right we will gain our independence, if wrong we will not. Oh, I wish it was ended now. I would rather have peace as anything else. If we are to be whipped, the sooner the better. If there is no hope, I do not see any use in killing up a large portion of our men and ruining the constitution of others if nothing is to be gained. A great many of this Brigade say that they are willing to fight here or in South Carolina, but to go help in Virginia they never will. This is my opinion. I have done some fighting and a heap of marching and suffering, while a good many are at home living at ease who have a better right to be here than many that are here. I hope we will not have another far trip, but if they should and the Regiment make a break I am there . . . I shall never think of Missisippi but with disgust. It is not the case with Georgia and Alabama; they treat us like home folks.

I understand that the Yanks are still fighting away at the Queen City of the South and say that it must fall. If Charleston falls Savannah must go, then where is the Confederacy? Our troops have despaired of success and say that all hope is gone. While we stay here or Charleston they will fight, but if taken away they will leave by hundreds. For my part, unless God has determined otherwise, all is lost. Sometimes I get so mad. I do not care to see the way some men are making money and living on the very best and the poor private nearly naked and not half enough to eat.

I am willing to stay here and do my best for the Confederacy, but if they should go to Virginia, I do not think that I will go. I think that we will be ordered to Charleston if they cannot keep the Yanks back. General Evans says that he is determined to rest his brigade. They are worn out and badly clothed.

The Macbeth Light Artillery was sent to Mobile for a few weeks before returning to Charleston. VIDI's account of the Macbeth's return to Charleston indicated the state of river transportation in the Confederate states:[19]

Our guns were put on the cars at Forest Station, and the horses were carried by the dirt road to Meridian. Securing transportation for our horses at Meridian we ran down to Mobile and went into quarters at Camp Beulah, in the western suburbs of the city. It was a lovely camp on a clear beautiful stream near some paper mills, just in the rear of the residence of Miss Augusta Evins, now Mrs. Wilson. The camp was so near to the residence of the author of Beulah, suggested its name. We had a remarkable easy time at Mobile. The enemy had not put his unhallowed tread on any of the southern part of the State, and the fortifications long the Mobile Bay guarded the water entrance to the metropolis of Alabama.

The only incident I have any recollection of in connection with the Macbeth at Mobile was the killing of one of our horses by lightning during a thunder storm. General Maury, commanding that military district, had but a small force at his command, and when it was supposed that an attack would be made on Mobile by the Federal soldiers then starting on an expedition from Pensacola, Florida, it was necessary for him to have more troops. Among the reinforcements sent was the Macbeth. It was in this way that we drifted to Mobile.

In obedience to the order for the Macbeth to return to South Carolina, we moved out of our quarters at Camp Beulah on the 30th August, 1863, and putting our guns and horses on board the *St. Waverly* and bidding farewell to the metropolis of Alabama, we steamed up the Alabama River, buoyant in spirits and full of hope. Montgomery, at the head of navigation, was our objective point. For miles the alligators, hideous ugly creatures lying on logs and rocks along the river banks, were objects of attraction, the more interesting because they furnished excellent targets for pistol practice. As long as the novelty of our mode of traveling lasted and the sight-seeing was new and refreshing, we enjoyed our quarters on the *St. Waverly*. As a visible evidence of the protracted drought that was prevailing out West at that time, the Alabama River was then running at her low water mark, and it was quite evident that the depth of water was decreasing as we ascended the river, our speed becoming correspondingly slow. Now and then we could feel the boat, as she dragged through the sand, quiver as a house shaken by an earthquake. Our interest in the *St. Waverly* grew monotonous as the depth of the river and the speed of the boat decreased. The third day our progress was so disgustingly pokey that we would have willingly exchanged the boat for the dirt road. Frequently the boat ran aground and hours were spent in pulling and tugging to get it afloat. Sometimes, after the ingenuity of the engineer and the physical powers of the men had been exhausted in their combined efforts to move the boat over a sand bar, our picket rope would be brought into requisition, and with one end of it fastened to a tree some distance up the river and the other to a pulley in the *St. Waverly*, we then, by the united efforts of steam, physical, and mental force, managed to inch our way up the river. We soon reached a point, however, that our efforts made no impression on the *St. Waverly*. She was in water too shallow and sand too deep—we could not move her . . . We were in a dilemma. Our boat was in the middle of the Alabama River, so deep in the sand that we could neither go forward or backward, and it was now quite evident that one of two things must be done: we had either to wait for a rain to flood the river and move us from our mooring or lighten the boat by taking off our horses and wade or swim them to the land. We adopted the latter plan, as the quickest way out of our trouble. The horses were taken to the bank and marched by the dirt road to Montgomery. As soon as the horses were taken off, the *St. Waverly* floated clear of the sand bars, and we had no more vexation on the Alabama River . . .

The Macbeth was landed safely from the *St. Waverly* at Montgomery on the 3rd September, 1863 . . . After waiting one day at Montgomery for transportation, we put our guns on the train the 5th of September and reached Charleston on the 8th. Lucky Macbeth. At home again.

8

THE FIGHTING ENDS FOR PRIVATE ELWELL

> Yankee surgeons took charge of the camp, and one of them poured a quantity of turpentine on my wound which almost made me crazy.
>
> Silas Elwell

Silas Elwell's story gives a graphic picture of the state of medical care on both sides of the battle lines, because the field hospital in which he was treated by Confederate doctors was soon captured by the Federals when the battle lines moved. In 1895 he related the story of his medical treatment, his escape to Confederate lines, and the many kindnesses shown him by local residents.[1]

Private Elwell described the course of events after he was wounded in Mississippi:

At about 4 o'clock on the afternoon of July 13, 1863, five days after the beginning of the siege of Jackson, Mississippi, they were attempting to storm our position with shell, having many batteries playing upon us, and their shell bursting about us, around us, and over us, in a furious storm. A piece of an exploded shell struck my left arm, about half way between the elbow and the shoulder, tearing it almost from the body. Only a small strip of flesh on the under part of the arm held it to my body. The day was hot and I had been much fatigued from the exercises of the day, and I bled very freely. The explosion of the shell near me had stunned me, and the first thing I heard when returning consciousness enabled me to hear, was the voice of Colonel H. N. Benbow calling for the ambulance corps. The Assistant Surgeon on the field corded my arm and stayed the bleeding. By this time, however, I had become very weak and almost blind. I was taken off the field on the same litter on which they had borne off only a few minutes before, my dear friend, Lieutenant Silas Spears of the 26th South Carolina Regiment. It was a singular coincidence we were both wounded at the same time and in the same manner and borne off on the same litter. He died, but by the mercy of God I continue until this day.

I was taken to the surgeon's stand, in a densely shaded part of the river swamp. Here I was laid on the ground and the surgeon of the regiment, Dr. Murray, examined the wound. I asked that it should be immediately amputated. He refused, saying it was not necessary, as I could live only a few hours at best. I insisted, but he turned away with some expression I could not hear. I then called for Dr. Logan, in whom I had great confidence, and for whom I entertained a very high regard. He spoke very kindly to me, and informed me that I was too weak from the loss of blood to undergo the operation. He told me to be content until morning; in that time I might sufficiently rally to justify the amputation. Stimulants and morphine were given me to allay the intense pain I was then suffering. Dr. Girardeau, the Chaplain of the regiment, came and knelt down by me and prayed very earnestly that my life might be spared and that I might be as true a soldier for the Lord Jesus as I had been for my country.

Most of the night and the day following I was unconscious; only at short intervals and when aroused by others, was I at all cognizant of transpiring events. About 10 o'clock the next morning, the brigade surgeon and four others came and examined me and consulted as to the propriety of the proposed amputation. This, I understood afterwards, was because of a personal difficulty between Dr. Murray and myself some time before. He was unwilling to assume the responsibility of the operation lest in the event of a fatal termination someone might attribute it, at least in part, to the aforesaid difficulty. I still insisted upon the amputation, believing that the removal of the torn and ruined arm would afford me relief from the agonies I was then enduring. In this time the parts were swollen, inflamed and very sore. My condition presented to the surgeons a puzzling question—whether or not it would be safest to use chloroform. In my very weak condition, with the heart action very feeble, I might not rally from the depressing effects of the chloroform; then on the other hand, the intense pain that I must endure under the operation, and the shock that must necessarily follow, might prove fatal. Of these conditions I was fully informed. I still insisted upon the amputation. I was not willing to wait any longer upon the hope of accumulating strength; I desired I should be done even though it proved fatal; for with the amputation I saw some hope of life, but if it were longer delayed I felt that death was certain. After some consultation they decided to perform the operation, and to administer chloroform to a limited extent, putting me partially under its influence, so that, for the most part, I endured the pain of the operation, supported by my determination to have it performed. God graciously sustained me in all this and no evil results followed. After the operation was performed my pain decreased, as I believed it would, and I slept soundly the greater part of the day, only awaking when some unusual noise or Adam Wells' familiar voice would arouse me to offer me stimulants or nourishment, such as he could procure. In the afternoon these kind attentions to me had to cease, as Adam's services were demanded entirely by the surgeons, and I was doomed to a new and trying experience.

General Johnston, having removed his hospital and commissary stores, determined to evacuate Jackson that night. Unable to remove the wounded beyond the enemy's reach, they put them in tents in Breckinridge's division camp, and made them as comfortable as circumstances would permit. The wounded men were gathered up from where they were lying about in the swamp and taken some distance in the ambulances to the camp. I was soundly sleeping and knew nothing of what was going on, and I suppose I was unintentionally overlooked. I did not wake during the night. No one can imagine, nor can I describe my astonishment and distress when I awoke next morning to find myself alone in Pearl River swamp, and utterly unable to move myself even to change my position. "What does this mean?" was my unanswered inquiry. "Shall I die here alone without help or attention? Oh! God, I have passed through the dangers of the battle; I have endured terrible suffering of the amputation, and now shall I die by inches in this swamp? Oh! God, Thou who art infinite in resources, in Thine inscrutable wisdom devise some way for my deliverance from what seems to be certain death." This and like prayers went up from my poor, weak, quivering lips. Oh! what a joy would have come to poor heart could I have seen a human form or heard a human voice! The day dragged slowly by, while I prayed, mused and suffered. My only company was a swarm of blow flies that deposited their eggs upon the bloody bandages that covered my inflamed, painful wound. I could not scare them away, not having strength to use my right hand, and was therefore forced to see the loathsome and distressing sight of having my flesh consumed while life yet remained. A burning thirst was fast consuming me. "Will I live till night? Must my last hours be rendered more gloomy because of the darkness and dreariness of the night?" These and many kindred thoughts engaged my mind as the day was slowly waning. The night approached and my feelings of sadness deepened. I felt faint, and a sense of nausea. Surely this was the approach of death. It will soon be over. "Oh! God, if I may not live until morning, let me die before night. The sun is almost down; his golden beams adorn the tree tops with a halo of glory as if to give me a beautiful vision before Nature's night and the deep gloom of death should deprive me of sight forever. This is my last look at the world. I shall soon see it no more until I shall see it wrapped in the flames of my kindred, and my comrades; I will soon be where there are no wars, no wounds, no suffering, no dying. I had fondly hoped that I would someday return to my home and family, but that hope, like all others, has now departed, and I would gladly dismiss from my mind, in this solemn moment, the thought of those whom I can never again see on earth. My poor body cannot be honored with interment in the burying place of my fathers, but must furnish a morsel for the wild beasts that inhabit this dreary swamp." Such were my thoughts as the sun was sinking.

From these thoughts, I was disturbed by a noise. It sounds like a step upon the dry leaves. Alas! it is some wild beast that has come, guided by the scent of blood, to hasten the process of death. The struggle now will soon be ended; but I hear a sound like the muttering of a human voice. Is it possible that God in His mercy has sent relief in this last moment? I call: "Come here." I hear distinctly one say to another. "Didn't you hear somebody?" and then they answered, "Who is that." Than I answered: "A wounded soldier; don't be alarmed; come and help me." It was two women who had come into the swamp to hide some of their valuables, whom God had directed to the spot where His servant lay almost dying. A few questions, accompanied with expressions of pity, and they hurriedly departed. Hope revived. They are surely gone to get someone to move me to more comfortable quarters, where attention can be given me, and immediate wants supplied. A half hour later, and they returned, bringing a cup of water and a bowl of mush and milk. They kindly raised my head and held it to my parched lips. Oh! how refreshing! for I was dying with thirst. I had no appetite and could therefore take but little of the mush and milk which they fed to me with a spoon. Having performed this office of kindness, they departed, saying they would return in the morning and bring me better nourishment. I felt much revived. Surely the hand of God is in this and I shall live. Glory be to be to His name! If I can endure through this night I will be cared for tomorrow as my condition and whereabouts are known to the living.

It was growing dark around me, but there was light in my heart. My position rendered more comfortable by leaves that those good women had gathered and put around and under me and for my pillow, I caught occasional naps of sleep. Some time during the night I was aroused by a noise. At first I was startled, but was soon composed when I discovered that the sound was that of the rumbling of a wagon. I called as loudly as I could. The wagon stopped, which indicated to me that I was heard. I called again. They came to me—two men with a wagon loaded with trunks which they were concealing in the swamp. One of them was intoxicated, the other seemed not only to be sober, but a man of generous impulses. He said he knew the way to the camp and proposed to take me there. His intoxicated companion protested, saying with an oath that I would soon be dead and that was as good a place to die as any. But the sober man's counsel prevailed and they took me very roughly and tumbled me into the wagon, which almost took my life, and then driving away across the swamp over logs, stumps and saplings, subjected me to indescribable suffering, with my wound inflamed, swollen and sore. The drive, however, was not very long. They reached camp and laid me on a bunk of shucks in a tent and departed. This was a luxury compared to my previous condition. My heart was in a measure resting from the distress and anxiety of a few hours previous. I slept little, but spent the remaining hours of night in thanksgiving to my gracious heavenly Father. I felt sure that God intended to spare my life, and I never again entertained any fear of dying there. Though my troubles were not ended I had an unshaken confidence that the Lord would bring me through safely.

The morning came and revealed another wounded soldier lying on a bunk of shucks on the opposite side of the same tent. He was asleep. I scanned him closely, but did not recognize him. He soon awoke and proposed an introduction. He gave me his name as Leonard Dryman from Pickens County, South Carolina. His company and regiment I do not now remember.[2] His arm was taken off below the elbow and he was doing well; he was able to sit up. I found him very helpful to me, assisting me up and down as necessity required, for the nurse to whose care we were committed was exceedingly trifling and neglectful. He spent most of his time away from the tent so as to avoid our needs, and we suffered much for water and for other attentions.

The women who had shown me such kindness the evening before came as they had promised. Missing me they followed the wagon tracks to the division camp. They brought me some milk and nicely prepared refreshments and also a long loose garment they had made, which was well-suited to my condition, and which I very much needed. After words of encouragement and sympathy they left me, promising to return the next day, but we were taken prisoners that day and they never returned.

The Federal troops came and took possession of the hospital. Some of the doctors and nurses escaped. Fortunately for me, however, Dr. Holley was captured. The Yankee surgeons took charge of the camp, and one of them poured a quantity of turpentine on my wound which almost made me crazy. They brought some of their own sick and wounded into the camp and scattered them among us. Many of them were sick with measles. I had never had measles, and I thought that I could not survive an attack of measles in my condition. About dark they brought into my tent a Yankee soldier with a high fever, and the next morning he was broken out with measles. I thought I would certainly be taken with that much dreaded disease, but through the mercy of God I did not take it. After breakfast was served, which consisted of a slice of bread and a spoonful of molasses, Dr. Hinkly, the surgeon of the post, on his round of inspection, came to my tent and entered into a lengthy conversation with me. A warm friendship at once sprang up between us. He had the measles patient removed and consented for Dr. Holley, my friend, to take charge of me and attend to my wound. As there was much gangrene in the camp and many were dying, the Doctor would dress my wound and that of my companion Dryman before day, before the other men's wounds were opened. He kept my entire shoulder covered with a piece of oiled silk. I improved very rapidly and was soon able to walk about. Dr. Hinkly, the post surgeon, visited me every day and spent much time with me in conversation. He showed me many kindnesses and treated me, not as a prisoner, but as a friend. Under the treatment of Dr. Holley, with the kind assistance of Dryman, I improved very rapidly. The daily visits of the post surgeon for social converse and interchange of ideas tendered my prison life more bearable than I anticipated. The topics of our daily discussion were mainly the *causus belli* and transpiring events. As to the first of these we were not well informed. I went out because I was led to believe it was my duty to obey the demands of my country, without considering the cause, or even at that time being able to understand it. With the latter I was somewhat more familiar.

A witty, humorous Irishman, familiarly known as Pat, frequented the camp. He had a wagon and would come every morning to haul out the dead, and as gangrene was prevailing, the death rate was alarming. With him I had frequent conversations. His manner and witticisms amused me very much. All these things detracted for a time my attention from my sufferings, and my improvement was rapid. In a few days I was able to sit up, and with Dryman's assistance walk around the tent. The blow flies, more numerous than I had ever seen house flies and much more annoying, prevented any rest in the daytime. Dryman had found a piece of muslin about four yards long and one yard wide, which we would use alternately to keep them out of our faces while trying to take a mid-day nap.

After some days had elapsed, an old countryman came into camp to sell fruit. He saw my destitute condition, and when he came the next day be brought me a pair of brown woolen pants, with both knees out. The holes in the knees were large enough to admit my head, and they were otherwise badly worn; however, they were a great help to me and much appreciated. I had found an old cap, and with this and the pants I felt like a little boy when first arrayed in such a costume. My diet was not altogether to my liking, as it consisted of a slice of light bread and molasses. Sometimes very little molasses remained after the flies were extracted. We did not complain, but tried to make ourselves as agreeable as possible. I had been there ten days and was strong enough to walk about over the grounds, yet I had not gone at any time ten steps from my tent door.

A rumor then circulated that the railroad leading to Vicksburg had been repaired, and that the next day we would be sent there and shipped to the prison at Elmira, New York. Certain maneuvering about the camp indicated that the rumor was well-founded. This caused me to feel much depressed and troubled. I began to pray that some way of escape would open up to me. I feared that I could not survive if carried to a Northern prison. As I could see no possibility of escape, I began to try to reconcile my feelings to what seemed to be the inevitable. Late in the afternoon the post surgeon made his daily visit to my tent and when leaving he advised me to take more exercise and gave me permission to walk as far as the cook's stand, which was just inside the guard line. This I did, and I saw where the guards were stationed and the careless manner in which they performed their duty. Without seeming to do so, I observed closely the length of the beat of the guard stationed at the cook's stand and the thick undergrowth just beyond, which formed a part of the river swamp. I thought I saw a way by which I could possibly escape, and believing that the hand of the Lord was in this, I returned to my tent, and upon my knees committed myself to God in prayer and thanksgiving. I then made known to Dryman (who remained at the tent during my stroll) all my discoveries, and told him of my intention to try to make my escape that night. He advised against it and entreated me to desist from such a rash purpose, saying I could not escape and it would cost me my life to undertake it; that we would be well cared for in the prison, and we would live and go back home together. But I was determined and told him that I would not ask him to go with me, but that I would go or be killed in the attempt.

I felt some anxiety as the hour approached for the undertaking, because I knew not in what direction to start. I had no knowledge of the country, or the location of the Federal camp. It was truly a hazardous undertaking but I felt hopeful of the final result. Dryman called my attention to another fact that was against my project, i.e., it was to be a clear moonlit night—but I noticed that the sky was thinly overcast with clouds and the moon would not rise until about an hour after dark. So I determined to make my escape, through the guard line before the moon arose.

It was dark—the time had come for the undertaking. I rose to tell Dryman good-bye, but he said he intended to follow me; I insisted that he should not, as I thought it easier for one to succeed than two in such an enterprise. Further, if we should meet with fatal consequences, I did not wish to feel that I had led another man to his death. However, with him no argument would prevail. He had determined to go with me and to die with me if it came to that. Such a result I did not expect, but a recapture would subject us to closer confinement, less considerate treatment and certain removal to a Northern prison. All this I was determined to risk, urged on by an irrepressible anxiety to get home. Not unmindful of the dangers attending the experiment, but encouraged by the hope of success and an unshaken confidence in God that

He would bring us safely through all the difficulties attendant, we left the tent at dark and walked slowly towards the guard line, in as aimless and indifferent manner as was possible under the circumstances. By the light at the cook's stand we could plainly see the guard as he approached that end of the beat. When he reached, as we thought, a safe distance, with his back toward us, we stole cautiously across the line and concealed ourselves in the thick underbrush near by, and here we awaited a like circumstance to favor our departure, lest our footsteps should be heard.

We were across the guard line, but the moon having not yet risen and the stars concealed by the clouds, we could not tell which way to go. We intended, when the moon appeared, or if we could determine at all the spot of her rising, to take our course by that, as we were intending to travel eastward. A bright spot in the heavens soon appearing indicated to us the direction we sought, and for some time we strolled along in a belt of thick wood that skirted the river, carefully and silently. We knew we were not far from the camp we had left, and feared that they would miss us. We came unexpectedly to a public road at the corner of a fence enclosing a yard fronting a large two-story dwelling. I hastened to cross the road, as I saw a thick wood on the other side, which I hoped would conceal us from any passer by. I had scarcely reached the middle of the road when I heard a voice clearly and distinctly calling out: "Who is that?" I turned and saw a man standing at the fence inside of the yard near a carriage house, which was built in the edge of the yard and formed a part of the enclosing fence. I recognized the voice to be that of Dr. Hinkly, the post surgeon. I turned and went to him.

Dr. Hinkly said: "What do you mean by coming out here at this time of night? I gave you permission to walk within the guard line, but not to cross it." I replied in a quiet tone: "I understand that, Doctor. I do not mean to tell you any falsehood, or conceal from you any fact. I am attempting to make my escape to our army with the hope of getting home. I can see no good it will do to keep me a prisoner while I am so disabled, and especially so, as it is permanent. My companion here is in the same condition. We concluded to make the attempt, feeling sure that if we were taken to a prison it would be death to us, and if killed in an attempt to escape, it would only be death. So while there is a chance of life in it, the other seemed to indicate certain death. And now I beg that you will not return us to the camp, but permit us to continue our journey. Maybe God will favor our flight." He stood for a moment reflecting, then said, "Do you know the country?" I answered: "I do not, but I know that South Carolina, my home, is east from this place, and I propose to travel in an easterly direction and take the chances. Said he: "Your army is somewhere about Brandon, twelve miles from here, and between here and there is a strong picket line that you could not possibly pass, especially so as you do not know the country. My advice to you is to return to the camp. These are my headquarters, and I can send you back to the camp and shield you from any punishment." "This," I replied, "is very kind of you, but I prefer that you will allow me to escape unnoticed into the woods and take my chances for a final escape." "Then," said he, "swear to me that if captured you will never reveal this meeting and interview." "You need not fear, Doctor," I replied. "I will die with the secret, and also will my companion." He took us inside of the yard and put us in the carriage house and shut the door and left us. "Now," said Dryman, "we will be sent back to camp. It would have been better for us not to have left." "No," said I, "he means us well, and will help us. Don't be so despondent. Wait and see; all will work well yet." In a few minutes he returned to us and gave us a luncheon which we relished, and for which we kindly thanked him. He gave me also a bottle of brandy which had never been opened, and said: "Now, don't be fools and get drunk, but take a little occasionally to keep your strength up. I can give you no information about the location of the picket line; the risks are yours. You will no doubt be brought back tomorrow morning, unless you should happen to get shot by some careless or scary picket, but trusting to your honor, I will let you try it. I will send Pat out with the wagon tonight. Good-bye." "Good-bye," said I. "God bless you for your kindness. Don't be uneasy about us, we will come out all right." Thus we parted at the gate. I have never heard of him since, but think of him often and cherish for him a feeling of gratitude and affection. We crossed the road and kept in the bushes, near enough to the road to be governed by its course, but far enough to be safe from the observation of anyone who might chance to pass. We had not gone far when we heard the lumbering of a wagon. Feeling sure that it was Pat we drew near road and watched the approach of the wagon. The moonlight was dimmed by the obscuring clouds, which, though thin, had completely overcast the sky. We were correct in our conjecture; it was Pat. I stepped out from my concealment and called out: "Ha, Pat!" He reigned up his horses and answered: "Who are you now?" Then in a familiar manner I addressed him: "Pat, we are trying to escape to our own army and home. We hear that there is a strong picket line somewhere in front of us, and we do not know where it is or how to pass through it. I have a bottle of brandy that has not been opened. If you will pass us safely through that picket line I will give it to you. Will you do it?" Pat replied: "Devil if I care who wins the day if I get the brandy. Get in the wagon." We were soon comfortably seated in the wagon, and Pat went on whistling some of his Irish ditties. We sat silent in deep thought and not a little fear.

We had gone a few miles in this manner when we reached a low place in the road. A gradual rise on the other side would bring us up again to the general level of the country. In this bottom Pat stopped his wagon and said to us: "Lay down now, and let me cover you with the wagon sheet, for the devils are at the top of the hill. Be sure that you keep still and make no noise." It is useless to say that we obeyed his every command, for our fears at this moment were exceedingly great. Will he betray us or will he be true to us? What a moment of anxiety! Our hearts beat fast and strong; to us it sounded so loud that we feared that the picket would hear. All is silence. Slowly Pat rises the long gravel slope; when near the top we distinctly heard what we were expecting to hear, but were nevertheless startled at the sound: "Halt!," Who comes there?" Pat promptly answered: "Hinkly's wagon." "Where are you going?" "To the mills for flour. The devils are perishing in the camp, so I had to come tonight." "What is that you have in the wagon?" I cannot describe my feelings when this question was asked. Pat answered very promptly, but the suspense of a single second was almost unbearable at such a time, but the Irishman was equal to the occasion: "I have the wagon sheet; don't you see that its cloudy and it may rain and have the flour all dough before I get back." This satisfied the picket and he said: "Pass on." What a relief! What a feeling of calm security! The danger is past, the much dreaded ordeal, and now I breathe easy. Pat passed on, all maintaining a perfect silence. When he had gone sufficiently far to insure the inability of the picket to see or hear us, he stopped the wagon and called out: "Hi, my man, come out from your cover and let's have the brandy." I very cheerfully handed him the bottle, for it had served a better purpose than if we had drunk it. Pat found considerable difficulty in getting out the cork, which was sealed and bound in with wire. Success, however, finally crowned his efforts, and putting the bottle to his lips, he began to swallow its contents so greedily that I thought he intended emptying it at one draught. From this he became very cheerful and talkative. I thanked him very kindly for his faithfulness to us, not intimating that any part of it was due to the brandy, and then made a movement to get out of the wagon. However, he insisted that I should not, that he meant to take us further. I assured him that we appreciated very much his purpose, but I feared that he might come unawares upon the Confederate line and be captured, and therefore I insisted that he should leave us to work out the problem ourselves; but he drove on, giving no heed to my remonstrance, only saying: "I know where I am going. There is no rebels this side of Brandon, but them pickets don't know it. They moved yesterday, and I am going to take you to Brandon. Be quiet and we'll have no more of your mouth, now." Silence reigned and Pat proceeded, quickening somewhat his horses' gait, as the effects of the brandy became more and more apparent. About the middle of the night we arrived at Brandon. Pat took us into the suburbs of the little town and as near to the guard line around the hospital as he could safely go.

He kindly helped us out of the wagon, and saying, "I wish ye gude luck!" drove rapidly way. I looked after him as far as the dim light would permit me to see his wagon, with feelings of profound thankfulness to the faithful Irishman.

Brandon was a small town, the county seat of Rankin County, situated on the railroad between Jackson and Meridian. Here we found the hospital. It was a large, two-story house, fronting the square, with open piazzas above and below, running the full length of the building. It was formerly a hotel. The walls separating the rooms had been removed to adapt it to the purpose for which it was then being used. In the upper story we found two unoccupied bunks near each other, and these we took. They were filled with shucks just as they had been taken from the corn; the sharp ends that attached them to the stalk remained. The reader can imagine what comfort we found in such beds.

During the eight days of my stay at Brandon I gained strength rapidly, being well cared for through the kindness of a Mr. and Mrs. Ferguson [who fed him and kept him in their nearby home each night]. Sunday, I spent the day in the ward reading my Testament. In the afternoon Dr. Parker passed through the ward and said that the railroad leading to Meridian had been repaired within two miles of Brandon, and the next day a train would come to take off the sick men—the wounded men would have to remain longer. This was cheering news in part, but not entirely satisfactory to me, as I desired to be among the first to go.

[On the next day, the ambulances came] and the Assistant Surgeon was in the ward selecting out the sick men that were to go. I caught Dryman's eye and beckoned him out and told him of my plans. He thought best not to undertake it, but said if I intended to he would follow me. We got into an ambulance and lay down under the seats and dropped the curtains down in front of us, which sufficiently concealed us. He on one side and I on the other. The ambulances were soon filled with sick men that had been selected to go and they were informed that Dr. Parker would be out to the road later and give them transportation. This we could hear and knew that we would have to conceal ourselves after reaching the railroad. The place we were to meet the train was in a wood near a branch. As soon as the others had gotten out of the ambulances we crawled out from under the seats and stole away in a thick place near the branch. From our hiding place we could see the Doctor when he came. Fortunately for us the train was late, and the Doctor grew impatient and returned before its arrival, which gave us an opportunity to come out from our hiding place and select a more comfortable situation. For some time Dryman had been complaining of feeling sick. He ate but very little of the breakfast I had taken him. It was now apparent that he had fever.

Poor fellow, he tried to bear up, but could not. At length he said: "I will be obliged to return to the hospital, and I know I shall die. There will be no one to secure me any nourishment, and no one will care for me; the nurses would rather I would die than live, for then I would be less trouble to them. I had hoped to be able to go with you and that we should not part until we reached Kingville, South Carolina, but poor me, my fate is to die here. Dear comrade, we must part. I will never see you again until we meet in Heaven." Said he: "You have been true to me and I know you would do anything possible for me. Good-bye. May God grant you a safe arrival home, and if you should ever see any of my family, tell them all is well with me. I go trusting in the Lord." We embraced each other and wept bitterly. He took off his canteen which he had kept, saying "Take this as a parting present from me. You may need it. I never will." I laid the canteen down and assisted him into an ambulance which was about leaving and when I turned again to pick up the canteen, an old gray-headed man, who was in the army as a substitute, had picked it up and run off with it. I could not recover it. The Lord reward him. I learned afterwards that Dryman lived only two days after his return to the hospital.

I looked after the departing ambulance until it was lost to sight. With a sad heart, I felt sure that Dryman would die, for he had himself despaired of life. We had been together in sufferings and danger and our souls had knit together like those of Jonathan and David. I had always found him cool, deliberate, and thoughtful. He was true in his attachments and firm and faithful in his friendships. He had a warm and confiding heart. It was sad indeed to part with him under such circumstances. My heart was already sad, having parted touchingly with Mr. Ferguson and his good wife. The revelation she had made to me of my favoring her son, which accounted for her preference for me, which Dryman seemed to discover.

Shortly after Dryman's departure the train arrived and everybody made a rush to get on board. After the sick men entered the car, I came and attempted also to board the train, but a Provost-Guard stationed on the platform of the car, forbade my entering. "Well, thought I, here it is again; difficulties seem to throng my pathway. Surely there is no smooth place in life for me." I was not discouraged at this, as I felt sure that the same God who had brought me safely through greater difficulties than this, would deliver me in this also. I stood at the steps holding to the rail, intending when the train moved off to take my seat on the steps, supposing that the guard would not be heartless enough to kick me off, and so I would go after all. The whistle blew and the train was about to start, when a tall erect, dignified looking gentleman came up to board the train. His hair and beard was gray, though from his general appearance I did not suppose him to be more than fifty. His beard was long and neatly trimmed; his manner commanding. He was polite, but decided in his bearing. He was quick spoken, seeming almost abrupt. I discovered that he was a physician. "Can I assist you?" he said to me in a kind, but quick tone. "I can get on sir," I replied, "but the guard there will not allow me." "Why?" he demanded of the guard in a commanding tone. "Because," said the guard in a hesitating manner, "this is a citizens car, and he is a wounded man, and his wound would be offensive to the ladies and gentlemen on board. They will send up a box-car tomorrow and he can come on that." "What; sir, must he, a wounded man, who has received his wound in the cause of his country, in defense of the property and homes of these very people, be left here in the woods merely for their pleasure? It shall not be sir; he shall go on this car," and drawing a revolver from his belt and presenting it at the guard he demanded, "Clear that door, sir, or you are a dead man." The guard stepped aside and he turned to me and said, "Now, sir, walk in," which I gladly did. The car was filled with passengers. Every seat was occupied. A brigadier general who was occupying a seat alone reading a newspaper, raised his eyes from his paper as we were about to pass him, and seeing my condition, he rose and said: "Take my seat." "No," I replied, "I can't afford to take your seat. I will be content to go in the baggage car, or take my seat on the floor." "No, sir," he replied, "I am better able to take care of myself than you are." In this time he had stepped out in the aisle and compelled me to take his seat, and turning to the Doctor, he said. "Sit here with him and take care of him." He went into another car and I saw him no more. A few minutes later the conductor came through the train taking up tickets. When he reached me he said: "You will have to get off, sir, but I won't put you off here in the woods. I'll take you to the next station." "He must go, Captain," said the Doctor, at my side. "But he can't go, it is against orders," said the conductor. "But he shall go," said the Doctor, "if this train goes." "Well sir, I'll put him off now," said the conductor, "if you are disposed to be obstinate about it," and he turned and went into the front car, returning in a few minutes accompanied by two guards. As they entered the door the Doctor rose from his seat with a revolver in his hand, and said, "Captain I see no need for battle on this train, but I notify you that somebody will die if you make any attempt to put this soldier off. I will kill the first man that approaches this seat, and you will never put him off until you kill me. If you wish to cause a tragedy like that, proceed." This created considerable excitement in the car. Ladies began to cry and beg that there be no trouble, and the conductor consented to let me go to Meridian, the place I desired to go. Some time between midnight and daylight we reached Meridian without further interference. Here I parted with my protector, whom I since learned was Dr. D. B. Gunn, of Brandon. He has since died.

I soon found the distributing hospital where, after breakfast, the doctor dressed my wound and assigned me to Lauderdale. I entreated him to send me to Macon, but he said Macon was full and could take no more. Lauderdale was a camp in an old field on the side of a creek of the same name. The sick and wounded were in small tents exposed to the unbroken rays of the sun, and they were like ovens for heat. To one of these I was assigned. At Meridian I met my brother-in-law, who was in search of me. It was my first information from home. The newspapers reported me mortally wounded and left on the field, and I thought they supposed me dead, but Captain Benbow knowing my real condition, kindly telegraphed home, without my knowledge, the facts. My brother-in-law, supposing me to still be a prisoner at Jackson, had obtained a permit to enter the line in search of me and was on his way there when I met him at Meridian. We went on together to Lauderdale where we found Captain H. H. Lesesne, then commanding the company, afterwards promoted to Major. He was sick but improving. While I tarried awhile at his tent, talking to him before going to my own, Dr. Thompson, commander of the post, came along and I asked him to transfer me to South Carolina. He said: "Certainly, you are able to travel. I will let you go. But let me first examine your wound." Which he did very casually, and then said, "Your wound is in too bad a fix for you to go." "Doctor," said I, "will it get any better by staying here in these little hot tents? I hope you will let me take the chances of the trip." "No, sir," he said, "my reputation is at stake: I would be held responsible if you should die on the way." "Well, doctor, who is going to be responsible if I die here, and what does your responsibility amount to?" "I don't care to discuss it with you," he rejoined, "go to your tent." I obeyed with a sad heart and great despondency. Here I was much neglected. The doctor never came to my tent during the ten days that I remained there. But for the kind attention of my brother-in-law, whom they compelled to board outside of the camp, I would have died. I feel sure. Every day he visited the doctor's quarters and begged him to let me go, but without avail. Captain H. H. Lesesne had in this time so improved that he could walk about over the camp, and was preparing to report for duty. He came to my tent to see me before leaving, and, as he said, to hear any message I wished to send to the boys. He was surprised to find me so much worse and went that morning with my brother-in-law to ask for my removal. The interview between the Captain and the Doctor was of a heated nature, involving almost a disregard for rank, but resulted well. An hour later he sent a messenger to tell me to send up for my papers, for my transfer to the College Hospital at Columbia, SC. We boarded the first train, which took us back to Meridian, thence to Selma, and thence to Montgomery. Then I traveled by steamboat up the Alabama river, which was the most pleasant part of the trip.

Rev. Silas Pinckney Holbrook Elwell
(*Twentieth Century Sketches of the South Carolina Conference, M.E. Church, South*, 1901)

In five days and nights traveling, with the hindrances incident to the times, we reached home, much exhausted, almost dead with fatigue and burning with fever. For many days after my arrival at home I seemed to be balancing between life and death, but God spared me for some wise purpose which I trust I will fulfill.

Silas Pinckney Holbrook Elwell would preach the gospel for the Methodist Episcopal Church South from 1867 until 1900.

9

GARRISON DUTY IN CHARLESTON

> President Davis asked him where his shoes were. His reply was, "By God, I ain't got none."
>
> William H. Edwards

In August 1863, Evans' Brigade returned from Mississippi and was assigned to assist in the defense of Charleston. Almost immediately, Brigadier General R. S. Ripley, commanding the First Military District to which the brigade had been assigned, had Evans arrested for disobedience. A court-martial acquitted Evans, but Beauregard refused to return him to command. Meanwhile, the brigade's six regiments and the Macbeth Artillery (which had arrived on September 8) served until April 1864 as almost independent units on James and Sullivan's Islands, at Mount Pleasant, and at Christ Church Parish.

Most of the accounts of the veterans make little mention of this period, probably because Evans' Brigade did not take part in any important military actions during this time. However, an account of the activities of the Seventeenth Regiment is found in the diary of Captain William Grafton Stevenson of Company D.[1] He was one of the soldiers who was wounded by his own troops near Legareville, South Carolina, in June 1862. He had recovered and returned to his unit, and his diary gives interesting insights into the everyday events of camp life. The diary begins when the Seventeenth Regiment was encamped near Savannah, as the unit was returning from Mississippi to Charleston:

Sunday—August 23rd: On guard today as officer of the day, hence could not leave camp to go to preaching. I read several chapters in the Testament; wrote to Sallie C. Gibson[2] and to Sallie Crawford; received a letter from May directed to Morton Trip. Orders read at Dress Parade this evening to have two inspections a week and policing every morning.

Monday—August 24th: Drew money for Company for May and June, the rolls amounted to $1033.96. [Note the amount of this payroll. The pay for a captain was $130 per month, but a private received only $11 per month. The payroll for a company of one hundred men for two months would total about

$2,500, if the unit was at full strength.] Also drew 42 coats, 19 pants, shoes, shirts, and drawers. We are now well clad. The news from Charleston is bad; the enemy have succeeded in throwing some shells into the city. Fort Sumter is said to be in ruins. The Company has packed up a box to send home, filled with clothing. Received a letter from home from Lizzie. The Regiment made quite a show at Dress Parade in their Confederate uniforms.

Tuesday—August 25th: Wrote a letter to Lizzie before breakfast; sent off the box which the Company had packed yesterday. While on Battalion drill this evening a courier came and delivered orders to Colonel McMaster to have two days rations cooked and be ready to march to Savannah tomorrow morning by five o'clock. We all suppose we are going to Charleston but do not know positively. The men are all busy cooking. It is reported that the enemy are shelling Charleston vigorously. About bed time another order came for us not to move until further orders, but to be ready to move at a moment's notice.

Wednesday—August 26th: Orders came for us to move at 10 o'clock; tents and flies were immediately struck and baggage taken up to be put in wagon. As soon as we were ready to march, it commenced raining very hard and continued for an hour. As soon as the rain cleared, the Regiment started. We had a sloppy road, but the Colonel rested us frequently, consequently we were not much tired when we arrived in town. We were ordered to camp in the rear of the Park. We went there and were just in the act of stacking arms when another order came for us to proceed to the Depot and get on the cars. Just as we got on the cars, it commenced raining very hard. Most of the men kept dry. I got wet attending to my trunk of provisions and my blanket. We had a jolly time. Everybody was in fine spirits, some having taken an undue allowance of the latter. The train our Regiment was on started at 9 o'clock P.M., before any other regiment of the Brigade. I went to sleep and slept all night, consequently did not see anything on the road.

Thursday—August 27th: Woke up this morning just before we got to our old Camp Simmons. Our old training ground thereabouts looked very natural; vestiges of the camp are still visible. Mr. Glover, the gentleman at whose house I stayed while wounded, is still living at the same place. I saw him sitting in the Piazza, and his daughters waved to us as we passed; they did not know it was our Regiment. From here to the city, everything looked as natural as ever and we felt like we were nearer home. Arrived at Fort Andrews Depot about 8 o'clock A.M. where we disembarked. Our Company was detailed to unload baggage. The Regiment was formed near old Camp Lee, stacked arms, and cooked. I went out to our old Parade Ground, where we could see some of the effects of the Yankee bombardment. The side [of Fort Sumter] we could see seemed to be demolished, and the boom of cannon could be heard at regular intervals. Received a letter from home by Captain Woods; he also brought me $125.00. Captain Edwards, Lieutenant Logan,[3] and myself walked over to the City, which we found almost deserted; it makes one feel sad to see so few citizens there. We went down on the Battery and saw our batteries on James Island firing. We could see a shell explode once and awhile over what we took to be Battery Wagner. The Yankees took our rifle pits on Morris Island last night; they are now within 400 yards of Battery Wagner.

Friday—August 28th: Had a good night's rest and woke this morning greatly refreshed. Shortly after we got breakfast, wagons came over from the City for our baggage, and we were ordered by the Colonel to get ready as he intended to move the Regiment, but he concluded afterwards to await written orders. I wrote a letter to Maggie and then went to sleep. Soon after I woke up, orders came for us to march to Northeast Wharf and take the boat for Mount Pleasant. We crossed Ashley River on New Bridge, went up the street, turned to the right at King Street and then to the left and went down John Street and then down Chapel Street to the wharf. The whole Brigade marched through together; the boys were all full of life and were a little noisy.[4] Several men from Company C left during the night, and also one from Company K; several left from various companies along the road, but Company D came through all right. Their deportment has always been good and of a soldierly conduct. Since we have been in service there has never been any one of the Company in the guard house or been convicted of any crime punishable by Court Martial; this is certainly praiseworthy. Their respect too for private property has been marked. Took the boat about 3 ½ o'clock P.M. and crossed the Cooper River to Mount Pleasant. While coming across we saw the Yankees shelling Battery Wagner. Just as we arrived at the Landing at Mount Pleasant it commenced raining very hard. We got off the boat and sheltered ourselves under the shed of a Hotel which is now a Hospital, but did not get to remain under it long; the Regiment was formed and the Colonel went off to see where to go, and we all got drenched. We then marched about a half mile on the Georgetown Road, halted, and stacked arms, but we had no shelter and in fact no place to lie down except the road. The Colonel finally concluded to go back. On the way back, several of the men fell out and stopped in houses. The Regiment halted under some trees, stacked arms, and the Colonel told us to make ourselves as comfortable as possible. We consequently scattered and got in houses. I met up with an officer who was quartered in a house. He had a good supper prepared for us, which we did full justice to. After supper, he took the men upstairs and gave them a mattress and dry bed clothes to lie on. I lay in the Parlor and slept soundly, although my clothes were perfectly wet.

Saturday—August 29th: Awoke this morning about daylight, got up and left the house. Went to where the Regiment stacked arms, washed my face, and ate some salt meat and bread. The Colonel soon came down and we started on the march and went about two miles to Lucas Mills, halted, and stacked arms, and the men all spread out their Blankets and wet clothes, but the Colonel started us off again and we went about a half mile to some beautiful shade trees, where all again spread out our blankets. I lay down and took a good sleep. Our trunk of provisions came up and we found the bottle of black pepper broken and pepper all over the sugar and meat.

Sunday—August 30th: Soon this morning the enemy commenced firing on Sumter. Captain B and myself got permission to go to the village and look on the bombardment. We got the Colonel's glass and could see the balls strike the Fort and some went entirely through. There is a terrible rent in the wall through which we could see light; the enemy continued firing all day, and our batteries did not reply except those on James Island. The fleet lay off at a respectable distance, quiet spectators. We could see the Ironsides. After we had looked long enough, we went and heard Mr. Girardeau preach. While he was preaching the firing was going on, and we saw the shells bursting. Made applications for two furloughs for the Company. Wrote to Pa; received a letter from Daniel. Will have a muster tomorrow for July and August. Saw one of my old classmates, Nettles, while at Mount Pleasant.

Monday—August 31st: Got up early and went to work on the Muster Rolls,[5] and finished two before breakfast, but the mustering officer did not come until late in the evening. A detail of five men was made up from our Regiment to put up telegraph posts, the authorities having determined to run a line from Sullivan's Island to Charleston. Last night, when the 20th and 23rd Georgia were returning from Morris Island, having been relieved, our guns on Fort Moultrie opened on the boat and sunk it; 160 men were missing from the 20th Regiment this morning. It is said that the boat did not signal as she passed the Fort. It was a serious and melancholy accident. The gunboats moved up today and fired at Battery Gregg and Fort Moultrie, but done no damage. They were struck several times and it became too hot for them and they finally drew off. Applied for furlough for Jesse McWalters. Drew $100.00 for James Wallace, being money due him for services rendered the Confederacy. We are ordered to start at daylight tomorrow morning and march about six miles to cut timber in front of the Breastworks on Georgetown Road. The firing in the harbor continued all day.

Tuesday—September 1st: Our Regiment started to the fortification early this morning. I did not go, and remained behind to finish the payrolls of the Company. The men had nothing but crackers to eat, and came back about 3 o'clock P.M., there being no tools to work with.

Wednesday—September 2nd: Sergeant [Wylie] and Bob Banks came in last night. Banks brought a box and shared it with us. Captain B also received a trunk of provisions; he went over to the City today. Court Martial convened today to try such cases as may be brought before it. Wrote to Mary. Very little firing today. The rations are very slim; the men have had no meat to eat since day before yesterday. They drew bacon and rice today and eat it all up at one meal. I bought a bushel of Potatoes for the Company.

Thursday—September 3rd: Got my uniform, which fitted me very neatly. Had nice white cabbage for dinner. Lieutenant Carlisle came over this morning and went back this evening, taking his trunk with him. At Dress Parade this evening the findings and sentences of the Regimental Court Martial were read out; one Gillam was sentenced to be confined to the Guard House for six days, his diet to be restricted to bread and water, to forfeit one month's pay, and to stand on the head of a barrel one hour each day for six days. Adjutant Connor and myself rode over to Mount Pleasant after night to see the shelling. There was, however, very little firing, it being mostly from Shell Point Battery on James Island. We returned and met the Colonel, Major, and Captain Means going over too, but we told them it would not pay, and we all came back to Camp together.

Friday—September 4th: Officer of the day today. No news of interest. Court Martial convened again today for the trial of Private Lanier who was charged with sleeping on Post and Drunkenness—found guilty—sentenced to ten days confinement and hard labor to dig well at Guard House. Private Gillam stands on head of barrel each day—one hour at a time. Captain Woods called to see us this morning. All quiet in the Harbor and on Morris Island.

Saturday—September 5th: A spirited cannonading kept up last night all night and continues this morning, slackened about 9 o'clock A.M. Bob Banks and myself got permission to go to the Landing at Mount Pleasant. About 10 o'clock the Ironsides moved up and commenced shelling Battery Wagner furiously and throwing an occasional shell at Gregg, and the enemy's land batteries on Morris Island also shell Wagner. The firing was very rapid and heavy; we could distinctly see where every shell exploded and the dust fly up in perfect volumes from Battery Wagner. One of the Monitors also fired one shot, but drew off. None of our batteries replied except once or twice from Moultrie and an occasional shell from Shell Point Battery on James Island. Bob and myself left about 12 o'clock, the firing having slackened somewhat, but in the evening it was renewed with vigor and continued until night when it again slackened. After supper Captain Edwards and myself walked over to the village and could see the enemy throwing shells into Battery Wagner from mortars; we could see the flash of the gun, and then the shell would go straight up and fall into the fort. We did not remain long. Orders came for us to march to the Breastworks at daylight tomorrow to throw up [additional works]. At Dress Parade another Court Martial was ordered. I am on the Court; to convene Monday.

Sunday—September 6th: A furious cannonading kept up all night last night. We left camp early this morning and marched some four or five miles to the works and found no one there to tell us what to do. We are waiting for someone to come and direct us. The Yankee Monitors and Ironsides are firing vigorously this morning at our Batteries on Morris Island. The Engineers came soon after we arrived. The Regiment was divided into two reliefs of 100 men each and we set in to work manfully; each relief works an hour at a time. Captain B and myself were invited to dinner by a gentleman who is manufacturing salt; the dinner was nothing extra, but we got a drink of good rum which sharpened our appetites. After dinner he (Mr. Long, for that was his name) showed us his salt works; the water is strongly impregnated with salt, it is pumped from wells dug on the beach which has been infiltrating salt from time immemorial; the salt made crystallizes beautifully. After we had satisfied ourselves with examining the works, we returned to the Regiment. Mr. Long insisted on us letting him know the next time we came and he would prepare for us a good dinner. We worked until [very late] when we grounded spades and left. My hands were blistered in several places. On our return to camp, we came a different road from the one we went, and got lost for a little while, but finally came out right. I found a letter to me from May. It is reported that the enemy landed in the rear of our works on Morris Island and made an assault, but were repulsed with heavy loss. We sunk several of the Barges in which they landed; our loss is said to be 160.

Monday—September 7th: Last night Morris Island was evacuated by our forces; the heavy bombardment to which Wagner and Gregg had been subjected made terrible rents in the above named Morris and it continued so our men could not repair damage. The heroic endurance of our soldiers will excite the admiration of future generations. I went up to Mount Pleasant this evening and found women and children coming in perfect swarms from Sullivan's Island. It is reported that the Yankees have said that they will not shell it until 8 o'clock tomorrow, but about sundown this evening their Gunboats moved up and opened a terrific fire. Our Batteries replied manfully. It continued for about an hour; the result not known. About 8 o'clock P.M. orders came to our Regiment for us to repair at once to the Bridge connecting Sullivan's Island with Mount Pleasant and protect it. No shelling from the enemy, so we passed the night in quiet. Our men shelled Morris Island all night.

Tuesday—September 8th: At daylight this morning the Regiment was taken off the Bridge, leaving a few behind who left in about an hour. We then marched back to town, sleepy and tired. Wallace soon prepared breakfast. After breakfast I took the Company out and fired off the guns, came back, and went to sleep. Was awakened by heavy firing in the Harbor, which proved to be the enemy firing on Moultrie, Battery B and C on Sullivan's Island. It continued until about 12 or 1 o'clock, when the vessels withdrew. The damage inflicted on our side was slight, but some of our own shells were exploded which killed several, and a few houses were fired by incendiary shells. The Bridge on which we picketed last night was shelled furiously. The extent of injury on the vessels is not known, but supposed to have disabled a Monitor and the Ironsides is thought to have suffered. One thing certain—they kept very quiet in the evening and a considerable stir was apparent among them. I was on a board of survey to condemn some spoiled Beef, 2300 pounds. Bought seven chickens at $1.50 a piece. Sent off trunk to Charleston to be shipped home. No meat rations today for the men.

Wednesday—September 9th: This morning was ushered in with good news—our men having signally repulsed an attempt of the enemy to storm Fort Sumter in Barges; the fire of the cannon and small arms was terrific. [Private Andrews reported that the defenders utilized hand grenades or "hand-bombs" to drive off the attackers.] Several Barges were sunk and 102 privates and 19 officers were captured. The killed and wounded is thought to be great; our loss small. Who would have thought that Infantry would be called upon to defend the noble old Fort after it proved not to be able to stand the heaviest cannon which the enemy could bring against it. Everything is remarkably quiet in the harbor today. Scarcely a gun to remind us of the momentous issue at stake. Our usual drills and roll calls were resumed today. Made application for leave of absence for 48 hours to visit Mr. Glover who was so kind to me when wounded. One of the chickens I bought yesterday was found dead this morning. I ordered Wallace to bury it with the honor of war.

Thursday—September 10th: Unusual quiet and stillness reigns. The enemy's Gunboats lie off at a respectable distance. Wrote a letter to Lizzie in which I sent a shell ring to Nanette. We are ordered to proceed to Bonneau's and throw up earthworks. Orders read at Dress Parade for each Commander to inspect his Company before going out to Dress Parade and to form the line at the double quick. Reverend Mr. Hawkins preached for us tonight and got up some excitement. Several signified a desire to be prayed for, but none joined the church as the invitation was only extended to those who wished to attach themselves to the Baptist Church.

Friday—September 11th: Started on working expedition about sunrise this morning. Waited sometime before the Engineer came. When he did come we went to work; left at 4 o'clock and came back to camp. The soldiers are now buying and sending home salt, but transportation will not be furnished now as troops are being transported over the road. Reported that the Big Gun is bursted.

Saturday—September 12th: Tom Lyles, an old college mate, came to our camp this morning. He is in the Quarter Master's department of the 20th Regiment. Went in bathing this evening. The boys drew some pickled meat which they swear is "mule" and will not eat it. I eat some of it and think it Beef. All quiet in the Harbor.

Sunday—September 13th: Went to hear Reverend Girardeau preach, and while at the 23rd called on Captain Woods and heard that the furlough system would be commenced again. Met up with White, an old college friend. Returned to camp and sure enough, orders had come for furloughs, two to each Company. I immediately wrote out two for our Company and one for myself. Mr. Girardeau preached for our Regiment this evening. Timmerman, an old college mate, came to our Regiment this evening. We have orders to guard the Bridge tonight, and left camp about 7 o'clock P.M. Received letter from Lizzie and Maggie. While on the Bridge the wind blew furiously. "Darkness sat brooding upon the deep, the heavens thundered, the lightening glared, all things threatened instant death to the men."

Monday—September 14th: Left the Bridge about daylight and came back to camp. Fired off guns and eat breakfast as soon as it was prepared. Drew some ordnance stores such as 3 Canteens, 5 Haversacks, 4 Knapsacks, 9 Guns, 10 Waist Belts, 9 Cartridge Boxes, 9 Shoulder Straps, 10 Bayonet Scabbards and 9 Bayonets, 1280 cartridges caliber 69, and 160 cartridges caliber 58, and caps. Turned over 1 Gun and Bayonet, 2 Knapsacks, 1 Waist Belt and Bayonet Scabbard, and cartridges caliber 69 and cartridges caliber 58 and caps. A Baptist preacher from Barnwell preached for us tonight. One man was restored to the Church, several were prayed for.

Tuesday—September 15th: Officer of the day today. No news of interest to record.

This statement in Stevenson's diary was the understatement of the year. This was the day that Ripley arrested Evans for disobedience of orders and gave Benbow temporary command of the brigade. Evans was tried by a court-martial and was informed unofficially on November 5 that he had been acquitted. Beauregard did not wish to restore Evans to command, citing "the moral and general condition of that brigade, the ill feeling pervading the regiments toward General Evans, and the evident lack of discipline and instruction, and the general defective organization and equipment of its several regiments. . . ." An inspection of the brigade by Asst. Insp. General Alfred Roman generally confirmed Beauregard's observations. Beauregard dragged out the process,

partly because Evans' seniority among the brigadier generals meant that if Evans' Brigade was transferred to almost any other command, Evans' date of rank (October 21, 1861) would entitle him to take command of the larger unit to which the brigade had been assigned. Evans appealed to higher authorities. The War Department ordered him reinstated on March 11, 1864.[6]

Wednesday—September 16th: After Guard Mounting, Bob Banks and myself went down to Mount Pleasant to meet Pa, staid there sometime, but he did not come. We came back and soon after we arrived we heard Ben Corden had come with several boxes for our Company. John Robertson took the wagon and went after them. He brought a box for me and also a letter from Lizzie and a few lines from Pa explaining why he did not come. We have orders to work on the fortifications tomorrow. We also received orders that a general inspection would take place today by General Ripley, but he did not come but sent another order that the inspections would take place tomorrow at 9 o'clock. I did not go to bed until late. Sat up talking with Major Culp and Adjutant Connor.

Thursday—September 17th: Had a terrible time of it last night; it rained in perfect torrents, the wind blew furiously, our "fly" was but a poor protection, and the water stood in puddles at our feet. Lieutenant Cornwell and Alex and Billie Beaty could not stand it and got up and dressed. Captain B and myself stood it very philosophically, drew up our feet, covered our heads, said nothing, but our actions implied "let it rain." Just at first dawn of day, Captain B poked out his head and said "Billy, lets get up"; we did so and found our shoes and Hats full of water. Several of the Company sat up nearly all the time, eating from boxes they had just received; they passed the time merrily singing, laughing, and trying to cook, but the rain "outed" the fire as soon as built. Tom Rattine, however, was indefatigable in his efforts to make some coffee and finally succeeded about daylight. The Company on the whole fared better than we did, having a splendid and commodious "Bell" Tent and also a Wall tent and a "fly." The rain continued all day, consequently we did not work and had an inspection. Everything in my trunk got wet, several of the Company Books ruined. Our blankets are all wet, hence we will have an uncomfortable night's rest. I went in the "Bell" tent and slept several hours today. I do hope the Yankee fleet may be blown to pieces. Wallace is complaining today.

Friday—September 18th: Went on a working expedition today. The roads were full of water and we all got wet going there; the framework of the magazine was put up today, and the boys all work well. Soon after our return to camp the Furloughs came back all approved except Captain Steele's and mine.

Saturday—September 19th: All the Furloughed men are jubilant this morning; every feature expressive of joy and pleasure. I took up the Furloughs of mine which came back disapproved, but could carry them no further than Colonel Benbow's Headquarters. I came back and went to sleep, woke up and found Mr. Eli Dawkins had come. Lieutenant Logan and myself walked up town and looked at the Yankee Batteries on Morris Island firing at Battery Simkins on James Island; on our return to camp we met Harper, the wagon driver, who had Lieutenant Logan's trunk and said that Logan's furlough had come back approved. With a shout which alarmed the women and children in the neighborhood, he bounced off the wagon and off he went, the last I heard or saw was him still hollowing. I felt sad and gloomy and greatly disappointed, for I had sent up an application too and mine had not come. Ordered to guard the Bridge connecting with Sullivan's Island.

Sunday—September 20th: The wind blew bitter cold last night. I like to have froze, and tried very hard to sleep but could not. Marched off at about daylight at a double quick in order to warm up, got to camp, eat breakfast, and lay down and went to sleep and slept to about 11 o'clock. When I awoke got dinner. Knocked about until 3 o'clock P.M. and went to hear Mr. Gamious preach in Captain Mills' Company. After supper the "Soldiers Christian Association" met for the first time though organized in Mississippi. The Furloughs I had sent up for Corporal Casey and Private Corder came back today and they went off as soon as they came. Mine did not come back.

Monday—September 21st: The large "Bell" tent, to which I alluded in some previous day, was taken away from us this evening; it belonged to General Evans and he sent for it. We will fare poorly now when it rains and the weather is becoming a little cool and frosty and plainly announces that summer is at an end. Major Culp and Adjutant Connor and myself walked up to the Wharf this evening. Our batteries were throwing shells pretty rapidly on Morris Island. We could see the Yankees fortifications and at every flash of our guns they hid, but as soon as the shells bursted they were up again. On our return Connor and myself stopped at Colonel Benbow's Headquarters to see if there was not some mistake in the orders for us to go to work tomorrow but found it was all right. We stopped and had a short conversation with Tom Lyles and Mr. Wannamaker of the 20th. When we got back to camp the Companies were forming for Dress Parade. Received a letter from Miss Sallie C. Gibson of Alabama. Mr. Hawkins preached for us this evening and Johnston of our Company joined the Church.

Tuesday—September 22nd: The Regiment went to the fortifications to work. Captain Edwards and myself went over to the City. I went to meet Pa, but he did not come, or rather I did not see him. We returned on the 6 o'clock boat. I met Tom Gibson who had been over with the Company during my absence. The news from the West is very encouraging and hopeful. We should be thankful for such a victory. [This probably refers to news of the Confederate victory at Chickamauga.] While in the City, I had my photograph taken.

Wednesday—September 23rd: Several of us walked up to the landing to buy a paper; Beauregard has ordered a salute to be fired in honor of the great victory in the West. Fort Sumter joined in the chorus, to our great surprise. I wrote to Sallie C. Gibson this afternoon. My application for a leave of absence came back disapproved. Orders to go on Bridge tonight; left camp about dark and when we got to the Bridge, the Colonel put only two Companies on the Bridge at a time, each to stand two hours, but our Company and Captain Steele's staid much longer than two hours on account of some misunderstanding.

Thursday—September 24th: On our return to camp from the Bridge this morning I called at the negro camp and saw Glasgow, Anderson, and Frank, who have been sent down to work on the fortifications. Officer of the day today. Wrote a letter to Lizzie, saw Major Rion [of the Twenty-second Regiment] at Colonel's Quarters. The company has been busy for the last day or two in erecting "shanties" made of pine poles and dirt which will protect them from the inclemencies of the weather. We have preaching nearly every night now conducted by different ones. Reverend Mr. Hawkins officiates the most; his labors have been blest with the conversion or rather the joining of the Church of several; they are to be baptized today at 9 o'clock A.M. Great interest is being manifest. The whole Regiment generally attends.

Friday—September 25th: Several of our Regiment were immersed this morning, having made an open profession of religion; among the number was L. Johnston of our Company. Orders to go to work tomorrow.

Saturday—September 26th: Left camp this morning about sun-rise. A detachment of four Companies were sent to the lines to fell timber. Our Company was among the detachment; the balance of the Regiment went to the Battery at Bonneau's. Our detachment was under the command of Captain Steele, and marched about 5 miles to a church where we found the Breastwork. The detachment was divided into three reliefs of 24 men each. The woods soon echoed with the sound of the axes. We left about 3 o'clock P.M. and arrived at camp a little before sundown.

Sunday—September 27th: Reverend John Douglass preached for us this morning. While he was preaching Mr. Banks came up, also several of the "old reserves" among whom were E. Gladden, Lovie Ingram, and Mr. Peden. We felt quite at home among our old friends and acquaintances. In the evening, Mr. Banks preached for us a short sermon; the old reserves left during he sermon on account of the boat leaving before the services would be over. Mr. Gladden did not, however, get over for when they got to the wharf the regular Steamer had left and their only chance was to go over in a small row boat. He and several others would not risk it; he came back and staid with Billie Beaty all night, the balance of us having to go with the Regiment on picket at the Bridge. Frank, one of Pa's boys sent down to work, came into our camp today and says all the rest are well.

Monday—September 28th: O. Nickels, J. Brown, and A. Morrison came into our camp this morning and are looking well. Our stay on the Bridge was much more pleasant last night than some of the previous nights. A Court Martial is ordered to convene tomorrow for trial of such cases which may be brought before it. A. G. Black unfortunately sat down at his post while acting as Sentinel and the Corporal supposed him sleeping and reported him; he was sick. Hugh Bigham, a member of Company A died yesterday morning at Regimental Hospital in Mount Pleasant. Reverend Mr. Banks left our camp this morning. I sent a letter home by him. There will be an election tomorrow for Tax Collector for Chester District.

Tuesday—September 29th: Pursuant to notice an election was held in the Regiment for Tax Collector for Chester District. Captain Edwards and myself managed the election; 57 votes were polled, and McFadden received 33 of them. We went up to the Hospital in order to receive some votes there who were unable to come to camp. I remained until nearly Sundown. We are ordered to move and camp on the Beach near the Battery at Bonneau and to fill requisitions for labor made by Lieutenant White, Engineer in charge; the orders were to move today, but Colonel Benbow agreed to postpone it until tomorrow provided we would work and move the same day, to which the Colonel agreed. A. G. Black was tried today and found guilty and sentenced to 3 days confinement in the Guard house. Received a letter from Cousin Lizzie. I understand that General Evans' trial will commence tomorrow. I do not know the charges against him.

Wednesday—September 30th: At 7 o'clock A.M., the Regiment was formed and moved off, having left behind a sufficient guard to attend to our Baggage; we went down the Georgetown road about 5 miles near the church at the lines, where we halted and awaited until the wagons came up with the axes. Soon after we commenced chopping. I unfortunately got cut by an ax flying off and striking my leg near the ankle. Captain B loaned me his horse and I rode with the Colonel to the camp which had been selected the day previous. When I got to camp, my leg was hurting me a good deal. I lay about until night, the place becoming sorer and sorer. Received a letter from Lizzie.

Thursday—October 1st: My leg pretty sore this morning. Cannot get about much. A detail of 130 men sent to work on fortifications. A pretty heavy rain fell last night and we were ill prepared for it. No news; the enemy open again on Sumter from land Batteries on Morris Island. Wrote to Lizzie.

Friday—October 2nd: Have concluded to apply for a short leave of absence, but did not get to send it up today. The wound on my leg very painful.

Saturday—October 3rd: Sent up my application for leave of absence for 15 days. Captain B went to town this morning. I am getting worn out doing nothing, though I consume my time in sleeping and reading Shakespeare.

Sunday—October 4th: A partial supply of hymn books, Testaments, and religious tracts was furnished our Regiment this morning by Catholic and Mount Pleasant congregations through Mr. Banks; the Testaments are beautiful English books and the hymn books just as such as we need. Alex Banks preached for us this evening. D. Brown, formerly of our Company, came over to see us. Corporal [Casey] and D. Corder came in today and brought several boxes for the Company and one for E. Cornwell; they both are looking well and deserve praise for the promptness with which they reported to their Company. Wallace is improving but slow. Orders for an inspection tomorrow by one of Beauregard's aids, Captain Fielding.

Monday—October 5th: The inspection came off at 10 o'clock A.M.; it was searching and rigid; the inspecting officer is an Englishman who has not been over here long. Drew one month's pay (September) from Captain Means. A lot of pants were issued to the Regiment today and two blankets to our Company which was a source of great contention who should have, there being some ten or twelve who said they had none. The camp at night echoed with the songs of praise to God, all having new books.

Tuesday—October 6th: Inexpressible delight! My furlough has come back approved. It however came too late for me to start this evening; what shall I do 'till morning! Oh! How impatient I am to get away and once more see my old home. I have made all arrangements to start early in the morning and hope nothing will interfere with me. I don't think I will sleep tonight.

Wednesday—October 7th: After a good night's rest which was not anticipated, I woke about daylight, got up, eat breakfast, bid all "good bye," and left. I wanted to get to Mount Pleasant in time to take the 8 o'clock boat, but we had a heavy load on the wagon and did not arrive in time. I spent the time very pleasantly in looking through my "Spy glass" at the Yankees on Morris Island. They were out in large force and seemed to be busy working on Battery Wagner and did not seem to pay much attention to our guns which threw an occasional shell among them. About 10 o'clock the boat left and soon landed in the City. I got all my Boxes and trunk off, being assisted by A. [McWatlers] who came over with me. I sent my trunk and boxes to the depot under charge of Wallace who will remain with them until I go down. I stopped and went to see the reserves. Found A. Nickles sick, being afflicted with neuralgia. All the rest were well; took dinner with O. Brown's mess, being kindly invited by Lovie Ingram to take dinner with him, but had previously promised Brown. After dinner the Company was paraded and marched up the street where each one was furnished with a gun. O. Brown went with me to buy a hat, but the price was so high I did not buy. We went down to Broad Street where I got a Provost Marshal pass out of the City and we came back where the reserves were stationed and supper was hurried up on my account. I eat with Captain Gill; after supper I left for the Depot. Arrived there in due time and found Wallace and all my things. E. Gladden and J. Brown walked with me down to the Depot and assisted me in getting my boxes aboard. I got a good seat by myself, but I wanted to sleep so I lay down on the floor and slept soundly.

Thursday—October 8th: Woke up this morning and found the cars had stopped and the engine gone, having been injured; we will consequently miss connections at Columbia which is about 28 miles from where we are. The place where we broke down is Fort Motte which was the scene of blood and death between Americans and British, and some vestiges still remain. A little after sun up an engine came down for us and started with us, but did not get more than two hundred yards before we met the down passenger train which caused us to back about 3 miles to a turnout. In this backing, the old engine broke, so we were worse off than before because we were not as near Columbia. The passengers seemed to take it patiently. I succeeded in getting something to eat from an old negro woman on the cars. About 1 o'clock P.M. another engine came and was welcomed with shouts. Arrived at Columbia about 4 ½ P.M. Went to the Charlotte Depot and found all my baggage in. When the train from the junction came up, I heard that Captain Beacham was on it severely wounded. Assisted in getting him on the train, but could find no seat for myself. Stood up nearly all the way to Winnsboro, where I got supper. Arrived at Blackstock about 1 o'clock in the night where fortunately for me Lumpkin gave me his horse and I rode home leaving my baggage and Wallace behind with the intention of sending for him tomorrow. Got home about day-light, woke up Pa and all the family; did not go to sleep.

The Seventeenth Regiment was apparently detached from the brigade during October and November of 1863 and sent to camp on James Island near Secessionville.[7] Captain Edwards of the Seventeenth Regiment noted the following event, which occurred while Captain Stevenson was on furlough:

On October 15th, while in camp at Secessionville, on James' Island, President Davis paid us a visit. He and General Beauregard reviewed our brigade, together with all the troops on the Island. In Company A one of the men, W. H. Kee, was barefooted. President Davis asked him where his shoes were. His reply was, "By God, I ain't got none."

Corporal Robertson remembered his assignment in Charleston:

At Charleston, myself and a good many others of the original Hatch's Battalion, under Lieutenant T. L. Swinton were detached from the Regiment and put in the boat-service on Charleston Harbor, moving troops to and from Fort Sumter and other points. The Fort Sumter work could only be done at night and the stars were our only guides. A certain one that hung over Fort Sumter I learned to know very well, and I picked up some additional astronomy in a crude state. This service was hazardous in every respect, liable to capture by enemy guard boats continually prowling around Fort Sumter, and shells falling around in close proximity, which from the noise made upon exploding I judge must have been about the size of nail kegs. The performance of this duty on a broad expanse of water in an open boat full of frightened soldiers was often very trying. One night, after landing my load of troops at Fort Sumter and returning to my quarters at Mount Pleasant, I was sailing right into the embrace of a Yankee guard boat. Fortunately the prowler, before I reached him, was captured by a Confederate guard boat. When I hailed the Confederate, he informed me that he had caught a Yank, and I at once offered up a silent prayer for my deliverance. Our transport crews carried no arms.

The barge that I was in charge of and the crew of five young fellows were under the control of the Quartermaster at Mount Pleasant. Only when troops from Sullivan's Island had to be moved did we have to do the night service to Fort Sumter. Our principal service was transporting daily soldier mail carriers to and from Charleston. This generally was not a very hard duty to perform. On one of my trips, I picked up a corked bottle which contained a document addressed: "To our friends off the bar." This paper was written by an intelligent person, giving a full description of fortifications and number of troops in and around Charleston. The South had traitors dwelling even in the Old City by the Sea.

When Captain Stevenson returned from his furlough, he continued his diary:

Thursday—October 22nd: After 15 days absence I this day left home to join my Regiment which has moved during my absence to James Island. The time I spent at home was very pleasant and I regretted very much to leave. I have under my charge several Boxes and two boys. On the way out to Blackstock, I stopped at Uncle William's who gave me a Bottle of Splendid Peach Brandy, also at Robert Caldwell's. At Blackstock saw Miss Fannie Douglass and had a pleasant conversation with her. The young lady who treated Zebulon Mobly so kindly when wounded at Dramsville was aboard. Zeb got on the cars and went as far as Columbia with her. Saw some of my old friends at Ridgeway. Arrived at Columbia about 5 o'clock P.M.; did not succeed in getting my boxes aboard and remained over at the junction with several soldiers, but finally concluded to walk up town and procure quarters. Went around and called on Dr. Edmonds, where I found Miss Janie McGregor and two Misses Smith. Spent a very pleasant time indeed. Dr. Edmonds and his wife insisted on me staying the night which I did.

Friday—October 23rd: About 5 o'clock this morning I was awoke and found the Doctor had horse and buggy to carry me to the Depot. Arrived there in due time, got a seat, got my Boxes on at the junction without any difficulty. Amused myself by reading the proceedings of Court Martial in the case of Colonel McMaster, which had been given me by the Doctor. Arrived in Branchville about 11 o'clock A.M. where while waiting for the Augusta train, I bought a cup of pure coffee, some chickens, eggs, and bread for $1.50; also bought some smoking tobacco. Left Branchville about 2 o'clock and run very slow; about 3 or 400 yards north of Summerville one of the brakes on the Engine broke but did not detain us very long. I saw Lovie Ingram and threw out his bundle and shoes for Mr. Brown, also letters; at the Depot the train stopped and Lovie and several of my acquaintances came up and shook hands, but had no time to talk. Arrived at Charleston about 8 o'clock P.M., and got all my boxes out safe except Mylie's which I had forgot to bring out of the cars. As soon as I got my boxes placed in a safe place, I left them in charge of my boys and walked up to the Charleston Hotel, where I got lodging for the night by paying two dollars.

Saturday—October 24th: Woke this morning much refreshed, got up, dressed and went down and bought a morning paper. Just then the bells rang for breakfast. I bought a ticket for $3.00, went into the dining room, got a poor breakfast, and came out and found Alex Ellerbe, an old college friend who I had not seen since I left college. We talked over old matters, and made inquiries of other of our friends. I gave him a copy of the Colonel McMaster trial report, walked down to the Provost Marshal's office, got passport, then walked down to the Depot where I left my boxes. I found John Robertson with a wagon and started off to Camp, but had to wait for some men who was going with us. A slow rain commenced falling. While waiting, Colonel McMaster and Captain Means came up and spoke to me; soon we started and the rain fell heavy and the wind blew hard. We stopped in some houses until it moderated, again started and arrived at Camp about 2 o'clock, where I found all the Company well. I was glad to see them so lively and cheerful. All the different packages I had charge of were delivered. I was not here long before I found out the duty was very onerous, about half the Regiment detailed each day for guard and picket.

Sunday—October 25th: Preaching this morning by our Chaplain, Reverend Carothers, a discourse on divine providence. He also preached in the evening, but I did not hear him. The Yankee tents are plainly visible to the naked eye and with a glass one can see what they are doing. Batteries Wagner and Gregg too can be seen better here than at Mount Pleasant, also the battered side of Fort Sumter. The regular firing from our Batteries keeps up and the enemy acknowledges it, killing and wounding four men each day on the average. The Yankee Batteries seem to be about complete, and we all expect them soon to begin operations.

Monday—October 26th: Everything was unusually quiet this morning, the wind blew bitter cold, and the sky was overshadowed with clouds. About 10 o'clock (so says the paper) Batteries Gregg and Wagner broke the deep silence by opening on Sumter and Fort Johnston. We did not observe it until about 1 o'clock. The firing was very accurate, and great volumes of dust was raised each time a ball struck Sumter. Two Monitors moved up and joined the chorus with their deep mounted guns. About dark the firing ceased on both sides. During the firing the Island was covered with Yankees.

At this point there is another gap in Captain Stevenson's diary. Captain Edwards noted that the Seventeenth was taking its turn in supplying troops to garrison Fort Sumter:

On November 9th, while we were still on James' Island, Companies B, E, K, and G were sent to Fort Sumter, where they remained until the night of the 22d. The enemy frequently shelled our quarters from Lighthouse Inlet, but did us but little harm barring the annoyance.

Captain Stevenson's diary resumed in mid-November:

Sunday—November 15th: A bright and beautiful morning. For the last week or two I have lost sight of my Diary, and I am now unable from memory to fill up the interval. The last day I recorded was the commencement of the bombardment of Fort Sumter from Gregg and Wagner. It has continued from that time up to the present, both night and day time. Sometimes it would slacken in its fury, but soon they would open with new energy and ferocity; the walls of Sumter have yielded to such an incessant firing. The Morris Island and Sea face is a chaotic mass of ruins, yet the papers tell us that every shot fired now only tends to strengthen it. There would seem to be some truth in the assertion, for Sumter, though robbed of her beauty, laid low in the dust, yet she still stands—a terror to the enemy and the pride of our State. Several men have been killed and wounded by mortar shells, but more by the falling in of the Barracks. The enemy's Ironclads have taken a conspicuous part in the fight. Four Companies of our Regiment were sent to Sumter last week. I do not know whether they have been relieved or not as I came over to Hospital. Pa came down to see me. Arrived in Camp on last

Saturday a week ago. He left Sunday evening and went to try and get J. L. Brown off home who was very sick from a Typhoid fever, but he had gone before Pa got there. Pa stopped as he came back, went out to camp and found that I had come to Hospital, so he came back and called in that evening. Billie Beaty and John Robertson were at the same hospital I went to, and they both got Furloughs of thirty days on last Thursday and went home in company with Pa. I was left then to myself. I felt pretty lonely for the first day or two but have made one or two acquaintances which breaks the monotony somewhat. Dr. Huges is the Surgeon in charge, and he is a kind-hearted gentleman. I am very pleased with him. The Ladies pay regular visits each day with refreshments for the sick. A young man from Virginia died in the room in which I am this morning about sun-rise. Mr. Varn, the mail carrier for the regiment, brought me a letter from May, and also one from Captain Beaty in which was enclosed $80.00, the amount due me for October. There was also information in it to the effect that one man in Company K has been killed in Fort Sumter. In the room adjoining mine is a very sick soldier who is delirious from fever; he cuts up some fancy tricks now and then. The nurse has had what they call a Straight Jacket put on him, which prevents him using his arms or stooping down. I amuse myself in reading tracts which the Ladies send to Hospital, also Captain Cook's voyages to the Pacific Ocean. Towards evening the weather becomes quite chilly and a fire would have been agreeable but none was built in our room.

Monday—November 16th: I did not rest well last night, but had strange dreams all night. Before I got up the newsboy came and I bought papers and read the news in bed. After I had finished reading the paper, I got up, washed, and felt much better. I am now ready for my breakfast. The Board of Examiners meets today to grant Furloughs. The firing this morning is somewhat more spirited and rapid. I ate pretty heartily of Fish and soft-boiled eggs and nice hominy—afraid I overdone the thing. Our Batteries on Sullivan's Island are firing very heavily on three Monitors, two of which are replying and the other firing at the Sea Face of Sumter. Got permission from Dr. Huges to walk up King Street a short distance to make some purchases. Met Captain Steele, who said that the Yankees had shelled Secessionville furiously that morning. Bought me a Pipe and smoking Tobacco, also two books "The Actress in High Life" and "Robert and Harold or The Marooned." On my return I felt very much fatigued and worried. As soon as I got back to Hospital, I went to my room and lay down and commenced reading "Robert and Harold . . ." which did not make a favorable impression at first.

Tuesday—November 17th: There is now no one in my room but myself, except at night. The Yankees are shelling the City this morning and it is reported here that they have fired one or two houses. I do not apprehend any danger here for this house is in the most N.E. portion of the City; strange to say, we cannot hear the explosion of the Shells. The mail carrier brought me in two letters this morning, one from Cousin Lizzie, the other from Lizzie. The enemy made an ineffectual attempt to shell the City but did no damage. Finished reading "Robert and Harold . . ."—not well pleased with it.

Wednesday—November 18th: Felt some better this morning though weak yet and dull. Dr. Huges told me this morning he would try to get me off tomorrow. In consequence, I got permission to go up town to see someone from the Regiment to send word to Captain B to send Jake over in the morning. I met up with an opportunity. The young man who went up town with me loaned me a book to read—"Camille" by Dumas. Did not rest well in the night.

Thursday—November 19th: Finished reading "Camille." I think that I am improving very slowly indeed. This is Thanksgiving Day in the City. Dr. Huges will recommend me before the Board of Furlough. Captain B and Major Culp called on me this morning, but did not stay long. Jake came with his things. The Yankees are shelling the City again today, and there is said to be great confusion in the City. One lady with a Baby and a little girl have come up here to get out of range. I went before the Medical Board, but on examination they recommended me to remain under treatment, and said that if I went home I would not get proper attention! What fools! Though I could not get off I concluded to send Jake. He got Strother Ford to arrange his papers and started last night. Strother came round to see me this evening and promised to come round tomorrow in a Spring Wagon and take me out in the City. I saw Dr. Huges this evening; he does not like it at all about the Board not giving me a Furlough but says it cannot be helped. Wrote to Lizzie and Jake. Received letter from Lizzie today. No injury from shells in the City. One struck the guard house, but fortunately no one was in the room at that time.

Friday—November 20th: I can see but little change in my health. I improve very slowly indeed. The Doctor has renewed my Bottle of Medicine—Ferric Chloride. Strother very kindly came round in a new little spring wagon and invited me to ride around town. As I thought it might be beneficial. I assented and had a pleasant ride and just got back in time for Lunch. He also brought me a letter from Maggie. Last night the Yankees came near Fort Sumter and commenced firing small arms. We replied from the Fort. When they withdrew there was no regular assault. A few harmless shells were thrown into the City this morning. Also a few shells this evening. I watched the Yankees as they were firing into the City, and could distinguish by flash of gun which one threw the shells.

Saturday—November 21st: Did not rest well last night; couldn't sleep; got up several times and walked about. My wound hurt me a little. Spent most of the day in reading the Memoirs of Josephine. The Doctor told me today to stir about and walk up town every day; he thought it would be beneficial to me. The Yankees threw shells into the City off and on all day. Said to have killed one negro woman. Bought some fish this evening. The shells flew so close to the house of the Sisters of Charity that they became frightened and Dr. Huges gave them permission to occupy a room in the Hospital.

Sunday—November 22nd: Rested tolerably well last night. Feel some better this morning. Early this morning a man wounded at Fort Sumter last night came in; his wound is slight. No lunch today. The Yankees still persist in effort to reduce Sumter, but all ineffectual.

Monday—November 23rd: The Board met this morning, but some disagreement caused them to adjourn until tomorrow. Dr. Huges intends sending me before them again. Cloudy and rainy.

Tuesday—November 24th: I went before the Board this morning and they granted me 30 days leave of absence and I walked up town and got dinner. Left for home, but had to leave trunk behind.

Stevenson made no diary entries during his furlough, but two friends from the Lancaster District, who were members of Company I of the Seventeenth Regiment, described the December situation in Charleston in letters to their wives from Sullivan's Island.[8]

Private Faulkner wrote in mid-December:

We are camped about two hundred yards above Fort Moultrie in a perfect sand bed. We have all got sand in our gizzards for our meat and drink is full of it. But for all this, I prefer staying here to marching in Mississippi . . . Lizzie, I wrote to you something in my last about salt. I understand it can be bought in Mount Pleasant for ten dollars a bushel. If Nick will come down be sure and send me word how much you want . . . You will see old Abe's Proclamation.[9] I am afraid it will do our cause harm. For my part, I look upon it as insulting to the South, but I am sorry to say there is a good many that will grab at anything even if it should only have the name of peace. I am anxious for peace, but I do not want such a one that will enslave my beloved wife and children for generations to come. It is very cold here. I was on guard last night. I suffered as much with cold as I have done for many a day. Mounting guns and standing guard is about all we do. We stand guard every other night. How the men stand it barefooted with cotton clothes is a mystery to me, for I have good clothing and can scarcely stand it.

We have no preaching. Our chaplain has played out and went home long ago. I wish Congress would conscript every preacher up to 50 and make them shoulder a musket and go into ranks. If they won't preach they ought to be made to fight. William Robinson after all his scoldings did not stay with our regiment but one night and preached one short sermon (what did I tell you when I was home).

Lizzy, I see by Congress act that all Black Smiths and Mechanicks will have to go in the Army, and all those that have furnished substitutes. This will increase our forces considerably. I suppose it is all right for we may as well all go in and fight it out and one man has as good a right to fight as another.

Private William C. Nesbit:

The Yanks have about give up Fort Sumter as a bad job, although it appears like it is in ruins. Yet the huge pile of brick and sand is visible to the naked eye, and yet every evening you can see the dense smoke and hear the sound of her signal from her parapet. The attention of the enemy is now drawn to the shelling of the City, but our batteries can silence them in one hour's time when they get at that. We have one 300 lb. Rifle gun on the Island, one on James Island at Fort Johnson. They wake things up when they open fire on the Yanks. I was detailed the other day to help move a gun from Battery Beauregard to Battery Marshall. It weighed 11,000 lbs. We hauled it 1½ miles by hand. It was hard work.

Upon his return, Captain Stevenson resumed his diary:

Friday—December 25th: After 30 days absence, I this morning left home. The time I spent at home was pleasant "in extreme" and I was loath to leave. I arrived at Blackstock Station just in time—15 minutes later and I would have been left. At Blackstock I found a great many negros who were spending Christmas on the train; they seemed to be the only ones enjoying themselves. Very few persons aboard the cars. At Winnsboro a great number of negros were at the railroad and the town seemed filled with them. At Columbia I hired a cart and drove to the Charleston Depot and got my boxes aboard without any difficulty. At Kingsville we heard that the Yankees had thrown 300 shells into the City [Charleston] and burned several houses. Arrived at Charleston about daylight.

Saturday—December 26th: Very cold. Had no fire to go to and "froze it out" until good daylight. Then Wallace and myself gathered up our baggage and walked up to Wayside House. I went in and registered and sat down to breakfast of cold beef and hominy—did not eat much. After breakfast we went down to Pavillon Hotel and then to Reid Street to see Strother Ford. Did not find him and went to get my boxes. While we were there Strother Ford came up and offered a wagon to haul them to the wharf; he said he would come to Wayside House in the wagon and take me down. Wallace and I are now waiting for him. Everything is well so far. Arrived at Camp on Sullivan's Island later in the day.

Monday—December 28th: Alarm! All are out at the breastworks. I am acting as Adjutant.

On this date, Private Faulkner wrote to his wife:

"I believe General Evans is Relieved from his command. It may be that the brigade will be broken up. I do not rejoice at this for we may not be bettered."

Captain Stevenson's diary recorded conditions at the start of the new year:

Friday—January 1st 1864: The New Year was ushered in by a cold windy day and the winds blew very hard. Sergeant Black started home today on a 20-day furlough. I sent Wallace with him.

Saturday—January 2nd: Last night was a terrible night. Some of the guard had to be sent to quarters to keep them from freezing.

Friday—January 8th: Went to Long Island in company with Major Culp, Captain Avery, and Lieutenant McConnell. We had some difficulty in crossing the Strait between Sullivan's and Long Island. The current was so swift we came near being carried by force out to sea. The waves were rolling mountain high, and the excitement at one time was intense but Captain Avery and Lieutenant McConnell worked the oars lustily. We finally landed safe on Long Island and then could laugh at each others fears and expressions. After we had secured our boat on the beach, we started up the beach in search of shells; we gathered a great many and of different variety. We saw the wrecks of several blockade runners, one a very large vessel with an amount of iron on her. After we tired of gathering shells we went out from the beach to the woodland part of the Island; we found it to be an almost impenetrable wilderness of Palmetto and dwarf live oak. The scenery was in some parts fearfully wild and truly grand; it would be a delightful place to stroll with young ladies who could appreciate the scenery. We returned late in the evening well pleased with the trip, but awfully hungry.

Colonel Lawrence Keitt of the Twentieth Regiment, which was also stationed on Sullivan's Island, noted the unrest in Evans' Brigade in a letter to his wife on January 17:

Last night, it seems that there was a disposition to mutiny among some of Evans' Brigade. When I came over this morning I heard of it, and at once instituted inquiries. I find that it has been exaggerated very much, but still it was necessary to do something. I have put a few under arrest—and have crushed it out. The pretext was a lack of rations. The supply here is very scarce.

Colonel Keitt had been assured of promotion to the rank of brigadier general as soon as a brigade command became available. He wanted this promotion

and was offered command of Evans' Brigade. However, he expressed his preferences in a letter to his wife on February 2:

"I will not have Evans' Brigade—and have so told the President. It is utterly spoiled, and it would take untill after the war to get it into any thing like good condition. The regiments I indicated to the President, I want."

February events are recorded in Captain Stevenson's diary:

Tuesday—February 2nd: The Steamer "Porsto" ran aground last night about 3 o'clock in front of Battery Rutledge. She was loaded with government Stores—blockade goods. The soldiers got a great many shoes, blankets, etc. off her, but are ordered to return them to Colonel Keitt's Headquarters. The Yankees are firing very rapidly at her this morning and have struck her several times. Four Monitors have moved up and opened on her.

Friday—February 12th: Just as the Regiment was formed for Dress Parade this evening, an order came for our Regiment to be prepared to march at 5 o'clock P.M. with four days of cooked rations. Soon after, another order came to leave camp immediately and march to Mount Pleasant wharf and take the Steamer for James Island. Major Culp sent me down to Colonel Keitt's Headquarters to see whether we would move all our baggage and go in light marching order, but I could get no information from his acting Adjutant General. He was under the impression that it would be a permanent move. He telegraphed General Ripley to find out, and I did not wait for an answer. I went back to camp, got supper, and went again to Colonel Keitt's Headquarters where a dispatch came for us to go "in light marching order" at dusk, so we left immediately. I rode Conner's horse. When we got to the Bridge our guard there had not been relieved. I went to see Colonel Butler who said that he would relieve it for us. In going across the Bridge I forgot the countersign, but prevailed upon the Sentinel to permit me to pass and caught up with the Regiment at Mount Pleasant. When I got there I found that the Bottle of Molasses which I had in my basket had nearly all spilt out in my clothes, the stopper having come out. Jake soon washed it off tolerably well. The Regiment was soon on board and the vessel landed us at the pontoon Bridge across Napper's Cut. After landing we marched a short distance and bivouacked for the night at James Island.

Saturday—February 13th: Early this morning we reported to General Taliaferro who said there was no further use for the enemy had gone back. We took the boat about dark and arrived at our camp about 10 o'clock. Late in the evening we were ordered to proceed to Green Pond, South Carolina. We took the boat and landed at the Savannah Railroad landing and lay over until morning.

Sunday—February 14th: We left early this morning in the cars for Green Pond, where we arrived in the evening.[10] We camped a short distance from the railroad.

Here there is a gap of two months in Captain Stevenson's diary. Captain Edwards of the Seventeenth Regiment chronicled some of the activities of the regiment:

On February 16th, the regiment was formed into line and Colonel McMaster made the men a speech and proposed that we enlist for the war, and asked all who were willing to step two paces to the front. The whole regiment moved forward like the work of a machine. We knew that there was no discharge in this war. Four men from each company were given furlough to go home for twenty days. The promise was made that this arrangement should go on until all the men should be allowed to go home. "But the best laid schemes of mice and men gang aft aglee, and leave us naught but grief and pain for promised joys." When the spring campaign of 1864 opened there was no time for any more furloughs, except to cross death's cold stream, as thousands of brave men did during that year of bloody conflict.

At this point in the war, Florida was supplying the Confederacy with 25,000 head of cattle annually, plus sugar, syrup, hogs, leather, fish, fruit, etc.[11] In early February 1864, Federal troops under General Truman Seymour landed at Jacksonville and marched westward in an attempt to cut off the Confederacy from these supplies.[12] On February 20, the Federal advance was stopped at Olustee by a Confederate force consisting of eight Georgia and two Florida regiments plus artillery.[13] The Eighteenth Regiment, S.C.V. was sent from Charleston on that same day to reinforce the Confederate forces in Florida. The Eighteenth arrived too late for the Battle of Olustee but was involved on March 1 in a minor engagement near Jacksonville.[14] On February 22, the Holcombe Legion left Charleston for Savannah, planning to go on to Florida. However, Federal troops attacked Whitemarsh Island near Savannah, and the legion was detained to assist in the city's defense. The legion never reached Florida.

Chaplain James of the Eighteenth Regiment reported on the engagements in Florida:

In February, 1864, the 18th Regiment was detached from the brigade and sent to Florida to check the advance of the enemy across that State from Jacksonville going toward Tallahassee. Just before we arrived they were met by General Finegan's Brigade at Olustee or Ocean Pond, near Lake City, and were repulsed with heavy loss, especially the colored troops, who had

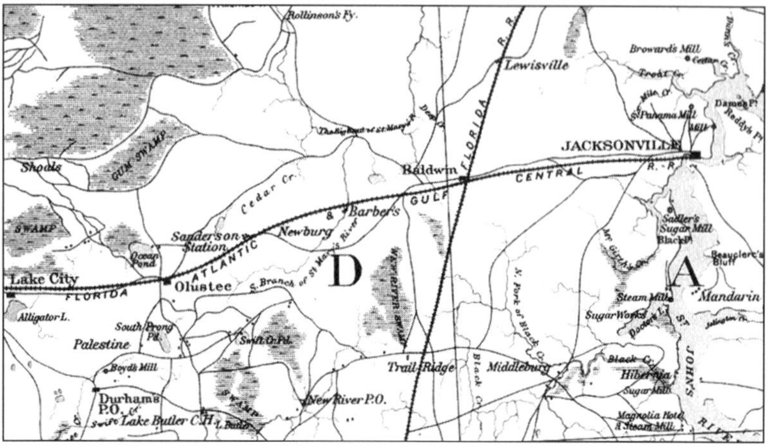

Map of northern Florida
(*Atlas to Accompany the Official Records*, Plate CXLV)[15]

been placed in front and forced up within range of our sharpshooters. The enemy, all that survived, retreated, and our regiment pursued them until they got under cover of their gunboats at Jacksonville. We had an engagement with them at Cedar Creek just before they arrived at Jacksonville. There were no casualties on our side. In April, 1864, we were ordered back to Charleston.

Evans was still awaiting reinstatement to the command of his brigade. Some time in late February, he challenged Colonel McMaster to a duel. McMaster, after considering the matter for a week, declined to fight, citing religious reasons.[16] On March 11, the C.S.A. War Department ordered Beauregard to restore Evans to command.

Private Faulkner's letters to his wife during this time mention McMaster's attempts to have his regiment transferred out of the brigade:

[March 29] Evans has been ordered to take command of his Brigade. Colonel McMaster is gone to Richmond to try and get detached here or go and join Jenkins Brigade (this is what I have learned) but one thing is sure, Colonel McMaster does not want to go under Evans. I hope he may succeed for if we have to go back into the old Brigade I am afraid we will go up [to Virginia]. I suppose we will know shortly our doom.

[April 3] Colonel McMaster is due here today, he having gone to Richmond to get out from under Old Evans. I wish we could get staying here. I know it is a sickly place, but I dread marching.

[April 6] Colonel McMaster has got back and tried very hard to get our regiment detached here but could not. They would not let him out from

General Evans, and it is thought the Colonel will resign. I hope he will, for I do not want him to command and it remain under Evans.

Private A. H. Lister of Company B of the Twenty-second Regiment described the rotation of soldiers into the garrison of Fort Sumter in his letters home. On March 8 he expressed his reluctance to serve there:

"Our men that was in sumter When I came back has come out and another de tail was made last nite to go thar an they say ther is another detail of one hundred and fifty men to be made next saerday nite and if ther is I shal Be one of them Ime afraid I don't want to go thar by no means the boys thats come from thar ses its a mity Bad place to stay they dont get half nuf to eat nor cant get a drank of water to without a pass from ther officer and ther is nothing to cook in all thay get is cookt and brote to them if we had eny thing to cook in I cold take provisions with me if I should haf to go the yankeys tuck nine of our sumter men prisners last sundy nite so I will quit that part of the subject."

His letter of March 29 confirmed the unpleasant conditions there:

"We come out of sumter last thirsdy nite about 2 o'clock all safe and soun I don't like the fort at all although our fiar about something to eat was beter than we draw hear we drawd light Wheat bread and bacon as mutch as I wanted but ide ruther stay hear on Bred than thar on bred and meat ther is so much hard dewty to do thar and the dewty is hard here but not like it is in sumter we have 2 nites to sleep hear and up one and thar it is up one and half the other and then up one and half the other we had power full cold wether while we was in Sumter I was cold nite and day all the time but if we stay hear we will haft to go back again in about a month"

Captain Edwards related the activities of the Seventeenth Regiment near Charleston:

We remained in the vicinity of Green Pond until April the 16th. Our occupation was felling timber, building corduroy roads and breastworks, at points up and down the coast. It was hard, irksome and very disagreeable work for volunteer soldiers. This kind of work all should have been done by the negro men of the South. What fools we mortals be! If the negro men had been enlisted to do all this hard manual labor, there would have been more white soldiers living at the close of the war, and fewer negro men to vote the radical ticket. But to our tale.

On the 16th of April we took the train for Wilmington, N.C.[17] Some time prior to this General N. G. Evans had been ordered to take command of Sullivan's Island. He refused to obey the order unless his brigade was sent with him. The regiments of his brigade were scattered at different points around Charleston. Because of this refusal he was placed under arrest. He was now released and given command of the brigade. He was injured in a runaway on the day we were embarked. The Seventeenth Regiment was on a train in Charleston, and the news came to us that the general was killed. It was sad to relate, but it is the truth of history that the men of the regiment, with but few exceptions, were glad to hear it. But he was not killed, but so badly injured as to incapacitate him for further service in the field, and we saw him no more.

On Monday, April 18, 1864, the *Charleston Daily Courier* reported the accident that essentially ended the military career of Nathan George Evans:[18]

A very serious and painful accident happened to General Evans between nine and ten o'clock Saturday morning. The General and his brother, Captain A. L. Evans, were in a light buggy, drawn by two horses, riding down Meeting Street, the General holding the reins. They had passed the *Courier* office, corner of Reid and Meeting, but a little distance, when one of the traces gave way, causing the horses to start off at full speed, jerking and breaking the shaft short off, and bringing down the front of the buggy with a crash to the ground. The General, in his effort to check the frightened animals, was drawn over the dash board, his head striking the paving stones with fearful violence. Several persons from the *Courier* office who witnessed the accident, ran to the assistance of the General, brought him in and sent immediately for medical assistance. When picked up he was found to be insensible, and bleeding profusely from a frightfully lacerated wound on the right side of the head, and with several severe cuts about the eyes and mouth. The whole frontal bone was laid entirely bare, the skin all being taken off . . . The General, although in a critical condition, somewhat revived towards Saturday evening, and afterwards passed a comparatively easy night . . .

The Tuesday edition of the paper reported on Evans' condition:

General Evans was much better Monday, and it was hoped that he had safely passed the most critical turn for which some anxiety was felt by his physicians.

Lieutenant Colonel Hudson of the Twenty-sixth Regiment noted the change in brigade leadership:

About the last of March, 1864, we were ordered to Virginia, under the command of Brigadier General Walker, bearing the sobriquet of "Liveoak" from the gallant fight he gave the Federals at a point of oaks near Pocotaligo. He was assigned to the command of our brigade instead of General Evans who, while hastening the departure of his brigade, was thrown from a buggy to the cobblestones of the streets of Charleston and severely injured.

William S. Walker
(courtesy of Library of Congress)

In his diary, Captain Stevenson described the train trip from Charleston to Wilmington, North Carolina:

Saturday—April 16th: This day eleven months ago we started to Mississippi. On arriving in Charleston we heard of the serious accident to General Evans falling from a Buggy. We also heard that the enemy were advancing on Goldsboro, and that General Beauregard would take command of the forces to meet him. I walked up the street and brought the General Orders from the Adjutant & Inspector General's Office. Came back; met Alex Beaty just from home, and he had a letter and box for me from home. Soon after we left the City some of the soldiers cut off the train and jumped off and left for home—they all belonged to the two Barnwell Companies—and the Engine went on with about half of the train.[19] While waiting for the return of the Engine the Colonel insisted on some of the officers singing in order to pass away the time pleasantly. "When this cruel war is over" was pronounced the best and was encored several times. Several other songs, some amusing, some sentimental, and all entertaining—so much so that we were sorry when we heard the Engine whistle. I slept on the floor between the seats. Arrived at Kingstree in Williamsburg District a little after daylight.

Sunday—April 17th: Several of us went into a gentleman's yard, got a big tub, and washed our hands and faces. Arrived at Florence, the junction of the Wilmington & Manchester Railroad, and the Darlington & Cheraw branch of the South Carolina Railroad from Kingsville about 20 minutes after 1 o'clock P.M. (distance from Charleston to Florence—102 miles; from Florence to Wilmington—106 miles). At Florence the officials said we could not go on until 7 o'clock P.M., but the Colonel insisted on being carried down as far as Mars Bluff. When we got there we had to go back to Florence on account of the turn-out being filled with cars and so there was no way for another train to pass. I went to preaching at the Hospital; several ladies present, none remarkable for beauty. The Holcombe Legion came up late in the evening. Went to preaching at the Presbyterian Church this evening. The Church was crowded and a Methodist preacher preached. After the services were over I came back and slept soundly until about 5 o'clock in the morning when we started.

Monday—April 18th: We left Florence about 5 o'clock A.M. Went as far as Mars Bluff and remained there until 9 o'clock at night. While lying over I wrote to Pa and walked a short distance to see Mr. Gregg, father of two of my college mates. Dr. Hartlie gave the Regiment several bushels of Potatoes, and Mr. Gregg gave us his tithe of Potatoes. Late in the evening Connor and myself went to see some young Ladies and had to double-quick nearly all the way back to be on time. We left about 9 o'clock and by daylight next morning we had gone about 60 or 70 miles. It rained during the night.

Tuesday—April 19th: Still raining this morning; we go very slow. Most of the cars have no covering—the soldiers all wet and cold. Our provisions nearly out, that is cooked provisions, as we made no calculation of being detained so long on the road. We arrived at Wilmington this evening, marched out two miles and bivouacked. Got acquainted with a Miss Flora McC . . . and we went to the theatre. Orders to go to Weldon.

Wednesday—April 20th: Orders to go to Weldon countermanded; went to the theatre.

10

NORTH TO PETERSBURG

> General Walker, who had taken command of the brigade that morning for the first time, thought the Eighteenth Regiment was in his front, and rode up to a line of Yankees who killed his horse, broke his leg, and captured him.
>
> William H. Edwards

Brigadier General William S. Walker was given temporary command of Evans' Brigade, pending General Evans' recovery from his accident.[1] Early in the war, Walker had defended South Carolina's coast as commander of the Third Military District of the Department of South Carolina, Georgia, and Florida. He had been promoted to brigadier general after the Battle of Pocotaligo, where his leadership had earned him the nickname "Live-Oak" Walker.[2] Walker would have the honor of becoming the brigade's second and most unfortunate leader.

The brigade arrived in Wilmington in late April 1864. For the next few weeks, the various regiments of the brigade were given different assignments in eastern North Carolina, along the railroad so that they could quickly move northward when needed. The Eighteenth camped near Wilmington on the river.[3] The Twenty-second was now under its new commander, Colonel Olin M. Dantzler, who was formerly the lieutenant colonel of the Twentieth Regiment.[4] It camped near Kinston and prepared to assist the Twenty-sixth in retaking Newbern.[5] The Holcombe Legion was sent to Weldon and assigned to guard the Petersburg and Weldon Railroad,[6] and the legion soon received a new commander, Colonel Stephen Elliott.[7] The Twenty-third camped near Masonboro Sound in the Wilmington area.[8] The Yankee prisoners recently captured by General Hoke at Plymouth, North Carolina, were sent up to Tarboro where the Seventeenth Regiment was to take charge of them.

Captain William Grafton Stevenson's diary recorded events in North Carolina:

Saturday—April 23rd: Passed through Goldsboro the next morning and at Rocky Mount on the Wilmington & Weldon Railroad we took the branch which leads to Tarboro. Distance from Rocky Mount to Tarboro—18 minutes. Arrived at Tarboro at 11 ½ o'clock A.M. Marched out to a beautiful grove and stacked arms, procured cooking utensils and prepared some rations. Walked out in town with the Colonel, who kissed every pretty girl he saw. We were ordered to cross the Tar River and encamp about one mile from the river, where we bivouacked for the night.

Monday—April 25th: On guard. The prisoners arrived about 11 o'clock A.M. A pen was made, one side being the river, the other many sentinels 13 paces apart—100 men on guard. The prisoners were worn out and hungry, feet blistered, nearly all barefooted . . . 2198 enlisted men, 98 commissioned officers, and 25 citizens. Great traffic between our men and the prisoners—we can buy most anything for a little bread and meat. I got an old cloth and silver pencil and gold pen. Officers allowed to go to town under guard, and there were a great many ladies to see the prisoners. I conducted several through the lines to get a good view. The ladies were very indignant and scornful. At night the crowd disperses and the prisoners sleep. Three Companies out as reserve and for emergency. No rations for the Commissioned officers, who take it well and don't grumble much. Expect to get off tomorrow.

Tuesday—April 26th: Seven hundred prisoners sent off this morning under Captain Avery. [They went by rail to Charleston, guarded by Companies A and F under Captains Edwards and Avery.] Trade still brisk. Made the acquaintance of Miss Blackwell and Mr. Floyd who invited me to call on them if I should ever be up here again. Rations nearly out. Our Company [Company D] ordered off together with Company E. The "modus operandi" of selecting prisoners to be sent off is as follows: the Orderly Sergeants form their different Companies, which are brought up to where a string of sentinels form a lane and as each man's name is called he walks out and continues as far down as he can get. We have under our charge the Sailors of the *Southfield* which was sunk by our ram, and the men swam ashore. There are only a few of these, the balance being Massachusetts, New York, Pennsylvania, and Rhode Island men. We passed through Wilson about dark, and a great many beautiful young ladies came out to see the prisoners, bitter in their denunciation against them. Mrs. D. S. Richardson invited me round to take supper. She gave me a splendid supper and loaded me down with provisions. She invited me to call on her whenever I should pass through again. Her husband is principal of a female school in the village, and their house is now a hospital.

Captain Edwards reported from Wilmington:

We left Charleston at 1 P.M. for Wilmington, N.C., and rejoined the regiment there on the 30th. On May 4th Companies A and F were detailed to do provost duty in the city, and, Captain Avery not being present with his company, I was again in command of the city as Provost Marshall for two weeks. On May 16th the regiment left Wilmington by rail for Petersburg, Virginia.

Private Faulkner of the Seventeenth Regiment wrote to his wife from Wilmington on May 3:

In my last I stated that we were at Tarboro, N.C. Companies I and B left there payday morning with 502 of the Yanks. We landed at this city Saturday about one hour before daylight. We did not stay but a short time until we took the train for Charleston. We stayed there one night and started back for this place and landed at 12 today. I do not begrudge my trip for I got to see a part of the country that I never have been.

The Twenty-second and Twenty-sixth Regiments camped near Kinston and prepared to assist Brigadier General Robert Hoke's North Carolina troops in retaking New Bern.

Sgt. William Martin of Company G of the Twenty-second Regiment wrote to his wife on April 30:

One of the rams which was to cooperate with the land forces in taking Newbern is aground between here and town. They started down the river and ran aground. Some think that the expedition is a failure. We have a rumor we leave for that place tonight, but I do not believe it. We left all of our baggage at Weldon and the Colonel telegraphed to Beauregard to know whether it would be proper to bring it here. He answered "no." So we are looking to go back there and from there to Petersburg or some where else in that direction. I do not care much where we go and would rather stay some where between Charleston and Weldon, but my druthers in the case do no good.

Private Lister, also of the Twenty-second Regiment, wrote to his family on May 9 that they had left camp on the third:

". . . last tuesday we left hear to go and take newbarn and thersday a bout 11 oclock we struck ther picket lines and run in ther pickets kild 2 and tuck 3 prisners went on tell about 12 and come to rail rode marcht down it bout 2 miles And met a gun bote on the rail rode our troops was formd in a line of battle and our artillery fierd on it and drive it back to the river then it and the Boats on the water comenst a fire on us and sutch a bumbardment I never heard the bumbs bursting over our heads continuly like thunder. . . ."

Lieutenant Colonel Hudson reported on the activities of the Twenty-sixth Regiment:

Reaching Wilmington, North Carolina, we were halted and placed in camp for a few days. Thence we proceeded to Weldon, North Carolina, and were again placed in camp for several days, whence we were ordered back by way of Goldsboro to Kinston, on the Neuse River. Here we were placed in camp to form a part of the command of Major General Hoke, who, after capturing Plymouth, North Carolina, was organizing an expedition against Newbern. On the second or third day we reached the enemy's lines, drove in his outposts and were preparing to storm his works, when an urgent dispatch from General Beauregard, recalled General Hoke and his command from Newbern, and ordered him to Petersburg, Virginia.[9]

Served by five railroads, Petersburg was the major supply point for Lee's Army of Northern Virginia and for Richmond, only twenty-two miles away. Beginning early in the war, a series of forts had been constructed in a semi-circle to defend the north, east, and south sides of the city. From mid-1862 until mid-1864, the city had been thinly defended by "home guard" troops. Now thousands of regular Confederate soldiers were brought to defend Petersburg when Grant began to threaten it and Richmond. Evans' Brigade (less the Holcombe Legion which was left guarding the Petersburg and Weldon Railroad) was among the reinforcements. In spite of Jefferson Davis' dislike of Beauregard, Lee had suggested that Beauregard be brought north to take command of the Department of North Carolina and Southern Virginia, and this had been done.[10] The initial attack on Petersburg came from the northeast and was known as the Bermuda Hundred Campaign.[11]

Lieutenant Colonel Hudson described conflicts in the Petersburg area:

General B. F. Butler with a heavy force had cut the railroad between Petersburg and Richmond and was sorely pressing the inadequate force under Beauregard. A part of Hoke's division reached Petersburg as early as May 10, 1864, but for the want of transportation the brigade of "Liveoak" Walker did not arrive until the evening of the 17th, the day after the battle of Drury's Bluff, in which General Butler was badly beaten and driven back toward Bermuda Hundred. This victory, though signal, was not so complete as the plan of General Beauregard promised, owing to the fact that Major General Whiting failed to come up from the side of Petersburg and Swift Creek in time to strike the enemy in the flank and rear. Had this movement been promptly executed as General Beauregard had ordered and expected it to be, in all probability the greater part of Butler's force would have been killed or captured.[12]

Remaining in Petersburg until the night of the 19th of May, we were moved across the Appomattox River and on to Clay's Farm or Warebottom Church. Shortly after daylight we were thrown against the enemy on the morning of May 20th, and throughout the day were actively engaged in

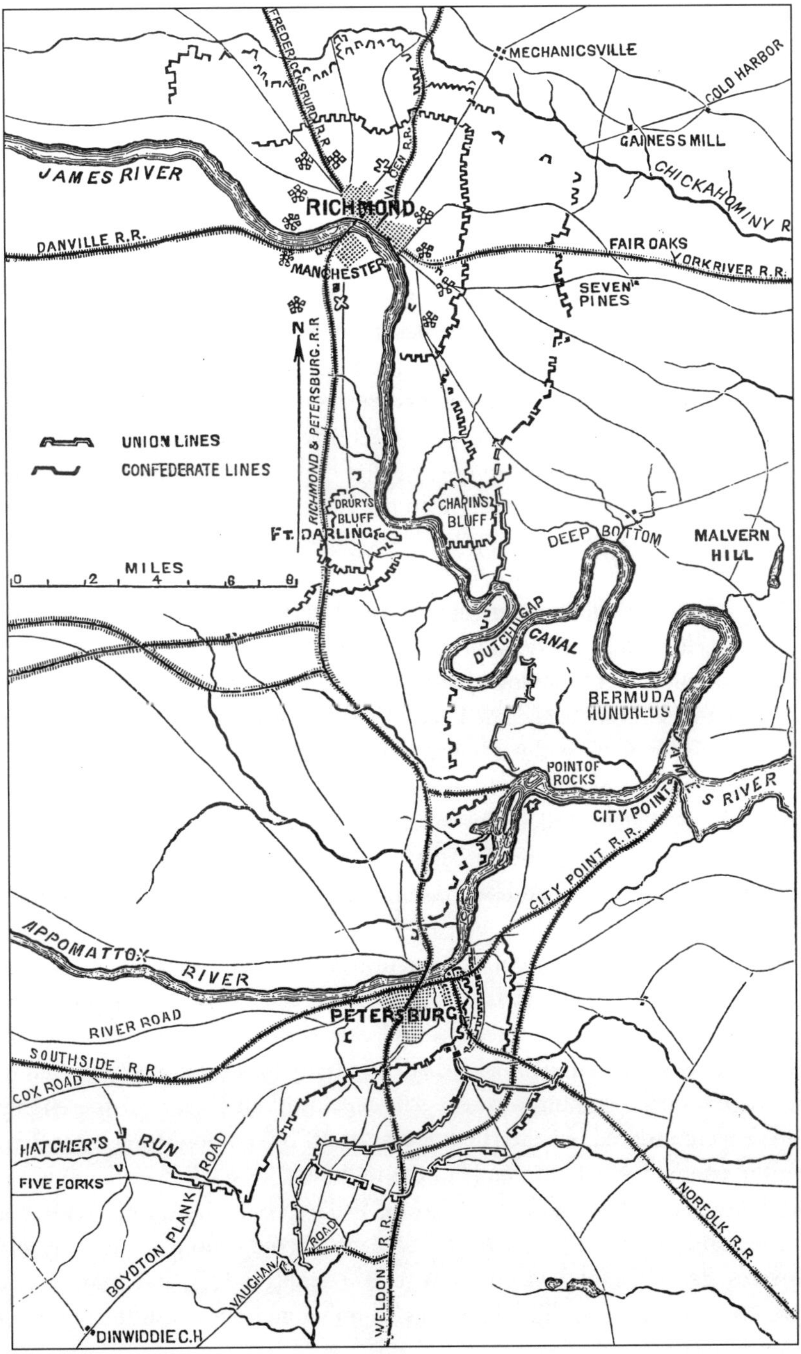

The Richmond–Petersburg area
(*Harper's Magazine*, June, 1864)

skirmishing and fighting, at times with great severity and loss. Among the slain of our regiment was Captain W. W. Davis, of Marlboro, a brave and efficient officer.

Captain Floyd of the Eighteenth Regiment wrote of the bravery of his men in battle:

On the 20th of May, 1864, Evans' Brigade, then under the command of General Walker, was ordered into battle at Warebottom Church, between Petersburg and Richmond. The battle was brought on by advancing our lines at this point, so as to strengthen them with the lines leading towards Bermuda Hundred. The brigade went into action by regiments successively, from right to left. The four regiments on the right pushed back the enemy's lines with but little opposition,[13] but when the two left regiments, the 26th and 18th regiments, went into line, we had hard fighting. The 26th wheeled into line first and had a hard fight to get there. While were moving on the position that we were to occupy, held by Clingman's North Carolina Brigade, we met Clingman's whole brigade running out, pursued by a Federal line, the Federals having driven Clingman from our line and were pursuing him. Our regiment charged the Federal brigade at once, striking them in the flank and causing them to break and fall back, but they re-formed again after retreating about 200 yards. It became necessary now for our regiment to wheel to the right so as to face the enemy. While we were making the wheel the enemy poured an enfilading fire into our line. As soon as we got into position Colonel Wallace ordered us to charge. The captains stepped out in front of their respective companies and led their men. When I stepped out in front of Company "I," hat off and sword in hand and asked my men to follow me, though half of the company and of the regiment had been shot down and though five times their number were in front of them pouring volley after volley into their ranks, they dashed forward at the enemy with that terrible Rebel yell, (which some writer has said that no living being yet ever heard unmoved) with such impetuosity that the enemy broke and fled, pursued by our regiment. We captured many prisoners and killed many of the enemy.

We were ordered back to the line staked off by our engineers, after driving the enemy for half a mile. Half the regiment were killed or wounded in this battle. Company I lost W. J. Brown, William Burris and John W. Burris killed, and Lieutenant J. T. Moore, Sergeants Pierce, Odom and Brown, and Privates Parnell, Hutchenson, Dewitt, Rhodes, [Hodge], and Moody, and seven others wounded. This battle lasted only one hour and fifteen minutes but was very severe.

Captain Edwards recalled General Walker's capture:

Stephen Elliott Jr.
(courtesy of Library of Congress)

The brigade was formed in line of battle with Wise's Brigade on our right. This line occupied by the Yankees was partly in the woods, but part of it extended across a large stubble-field to another large body of woods. This part of the line was entrenched, the Yankees using a field ditch that ran all the way across the field with an old straight fence on the top of the ditch bank. On the Yankee side of the fence it was quite a good breastwork, but on our side it was very poor. We charged three or four hundred yards through an open field and captured this line and held it, although we had poor protection from the bullets of the enemy. But it is astonishing how quick a Confederate soldier could go in the ground with his bayonet and a tin plate. In charging, the Eighteenth South Carolina Volunteers was opposite the body of woods on our left, and they had gone in an oblique direction and left a vacancy in the line between the Seventeenth and Eighteenth Regiments.

Olin M. Dantzler
(courtesy of Calhoun County Museum)

General Walker, who had taken command of the brigade that morning for the first time, thought the Eighteenth Regiment was in his front, and rode up to a line of Yankees who killed his horse, broke his leg, and captured him.[14] He refused to surrender and hoped to ride away from them. We saw him for the first and last time that morning. He was a great loss, and was a fine officer, and we needed him. Our regiment lost several good men, killed and wounded, but the Eighteenth suffered far more than we did. The enemy made several charges during the day to dislodge us from the position, but were repulsed with heavy loss each time. We built good fortifications and held the line from river to river. This was the last lick that drove in the cork that bottled up the immortal "Beast" Butler—the cowardly old skunk!

Lieutenant Colonel Hudson noted the change in the brigade's command:

General Walker recovered with the loss of a leg and still survives. He was succeeded in command by Brigadier General Stephen Elliott, the hero of

Caleb Glover
(courtesy of Calhoun County Museum)

Fort Sumter, who for distinguished gallantry was promoted from the rank of major of artillery to the rank of brigadier-general, and was assigned to the command of Walker's Brigade.[15]

Because it had been determined that Evans would not be able to resume command, this appointment was considered a permanent one, and the name of the unit was officially changed to Elliott's Brigade. The brigade remained in the lines at Bermuda Hundred for a few more weeks. On June 2, Beauregard ordered a reconnaissance of the enemy's strength, and Colonel O. M. Dantzler was killed leading the Twenty-second Regiment into battle near Warebottom Church.[16] Dantzler's manservant, Caleb Glover, brought Dantzler's body home to Lewisville (now St. Matthews), South Carolina for burial.[17] On June 13, 1864, Beauregard ordered the battery of heavy guns that overlooked and controlled the James River from Howlett's Hill to be named Battery Dantzler in his honor.[18]

Now the focus of the Federal attacks shifted southward. On June 9 Federal general Benjamin F. Butler ordered an attack on Petersburg by infantry

attacking from the north and east and cavalry attacking from the south. The city was poorly defended by a home guard consisting of old men and boys, a few veterans, and a small artillery unit, but they and a few late-arriving reinforcements managed to repel the half-hearted Federal attacks. A few days later, Grant would elude Lee and begin to move his Army of the Potomac from the battlegrounds at the Wilderness and Spotsylvania Court House to join Butler on the east side of Petersburg.

On June 16 the guns of Battery Dantzler were buried to avoid their capture, and the Confederate "Howlett Line" was abandoned as Confederate troops were pulled back to help to defend Petersburg. Because this line held Butler's forces back from the city and also defended the railroad to Richmond, it was retaken a few days later. The heavy guns were recovered and put back to use in blocking the James River.

Captain Edwards described the early days of the defense of Petersburg:

On the 16th of June it was ascertained that the van of Grant's army was nearing Petersburg. General Lee's army, except the troops between the two rivers, all being on the north side of the James, General Beauregard rushed our brigade to Petersburg, evacuating the lines in front of Butler, who sent troops to occupy our lines, and Pickett found them tearing up the railroad leading from Richmond to Petersburg. Fortunately Pickett came on them before they had done much harm. He thrashed them and ran them back to Butler's main line and left a few regiments in our old lines to hold Butler in his bottle. Our folks were not afraid of Butler, as he had no reputation as a fighter. He was very brave among Southern women and children, but did not care to come in close quarters with Southern men with arms in their hands.

We left these lines at 3 A.M. on the 16th and marched rapidly to Petersburg, where we arrived about 8 A.M. This was what is known in army parlance as a forced march. When we got to Petersburg I saw no other organized regular troops there and don't think there were any there until late in the evening. We had some batteries of artillery and a large company of old men and boys from the city.[19] There was a whole corps of Grant's army in our front. They could have run over us and gone into the city, but somebody would have got hurt and many a man would have bit the dust. But there was no fighting of any consequence done around Petersburg that day. With the Wilderness, Spottsylvania and Cold Harbor fresh in their minds, Grant's army did not seem at all eager for fighting. It is a fact of history well established that Grant knew he could not defeat Lee's army in battle, and another fact of history is he never did. When day dawned on the morning of the 17th of June General Lee had at least twenty thousand soldiers in Petersburg, and all that day the fun grew fast and furious. The two armies were sparring for positions, Grant trying to establish his lines in shelling distance of the city and Lee as determined not to allow him to do it, and he didn't. There were a number of sharp conflicts that day and many men killed and wounded. One of these occurred between Mahone's command and a large body of Federal troops. This fight was in a body of dense woods, about four miles from the city. It was their purpose to establish their lines in the edge of these woods, but Mahone struck their flank and routed them, with great slaughter.

Our brigade, while in no close conflict with the enemy, was under fire all day, and in the evening the Seventeenth Regiment lost several men. Among them Adjutant J. W. Connor and also Joseph Lock, of Company A, was mortally wounded, and I was severely wounded. About this time Stephen Elliott, of Fort Sumter fame, was promoted to Brigadier General, and placed in command of our brigade.

Captain Floyd recalled some of the brigade's successes:[20]

On the 16th of June our brigade, now under General Stephen Elliott, was ordered to Petersburg. When we arrived we found that Grant's whole army was in our front. General Beauregard was holding our lines with about 10,000 men. Our brigade was in reserve and we were hurried from one position to another, whenever an attack was expected, all day long. On the morning of the 17th we were aroused by tremendous firing on the lines. A staff officer of General Johnson's soon made his appearance with an order for our brigade to move up to the line at double quick. We soon learned that Johnson's Tennessee Brigade had been driven from the lines, most of them being captured. We met men, officers and artillery running out, and we were told that the enemy had our lines and were pressing on towards Petersburg. We formed a line of battle and moved forward, soon meeting the enemy. We gave them one tremendous volley, then with a yell, gave them the bayonet, drove them back and reestablished the lines. Things remained comparatively quiet until late in the afternoon, when the enemy commenced a series of charges on Wise's Brigade just on our left. At the fifth charge Wise's men gave way and were driven from the works. Our brigade was forced to the left and moved by the left flank at double quick until we gained position to the rear of Wise's works, (now occupied by the enemy) then faced to the right and moved forward at the run, using the bayonet, driving the enemy from the works, capturing them with hundreds of prisoners. Lieutenant Jordan, of Company "I," and several men were wounded in this charge. That night we fell back to a new line that had been laid off by our engineers, and by morning had a pretty formidable works built. Those were the lines that we held until Petersburg was evacuated. Early on the morning of the 18th the enemy charged our whole front, but were driven back with heavy loss. All day long, at intervals, some part of our lines were charged.

Lieutenant Lowry of the Seventeenth Regiment described the final battle of the day:

This evening about five o'clock the enemy commenced massing in our front. At first they threw out a skirmish line, but our line, under Major Betsil of the 18th, charged them and ran them back. They displayed a line a little to our right and drove in our pickets. Shortly after this they threw a line of battle in the edge of a piece of woods, and making them lie down massed four lines behind them. They then deployed another skirmish line and advanced it forward. It was at this juncture that we lost our much lamented company commander, Lieutenant David J. Logan.[21] He ordered the men to keep down their heads for the enemy were sharpshooting fast, and in his zeal for his men, exposed himself when a stray ball struck him square in the forehead killing him instantly. He never groaned, but was dead in a minute. It threw a gloom over every countenance and cast a damper over the whole company. His bloody corpse was borne away by our ambulance men, which was the last of our lamented Lieutenant. He was an officer and a gentleman, a man of brilliant intellect, who by his kind heart and gentle ways, had attached himself to every one of us. I can say no more, but his death was a shock so unexpected as to almost overcome my discretion. He is gone, and I trust is with his God in heaven. Shortly after he had been borne off the enemy began to make furious demonstrations in our front. In a few moments their front line appeared and came forward at double quick, followed by four other lines seemingly bent on taking our lines, but they did not count the cost.

"Fire" came the word, and our whole line was a sheet of flame. The Yankees in line began to dwindle down and before they had got within one hundred yards of our works, we turned their tune, and they broke and fled in utter dismay, followed by the shouts and bullets of our victorious boys. Every now and then after the main body had reached the woods a solitary Yankee would rise and make for the woods, followed by shouts of laughter by our boys. Again the Yankee officers attempted to renew the charge, acting, I must say, with considerable bravery, but forming a line as they did, still they could not prevail on the Yanks to charge us again. After two or three more futile attempts, they desisted altogether. We had one man in our company wounded by his own gun, E. W. Bridges, finger and thumb shot off. This was our only casualty, while many a Yankee bit the dust in our front. I do not know the number of enemy killed and wounded.

Captain Floyd's men held their line against repeated enemy charges:[22]

On the morning of the 19th a heavy charge was directed against our brigade front and a desperate attempt was made to carry a portion of our lines occupied by the left of the 18th Regiment and the right of the Holcombe Legion.[23]

Colonel Wallace being wounded and absent, Colonel Allison had ordered me to take charge of the left wing of the regiment, and when the enemy made the charge mentioned and were almost on our main works, having already taken our picket lines, I ordered the left companies to fix bayonets and prepare to charge . . . Our men dashed over the works and hurled the enemy back to their main line. Our picket lines being reestablished, we rested comparatively quiet for the remainder of the day. Early on the morning of the 20th, the enemy again charged our lines, but were again driven back with heavy loss. Lieutenant M. W. Hunter, commanding Company I, was severely wounded in the head and five privates were also wounded in these charges.

Our company was now without a commissioned officer, as I was still in command of the left wing of the regiment. I considered it a compliment to be ordered to act as a field officer, especially so when it is remembered that there were six captains in the regiment my senior. Late in the evening Longstreet's Corps marched into our lines and we felt relieved. I was ordered to return to my company, Colonel Wallace having returned. For several days things were comparatively quiet in our front. On the next day, our brigade was sent to the Ice House ravine to rest for a few days. Shortly afterwards we were again ordered into the lines opposite Cemetery Hill. The sharp-shooting was very severe on this part of the line, in fact there was a continuous rattle of musketry, booming of cannon and crashing of bursting shell, night and day.

On June 22 Federal infantry and cavalry troops launched the "Wilson-Kautz Raid," an attempt to destroy the railroads which brought Confederate supplies from the south and west to Petersburg and Richmond. On June 28, after tearing up over sixty miles of track on the South Side Railroad and the Richmond and Danville Railroad to the west of Petersburg, these troops were withdrawing towards the east when they approached the Stony Creek Station of the Petersburg and Weldon Railroad. This station, about twenty miles south of Petersburg, was guarded by four companies of the Holcombe Legion, and reinforcements had just arrived in the form of Wade Hampton and his cavalry division. Together they successfully defended the area, forcing Wilson and Kautz to divide their forces and to scramble eastward by different routes to rejoin the Federal forces east of Petersburg. Lieutenant Colonel William J. Crawley was severely wounded in the fighting on June 28 and would not be able to return to command the Holcombe Legion. This action was the most noteworthy activity of the Holcombe Legion during its assignment to guard three bridges of the Petersburg and Weldon Railroad during the summer of 1864.[24]

Private Faulkner wrote on July 3 of the continuous fighting in the trenches at Petersburg:

This is a miserable place, lying in the fortifications in the sun and dust, with the enemy two hundred yards in our front continually popping away at us every minute day and night and our men returning the fire. We are so close we can talk to each other, but it is against orders. Some of our regiment is killed or wounded every day . . . All the men that are hit are shot in the head. If a man sticks his head above the breast works "he goes up." We get little or no sleep. Three men out of every company stands and shoots all the time through the night. I stood up from midnight until day this morning, and shot until my gun got so warm that I could hardly hold it. If the roar of our guns would stop, we would soon get orders to pitch in. I thought of it being the Sabbath and what a dreadful way it was to spend it, but the sin will not lie at my door. This beats anything of war I have ever seen . . . I have got so used to it I can lie down on the ground and sleep, the guns not disturbing me. The night before last we were all ordered up as "the Yanks ware coming." The boys rolled out of the sand and went to work. It was a perfect sheet of fire. After firing ten or twelve rounds, it was ascertained that "they ware not coming." I think they do this to try us, but if the Enemy advances on us somebody will be hurt. Our men have not any idea of giving up the works.

On a brighter note, Colonel McMaster wrote to his wife on June 28:

My orderly has brought me my dinner regularly the last four days and each day he brought me a pie. He had for a few days before brought $1 worth of beans each day—yet a pie would sell for $4 or $5. I was imagining it was some kind lady of means who desired to attest her devotion to the cause by feeding the poor soldier and felt some compunction about taking the cherry and gooseberry pies without paying for them and that was out of the question as I had no money. Yesterday I learned it was a <u>fine</u> <u>woman</u> <u>of</u> <u>color</u> who had fallen in <u>love</u> with Sam and gives him a nice pie every day which he sends to us. May her love continue—at least, may the pies continue as it is the only comfort we look for during the 24 hours.

After commanding the brigade for a little more than a month, Brigadier General Stephen Elliott described his officers in letters to his wife:

[July 6] I like Colonel Wallace very much, having known him well in college. He is a placid but firm and intelligent man with perhaps not enough "vim" in him, but his ambition lies more in the political than in the military line. McMaster is just about what you might expect—a man who has been writing pamphlets against his superior officer to be—but I have had no trouble with him and do not expect to have. Benbow is a high-spirited tall gentlemanly man rather weakly in health and not a very thorough officer. I suspect though a gallant man. Fleming is a regular, steady and slow and reliable, but you must not crowd him with ideas. Hudson reminds me, so far as I have seen him, of the party who set Othello, Cassio, Desdemona, and the rest of them so much together by the ears.

[July 14] McM is still nibbling at trouble. He shall have a plenty of time and will be well hooked before he knows that any one has a line out. He is a hypocrite and I strongly, yea powerfully, suspect that his regard for his hide is paramount, and that Genl. Evans account of the big rock at Boonsboro is not quite so much a myth as he would like to make out . . .[25] If you do not think much of a man in college the chances are that you never will at any subsequent time. I believe that he will behave creditably when he cannot avoid it without disgrace, but he certainly has instinct—Pshaw! I ought not to waste half a page on so poor a subject.

[July 21] I have commenced however and will succeed if the war last two or more years longer in getting at least one reliable officer in each company, that is unless they are killed sooner or I. Those companies that have good officers do well. The others do not. The brigade has not a good reputation in this army and anything that is accomplished will be placed in a great measure to my credit.

Toward the end of the first month of the siege, Lieutenant Lowry described life in the trenches in his diary:

July 15th—All quiet along the lines except continual sharpshooting and mortar shelling. Nobody hurt in the regiment. Early in Maryland and created a great disturbance in Yankeedom. Awful hot and dusty in the ditches.

July 16th—Nothing unusual. Sharpshooting still going on. One man of Company D killed by sharpshooters, William Ritchey. No one else hurt. Rumors are rife, but nothing reliable. See no prospect of relief. Rations very scarce, and men all anxious for a change.

July 17th—Re-act again the monotonous scenes of yesterday. Another man of Company D killed killed, Joe Armstrong. It is Sunday and contrary to their usual mode of acting, the Yankees are rather quiet, only threw a few mortar shells in the ditches.

July 18th—A mortar shell fell in the ditches this morning causing some tall skeedadling, but fortunately did not burst. Very anxious to hear from Early in Yankeedom. Cannot hear a word of news. Another man wounded in the regiment this morning. The Yankees keep balls continually flying over our heads, and no man can expose his head a minute above the breastworks without being struck, and most probably killed. We have had no rain in about two months, and the dust is stifling. Living on corn bread and bacon, with cow peas occasionally. Will not be apt to get anything better this summer. Here is General D. H. Hill just passing by inspecting the works, a stern looking old warrior in full uniform. Brigadiers and Colonels are as thick as blackberries and hardly arouse attention, they are so common.

July 19th—Today a change, long looked for, but very unpleasant to the weather worn soldier, took place. The clouds were overspread by a gloomy pall, the atmosphere became dull and sultry, and at length the flood gates of heaven were opened and rain, rain, descended in torrents, as if venting its long pent up rage on our devoted heads. Blankets, tent clothes, oil clothes, etc. were greatly in demand, and everyone was busy amid the pelting storm fixing up a shelter. But the wetting was the least of our inconveniences. Remember, we are in ditches of red clay, and as the rain mixed with the sticky clay, mud became the consequence. It rained all day and by evening the mud was actually in places knee deep, and if we moved at all we were compelled to walk in mud ankle deep every step. It was truly an inviting prospect (knowing that if the mud became waist deep we would have to stay here). Imagine our appearance, clad in all the beauty of our clay colored habitiments, sheltering under the kindly protection of a diminutive oil-cloth from the pelting rain, and standing with stoic composure knee deep in mud and water. But it is all "Pur Palaria," and you would be surprised to hear peals of laughter at the unfortunate fall of some clumsy individual, and the jokes cracked with all the jovial mirth of better days. Gradually the rain ceased and the men, ever ready for improvement, began to remove the muddy clay until he came to more stable ground. Thus we passed the day. Nothing occurred to excite attention, and the night closed in all quiet. Early is now safe out of Maryland after having frightened old Abe to death, captured an immense amount of plunder, horses, cattle, etc., whipped the enemy in a pitched battle at Monocacy, and accomplished the greatest raid on record. I was in hopes his designs were against Washington or Baltimore, but it seemed not. Grant is still in our front and keeps up a liberal display of men and wagons. The enemy throw a few more shells but to no effect. Nobody hurt in the regiment today. Received a letter from home today with some much needed funds, $150.00.

July 20th—A few mortar shells were thrown into our lines this morning but no harm done. The usual sharpshooting going on. It is feared that the enemy are tunneling under our lines, and as right in our front is the most favorable spot for such works and as a battery is also here, we are preparing for such a device by digging a tunnel all along the whole face of the battery to meet theirs if they have any. Not quite so muddy today, but warm and sultry.

July 21st—Today I got leave to visit the City of Petersburg and found it a great luxury to get in the rear for a short time to clean up and get a good dinner. Nothing new occurred in the trenches today.

July 22nd—Very warm and sunny. The enemy threw a good many mortar shells at us this morning but hurt no one. Sharpshooters still at work.

July 23rd—Last night we were relieved to rest for a day or two and retired about one mile in rear of the works. Today I am on guard so I get but little rest. Good news from Georgia. Sherman thoroughly whipped by Hood.

July 25th—All quiet. Go back to the ditches tonight.

This was Lieutenant Lowry's last diary entry. He was killed five days later during the Battle of the Crater.

11

THE BATTLE OF THE CRATER

> . . . there came another blast and
> God only knows how high it sent me.
> I spread my wings to see if I could fly but
> the first thing I knowed I was lying on
> top of the works . . .
>
> J. Warren Pursley

For two years, the brigade had been wandering about, fighting where it was needed. Its wandering days, except for the retreat to Appomattox, were over. July 30, 1864, would be its day of glory.

After the siege of Petersburg had lasted for over a month, the Battle of the Crater took place approximately one mile east of the city, where the brigade, now under the command of Stephen Elliott Jr. and officially called "Elliott's Brigade," occupied the trenches. The Federal plan called for the use of explosives in an underground tunnel to blow a gap in the Confederate defenses.[1] A large force would then rush forward and take the hilltop at Blandford Church, about one-half mile to the northwest.[2] This hilltop overlooked Petersburg, and its capture would break the siege of the city. Although the Federal troops employed great secrecy in digging the tunnel, the Confederates believed that the enemy was digging somewhere under their trenches, and they began to dig countermines.[3]

Elliott's Brigade was in the trenches directly over the Federal mine. Its regiments were deployed in the following order from left to right: the Twenty-sixth, Seventeenth, Eighteenth, Twenty-second, and Twenty-third Regiments. (The Holcombe Legion was still detached and guarding the railroad south of Petersburg.) After the battle, the brigade adjutant would estimate that Elliott's Brigade had lost 667 men as follows: Twenty-sixth Regiment, 72; Seventeenth Regiment, 135; Eighteenth Regiment, 205; Twenty-second Regiment, 216; and the Twenty-third Regiment, 49. These total nearly one-half of the Confederate losses on that day.[4]

Captain Floyd related the activities of the Eighteenth Regiment on the evening before the battle and told how it was moved into position over the mine:[5]

A Confederate countermine
(courtesy of Library of Congress)

We were in the trenches about three hundred yards to the left of the "Elliott Salient" and were near Wright's Battery of Coit's Battalion, where we had been for several days. The artillery fire was very severe at this point, as was always the case near batteries. Privates W. F. Timmons, J. W. Windham and Thomas E. Colvin were severely wounded in the early part of the day. Just before sundown the enemy opened fire upon us with their mortar batteries and one of their shells fell into the trenches just where Company "I" was stationed. Private Odom had his skull fractured and several others were wounded by this shell. We received orders about dark to follow the movements of the troops on our right and moved along the trenches until the right of our line rested upon Pegram's Battery at the "Elliott Salient." Just as we halted Private J. T. Vann was badly wounded in the face. The sharpshooting was unusually severe all night. It had been reported by deserters coming into our lines that the enemy were tunneling under Pegram's Battery, and our people were counter-tunneling but had failed to find the enemy's tunnel. We all went to sleep, however, except the sharpshooters, one every five paces.

Captain B. Lewis Beaty of Company K of the Twenty-sixth Regiment told of the Battle of the Crater in his 1903 address to the Horry County Confederate Soldiers Association:

The uniform failure of the assaults of our enemies upon our lines around Petersburg had caused them to come to the conclusion that they could only succeed after a breach had been made in our works. For this purpose a subterranean gallery for a mine was run under one of our earthworks or forts, situated at the angle of the Confederate works around Petersburg, Virginia, known as Elliott's Salient. The site was east of the Jerusalem plank road, about one-half mile southeast of Cemetery Hill, where Blandford Cemetery was located—a short distance beyond the city limits of Petersburg. The Federal General Burnside, who conducted this operation against us, thus described the work: "The main gallery, extending to a point under the Confederate line, was 522 feet long. From the inner end of this main gallery extended side galleries for forty feet in each direction. At the outer end and middle of these side galleries, short galleries were run and chambers or magazines were made to contain the explosives. This was first intended to consist of 1,200 or 1,400 pounds of powder in each of the eight magazines, to be connected by a trough half-filled with powder. It was afterwards decided to put only 320 kegs of powder containing 1,000 pounds, in each of the eight magazines, making a charge of 8,000 pounds."

We knew the enemy was undermining our line at this point and had endeavored to countermine and blow up the workmen, but failed for want of proper tools to do the work. Our brigade had been stationed on this part of our line, or near to it, since it was established. We fell back on the 18th of June after stubbornly resisting Grant's army when he moved to the south side of the James River, and christening with the blood of our men this new line by resisting several heavy assaults of the enemy before we had completed our breastworks, and by holding the enemy in check until General Lee could come to our relief. Our regiment, the Twenty-sixth, was then fighting to the right of the hill where Pegram's Battery was stationed. The earthworks in which this battery was located was afterward blown up, forming the Crater. On the morning of Saturday, the 30th of July, 1864, the brigade of General Stephen Elliott, composed of the Twenty-sixth, Seventeenth, Eighteenth, Twenty-second, and Twenty-third South Carolina Regiments of infantry, occupied the line at Elliott's Salient. The regiments were located from left to right, as here named, with Ransom's North Carolina Brigade [under McAfee] joined to the Twenty-sixth Regiment on the left and Wise's Virginia Brigade [under Goode] joined to the Twenty-third Regiment on the right. Our line at this point was very close to those of the enemy—only 130 yards by actual measurement afterward made.

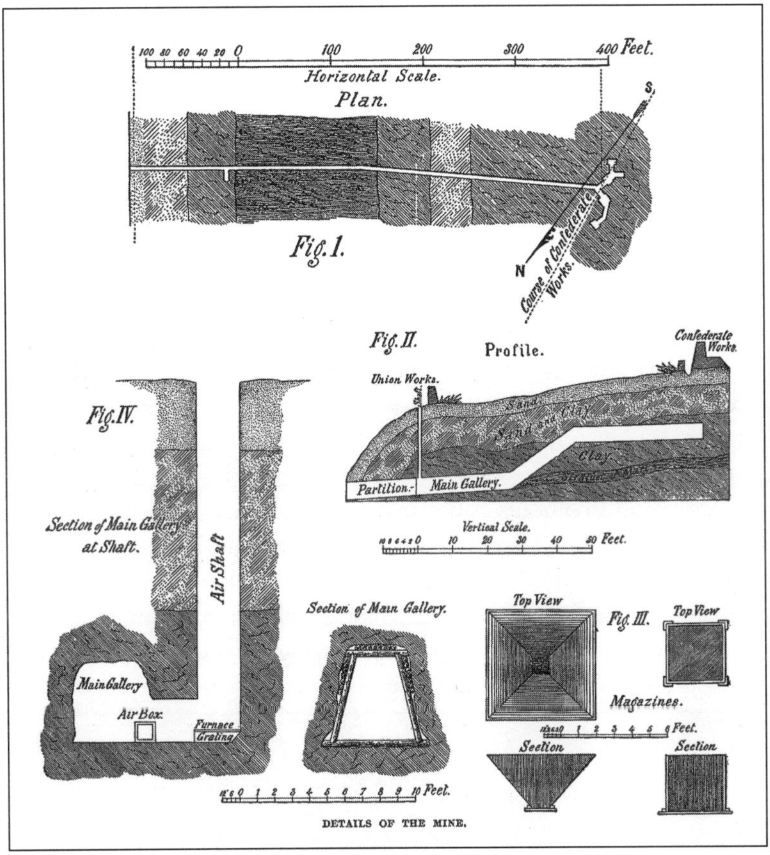

Detail of the Federal mine
(*Battles and Leaders of the Civil War*, vol. 4)

To drown any noise made by their miners, the Yankees kept up a constant firing day and night, and our men were equally vigilant, not allowing one of them to expose himself without receiving our fire. Many deaths and narrow escapes occurred here. So accurate became their aim, that to hold up one's hat on a ramrod was to have several holes through it very quickly. This constant watching and exertion day and night was very exhausting, so much so that the infantry and artillery stationed here had to take duty by turn in the battery and breastworks immediately adjoining. Our regiment, the Twenty-sixth, had not long been relieved from duty in the fort by the Eighteenth Regiment. We were occupying the line on the left of the brigade.

We later learned that the enemy's plan of attack was for the colored division of the Ninth Division of Burnside's Corps to make the advance. The location of our fort was pointed out to them and the part they were to perform was given to their officers in detail, as was the work of the other troops.

The Thirtieth U.S. Regiment, Colored Troops, was to advance immediately after the explosion as rapidly as possible through the Crater, turn to the left, sweep down our line of breastworks and hold the farthest point gained. Another regiment was selected to do the same on the right. This would make a fair opening for their troops following to make a bee line for our battery on Cemetery Hill, which was understood to be the key to this part of our line. This hill also overlooked the city. For several days their troops were drilled in the movements they were expected to perform when the explosion occurred. Time after time did they go through the imaginary advance, turn to the left and advance along the line of our breastworks. Every officer and private knew his place and what he was expected to do. Without a single command, the part assigned to each could have been carried out. However, the night before, their plan was changed and white troops were sent in, apparently without knowing what to do, while the colored division was not ordered forward until a full two hours had elapsed and then had no definite idea what was expected of them. The intention was to spring the mine at 2 o'clock Saturday morning, but the fuse twice failed. For the grand assault on our lines the enemy had massed 65,000 men. It was well planned, and if carried out without the confusion resulting from their change of plans at the last moment,

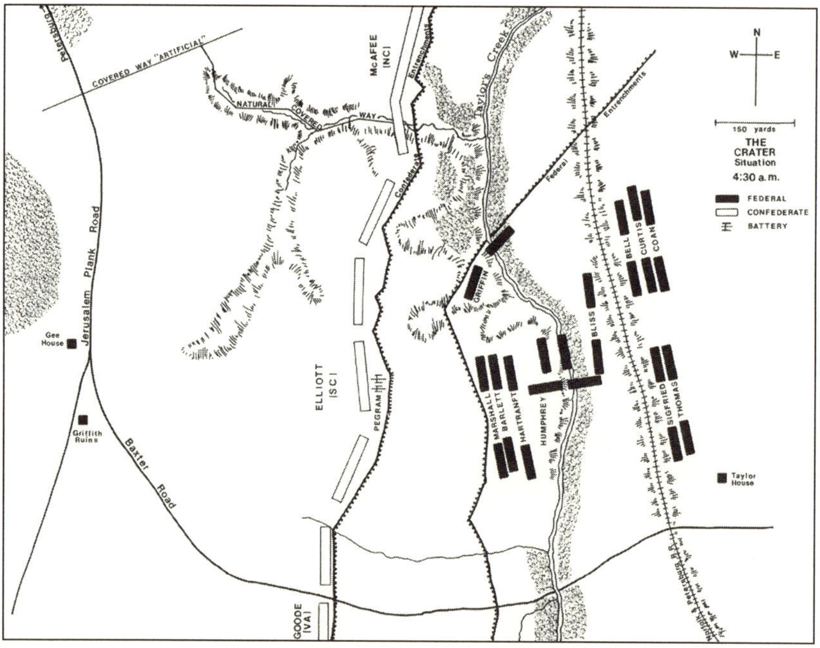

Situation at 4:30 A.M. on July 30, 1864
(*The Battle of the Crater "The Horrid Pit,"* 1989)

would have proven very disastrous to us, indeed. The explosion, which occurred at 4:45 A.M., by the records, overwhelmed Pegram's Battery of four guns, most of the Eighteenth Regiment, three companies of the Twenty-second and part of Company A of the Seventeenth Regiment[6]. These all were in that part of the line that was blown up, or immediately adjoining it.

Lieutenant Pursley of the Eighteenth S.C.V. wrote home on August 1:

"I had lay down & had just got to sleep when it came it commenced on the right. The first jar I felt I thought it was a boom had lit on my little boom proof. John Jackson was lying in with me he hollowed at me to get out of the boom proof & we both jumped out. Just as I lit in to the ditch there came another blast & God only knows how high it sent me. I spread out my wings to see if I could fly but the first thing I knowed I was lying on top of the works . . ."

Colonel McMaster noted in his 1895 account of Elliott's Brigade at the Crater:

An amusing incident occurred at this time illustrating how even the bravest men are affected in a panic. Lieutenant Moss of Company E had gone off to sleep with his coat off, which was contrary to orders. In relating personal experiences after the battle, he said that without coat and shoes he had run down to Ransom's Brigade, but coming to his wits he cried out: "What! Old Moss running?" and immediately returned to his company. The panic was not confined to our men. The Federal lines were formed for the assault, but were so frightened with the sight of the earth, timber, cannon, and falling human bodies that they broke ranks, and it took ten minutes to reform them.

Captain Beaty continued his account of the Twenty-sixth Regiment:

For a short time immediately following the explosion, great consternation prevailed among our men close to the "Crater." Some being awakened from sleep, and others taken completely by surprise, were filled with consternation at the terrible calamity and awful destruction caused by this, to them, new and powerful mode of warfare. Some, partly stunned, and others who had been partly buried or tossed about by the explosion, came rushing down the line covered with earth and wild with fright. But this condition did not last long. Within ten or fifteen minutes our men recovered from their panic, the few left of the Eighteenth Regiment falling in line with the Seventeenth, and these, with the Twenty-sixth, were ready and began the fight almost as soon as the enemy made their appearance in the Crater. So demoralizing was the effect of the explosion upon the enemy that it was fully ten minutes before they came over their breastworks and made a rush for our lines. At the same time two guns of Wright's Battery to our left and rear began its work of death, sweeping with grape and canister the open space on the hill between our lines and those of the enemy, over which they had to pass, also enfilading the Crater. This battery, being on an eminence above the elevation of the Crater, could fire over our line, which it did with remarkable accuracy and effect in the destruction of the enemy all through the fight to its close, throwing during this time between 500 and 600 shell and canister. Immediately following the explosion, the enemy opened fire upon our lines as well as upon the city of Petersburg, with all of their cannon in range of these points, hurling shot and shell heavily and furiously upon us, burning several houses in the city, tearing up the earthworks and ground all around us and our artillery, and with the heavy infantry fire killing and wounding many of our men. The roar of the guns, the bursting of shell and rattle of musketry was deafening, yet the men of Elliott's Brigade bravely manned the works up to the borders of the Crater, leaving no front for the entrance of the enemy except such as had been made vacant by the upheaval of the earth.

Captain Floyd gave this account of the early part of the battle:

When I awoke the next morning it seemed to me that the whole world was going to pieces. I started to rise up but was hurled to the ground so violently that I lost consciousness. When I came to myself again I saw masses of earth and pieces of large timbers lying all around me and I was covered up from head to foot with earth and debris. Tremendous firing and shouting was going on and the fierce, defiant yells of contending men, intermingled with the groans of the wounded and dying constituted a perfect pandemonium, not inferior in intensity to "Dante's Seven Circled Hell." I saw that the battery on our right had been blown away and that a hand-to-hand fight was in progress, just in rear of where the battery had been located. I, Adjutant Sims, Lieutenant Anderson, Sergeants W. D. Kirvin, W. W. Pierce and T. W. Berry were among them and about fifty privates of the regiment were there. I, Sims, and Berry were bareheaded and looked like we had just emerged from a clay hole. There were about two hundred Federal officers and men contending with us. Swords flashed, and bayonets and the butts of rifles were freely used. It was a hand-to-hand fight in every sense of the word. Just then a bomb shell, thrown from our mortar battery in the rear, fell in the midst of the contestants and burst with a crash, hurling the Confederates and Federals right and left, killing and wounding several, and causing the contesting parties to separate. This was a critical moment for the Confederates. Both parties now commenced loading their guns and other Federal troops appeared on the banks of the Crater. The enemy now dashed over the bank and into the Crater and I gave the order for my men to fall back to a ravine or cross ditch about one hundred feet to my rear. It was about one hundred

The Explosion of the Mine
(*Battles and Leaders of the Civil War*, vol. 4)

and fifty feet from the main breastwork and was a good cover to fight from. Our men fell back, walking backward and firing as they retired, the officers using their revolvers and the men their guns. They finally reached the ditch, after losing half their number. Lieutenant Anderson and many of the men were killed before they got halfway to the ditch. Adjutant Sims was shot through the lungs and died in a few days. Sergeant T. W. Berry was pierced through the head with a rifle ball and died shortly after. A number of the regiment were already in the ditch when my party got there and the rest were not long in coming. Orders then came from General Elliott to hold and fight from the ditch and to fire only when the enemy showed themselves or attempted to cross the hill towards Petersburg. Several attempts were now made by the enemy to cross the hill toward Petersburg, but the fire of our men was so severe that they quickly returned to the Crater. Wright's battery of Coit's battalion was stationed on a hill about three hundred yards to our left and they opened on the enemy at the first onset and continued to sweep the hill in front of the Crater with grape and canister during the whole fight, thus impeding the progress of the enemy's reinforcements. If the battery on our right had done half so well there would not have been so many Federals in the Crater, but the lieutenant in command (I think his name was Otey) with his whole detachment acted as cowards and left their guns without firing them as soon as the mine was sprung. General Elliott brought the 26th Regiment from the left of the brigade and made a direct charge, but Elliott was shot down and the regiment, after tremendous loss, was driven back. Colonel Smith then attempted to lead his regiment to charge, but Smith was wounded and his brave men again driven back. At this time there were eleven stands of colors on the banks of the Crater.

Captain Beaty reported the swift and terrible loss of men in this battle:

General Elliott now, about six o'clock, with Colonel Smith, followed by his regiment, the Twenty-sixth South Carolina, marched up the line of breastworks under a very severe enfilading fire from the enemy, to within fifty or seventy-five yards of the Crater. They filed the regiment out of the entrenchments to the rear into the open field in full and complete exposure to the masses of the enemy in the portion of our lines captured by them, as well as those in their own lines who redoubled their fire on us, until it was a terrific hailstorm of death. So severe and destructive was this fire that we did not wait for the entire regiment followed by the Seventeenth, which was ordered to form with us for the purpose of driving the enemy from our lines. So fast were our men being killed that as soon as five of nine companies were formed we charged upon them. It was indeed a forlorn hope. Our men were literally mowed down, losing large numbers of officers and men. General Elliott was among the first to fall, within thirty yards of the Crater, and was carried from the field badly wounded.[7] In this charge the few of us making it pushed clear up to the Crater and one or two going inside were made prisoners. Company K being on the left of the line in this charge struck a little to the left of the Crater where it joined on our trenches. After our line had been repulsed with terrible slaughter, we found ourselves in the traverses, close up to the Crater, between our men and the enemy. Though but few of us were left, we held our position, loading and firing into the masses of the enemy in our immediate front by elevating our guns over our heads, as there was a constant stream of death-dealing missiles passing over our heads from front and rear of us, from friend and foe.

The command of the brigade now devolved upon Colonel McMaster, of the Seventeenth Regiment, who counted fourteen to sixteen of the enemy's regimental flags in our front.[8] Seeing the rashness and hopelessness of the efforts to dislodge such a large number of the enemy in our lines, he countermanded the order. The enemy was so well protected from our fire by the position which they occupied in our breastwork in the rear of the Crater and the Crater itself, while our men were so few and exposed from head to heels. Fearing that the enemy massed so heavily in our works would rush down the hill and get in the rear of our lines and push on across the fields to the City of Petersburg, only about a mile away, he ordered Colonel Smith to take all of his regiment that he could gather, immediately go down the ditch to where General Elliott's headquarters were, go up the ravine extending somewhat parallel with and in the rear of our lines, form in line, and resist every

Fitz William McMaster
(*War Talks of Confederate Veterans*, 1892)

effort of the enemy to advance. He believed that the fate of Petersburg, as well perhaps as the entire line of defense, depended upon filling up the gap in the rear of the Crater and holding he enemy in check in this direction.

In 1895 Colonel McMaster gave this account of his actions:

Colonels Benbow of the Twenty-third and Wallace of the Eighteenth were absent on sick furloughs. Adjutant A. L. Evans [Nathan George Evans' brother, who had challenged McMaster to a duel six months earlier] and Captain James Lowndes of General Elliott's staff promptly reported for duty and served faithfully throughout the day.

Believing that the only way that the enemy could reach Petersburg was by dashing to the ravine, thence taking the covered way to Cemetery Hill, which they could do without the loss of a man, I immediately ordered Colonel Smith with his regiment, the Twenty-sixth, and Captain Crawford with the three largest companies of the Seventeenth, to hurry down to the ravine and cover the gap caused by the crater, and to lie down and wait for the attack of the enemy in that direction. This order they faithfully executed. I sent couriers to General Johnson for reinforcements and sent Phillips, a faithful soldier of Company I, to the right of the crater to inform the officer there that General Elliott was shot and I was in command, and to report their condition as soon as possible.

About this time the Federals began to advance from the plateau adjoining the crater. They first attacked Company A, which had been so near to the mine that some of the men were covered with earth. Notwithstanding this, the feeble squad resisted and Private Hoke, refusing to surrender "to a damned Yankee," knocked down four of his antagonists with the butt of his musket and was bayoneted. They next attacked Company D, which was surrendered by its lieutenant, and 27 men were captured. These men were sent to Elmira Prison—14 died of scurvy and two died soon after their release.

Captain Beaty described the battle in the aftermath of the explosion:

The Twenty-sixth Regiment being very much reduced by the heavy loss sustained in the charge just made with the other fighting of the morning, three companies of the Seventeenth Regiment were detached to go with it, and altogether they numbered not over three to four hundred men. The remainder of the Seventeenth, with the remaining few of the Eighteenth, were spread out along the line of our breastworks until they struck Ransom's North Carolina Brigade on the left, and fought the enemy from behind the traverses. So heavy and close was the fighting here that about all of the men of the two companies on the right were killed, wounded or captured. Though so few, they held their lines until driven by the charge of a negro brigade, about 8 o'clock, who thus captured about 100 yards of our lines. From the time the firing began ten or fifteen minutes after the explosion, until the final recapture of our line, the infantry fire north or left of the Crater was unceasing, and did great execution. The fighting on the right or south of the Crater, I can give only a small account of, as we were cut off therefrom.

The enemy threw into our lines three white divisions, "Ledlie's," "Potter's" and "Wilcox's," of the Ninth Corps, excepting about four regiments, making 6,000 men. To this add 4,400 colored troops and we have 10,400 men, and this without counting a brigade of Turner's Division of the Eighteenth Corps, which took possession of about 100 yards of our line north of the Crater. One report of the enemy put the number at 10,000 to 12,000 men that crossed over into our lines. The Ninth and Eighteenth Corps made the charge, the Fifth in reserve. They filled our line to overflowing for about 100 yards on each side of the Crater. They became so packed therein that it was difficult to move about, and made repeated efforts to move out, form line of battle in rear of our lines they had captured, and charge through to Cemetery Hill and the city. The first effort was broken up by our men firing into their backs from our line of breastworks immediately adjoining the Crater, before the Twenty-sixth and part of the Seventeenth were ordered to close and hold the vacant gap in rear of the Crater. While we occupied the latter position in the ravine to the rear, we were continually firing into the enemy crowded into our line and receiving their fire in addition to that of many of their batteries of artillery being drawn upon us by the fire of our mortars and cannon near and in line with us. This was killing and wounding our men continually. Their officers repeatedly and continuously endeavored to have their men leave the Crater, where they were so packed and being slaughtered so terribly, and move out in accordance with original plan of attack, but whenever they began to do so the men of the Twenty-sixth and Seventeenth Regiments rising up from the depression or ravine where they lay would pour in their fire so rapidly with that of our artillery that they would waver, break and rush back to cover in the line of captured breastworks and Crater. There was a line of breastworks running immediately in the rear of the salient occupied by Pegram's Battery. This rear line was not completely destroyed by the explosion and it was back at this rear line, in the open field, they would attempt to form their lines of battle. Every effort made by the enemy thus to advance was foiled and broken up. The balance of our South Carolina Brigade, aided by Ransom's on the left and Wise's on the right, hemmed them in to within about 100 yards on each side of the Crater, while our cannon and mortar hurled and rained shot, shell and canister upon this seething mass of humanity. Their commanding officers continuing to rush their men into the Crater, with the intention to form and charge to the right and left and double up our line, hold as far as captured, and then with the balance of the 65,000 men massed for the occasion, push on through, take and hold Cemetery Hill, break up our line of defense, and capture the city. For four hours, from about 5 A.M. until about 9 o'clock, we fought them foot by foot, from the line of our breastworks and the ravine in rear of the Crater, succeeding in confining them to and adjoining the breach in our line made by the springing of the mine. Then Mahone came to our assistance. It must have been only a question of time how long the artillery and the few men we had, and they becoming more and more reduced by death and wounds, could have kept up the unequal contest. It must have eventually resulted in the enemy finally rushing over us.

The mine exploded at 4:44 A.M. Beaty states above, and most authorities now agree, that Mahone's troops arrived and attacked at about 9 A.M. Elliott's Brigade and its supporting artillery, greatly outnumbered by the attacking Federal forces, held the Confederate line for at least four hours after the explosion of the mine.

Captain Floyd described the confusion among the Federal forces:

The Federals now charged from our front to the left of the Crater and in the position we occupied an enfilading fire was opened upon us by a division of drunken negroes and we were pushed back to another ditch 100 feet to the rear, but we made a stand here, and though the negroes were drunk and charged as though they were going to eat us up alive, yelling "no quarters, remember Fort Pillow,"[9] we gave them such a volley they were glad to seek shelter in the Crater. There were 11,000 Federals now in the Crater without orders, their officers having lost control of them when they jumped into the Crater. All organization had been lost and they were helpless. One more attempt was made to cross the hill towards Petersburg, this time by about 500 negroes led by a white officer, but before they got hardly out of the Crater the officer was killed and the negroes threw down their arms, holding up their hands as a sign of surrender, dashed across the hill towards Petersburg.

General Mahone appeared in the ravine between the Crater and Petersburg at 11 o'clock [disputed, probably around 9 A.M.] with his two brigades, deployed and charged the Crater at once. So far as our side of the Crater (the left) was concerned he had a "walkover." He ran his men up to the bank with scarcely any resistance, but he had considerable fighting on the right, though in a short time the enemy were all inside the Crater. A few small mortars were brought up and shells were hurled from them into that mass of humanity inside the Crater, when they surrendered. This was a sad day for Company I. Sergeant. T. W. Berry, Privates J. J. Timmons, William Hill and James Wadsworth were killed and I, Sergeant Brown and twenty-two men were wounded. Twelve more were captured by the enemy, leaving only two men for duty in the company: W. D. Kirven, the regimental color bearer, and W. W. Pierce, one of the color guards. There was only one commissioned officer with our company, Lieutenant Jordan, since Moore and Hunter had been wounded in previous battles. When the mine was sprung Captain [Jefferies] was in command of the regiment. He was wounded, and Captain Ferguson next in command was wounded. Lieutenant Johnson then was in command until the battle ended.

Although Captain Floyd and others make a good case for the fighting abilities of the brigade, it is clear that by mid-morning the Confederate line was weakening and required reinforcement. Earlier, at about six o'clock when

he was informed of the battle, Lee had bypassed his lethargic division commander, Major General Bushrod Rust Johnson, and had ordered Brigadier General William Mahone to send two brigades from Anderson's Division, which Mahone was commanding about two miles away.[10]

Captain Beaty's account noted the arrival of Mahone's troops:

A little before 9 o'clock, while we were holding the enemy in check, confining him to as small portion of our lines as possible and doing all in our power to make it as hot for him as we could, General Mahone came to our assistance with his men. "Arriving on the ground," General Mahone says, "I saw the Confederate works filled to overflowing with Federal troops, and counting eleven regimental flags, estimated the federal force in possession as at least 3,000 men. The situation was an extremely grave one." One of his men says, "As we approached the ravine from which the charge was made I saw the works north of the Crater filled with thousands of the enemy. I counted twenty-one flags flying from the Crater and these works."

The first that arrived were Mahone's old brigade of Virginians. These came up out of the covered way, cautiously approaching the ravine where we lay, forming on the right of the Twenty-sixth, and three companies of the Seventeenth South Carolina Regiment. At the openings where the enemy could see them, they were ordered to run quickly, one at a time, to conceal their approach and lessen the danger of being shot. Soon the line of battle was formed.

General Mahone ordered the men to fix bayonets and lay down, and when we charged to oblique sharply to the right, so as to strike well up the line and into the Crater, and to reserve our fire until we reached the ditch, then give them one volley and use the bayonets. At this point, while waiting for the Georgia Brigade to get in position on the right, one of Mahone's men says, "The battle flags seemed as thick as corn stalks in a row and the whole face of the earth, including the ditch which our men formerly occupied, fairly teemed with the enemy." Wright's Georgia Brigade had not got into position when many of the enemy began jumping in line. Suddenly we heard a shout, as if the enemy was about to charge us. We could delay no longer. It was life or death with us. "Charge!" rang out along the line, which we did with a yell, with bayonets fixed, arms at a trail, reserving our fire. It was a glorious sight to see that line of veterans with their tattered uniforms, as it swept across the open field, in the face of a tremendous fire, that was thinning its ranks at every step and every man appreciating the vital importance of getting to the works and closing with the enemy as quickly as possible. The charge was possibly as splendid as any of which history had made record. The line of battle beginning on the left consisted of the Sixty-first, Forty-ninth and Twenty-fifth North Carolina Regiments; the Twenty-sixth and part of the Seventeenth South Carolina Regiments, all under Colonel Smith; the Sixth,

Twelfth, Sixteenth, Forty-first, and Sixty-first Virginia Regiments[11] (Mahone's old brigade), and one and a half regiments of the Georgia Brigade. We captured the line equal to our front—three-fourths of the line around the rear of Crater and all of that part of entrenchments on the left of it occupied by the enemy. Many of them, white and black, abandoning the breach, fled to their lines under a terrific flank fire from our infantry and artillery. But the works were not ours; the Crater itself was held by a large number of the enemy, not yet ready to surrender; also some fifty yards of our works south or right of it was in their possession. We were also suffering very severely from an enfilading fire poured from the Crater that projected far to the rear of our line, as well as from their main line of battle in their works. To drive out these in our lines, at 10 o'clock, about an hour after the first charge, Wright's Brigade, of Georgia, was ordered forward from the ravine from which the previous charge was made.

But such was the severity of the fire from the enemy they were forced to oblique to the left and take shelter, partly in the works previously captured by us. When this charge was about to be made, our men were all ordered to fire on the enemy as rapidly as possible to keep their heads down, which was obeyed with a will, as there were many captured guns lying around which were used in addition to our own. About 11 o'clock the Georgia brigade was called to make another attempt to carry the works about the Crater and south of it, but this, like the first, was unsuccessful. It was agreed between General Bushrod Johnson and General Mahone that a combined assault should be made at 1 o'clock, Johnson from the south and Mahone from the north, from the rear in the Crater. In meantime the fight was continued with terrible effect on both sides, and fears were entertained that the enemy might from a reinforced effort regain the breach in our line.

Colonel J. C. Haskell, always hunting a place where he could strike the enemy with telling effect, brought up two mortars to a ditch within a few yards of the Crater, and was quickly pitching shell after shell over among the crowded masses of the enemy in this terrible pit. While this deadly work of the mortars was going on our sharpshooters sent back to the pit dead or wounded every man who exposed himself or attempted to get away back to their lines. Bayoneted muskets of the dead were also hurled like javelins into the pit upon the enemy, who would send them back upon us. The hour of 1 o'clock having arrived, the combined movement before mentioned was made and our line restored. The enemy in the pit, finding they could not escape, surrendered.[12]

Mahone's final charge was made after Wilcox's Alabama Brigade under Colonel John C. C. Saunders arrived around 1 P.M. Even with the addition of

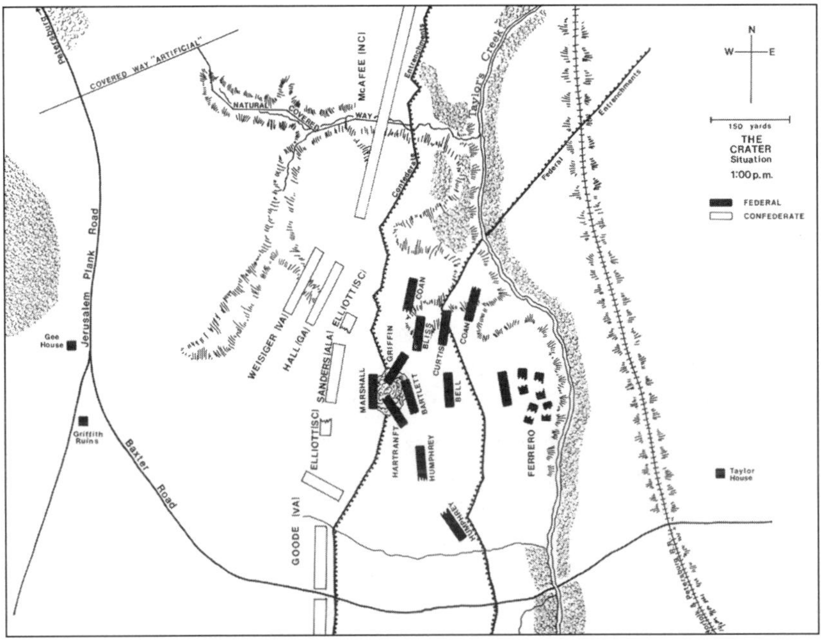

Situation at 1:00 P.M. on July 30, 1864
(*The Battle of the Crater "The Horrid Pit,"* 1989)

these five regiments, Mahone's attackers were outnumbered by perhaps two-to-one. However, the Federal soldiers in the crater were by now completely demoralized, and after an hour of hand-to-hand fighting the Confederate troops re-established their line along the far side of the crater. As company F of the Ninth Alabama Regiment went into this charge, its captain gained an additional soldier:[13]

"Captain, can I go into this charge with you?"

"Yes, who are you?"

"I am [Smith Lipscomb], and I belong to [the Eighteenth] South Carolina Regiment. [I] was blown up in that fort and I want to get even with them. Please take my name, and if I get killed inform my officers of it."

"I have no time for writing. How high did they blow you?"

"I don't know, but as I was going up I met the company commissary officer coming down, and he said: 'I will try to have breakfast ready by the time you get down.'"

Captain Beaty continued:

Saturday night 55 negroes and 178 whites of the enemy were buried in the Crater. Sunday a flag of truce was sent in with a request to bury the dead. On

Monday morning from 5 to 9 o'clock they buried 700 of their men who had been killed on the hill between their line and ours. Only twelve of our men were found here, probably thrown there by the explosion.

Captain Edwards of Company A of the Seventeenth Regiment later summarized and commended the efforts of the brigade:

On the morning of the 30th of July, 1864, no command ever passed through such an ordeal, and sustained itself with more gallantry and honor than fell to the lot of Elliott's Brigade on that awful and bloody day. General Elliott was wounded immediately after the explosion of the Crater. Colonel F. W. McMaster, being the senior field officer present, commanded the brigade during the battle, and Lieutenant Colonel John R. Culp commanded the Seventeenth Regiment. I don't care what may be said of Mahone and the brave troops under his command, and they deserve great praise for valor, not only on this day, but on many other occasions, but to Elliott's South Carolina Brigade belongs the glory of the Battle of the Crater and the maintenance of the integrity of Lee's line of battle around the city of Petersburg. If Elliott's Brigade had been driven from its position that day the integrity of our line of battle would have gone, and with the weight of Grant's army against us our whole line would have been untenable. The hill upon which the Battle of the Crater was fought was the key of our whole line of defenses. Elliott's Brigade held the line from early morning until the turn of the day and confined the enemy to the crest of the hill. Wherever the attempt was made by the Federals to form in line for an advance movement, Elliott's rifles and grape and canister from Wright's Battery would mow them down like wheat in a harvest field.

When Mahone came and reinforced Elliott's shattered brigade, the charge that recaptured our works was the smallest part of the day's work. The dead and wounded in Elliott's Brigade tells the tale more eloquently than words can speak or pen write. In Company A of the Seventeenth Regiment, four men were killed on the field, and the casualties during the day were at least fifty per cent of those present for duty. Our other nine companies fared no better. No command during the Confederate war or any other war of modern times ever opposed successfully greater odds or fought with more distinguished gallantry than did Elliott's Brigade at the Battle of the Crater.

Private Andrews of the Twenty-third Regiment noted the thin line between life and death:

We carried away 500 prisoners (black and white) together with a few Indians from the West. And oh! what a spectacle to behold! in this Crater, 30 or more feet deep and more than 100 feet in length. More than one of the

Twenty-second Regiment, South Carolina Volunteers, was taken out alive, where he had been buried under the debris all day. In each case a board of timber of some kind had kept the pressure of dirt from him and a little air had spared him from being buried alive.

Captain Beaty described one happy survivor of the Crater:

There was one very happy man on the field that afternoon. His clothes were saturated with red mud made of red dirt and sweat. He was bareheaded and his hair was matted with the same red mud, and his face was covered with it, except here and there were streaks washed clean by perspiration. But his eyes showed happiness to their very bottom. He was one of Elliott's Brigade, and he had been buried close by the side of the Crater, had been stunned by the concussion and when he came to himself he had been buried, but how or when he knew not. He could move a little, and he saw near him a crack through which daylight came. He had finally worked his way out with his hands and nails. He had emerged from what he feared would be his grave and was happy.[14]

Private Andrews gave a grim account of the scene at the Crater during the weeks after the battle:

Then the burying of 500 human beings in this Crater and around it. For months after this the Twenty-third Regiment was on duty at this point, and "oh! what a stench!" as the partially covered bodies would open the earth for the gas to escape. The hills were whitened with lime to enable us to remain on duty there. The two battery guns were blown about 90 feet from their position near the enemy's lines. A 60-day furlough was offered to any one to place a rope around them, so that they could be pulled back and gotten in our possession, but no one was found daring enough to try it. The orderly saw in the Crater two men (one a Confederate, the other a negro). They were on their knees, with their guns clenched in their hands, their bayonets thrust through their bodies (the Confederate's through the negro and the negro's through the Confederate), their backs against a clay wall, both stiff in death. There was blood in the Crater. Several Confederates dug into spots of blood to find how deeply it had soaked. One spot showed blood at five inches depth.

For weeks we suffered much. The Yankees refused, on application, to grant a flag of truce to remove the dead and wounded. We removed ours at night. The next day we made negro prisoners drag the bodies of their dead and throw them into holes dug for their reception, filling many of them to within two or three inches of the surface and spreading a little earth over them. These pest-holes and pools of blood, coupled with the beaming, scorching rays of an August sun, filled the whole atmosphere with a foul vapor, which we inhaled at every breath. Green flies without number buzzed audibly all

The Confederate line as reconstructed at the Crater
(*Battles and Leaders of the Civil War*, vol. 4)

around us and added to the hideousness of the scene. Every attempt to eat or even open one's mouth caused nausea. This was not confined to one or two days, but for weeks it was the same daily endurance. Our duties were increased, for our ranks had been thinned and no recruits came in to fill the vacant places. None, save those who were in or near the Crater in this trying time, can have any adequate conception of what we endured. Who would have thought that mortal man could stand up in so trying a position.

Colonel McMaster reported the losses suffered by the brigade:

According to an estimate made by Adjutant Fant, Elliott's Brigade lost 667 men as follows: Seventeenth Regiment, 135; Eighteenth Regiment, 205; Twenty-second Regiment, 216; Twenty-third Regiment, 49; Twenty-sixth Regiment, 72—nearly one-half of the Confederates' loss that day. General Grant estimates his loss at 5,000; the loss of the Confederates was 1500, I think.

The Federals that crossed our breastworks to attack our lines were about 18,000, with a reserve of 30,000 more. The Confederates, including Mahone's, [Wilcox's], Wright's, Elliott's, and parts of Ransom's and Wise's brigades, amounted to about 3,300 with no reserve. The enemy used 81 of their 144 cannon and shot 3,833 rounds and 75 tons of iron. The Confederates used about 25 cannon and shot at a guess, about 1600 rounds.

One account placed the Federal losses at about 504 killed, 1,881 wounded, and 1,413 missing, for a total of 3,798 out of 16,772 men engaged.[15] Confederate

losses were reported as 361 killed, 727 wounded, and 403 missing, for a total of 1,612 out of 9,430 men engaged. In terms of the amount of lead flying through the air in a small place and in a short period of time, this battle may take the prize. Curiosities found later on the battlefield include two bullets which met point-to-point, flattening into a small lead pancake, and a rifle whose barrel exploded when the bullet fired from it met an incoming bullet halfway down the barrel.[16] These items are now in the museum at the Petersburg National Battlefield Park. Captain Beaty also reported that "one battle flag, by actual count, was found to have had seventy-five shots pass through it, while nine had struck the staff."

On September 20, 1864, William Henry Wallace of Yorkville was placed in temporary command of Elliott's Brigade. Even though orders converting Wallace's appointment to a permanent one cannot be found, the brigade was generally referred to as "Wallace's Brigade" for the remainder of the war.

Captain Edwards saw Wallace's promotion as a slight to McMaster:

> General Elliott and Colonel Smith both received severe wounds at the Crater which disabled them for the rest of the war. Colonel W. H. Wallace, of the Eighteenth South Carolina Volunteers, was promoted to Brigadier General and put in temporary command of the brigade. Many officers of the brigade never did understand it, and many of us thought, and will always think, that Colonel McMaster ought to have had the promotion. He had done more service and was the senior officer.[17] We thought it was perhaps because of the trouble between Colonel McMaster and N. G. Evans. And then again, Colonel Wallace's father had been a Congressman, and that may have given him a pull. Whatever was the influence, the fact remains that Wallace got the promotion. He was a brave man and a high-toned gentleman, and was highly respected by all the officers and men of the brigade.[18]

SIDES AND EDGE OF TWO BULLETS THAT MET POINT TO POINT AT THE CRATER—THE SIDES FROM PHOTOGRAPHS OF THE ORIGINAL IN MAJOR GRIFFITH'S MUSEUM AT THE CRATER.

Battlefield relics
(*Battles and Leaders of the Civil War*, vol. 4.)

William H. Wallace
(courtesy of Library of Congress)

For at least thirty years after the war ended, the Virginians who survived told how they had rescued the South Carolinians from defeat by charging the enemy at 8:45 A.M. A leading advocate of this theory was George S. Bernard of Petersburg, who had served in Mahone's Brigade. He and Colonel McMaster exchanged a number of letters about the details of this battle; however, they never came to agreement on the time of Mahone's initial charge. Colonel McMaster claimed in 1882 that Mahone's attack took place after ten o'clock,[19] and Federal brigadier general Humphreys' 1883 book, *The Virginia Campaign of '64 and '65*, supported this view. In 1892 Bernard edited a book, *War Talks of Confederate Veterans*, and included in it a lengthy section that he had written about the Battle of the Crater. In 1898, Captain John Floyd of Darlington, having heard about all that he wanted to hear from the Virginians and now hearing a similar story from a South Carolinian, wrote a letter to the editor of *The State* newspaper of Columbia, South Carolina:[20]

To the Editor of *The State:*

I have often noticed that whenever there is a reunion of the Virginia survivors of the War Between the States the orators invariably claim the victory at the Crater in front of Petersburg, Va., on the 30th day of July, 1864, for General Mahone and the Virginians.

We are not surprised at that, in fact there has always been a contention between Elliott's men and Mahone's soldiers as to which of two the commands did the most fighting on that day. But when a prominent South Carolinian, before a South Carolina audience, not only follows in the same line, but says that Elliott's men were so demoralized that they were replaced in the lines by fresh troops brought up from the flanks by General Lee, I think that it is time that the survivors of the old brigade come forward and tell what they know about that battle. It is evident that the people of our own State do not understand how that battle was fought, who conducted it, what troops were engaged, or how it was possible for Elliott's Brigade to hold the lines at the Crater against such fearful odds. The battle of the Crater was one of the most important battles of the war and its result had more effect upon the minds of the Northern people than any other battle of the war. On the next day the propriety of offering terms of peace to the South was freely discussed in the Northern cities. Gold went up to 2.90, the highest point it ever reached. But the battle of Altoona[21] was fought and lost by our Western army a few days afterwards, and the prospects of peace went down with their defeat. How can our people understand how Elliott's Brigade held eighty thousand troops with eighty pieces of artillery, concentrated at that point by General Grant, no doubt for the purpose of breaking through our lines at the Crater and then swinging his tremendous army right and left and thus destroy our army lines until it is told by the old survivors who were there?

The mine was sprung on the 30th day of July, 1864, at 6 o'clock in the morning. Four hundred and fifty-seven of Elliott's Brigade were killed or wounded by the blow-up. Elliott's men held the lines, fighting the enemy without assistance except from the artillery, until General Mahone arrived with his two brigades five hours after the mine was sprung. When General Mahone arrived he deployed his troops and charged the Crater, it being packed with 11,000 Federal troops that had been driven there by Elliott's Brigade and the artillery under Colonel Haskell and Major Coit.

Major Coit's guns were on the next hill to the left of the Crater, and had swept the hill in front of the mine with grape and canister from the time the mine was sprung to the close of the battle. Colonel Haskell was posted just in rear of our position near the Crater and did heroic work with his mortars and other guns. General Mahone ran his men up under the very banks of the Crater. Small mortars were brought up and bursting shells were hurled into that huddled up mass of humanity inside the Crater, the white flag was hoisted in due time and they surrendered.

It had been learned since the war that when General Grant arrived at the headquarters of General Meade at 10 o'clock, on finding that our lines still held out, he ordered his troops to retire from our lines, saying to General Meade, that if he (Meade) could not break through our lines when the mine was first sprung he could not expect to do so four hours afterward. It may be asked why the Federals had not retired from the Crater before General Mahone made his charge? They could not leave without being exposed to almost certain death. When the mine was sprung the enemy had been brought up very near our lines, in fact they were so close that some of them were killed and some wounded by the explosion. They rushed into our lines at once, expecting that the Confederates would be so demoralized that they would desert their works and that they, the Federals, would have a "walkover," but they were attacked at once by the 22nd S.C.V. on the right and the 18th S.C.V. on the left so vigorously that they were astonished and jumped into the Crater to protect themselves from the bullets of these regiments. More troops were now brought up from the Federal lines and broad lanes were cut through their columns by Coit's Battery on the left as they advanced, and also by a two-gun battery on the first hill to the right of the Crater. This battery had been commanded at first by a Lieutenant Otey, but when the mine was sprung Otey, with his whole detachment, ran and left their guns without firing them, but they were moved and fought later by men from General Wise's Brigade. When the reinforcements of the enemy got in reach of Elliot's men they poured volley after volley into their ranks and they then jumped into the Crater. It continued much the same, as the reinforcements of the enemy were brought up they would be subject to the same dangers and would invariably jump into the Crater until, as I said before, 11,000 Federal troops were in that Crater, two hundred feet long, thirty feet deep and thirty feet wide, with a bank surrounding them fifteen feet high. All organization was obliterated, their officers had lost control of them and they were as helpless as so many cattle. In their position they could not retire. They were hemmed in on three sides by Elliott's men and Haskell's batteries and could not advance, while if they attempted to retire they would be mowed down like wheat before the scythe by the batteries on the right and left. There was nothing left for them to do but to surrender.

I had the honor of being the commander of a company in the 18th S.C.V. and was officer of the day of my regiment on the 30th of July, 1864. The right of my regiment rested on the battery (Pegram's) that was blown up, and the whole right wing was enveloped, covered up with timbers, earth and debris. Those of us who were not struck by flying timbers, emerged from the debris and attacked the enemy at once. Being officer of the day of my regiment I deemed it my duty to assume the direction of affairs in my immediate neighborhood and if possible grasp the key to the situation before it was too late. The air was so filled with smoke and dust that we could not see ten feet away, but I was satisfied that the enemy were upon us. I ordered the men to commence firing over the breastworks. I then, with the assistance of Adjutant Sims and Lieutenant Anderson, gathered as many men as could be spared from the left of the regiment and with them occupied a line of works running around the rear of the battery, now the Crater. The dust and smoke were still dense, in fact we were groping in the dark. Suddenly we came in contact with about two hundred of the enemy. They ordered us to surrender; in reply we gave them the contents of our rifles. They returned the fire and now that the guns were all empty a hand to hand contest ensued. Swords, bayonets and the butts of rifles were freely used. This lasted only for a few moments, however, for a shell thrown from our mortar battery in our rear fell among us, and bursting with a crash it hurled Confederates and Federals right and left, killing and wounding several and completely separating the contesting parties. The Federals now dashed over into the Crater where they could fight from cover while we were unprotected. We fell back to a cross ditch that had been laid off and prepared by our engineers to fight from in case of disaster. The fire from the Crater was very severe and we retired walking backwards, fighting as we fell back, the officers using their revolvers, while the men fought with their rifles. Adjutant Sims was mortally wounded and Lieutenant Anderson and half the men with us were killed before we reached the ditch. The balance of our regiment had taken position in this ditch before we arrived under Captain Bridges. We now received orders from General Elliott through Adjutant A. L. Evans to hold and fight from the cross ditch and to fire only when the enemy showed themselves. Then General Elliott drew out the 26th S.C.V. from the left of the brigade and made a direct charge on the enemy in the Crater, but Elliott was shot down and his men driven back. Colonel Smith made another attempt to charge the Crater with the 26th S.C.V., but Smith was wounded and his brave men again driven back. The enemy then hurled Ferrero's Division of drunken negroes against our left and they did succeed in driving back our line near the Crater, so that the line or ditch that we occupied was enfiladed by their fire and we were compelled to fall back to another cross ditch 100 feet to the rear. Seeing us fall back the negroes charged us, yelling "no quarters, remember Fort Pillow." We gave them our "broadside" and they, too, dashed into the Crater for protection. Several attempts were now made by the enemy to cross the hill towards Petersburg, but the fierce firing of Elliott's men from the right and left and from the rear—for Colonel McMaster, who was now in command of the

John Floyd
(*Men of the Time*, 1902)

brigade, had placed his regiment, the 17th S.C.V., and also the 26th S.C.V. in a rear line between Petersburg and the Crater, about 100 yards in rear of the Crater, prepared for just such an emergency by our engineers—drove them back into the Crater, dripping with blood. No other attempt was made by the Federals to leave the Crater. General Mahone appeared in the ravine between Petersburg and the Crater at 11 o'clock.

Please publish this and oblige, Respectfully,
John Floyd, Captain 18th S.C.V., late C.S.A.

Colonel McMaster may have had the last and best word in this dispute in 1899:[22]

I dislike to differ with Mr. Bernard, who has been so courteous to me, and with my friend, Colonel Venable, for we literally carried muskets side by side as privates in dear old Captain Casson's company, the Governor's Guards, in Colonel Kershaw's Regiment, at the first Battle of Manassas . . . But I can't help thinking of these gentlemen as being like all Virginians, which is illustrated by the remark of a great Massachusetts man, old John Adams, who in answering some opponent, said: "Virginians are all fine fellows. The only objection I have to you is, in Virginia every goose is a swan."

12

The Siege of Petersburg

> They commenced begging for quarter and inquiring for Masons and Odd Fellows.
>
> John Floyd

After the Battle of the Crater, Confederate troops occupied the trenches around Petersburg for another eight months. There were at least nine major battles around Petersburg before winter and another four in February and March.[1] Although Grant's continued assaults were not successful in capturing Petersburg, they were successful in keeping Lee's Army of Northern Virginia in the vicinity of Petersburg and Richmond.[2] Meanwhile, other Federal forces were winning battles at Mobile Bay, Atlanta, Cedar Creek, Nashville, Savannah, Charleston, and Wilmington, and Sherman's troops would march through Georgia and the Carolinas.

Captain Floyd described a small victory over the Federals:

Our division (Johnson's) remained in the trenches in front of Petersburg during the winter of 1864 and up to the first of April, 1865. Our brigade held the lines at and near the Crater and it does seem that a worse place could not be imagined. The thunder of artillery, the rattle of musketry, the crash of bursting shell, the groans of the wounded and dying, were scenes by day, lightning flashes of thousands of small arms, the lurid glare of bursting shell and exploding artillery, the fierce, defiant yells of contending men, the prayers of the wounded and dying made up the dreadful scenes by night, and this continued for nine long months.

On the 1st of Oct., 1864, a reserve picket was organized in the trenches at Petersburg, Va. The duty of the reserve picket was to be in readiness at any moment during the night to charge and recapture any part of the picket line that might be taken by the enemy in front of the division. This was done for the reason that the enemy had been in the habit of capturing portions of the picket line wherever they could find a weak place or new troops on the line. This was very annoying to the Generals, as it was always necessary to make a detail from the different brigades, as we had no reserves—every man being in the line. Two hundred men were organized for this reserve picket and were placed under my command. This body of men were detailed from the different brigades of the division and reported to me at my tent in the trenches every evening at sunset and would remain under arms until sunrise next morning.

On the fourth night after the organization of the reserve picket, about 12 o'clock, the enemy charged and captured the picket line of a Florida brigade on our right, driving the Floridians out. I was notified at once by a courier and moved with my charging party up the line to the scene of the disaster, deploying my men in a wheat field in front of the Florida brigade, so as to cover the length of the line now in possession of the enemy. I directed my men to move forward stealthily so as not to attract the attention of the enemy, who were busy reversing the works, until they arrived in 30 yards of the enemy, then to halt. It was a very dark night and was drizzling rain. The men were then ordered to yell with all their might and then to fall flat on their faces. Every Yankee fired his gun when he heard that yell, but their balls went harmlessly over us. I then ordered my men forward at the run, and before the enemy could reload their guns we were on them. They commenced begging for quarter and inquiring for Masons and Odd Fellows. We captured all of them—200 and sent them to the rear. The Floridians were again put in possession of their lines and we returned to our quarters to find a fierce artillery duel in progress. Though we made a desperate charge, capturing the lines that had been lost by the Florida brigade and two hundred prisoners, we never lost a man or fired a gun.

Private Andrews tended to an injured fellow soldier:

Albertus S. White was wounded by a fragment of mortar shell while lying down in the trenches reading a home letter on October 12, 1864. The piece of shell broke his left jaw-bone, severed two arteries on that side of his face, tore out several teeth and lodged there. He was laid out as dead. Providentially the blood clotted and prevented his bleeding to death. In about two hours' time he was carried to our regimental infirmary. Drs. Murray and Dick examined and dressed his wounds, after tying up the arteries. Afterwards he was sent to the Confederate State Hospital on Washington Street, Petersburg. I, having chills and fever, was allowed to nurse him, and for several weeks my sole duty was the care of my brother. Eggs fed to him cost only ten dollars per dozen. I nursed him six or eight weeks. As soon as he could walk about well he was sent home, and I returned to duty in the trenches.

Colonel McMaster noted in his October 19 letter to his wife that he and Colonel Benbow had been elected to the South Carolina General Assembly. Brigadier Generals Wallace and Elliott (at home recovering from his wound received at the Crater) were also elected.

On October 17 the strength of the brigade was increased by four hundred to about eighteen hundred men when the Holcombe Legion, which had been at Stoney Creek since May, rejoined the brigade.[3] Shortly before midnight on November 5, about 250 men of the legion attacked Fort Morton, which was just south of the Crater. They captured and held about one hundred yards of the Federal line until daybreak but were then driven back with considerable losses, and forty men were taken prisoner.[4] A month later, Captain Floyd led a mission to capture Federal pickets:

On the 20th of Dec., 1864, I received orders to dash over the enemies' lines with my charging party and capture as many prisoners as we could and bring them to the headquarters of General Johnson. The enemy had been moving for several days in our front and as there were no deserters coming over at the time, the General did not know where they were moving to, but judging that they were concentrating their forces at some point for attack, it was necessary that we should have some prisoners to learn from them what point they were concentrating upon. After night had set in, it being dark and cloudy, I and my 200 reserve pickets set out for our picket lines. On arriving at our lines I left 100 men under the charge of two lieutenants with orders that if I was engaged with the enemy to come to my assistance. Then I, with the remaining 100 men, proceeded to the enemies' picket line. The enemies' lines consisted of a line of rifle pits, ten paces apart, with four men in each pit. I, with my men, passed between two of these rifle pits unobserved by the enemy and turned to the right and commenced the process of "relieving the Yankee pickets," as it was afterward called by the men. We captured the men in the first pit without trouble, also the men in the second, third, fourth, fifth, sixth and seventh pit. The fact is the Federals thought that we were their relief guard. When we got near the eighth pit, however, the enemy perceived their mistake. The men fired upon us, jumped out of the pit and ran, yelling "Rebels, Rebels." We then made for our picket line as fast as we could with our prisoners. A tremendous cross fire was opened on us. We reached our lines, however, with the loss of one lieutenant and two privates and three men wounded. I placed the prisoners under the charge of a lieutenant with twenty men, with directions to take them through the "covered way" (a zigzag ditch running from the main line to the picket line for the purpose of relieving pickets) to the main line and to General Johnson's headquarters. The whole line of the enemy had opened on us by this time and there was a continuous blaze of artillery for miles to the right and left. Our artillery had also opened all along the lines and such a thunder of artillery I have never heard before or since. The landscape was lighted up as light as day. I remained on the picket line with the remainder of my men to assist the pickets in repelling the charge, which I knew would be hurled against them, nor were we mistaken in our supposition. In about thirty minutes after we got to the picket lines a tremendous line of battle was hurled against us, but was repulsed. Again they hurled a heavy line against us, but they were again repulsed and the result was that the ground in front of our lines was piled up with dead and wounded. We were not attacked any more after the second repulse, and in two hours time things quieted down except the picket firing. We then returned to our main line and found the brigade preparing to move to the right. We moved one mile and halted. R. G. Parnell was brought from the picket line during the night frozen stiff, but a warm fire with warm blankets and medical aid soon brought him out. Bob was not to "hand in his checks" yet.

The brigade spent a miserable winter in the trenches around Petersburg. The soldiers' letters to their families describe the hardships of life in the trenches.

William C. Leak of Company F of the Seventeenth Regiment wrote to his wife on January 30, 1865:

As to the times here, they are bad enough. We have the coldest weather I ever felt. It rains, sleets, and snows. We have mud in abundance. It is just like living in a hog pen. We are nearly on starvation. I draw one tin cupful of corn meal every day. It is piled in loosely and struck off at that, and a half pound of beef, bone and all. I don't think that we can stand it much longer. I buy one dollar's worth of meal a day, and I don't have nearly enough at that. I have to pay a dollar for a tin cupful and I am always hungry.

Our duties are hard. I have to go on picket every other night. I have to sit up all night in the cold and smoke. I get so hungry that it makes me sick. I stand it much better than I thought I could, but I don't know how long I will hold out at it. The reason they do not feed us any better may be they can not get it. I told you last fall that I thought this Confederacy was on its last legs, and I think that they are nearly worn out . . . I fear the supplies are not in the country to be had.

Captain John C. Evans (no relation to General Evans) of Company A of the Twenty-third Regiment wrote the following in letters to his wife during January and February of 1865:

Our duties are very hard. I am on picket one day, then the Officer of the Day, and rest one. Then commence the same routine. When on duty we are compelled to be up the whole night. We are having a heavy snow. I had to pass up and down our picket line repeatedly in the night when the snow would almost cover one side of me. We are building small pens on the picket line to protect us from the weather. Rain or shine the men have to stand out in the cold en vidette. It makes me sorry to see so much suffering. Yet still we are compelled to require it of them or be arrested our selves . . . Some of our Captains have gone home and some are under arrest. This makes the duties very hard. I was awake all night until 5 this morning. Today I am on picket. I generally sleep about 2 hours. Who would ever have believed that I who loves to sleep so well, could have been brought to this small allowance . . . The North Carolina troops fired on the enemy picket on the right of our pickets last night. I went to the right expecting that the attack might be general, but it stopped after a few rounds. The enemy were taunting the North Carolina troops about the fall of Fort Fisher and this caused the disturbance . . . we poor fellows are in the mud and water. The duties are harder every day. It is very trying to me to have to require the duties of the men. I feel that I would rather be a private myself than to have to do what I have to do . . . The dissatisfaction is spreading fearfully and especially in the North Carolina brigade it looks like a general stampede for home will take place before spring. I don't write this to frighten you but to give you the true state of affairs here. Rations are short. For sometimes days without meat and a very short allowance of bread. A soldier endures a great deal, much more than people are willing to believe. We officers have men over us that we fear as much as the men do us and more so. We hear heavy cannonading on our left today, but this is so common that it attracts no attention . . . We had 2 men to desert last night from the pickets. The 26th Regiment is losing men every night. Short rations and hard duties they say is the cause. If they would only be true a little longer they would see the dawn of brighter days . . . I put a coal grate in our tent today. It makes a very hot fire. Since I have been in command of the Regiment, I have no picket duty to do and consequently some rest . . . We have not been allowed to go to Petersburg for some days, probably on account of the fighting on Hatcher's Creek near us, and partly on account of numerous desertions. The men are going home. Twenty-five went night before last from the Brigade, eight from our Regiment. I don't know how many left last night.[5]

Colonel McMaster mentioned desertions from the other regiments in his February 10 letter to his wife:

The weather remains intensely cold, the ground frozen hard all the time. Night before last 28 men left the 23rd, 18th, and 26th and the reserve pickets were sent for them but without catching them. Last night some left the Holcomb Legion and 8 left the 26th, the last however became alarmed and came back. We now have pickets at night deployed as skirmishers in the rear of the brigade to stop this shameful desertion. I am glad that the 17th still bears the policy of doing her duty. I haven't lost but one man thus far, and he was a worthless Irishman.

It is lamentable that at this time while so many of our soldiers are pledging themselves anew to fight out this bloody continuing war to the death that there are such a number who are ready to bring eternal disgrace on themselves and country by their ignominous conduct. It makes me tremble to contemplate the result of such conduct. We have not a man to lose and still so many scoundrels are deserting us.

By March 12, however, McMaster was forced to admit:

In the last month even the 17th has disgraced itself by deserting on an average one a night.

On January 19 General William T. Sherman ordered his troops then occupying Savannah to begin to march into South Carolina. He initially moved toward Beaufort, with feints toward Augusta and Charleston. By February 1 his objective was clearly Columbia, which his troops occupied on February 17. Sherman's troops then moved on to Winnsboro, Camden, Chesterfield, and Cheraw, leaving South Carolina on about March 6.

Captain John C. Evans' letters reflected his concerns about his family in Cheraw, South Carolina:

I read with great concern of the movements of Sherman. I pray God to avert the storm from you. We must trust him. I, however, think that there is no danger to you until after he has succeeded in establishing a base in South Carolina . . . My dear one, my heart swells with emotion when I think of you and the dear ones. I hope God will protect you from the calamity that has befallen so many in Georgia. Sherman will show very little favor to South Carolina . . . The news from South Carolina makes me uneasy and since the fall of Fort Fisher makes me tremble for our part of the State. However, we can't conjecture the probable route of Sherman . . . Sherman I am afraid will strike where our men are not looking for him . . . My anxiety is very great about my dear ones at home. I hear that the enemy are in Cheraw. I pray that your lives and persons are spared if this is so. I can't express my feelings but can only rely upon our heavenly father for help. We know nothing that is occurring in South Carolina, as the papers don't publish any movements of the enemy, in order to keep information from the enemy . . . There appear to be no letters coming from South Carolina at this time, and from this I judge that mail communication is interrupted in a good many ways. If you do write, you will find the Salisbury route via Wadesboro the surest . . . You can't imagine my anxiety about you at this time. We hear rumors about the occupation of Cheraw by the enemy, and if so, there is no telling how many privations you are enduring . . . My anxiety on your account is very great as we hear that our army is at Cheraw and that there has been a battle fought near you. I can only pray God that you and the dear children may be spared from suffering violence in these troublesome times. It is useless for me to urge you to write as I know you will do all you can to let me hear from you . . . We hear nothing reliable from the South. We wait and hope on . . . I hear that Cheraw has been entirely destroyed. If I could only know that you are all alive and suffered no bodily harm, I would be so glad, but here I am without one word from you since the 24th of February.

The privations for Sherman were not so bad. He noted that Cheraw was found to be full of stores . . . "including eight wagonloads of the finest Madera I ever tasted . . . the wine of some of the old aristocratic families of Charleston, who had sent it up to Cheraw for safety." A large cache of fine carpet from Charleston soon became Yankee tent rugs and saddle blankets.[6]

Colonel McMaster wrote to his wife on February 19:

I feel the deepest solicitude for your welfare and I hope before this time you are on your way to Union to Mrs. Rice whose hospitable roof will shelter you from all privations. I can only now commit you to the grace of our merciful Father. When man's aid fails He can still protect and comfort.

The South Carolina troops here are all in a state of great anxiety and long to be sent home to meet Sherman who seems to be the Jackson of the Yankee army. But General Lee, I suppose, can not spare us from the lines and I see no prospect of our places being supplied.

Yesterday and today are the first springlike weather we have had since winter set in and everything looks favorable for Sherman's advance. Today we have had rumors that Columbia is burnt, but although the Yankees feel peculiar hatred to South Carolina I can't think they will be so inhuman as to lay such a pretty city in ashes and turn out of doors so many women and children.

It is probable that they will burn the public works and great destruction will be done by their contiguity to private residency and that the city in its main street will suffer much, but I can't believe they will burn private residency on the back streets. If they do I believe the curse of Heaven will follow the men and some great calamity will yet befall them.

Captain John A. F. Coleman of the Seventeenth Regiment noted similar concerns in his diary during the period between February 19 and March 13:

Very bad news from home. Sherman has taken Columbia and probably will overrun and lay waste to the whole state . . . Gloomy times for all South Carolinians as Sherman is marching through their state with weak opposition . . . From Wednesday the 24th to the last of the month was passed quietly in the trenches . . . Has rained a great deal. I have had no letters from home for a long while, the communication being cut. I fear the enemy have been at my home and probably burned my house. I never did want to hear from home so bad before . . . A great many of our men have been deserting for the last three or four weeks . . . No news from home. In great suspense. Never wanted to hear so bad before since the war began. Fear that my all is destroyed, my wife and children without food or shelter . . . Preaching in the barn by Mr. Morse. Read Bible all day, and much thinking of home . . . I have not felt disposed to follow my journal daily from the fact of hearing no news from my family and knowing that the enemy were marching through our State. Have no reliable news yet. This is Monday, March 13, 1865. Have had a great deal of rain, until the last few days, when the clouds have disappeared and the winds of March are drying the mud very fast. Since the 7th I have made out a list of all the members that have ever belonged to our Company, both living and dead, in all numbering one hundred and twenty-five (125), while our aggregate at this time is only fifty-six.

At this point, Lee's army of about fifty thousand men faced Grant's army of about 150,000 men. The wet winter had made the roads nearly impassable, and Lee was waiting for them to dry before abandoning Richmond and Petersburg and moving southward to join Johnston in North Carolina. In an attempt to buy some time, Lee sent John B. Gordon's Corps of three divisions, plus a division of cavalry and six brigades (including Wallace's and Ransom's Brigades of R. H. Anderson's Corps) to attack Fort Stedman. This fort was in the Federal line about a mile south of the Appomattox River and about a mile north of the Crater. At a minimum, Lee hoped that this attack would cause Grant to withdraw forces from his left, shortening his line so that Lee could hold him with fewer men.[7]

Private McLaurin saw the end of the Confederate cause at hand:

As the spring opened, General Grant began mobilizing his entire force before Petersburg for the final struggle. The Confederate lines had been stretched until they were almost ready to break of their own weight. To the far-sighted the fall of the Confederacy was imminent and inevitable. Only that hope which "springs eternal in the human breast" was left us. The South must succumb to the overwhelming numbers and powerful material resources of the North, despite its courage and sacrifice.

Captain Edwards readied for the next battle:

On the morning of the 24th of March, 1865, we got marching orders. We were then camped twelve miles from Petersburg, on the right of our lines. After dark we took up the line of march for Petersburg, where we arrived about midnight without ever halting for minute. Many were the surmises as to what the forced march meant, but we were all agreed on one point, that it

The interior of Fort Stedman
(courtesy of Library of Congress)

meant a fight. We rested a short time in the city, and then marched through the city to the valley at the iron bridge, in the vicinity of Hare's Hill on which was built a strong fort, called Fort Stedman, which was occupied by the Yankees. It was named for the Colonel of the Sixth South Carolina Volunteers, because the Sixth Regiment had built the works some two years prior to this date.[8] When we rearranged our lines around Petersburg in the summer of 1864, our engineers left this fort in the Yankee lines.

Captain Floyd gave an account of the Eighteenth Regiment's experiences:

Our line was then faced to the front in single file. We did not know what was up, but supposed that there was heavy work ahead. I said: "Lieutenant, have the file closers to keep the men well up." I mounted the works at once, and taking off my hat, said, "Men, forward." The men mounted the works and dashed across the field towards the fort, 400 yards away. As we neared the fort we saw that some regiments of our brigade were ahead of us and were scaling the walls. When we arrived the fort was in the hands of our troops and the garrison had surrendered. Brisk firing was going on in rear of the fort, however, and it grew terrific. Our troops in front were deployed in the traverses and redoubts near the Fort and in a few minutes a terrific battle was raging. The Colonel ordered the 18th S.C.V. to form in the Fort and I formed Company I, the color company of the regiment, under the most terrible rain of shot and shell that we ever experienced. A piece of shell carried away my overcoat cape and part of my coat sleeve, slightly wounding me in the arm, then killed Captain Goode, who was standing near by, and broke Lieutenant Pressley's leg. Sergeant A. B. Odom, Privates Nat Odom, W. F. Wilkes and nine others of Company I were wounded. The fire was so terrible that General Wallace ordered me to allow my men to shelter themselves and to select their own positions to fire from. The idea of formally forming the regiment was abandoned and the men were allowed to fire from every available point. We remained in the Fort about two hours, when it became necessary for us to retreat, being charged in front by twenty times our number and in danger of being cut off by flanking parties on the right and left. When we left the Fort, six men of Company I were left behind and fell into the hands of the enemy, being too severely wounded to attempt to cross the field between the Fort and our lines. We retreated across the field, under the most terrible cross fire of shot and shell imaginable, to our lines and then returned to our position on the right.

Private George R. Jones recorded the actions of Company I of the Twenty-third Regiment at Fort Stedman:

On reaching our intrenchments we saw some of the troops leaving the fort and making it back to the lines where we were. General Johnson, on seeing this, jumped upon our works and said to General Wallace: "General Wallace, don't you see those men leaving that fort? Have your men take it and hold it." At this order, General Wallace gave the order to the brigade to go forward. Colonel Benbow mounted the works and shouted, "Forward 23rd," and in a few moments the 23rd were out of their works, and at a "right shoulder, shift arms" were on the doublequick for the fort. The brigade advanced under a scattering fire of the Federals. A short distance in front of the fort and works of the Federals, we encountered a line of Chevaux de frise, strongly linked together, and after getting through, and passing this line of Chevaux de frise, a ditch of about twenty feet wide and four or five feet deep was crossed. On reaching the fort, the 23rd, or a part of the 23rd, poured over the works and into the fort. The rest of the 23rd had to stop on the outside of the fort. The fort did not cover much ground, so for all to have crowded into the fort would only have increased our casualties. As soon as the fort was reached, the Confederates on the right and left of the fort pushed forward and captured the Federal line extending right and left of Fort Stedman. The Confederates were now in possession of three quarters of a mile of the

Federal lines. On reaching and possessing this much of the Federal lines, the Confederates found they could proceed no further for they now found themselves confronted by impregnable earth works, works that Grant had been nearly a year in constructing. Just as the 23rd reached the fort, the Federals opened up with a rapid fire upon the fort from their batteries, increasing their fire, it seemed, every minute. The Federals poured a right and left cross on the fort, also raking the fort with a heavy front fire for the fort being in the possession of the Confederates now turned the rear of the fort into its front. The 23rd now found itself under three heavy fires. The Federals were pouring their fire into the whole length of their line that the Confederates were now in possession of, but their heaviest fire was directed against and on Fort Stedman. At the fort were a great many oak trees, as well as I remember, the fort being among these trees. The place had the appearance from the trees and their size of having been a settlement at some time. The Federals did not for one minute cease their fire to the front. The missiles were coming, it seemed, from every direction. The Federals were pouring into, on, and across the fort a storm of mortar, shrapnel, rifle, shell, and grapeshot the whole time, and for four hours and one-half the Confederates stood their ground and held the works nobly, sustaining heavy casualties nearly all the time, and I will venture to say we were under as heavy fire as any troops ever were. In this fort there were several guns and the Confederates turned some one or two of them upon the Federal works and kept up a constant fire upon their works. I will never forget seeing General Wallace with his coat off and helping to man one of these guns, the whole time like a true and brave Confederate soldier, which he was.

At the end of the four hours and a half we discovered that the Federals were massing a heavy body of troops, and numbering, I will venture to say, five to one, to charge and recapture what they had lost. Seeing this, the order was given to the Confederate line to get out of the Federal works and back to the Confederate line as best they could . . . On the Confederates leaving the fort and the Federal works, the Federals commenced using grapeshot, it appeared, altogether. The Confederate and Federal works at this place, I suppose, were about two hundred yards apart and perfectly open. At the order to get out of the fort and back to our lines, the 23rd got out and most of them made for the Confederate works the best way they could, under a heavy fire from the Yanks. The Federals were sweeping the whole of creation, it seemed, with grapeshot . . . The 23rd lost a few who were taken prisoner [including Private Andrews, whose prison story is related in the next chapter] . . . it was reported that Wallace's Brigade had one hundred and one men killed, and the number wounded I do not now remember, though it must have been large.

Captain Edwards reported heavy losses among the Confederates:

We took about twelve hundred prisoners, and got one Brigadier General in his night clothes.[9] It was a complete surprise, and was a cheeky thing for General Lee to do. We were in possession of nearly half a mile of Grant's works, that is, the works nearest our lines. But the forts on our right and left were not taken, and there were soon a hundred cannon massed on the hill in front of us (the rear of Fort Steadman). If ever Sherman's definition of war was realized it was fully met that day. About 8:30 A.M. our regiment was sent out in front and to the left of the fort, ostensibly to support a North Carolina regiment, but without accomplishing anything, except to get the regiment mutilated by shot and shell. My company, being on the right of the regiment, went in front. I did not go more than twenty yards before I was shot down, and I lay there and saw the men of the Seventeenth Regiment falling along down the line. My company had four men killed or mortally wounded and many others wounded, and the other nine companies fared no better. When orders were extended to retire from the Yankee lines, many of our troops got back to our lines, but many, very many, were captured. All of our regiment that fell back straight to our works got into our trenches except those who got shot. All who undertook to come out by way of Fort Steadman were captured. Colonel McMaster and quite a number of others not knowing that the Yankees had captured the fort came that way and were captured.[10] It was impossible to hear or see what was going on. Smoke had covered the earth and sky and the roar of cannon and the rattle of musketry was awful beyond expression by word or pen. It was reported that our division lost twenty-six hundred men in killed, wounded, and captured.[11]

The explanation of the attack on Grant's lines as we heard afterwards was to draw his troops from our right and give Lee time to get Pickett's Division from the north side of the James. General Lee accomplished his purpose, but at a fearful sacrifice, and only prolonged the agony.

Bruce Catton characterized the Battle of Fort Stedman as Lee's "last great counterpunch," after which "Grant would take and keep the initiative." The siege of Petersburg was almost over.

13

The Fighting Ends for Private Andrews

From the 25th of March to the surrender . . . over twenty of Company K were gathered within the wooden walls of Point Lookout Prison.

Welborn James Andrews

Private Welborn James Andrews was captured at the Battle of Fort Stedman, and he was taken to Point Lookout Prison. This prison was established on August 1, 1863, at the extreme southern tip of that part of Maryland that lies between the Potomac River and the Chesapeake Bay. It was the largest prison in the North, and at one time it held 20,110 inmates.[1] It was located on land which was barely above high tide, and the water from the prison's wells was often brackish. One cartoon shows inmates catching rats for food. Winters were especially harsh, with the bitter wind blowing in from the water. Andrews' story gives an insight into prison life there; however, it must be understood that his account depicts a short springtime stay in this prison.[2]

Private Andrews gave this account of his capture and imprisonment:

Our regiment had just reached Fort Steadman when Lieutenant Scarborough was wounded in the thigh. Ten or fifteen minutes later, William Gregg was shot in the head and killed. The regiment began spreading out on the right. The Yankees advanced in our front and right, firing as they came. In a short time our troops on the right began to retreat. The orderly of Company K (who was in command of the company as the only commissioned officer present had been shot down and removed from the field) inquired if there were any order to retreat. The reply was "no," still the retreat continued. The orderly determined to remain and was with five or six others captured. We were taken to General Meade's headquarters; after a little rest were put on cars and conveyed to City Point, where we stayed until afternoon of the next day. The orderly, after eating supper Friday evening the 24th, did not get another meal until 11 A.M. on Sunday, the 26th. On the 27th of March the prisoners at City Point were divided.

The commissioned officers were held presumably for Johnson Island, while we non-commissioned and privates were carried to Point Lookout, Maryland. In a few days others of Company K arrived at the same prison. From the 25th of March to the surrender, April 8th, over twenty of Company K were gathered within the wooden walls of Point Lookout Prison. Wightman Durant, John Huggins, Tom W. McDonald, John Pearson, Legrande Joye, Ed and Frank Mathis, J. Grier White, Ed, Lem, and Hub Scarborough, Elijah, Lafayette, Tom, and Wilson Josey, Morgan Baker, Josiah Fleming, and others.

Point Lookout Prison was at the extreme point of land between the Atlantic Ocean on the east and Chesapeake Bay on the west, enclosed by a high wooden wall. None were allowed to go between the ditch and the wall. The ditch was called the dead line, for if a prisoner crossed it, he was shot down unceremoniously. We all occupied tents arranged in rows; two lines faced each other. The double lines formed a company. We were formed in line every morning and the roll called. We were permitted to go through gates on the bay side and walk about between sunrise and sunset, when the gates were closed. We were given two meals a day, mostly bean soup and baker's bread, yet it was fully as much as we had before our capture. Wells eight or ten feet deep supplied the water we used. It was very brackish and frequently scarce. Major Brady, the commander of the post, was very humane and as kind to the prisoners as the circumstances permitted.

About the first of April, 1865, General Grant, bent on surrounding General Lee's army, moved all the white guards from our prison to add to his number, and substituted negroes as guards for us. The very first night they behaved badly. In the daytime we had only an outer guard on the prison wall. At night a guard was placed within to keep the quiet and promote decency and the welfare of the prisoners. The second night the negroes threatened some, shot at others, and made a few kneel and pray for Abraham Lincoln and do other foolery of like kind. Their conduct was reported to Major Brady, who immediately replied that he would remove the night guard within the walls, provided the prisoners would form a guard for the service within the enclosure, offering to place said guard in separate quarters and give them separate rations. The guard was formed—100 in all—with two lieutenants and one sergeant. The orderly of Company K was the sergeant. At his suggestion to one of the lieutenants (a native of Sumter, S.C.), as many of Company K as the sergeant could induce to join the guard were placed on it. Our ration was much enlarged. Even sugar, coffee, and tobacco were given us and we were allowed three men to do our washing. A fifty-gallon caldron was given for that purpose. We felt the benefit of the change. Having nothing to do when first imprisoned our time hung heavily on our hands. Some New York ladies conferred with Major Brady and sent school books to him for the use

Welborn J. Andrews
(courtesy of Celeste Phillips)

of the prisoners. He furnished a house for school purposes and gave to capable prisoners, who would instruct the illiterate, an extra ration daily. Soon everything was working right—plenty of teachers, scores of scholars. Many, totally ignorant, learnt to spell, read, and write; others increased their limited knowledge. The Confederate Government, with the aid of Baltimore ladies, sent clothing for the prisoners. It was distributed by two old prisoners to the most needy. Alonzo Morgan (youngest son of Reverend Jesse Morgan of Sumter, S.C.) was one of the clothing committee.

After General Joseph E. Johnston surrendered, the Federal Government soon began to parole prisoners. Some after capture wished to desert. They were released first. Major Brady, being approached about our release, replied that as soon as he could get rid of the rascals (deserters), then he would have only gentlemen to deal with and would parole them as rapidly as practicable. After our release began, the prisoners who had been there longest were paroled first. It was done alphabetically. The orderly of Company K was in command of the inner guard from that time until the 23rd of June, 1865, when he was paroled. He left Sergeant Legrand Joye in command. There were many captives within those walls, estimated at 25,000.

On the north side a commodious hospital was erected. Surgeons and nurses seemed plentiful. We had preaching in the school house two or three times a month.

After release, transportation was given us as far towards our homes as conditions warranted. Three Sumter men (John Brunby, Morgan Baker, and J. Grier White) came [with me] from Point Lookout Prison. Leaving Monday evening by steamer, we reached Charleston on Thursday morning. We left Charleston by the South Carolina Railroad for Orangeburg, where the cars stopped because the bridge over the Congaree River had been burnt. We footed it to the river. It being night, we waited until morning. We found a man named Mitchell living in a shanty on the river bank. He had the only boat (bateau) to be seen. Though we were old soldiers, he would not take us over the river without pay. The orderly was the only one of us who had anything to pay with. He gave a good pair of blankets and about fifty cents worth of tobacco to the skinflint to take us over the river.

As soon as we reached the opposite shore we saw a hand-car on the trestle. A young man named Ligon, who was the telegraph operator at Kingsville, had come to the river with a friend. They appeared and offered to carry us to Kingsville, two miles distant. At Kingsville we met Marion Lafar (formerly of Sumter) who was the railroad agent. He gave us free passage to Sumter, where we arrived between noon and 1 P.M. Sunday. We passed the First Methodist Church just as the morning services were over. This was the first Sunday of July, 1865.

14

The Battle of Five Forks

> . . . we will say right here that every man in Lee's army at this stage of the war was a hero. The "dross" had been skimmed off and the "chaff" sifted out.
>
> John Floyd

During the first three months of 1865, Lee's Army of Northern Virginia lost nearly 40 percent of its strength, or about 25,000 men, to desertion, combat, and transfer. The combination of the bitter cold winter of 1864–65, Sherman moving north through the Carolinas, and the long series of battles which were a part of the Siege of Petersburg were contributing factors to the low morale of the troops.[1] In late March, Grant began his spring campaign by sending his troops around the south end of the Confederate line toward Five Forks. Grant's purpose was to break Lee's railroad supply lines to the south and west of Petersburg, leaving the city indefensible. Also, if he could control this area, he would have interposed his troops between the armies of Robert E. Lee and Joseph E. Johnston.

By this time, Lee's Army of Northern Virginia was stretched too thinly to defend its flanks. The last two miles of the right end of Lee's line was held by Richard H. Anderson's Corps, which consisted of the Division of General Bushrod Johnson (about 4,800 men) and four battalions of artillery. On March 29, Lee sent Samuel McGowan's Brigade to bolster Anderson's Corps. To strengthen his right flank, Lee moved to create an independent mobile force of perhaps ten thousand troops under General George Pickett. Pickett was ordered to bring his five thousand infantry troops from the Bermuda Hundred area to Sutherland Station, a railroad station about two miles behind of the south end of Lee's line. There he was to link up with about 4,400 Confederate cavalry commanded by Fitzhugh Lee, Rooney Lee, and Thomas Rosser and then move toward Dinwiddie Court House. Before these units could arrive and join together, the Battle of Lewis Farm took place. This battle can be considered as the first of four parts of the Battle of Five Forks.[2]

Captain Floyd commended the efforts of the experienced Confederate soldiers:[3]

Our brigade (Wallace's) was stationed on the right of Petersburg, near Gravelly Run, with a heavy picket line a half mile to the front. On the morning of the 29th of March we were notified that the enemy were advancing in heavy force, and that our pickets were falling back. The brigade was formed in line of battle at once and moved forward to meet the enemy. We met our pickets fighting as they were forced back by a heavy line of battle and met the enemy shortly afterwards. We exchanged shot with them and then charged, driving them for a mile. The enemy having crossed a field of about four acres with a fence on both sides, made a bold stand and having brought up a battery of artillery, and having been reinforced with another brigade of infantry, we failed to move them from their position, though several bold attempts were made, led by myself, Major Betsel, and [Lieutenant] Munro, who was then acting Adjutant of the regiment. We held our ground, however. The enemy then sent a regiment to our left for the purpose of flanking. Major Betsel, with 200 men, went to meet them. In a short time we heard heavy firing on the left. We knew that the Major had engaged the enemy. We then received orders from General Wallace to have a heavy skirmish line at the fence and for the brigade to fall back. The skirmish line was under my command and my orders were to hold my position as long as I could, and not to allow any skirmish line to move us. We were to fall back only when attacked by a regular line of battle and then to retire fighting. As soon as the brigade commenced falling back the enemy sent a heavy skirmish line forward and attacked our skirmishers, but they were repulsed. Three times they attacked our skirmishers but were repulsed each time. They then retired their skirmish line and attacked us with a heavy line of battle but that also failed to move our line of skirmishers.

The fact is that the men who held that line were veterans; they were heroes true and tried, and we will say right here that every man in Lee's army at this stage of the war was a hero. The "dross" had been skimmed off and the chaff sifted out. Our brigade had been under the fire of the enemy for nine months without intermission, night and day, and every day of that nine months men were killed or wounded in our regiment. It was not unusual to see a private lead a charge, for every man was educated, by experience, in the art of war. R. G. Parnell, W. W. Pierce, Nat Odom, Blany Miller, J. D. Brown and many others acted with the greatest bravery on this occasion, as they always did in battle. Lieutenants Jordan and Moore showed very great nerve. The enemy was no match for our men and had to reinforce their line three times and had to make three distinct charges before they moved our skirmishers, and when we did retire we did so fighting. The skirmish line fell back slowly;

every other man would fire and fall back twenty paces, loading as they retired, and then the others would fire and fall back twenty paces, passing the line alternately with such precision that they looked as though they were drilling. We fell back through a piece of woods with thick undergrowth, giving General Wallace time to make his dispositions for battle. The brigade fell back about half a mile, then halted and concealed themselves in a thick chapparal by lying down. I had received orders from General Wallace to fall back over the brigade line and make no halt, but to have the men pass to the rear without noticing the line. The object was to draw the enemy up very close before they were aware of the presence of the brigade. The skirmish line passed over the line with the greatest precision and the enemy got up in thirty feet of our line before they were aware of our presence. General Wallace then ordered the brigade to rise and fire, which they did, delivering a tremendous volley. Then before the enemy recovered from the shock General Wallace hurled his entire line against them with the bayonet. The enemy fled and we fell back to our lines, established a picket line and threw up breastworks. Company I had eight men wounded in this fight.

Lieutenant Colonel Hudson reported the activities of the Twenty-sixth Regiment:

On the night of the 28th and during the day of the 29th, the rain had been very heavy and we suffered much discomfort. . . . Sheridan's advance forces, aiming to reach and destroy the South Side Railroad, struck us at the sawdust pile on the Boydton plank road, near our camp. A stubborn fight ensued between our three brigades: Gracie's Alabama, Wise's Virginia and Wallace's South Carolina on the one hand, and two divisions of Federals on the other. We made the attack on their superior force by single brigades in the woods, but with only partial success, the opposing forces camping within easy range of small arms.

On the following morning by break of day we moved along the White Oak road, parallel to the march of the Federals and skirmishing with them all day. On the night of the 30th we went into camp at Five Forks, the enemy having moved off in the direction of Dinwiddie Courthouse, and they were much harassed by our cavalry. On the last day of March our infantry, consisting of only 7,000 men under General Pickett, moved in the direction of Dinwiddie Courthouse, where Sheridan with his 25,000 fresh and well equipped troops lay in camp. Late in the afternoon a severe cavalry engagement occurred in that vicinity with the advantage on the side of the Confederates.

The Battle of White Oak Road (or Gravelly Run) was the second of the four parts of the Battle of Five Forks. It took place on March 31 and did not

involve Wallace's Brigade. Part three of the Battle of Five Forks, the Battle of Dinwiddie Court House, took place on the same day about four miles to the southwest. Wallace's Brigade was involved to a limited extent in this battle.

Captain Floyd recalled the musical accompaniment to this battle:[4]

On the 31st of March, 1865, we were ordered from the lines near Gravelly Run to Dinwiddie Court House. When in half mile of the courthouse we halted and formed line of battle across the road leading from Five Forks to the Court House. We were aware that General Fitz Lee's division of cavalry were in our front, and we also knew that General Lee had engaged the enemy, for there was heavy firing going on just in front of us, and we knew that we were brought there to support Lee's Division. The strange part of the proceedings however, was that a fierce a battle was raging and the enemy's works were stormed and carried by Lee's Division, while all the bands of the division were on the line playing Dixie with all their might, and really made fine music. It was not long till the wounded commenced to pass us, then we learned that General Lee had told his men that they must dismount and carry the enemy's works, or that he would take their horses from them and make infantry of them; and had also made the bands go upon the lines and play while the fight was in progress. The division of Lee made a brilliant charge and captured the works of the enemy. We went into camp after the battle was over and remained until morning. The cavalry commenced passing to the rear early in the night. They evidently did not know that the infantry was near enough to support them, for you could hear all kinds of remarks of surprise as they passed by. One fellow would exclaim, "Good gracious, here are the infantry. If we had known that they were so near we would not have been so frightened." This remark, of course, elicited a storm of abuse from the infantry.

The main Battle of Five Forks occurred on April 1, 1865. The Confederate trenches extended westward and eastward from Five Forks along the White Oak Road. Fitzhugh Lee would later report that Pickett's seven thousand men were facing twenty-six thousand Federal troops.[5] Wallace's and Ransom's Brigades were stationed at the eastern end of the Confederate line where the trenches turned sharply to the north, in an area called "The Angle." The Federal Fifth Corps began the battle by attacking The Angle, and they quickly overwhelmed the Confederate line and captured between one thousand and fifteen hundred Confederates, many from these two brigades. In his report of the Appomattox Campaign (March 29–April 9), General Wallace would refer to "the remnant of the brigade which had escaped from the affair of April 1 at the Five Cross-Roads." Overall, the Confederate losses in this battle were estimated at 545 killed and wounded and 2,000 to 2,400 captured. Federal losses totaled about 830.

Lieutenant Colonel Hudson described the efforts of the outnumbered Confederates:

That night [March 31] we encamped in the woods within two miles of Dinwiddie Courthouse, but since we were within the Federal lines and practically surrounded by portions of their troops, no fires were allowed and silence enjoined. Before day we began a retrograde movement towards Five Forks, pursued by the enemy. About noon we reached our camp of the night before at the Forks, and at once began to prepare dinner, being very tired and hungry. Before we had finished the meal we were hastily called to arms and thrown into line along the main road of the Forks—Wise's Brigade covering the Five Forks, Wallace and Ransom on the left and Gracie to the right. By the time we had cut bushes and with bayonets and pans had thrown up dirt knee high, the Federals ran upon us in force. The fighting was close and severe. By the middle of the afternoon Sheridan's 25,000 men were up, and greatly overlapped us on the left, when we were completely flanked. Warren's entire corps was thrown on the left flank of Pickett's meager force, and the onset had to be met by the thin brigades of Ransom and Wallace which were attacked in front and flank simultaneously in an open stand-up fight, for we had scarcely the semblance of protection in front and none whatever on the flank. The fighting was fierce and bloody until we were completely overlapped by superior numbers and stood as it were between the blades of scissors, the enemy being within twenty steps of our front and rear. Just before this extremity arrived a tragic incident occurred. For several days it was known that spies and scouts of the enemy had been among us afoot and mounted, but none had been caught. In the rear of the 26th Regiment was a thicket of old-field pines behind which were our ambulances and ordnance wagons. Through this thicket a soldier with a Federal overcoat dashed up to us on horseback. Some one cried out, "Shoot the Federal spy." Instantly a half dozen bullets pierced his body, and he fell from his horse dead. It was then discovered that he was General Ransom's young adjutant, McGhee, who had been but recently married. His fate was never definitely known to his people or his general until I narrated it to General Ransom in 1896. But the enemy had doubled upon us, and the rout began in an effort to retreat by the right flank, where there was the only possible chance to escape the storm of bullets pelting us in front and rear.

Captain Floyd continued his account:

On the morning of the 1st of April we fell back to Five Forks, formed a line of battle and commenced to strengthen our position by fortifying the best we could and by the time the enemy made the first charge, about 3 o'clock P.M., we had pretty good works, and repulsed them with ease. They doubled their

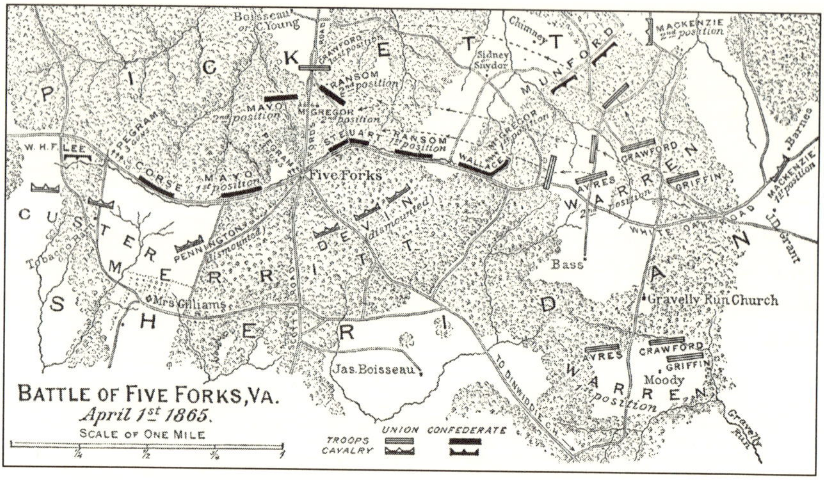

Map of the Battle of Five Forks
(*Battles and Leaders of the Civil War*, vol. 4)

lines, however, and charged us again and again, in fact they continued to charge us at intervals until late in the evening, when they made a tremendous effort to move our line, some of them actually climbing upon our works and were bayoneted. We repulsed them with very heavy loss.[6] They sent a strong column and attacked our cavalry on the left flanks, and though the cavalry were dismounted and fought with the greatest courage they were overwhelmed by numbers and finally gave way. The enemy then pressed a heavy column forward and penetrated our rear, and had almost surrounded us when General Wallace ordered our brigade to "charge front rear," so as to meet the enemy, but while we were executing the command, Ransom's North Carolina Brigade became demoralized and ran through our line, causing the greatest confusion. The enemy pressed their advantage and the consequence was that our line became a confused mass and we were compelled to retreat as best we could through a thick swamp, so as to save ourselves from capture. Private Samuel Parker of Company I was killed and twelve men were wounded and captured. I was wounded in the left arm, but remained with my command. On the next morning the regiment numbered three officers and fifty-two men.

Lieutenant Colonel Hudson escaped capture but was wounded:

Lieutenant Colonel Culp, of the Seventeenth, and I, of the Twenty-sixth, had stood our ground until it was almost too late to escape, but we began to retreat by the right flank. We were uncovering the Five Forks when General Matt Ransom dashed up on a fine bay horse, hat in hand, and called for volunteers to return and beat back the foe. We had then retreated less than one hundred yards from our original position. I responded and gave the order to counter-march. I supposed the regiment had obeyed, but owing to the confusion and panic not more than the two companies of the right followed me into the place of peril and confusion. The ambulances and ordnance wagons had been driven from shelter and stood deserted by their drivers near the line then being occupied by the enemy, who likewise filled the pine thicket. The dead and wounded lay thick upon the ground, and the bullets were flying and shells bursting in every direction. Into this pandemonium we rushed and regained our position in the lines, but only to become targets for the close cross-fire of the Federals massed in front and rear at twenty paces distant. I was shot down, as were many others, and the rout of Pickett's entire command became general, a few escaping, but most being captured. Now, the way to the South Side Railroad was open to Sheridan.

Captain John C. Evans of the Twenty-third Regiment was among the large number of men captured at the Battle of Five Forks. He wrote to his wife from Johnson's Island Prison near Sandusky, Ohio, on April 30:

On April 1 we were pressed by the enemy at Five Points near Dinwiddie Court House. After passing through one of these terrible scenes, in which God in his mercy has shielded me from harm, the enemy flanked us and cut us off from the Brigade, and captured all of us who stood up manfully according to orders . . . As soon as captured, the Federals marched us day and part of the night to City Point, about 40 miles. There were about 4000 captured during the day and we were all marched together. From City Point we went to Washington and were confined in the Old Capitol Prison—a miserable place. We remained there a few days and then were sent to this point. Although this is a prison, yet in a great many things it is comfortable. The rations are short, but enough to sustain life. I shall ever remember Lep Godfrey for his kindness to me. He has given me some provisions and clothing and does, very frequently, ask me to partake of his meals. He and his mess live very well. They have been here long enough to get funds. I have written to some of my friends and expect surely they will aid me. Thank God I have health.

We spend our time very pleasantly all things considered. Between drawing rations, cooking, bringing water, cutting wood, sweeping, loading carts with refuse, and occasionally patching and sewing, we feel as if we are always in a strain and yet accomplish apparently nothing. The prisoners, all officers from Generals down to Lieutenants, have to take their regular turn at all these things mentioned. Besides we sit up and wait on the sick and for them we have to do everything, even to carrying out the chambers and washing them. Colonel Henagen of Marlboro who was a special friend to me when I

Henry L. Benbow
(courtesy of United States Army Military History Institute, Rod Gragg Collection)

first came here has since taken sick and died. I sat up with him his last night. His disease was pneumonia. Sometimes you will see a Colonel or perhaps a General cooking: he gets his rations and rushes to the kitchen with his little tin bucket and loaf bread to toast . . .

Our pen is about one-fourth of a mile square. There are twelve houses, each house containing 7 or 9 rooms. Generally the rooms have bunks to contain about from 12 to 50 men according to size. We are allowed to roam at large within certain limits in the day time, but at night all must be in their rooms. At 9 P.M. every light must be out or the Sentries will shoot at your window. The fence around is about 15 feet high. In wet weather it is a miserable dirty place, but when dry it is a pleasant grounds.

Colonel Henry Benbow of the Twenty-third Regiment was wounded and captured at Five Forks, and he was taken to Lincoln General Hospital in Washington. During his stay there, the hospital received a prominent visitor, who approached and offered his hand. Colonel Benbow asked: "Does President Lincoln know that he offers his hand to a Confederate colonel?" Lincoln replied: "Let me hope that a Confederate colonel will not refuse to shake my hand." The president then sat beside Colonel Benbow and talked for some time.[7]

Many years later, Lieutenant Colonel Hudson reflected on the brigade's final battle:

I have thus attempted to give a brief narrative of the battle of the afternoon of April 1, 1965, at Five Forks, where fewer than 8,000 foot-sore, ragged and half-starved Confederates for four hours and in the open held at bay 25,000 well-clad, well-fed Federal troops, and gave way and fled only after more than half the force had been killed, wounded and captured. The rout of the survivors was complete, and night and the woods and impassable roads alone enabled any to escape.

The able and gallant Federal corps commander, Warren, incurred the displeasure of General Sheridan for not destroying or capturing Pickett's entire force, and he was relieved of his command, which was given to General Gibbon. Could the verdict of the Confederates have been rendered Warren would have been vindicated, for in our judgment his corps was never better handled, and never fought better. Warren by a court of inquiry was after the war fully vindicated. This disastrous battle led to the evacuation of Richmond and Petersburg on the night of April 2nd, the retreat of Lee's skeleton of an army, and his surrender at Appomattox on Sunday, April 9, 1865.

Private Andrews noted his regiment's service with pride:

In the Battle of Five Forks, the Twenty-third Regiment was sacrificed to save the balance of the army. All of Company K who had not been previously captured fell into the enemy's hands, save Joe Lewis and Randolph Bracey; they were at Lee's surrender.[8]

15

The Fighting Ends for Lieutenant Colonel Hudson

> General Grant . . . inquired my name, rank, and nature and circumstances of my wound, and then asked me if he could do anything for me.
>
> Joshua Hilary Hudson

Lieutenant Colonel Hudson's account of his care (or lack thereof) following his wounding at the Battle of Five Forks almost creates the image of a slapstick comedy. Nevertheless, he did manage to survive until Federal troops captured the house where he was being treated. Federal medical care proved to be somewhat better. General Grant and his staff stopped to rest and have lunch, and they visited him. Lieutenant Colonel Hudson relates the story of his slow recovery, his journey via boxcar to Greensboro and Charlotte, and then his journey home via rockaway and wagon to Cheraw and Bennettsville, South Carolina:

I will relate my experience after being wounded. The wound I received was from a Minié ball at the distance of fifteen steps, the ball passing through my left side below the lungs, and just missing the entrails. It knocked me down. In a moment, two men of the ambulance corps, one of them being from Chester, S.C., ran and hastily threw me on a stretcher and shoved me and my stretcher into our ambulance, standing without a driver within twenty steps of the enemy and in the line of the crossfire. I remonstrated with them, but all in vain, and in a twinkling they were gone. As apprehended, the bullets were passing through the covering of the ambulance, and in desperation I raised up, slid from the ambulance in face of the battle line of the enemy twenty steps off, crawled under the vehicle and horses, and toddled off through the small pines, every one of which was being scraped with bullets. How I escaped being riddled, Providence alone knows. Having hobbled off one hundred yards, I fell down in great pain exhausted. Passing pell-mell rushed the routed Confederates, when Lieutenant Kennedy and two of his men, of Company

F from Horry County, saw and picked me up, telling me to run. I cried out, "I cannot walk, much less run. Carry me away. I do not wish to die and be buried here." Replying that the enemy is upon us, they ran on, leaving me under fire. Rendered desperate, I regained my feet and trotted on through the pines. I had gone about one hundred yards when General Matt Ransom (mounted on a bay horse, one having been shot under him at the Five Forks[1]), followed by an orderly, came dashing by. I shouted to him my condition and begged him to save me from capture. He cried out to his orderly to dismount and give me his horse. On his dismounting, I laid hold the mane of the tallest of black horses, and bare back, no saddle nor blanket. I begged him to help me on. With an oath, he cried to me to mount or turn the horse loose for him. He did not know me and was excusably alarmed. Making a desperate effort I climbed astride and the black horse went in pursuit of the bay, I giving him the rein and holding to the mane.

At the distance of three hundred yards, having passed beyond the line of fire, I came to two ambulances standing on the road that leads towards Ford's Station on the South Side Railroad. Dropping from the horse, I attempted to get in the rearmost vehicle, when the driver objected and raised his whip to strike me. At that moment, someone, I know not who, cried out, "Let him in; that is Colonel Hudson, Twenty-sixth S.C.V., wounded." He at once lowered his whip, and I crawled in the rear end of the ambulance. In justice to this driver I will say that I had on a dingy, thread-bare fatigue suit, and the stars on the collar of my jacket were scarcely visible in their dark rusted state. The same must be said in explanation of the rude words of General Ransom's orderly.

I threw myself on my back in the ambulance and begged the driver to move on. He said he would do so as soon as the one in front moved, telling me that in it was Lieutenant-Colonel Pegram, of the artillery, who was shot through the lower part of the left lung, and could not speak.[2] I began to regret abandoning the black horse, for I knew we were pursued by the enemy. However, in a few minutes the ambulances moved off. This was about sunset, and it was seven miles to Ford's Station. I lay flat on my back in great pain and fully believing my wound to be mortal. I could hear the noise and confusion of the route all along the road, and from the driver's talk could get some idea of the panic of the retreat and the condition of the terrible road. Twice the ambulances stuck fast in the mire and were on the eve of being abandoned. I believe they would have been but for the wounded officer in each. By the aid of the artillery horses as they passed us the vehicles were extricated from the mire, and we reached Ford's Station at midnight, having made seven miles in six hours. The driver of the ambulance in which I rode was a soldier from Louisiana and a noble fellow. At Ford's Station I was lifted from the ambulance by Dr. Girardeau, our chaplain, and others, and laid on a mattress in the house of Mr. Pegram, the depot agent, while Colonel Pegram was laid upon the bed in the same room. Surgeon Dick, of Sumter, gave me a dose of morphine and left with me some more in a paper, with instructions not to take any of it unless my pain demanded it. The effect of the medicine soon put me to sleep, and my surprise was great next morning when I awoke to find myself alive. I at once inquired for Colonel Pegram and was told that he was dead and buried in the yard. This was unpleasant news to me, as our wounds were alike, save that my lungs escaped, but I fully believed my intestines were cut. In an hour a private cavalryman from North Carolina was brought in and laid on the bed on which Pegram died, wounded precisely as I was, except that the ball did not pass through and out of the body. He suffered much, and asked me if I had anything to ease pain. I told him I had morphine under my mattress. He begged me to bring him a dose. I informed him that I could not rise up or turn over, whereupon he got down from his bed, came to me, took some of the morphine, returned to his bed, and soon asked me to get some one to come and adjust his pillow, as he was in great pain. I tapped on the floor with my knife and Mrs. Pegram came in. I told her of the soldier's request. She went to arrange his pillow, gave a look of alarm, saying he was dying. I expressed my surprise, telling her that he had just left my bedside after taking a dose of morphine, but she threw up her hands, exclaiming, "My God! He is dead!" and so he was. Of course I feared that my turn would come next, as these two with wounds similar to mine had died. But night came, I slept, and awoke next morning again rejoicing to find myself alive.

Early on the 3rd day of April, Spear's cavalry, the advance guard of Grant's army, arrived and dispersed the last of Pickett's stragglers. They scoured the premises and sacked the house of all vestiges of food. An assistant surgeon came in, examined my wound and told me I would soon die of peritonitis. In spite of the fright this gave me, I slept some that night and again found myself alive next morning, but Grant's main army was passing by in pursuit of Lee's remnant of a once proud victorious band. The tramp of infantry and cavalry and rumbling of artillery was incessant and seemed never-ending. I could hear all but see nothing as I lay on the floor, feeling deeply anxious for the coming fate of our brave boys.

About noon General Grant and staff and several of his corps commanders came into the room where I lay, to rest and lunch. Of these General Grant was most plainly dressed, and bore a weather-beaten appearance and careworn look. The others were more gaily dressed, and more garrulous. General Grant was calm, quiet and reticent. After taking a seat he inquired my name, rank and nature and circumstances of my wound, and then asked me if he could do anything for me. I asked for a surgeon to examine my wound. He promptly had one called, who came in and made the examination, inquiring particularly as to the time, place and circumstances of the wounding. I informed him, and anxiously awaited his judgment. His appearance and manner pleased me, and a feeling of great relief came to me when he informed me that I had made a narrow escape, and that if well cared for I would recover. He then told General Grant that I must not be moved; that it might be fatal to send me to a hospital with other wounded. General Grant replied that he would see that I was not moved. The surgeon then directed me to do nothing for the wound but to keep a wet cloth across my left side so as to cover both orifices of the wound, and left me. General Grant then kindly asked if he could do anything else for me, to which I replied that I knew of nothing else, and thanked him for his kindness. He smoked a cigar while sitting in the room, but not till he learned from me that it would not annoy me.

I never saw a happier looking military family than were the other Union officers in the room, and they plied me with numerous questions about the Confederate army. General Gibbon sat by me, and learning that I was a native of Chester, S.C., informed me that he was a native of Charlotte, N.C., and knew men of Chester, while I knew men of Charlotte. We talked much of our mutual acquaintances, and several of the gay company wished me to drink of the fine liquor in their full canteens. I longed for it, but had the will to decline with regret, fearing its effect upon my wound.

General Grant asked me but few questions, and among them he asked if I thought General Lee ready to surrender. My answer was, "General Grant, our army is thinned to a skeleton and worn down. General Lee cannot resist much longer your vastly superior force, but when he surrenders or is captured, you will get only a fragment of this skeleton. I know that a number of his soldiers will make their way South as best they can in spite of your army and will not surrender. Their faces are turned homeward; they will stand by General Lee as long as there is hope, but when despair comes, they will take to the woods, homeward bound, and will never surrender." He seemed thoughtful, and asked no more. He was, during the hour he remained with me, the most calm, quiet and modest man of his rank I ever beheld.

As the Federal army passed on, the corps of pioneers and laborers changed the gauge of the South Side Railroad to conform to the City Point Railroad, and so rapidly as almost to keep abreast of the army. At each depot a garrison of a company, or part thereof, was left on guard. By the small garrison thus left at Ford's Station, the family of Mr. Pegram, consisting of himself, wife, daughter, and servant, were fed, as was I and any other wounded soldier who happened to be brought in, and they were brought in daily, but as rapidly were hauled off to hospital or prison, I alone being left undisturbed, although the garrison was changed every week or ten days. The coming and going of the captured and wounded continued for at least two weeks, and at times the floor of my room was covered with soldiers wounded variously, and not a few like unto myself, but I at last was left alone with Mr. Pegram and family, and received uniformly kind treatment at the hands of Federal officers and soldiers. I think the kindest, most sympathetic and tender-hearted human being that ever slept by my bed and administered to my wants was a freckled-faced private Federal soldier who, in the first week of my suffering, nursed me day and night; and the sweetest food I ever swallowed was the beef tea he made for me in his tin cup. A surgeon examined my wound about once in ten days, but no change of dressing was prescribed.

During the fifth week of my prostration my greatest torture came in the form of bed pains, and through ignorance I narrowly escaped death from morphine. I knew not what quantity to take, and in my torture took all I could hold between thumb and forefinger. But for my suffering, this would probably have killed me, as a surgeon afterwards told me of my narrow escape, and urged me to take no more.

At the end of six weeks I was able to walk a little, and was paroled by General Chamberlain, of Maine, as he happened to pass that way. With this parole I took the train (box car) and managed to get as far south as Greensboro, N.C., where, owing to increasing pain, I went into the hospital. On the third day, learning by accident that I was lodging within fifty yards of three tents of smallpox patients, my pain left me, and I fled to the depot, where I took the first train going south towards Charlotte, N.C. After walking several miles over a break in the railroad, in company with other returning soldiers, I arrived in Charlotte about 10 o'clock on a fair May morning. My aim was to get to my mother's home in Chester, and then wait for a chance to reach Bennettsville, when the railroads had been repaired.

Here a Confederate soldier and road companion, Praither by name, from Laurens, S.C., left me on some loose cotton in the demolished railroad roundhouse, and went in search of a meal. In due time he returned with a promise from a good lady—an angel of mercy—to send us a meal, and presently a negro boy came bearing a waiter covered with a snow-white napkin and filled with such victuals as I had not seen or tasted in four years. With sharp appetites and hearts of gratitude Praither and I ate as only the hungry can, and sent the boy and empty waiter back to our benefactress with sincere thanks. Praither here left me, and I have never seen him since, nor did I ever learn the name of our angel.

Being alone in this desolate spot my wits began to work and I remembered that my colonel, A. D. Smith, once told me if I ever stopped in Charlotte to

Judge Joshua Hilary Hudson
(Marlboro County Court House, Bennettsville, S.C.)

be sure to call on Mrs. Holton, and I would find a friend to the soldier. This brought me to my feet, and with my little bundle of Confederate cloth received at the hospital at Greensboro to make me a suit of clothes, and clad in my blood-stained army fatigue suit, I wended my way up to an old freight warehouse still left standing. There I met a solitary negro boy, who pointed out to me the home of Mrs. Holton.

Going straightway to it, I knocked and the door was opened by Mrs. Holton. To her I introduced myself, made known my forlorn condition, and repeated what had been told me by Colonel Smith. I had not seen Colonel Smith since January, 1865, he being at home on leave of absence that month and, being cut off by Sherman's army, had not been able to return to Virginia, and hence had no part in the closing acts of the war in Virginia; but at home had gallantly aided in striving to check Potter's raid to Sumter and Camden. Imagine my surprise and delight when Mrs. Holton told me that Colonel Smith was then in Charlotte and a guest of her house—he and a Mr. Tuomey. In a half hour Colonel Smith came in and in great surprise and amazement found me, whom he had heard was killed at Five Forks, there. He and Mr.

Tuomey had made their way to Charlotte late in May in a rockaway drawn by two weather-beaten horses, for the purpose of buying items on which to trade. How happy was I to be told that in two days they would start for Marlboro, South Carolina, and could carry me! At the appointed time we bid adieu to kind Mrs. Holton and family of sons and daughters, and after an adventurous journey, arrived on the third day in Cheraw. Here I met Chancellor Inglis, Captain Henry McIver, and others, who greeted me heartily and earnestly inquired of me what would probably be done with the slaves, etc. I told them that absolute emancipation was an accomplished fact, and that the whites would be placed under military rule at least for a season. After getting a free lunch for ourselves and horses, Mr. Tuomey, to whom the vehicle and team belonged, bade us good-by and left for Society Hill, he and Colonel Smith having divided their goods.

As good luck had it, an empty wagon drawn by two horses and belonging to the Rev. Mr. Beattie, a neighbor of Colonel Smith's father, was about to start home, and the driver took aboard Colonel Smith and myself. After a rough jolt of two hours we arrived at Mr. Smith's, who then lived at the Terrel place and ran a distillery during the war. There I was kindly received by Mr. and Mrs. Smith and fed. Mr. Robert Hamer, called "Little Bob," drove up alone in a buggy to get some whiskey. He kindly gave me a seat in his buggy and before sunset landed me in Bennettsville, South Carolina, in the bosom of my family, who were surprised and rejoiced to greet the "dead come to life," for all reports had left me dead on the field at Five Forks. So ended my army experience.[3]

16

ON TO APPOMATTOX

I shall "swallow the Eagle" and come home.
John C. Evans

On April 2, 1865, the day after the Confederate defeat at Five Forks, Federal troops broke through the defenses of Petersburg near Fort Gregg on the south side of the city. The Army of Northern Virginia then began its withdrawal from Petersburg and Richmond. Lee attempted to save his army by moving westward along the Appomattox River, hoping to turn to the south and join with Joe Johnston's forces in North Carolina. For the next week, Lee's men fought a number of rearguard actions with the pursuing Federal troops. The brigade retreated westward with Richard Anderson's Corps through Amelia Court House and Farmville to Appomattox,[1] and Wallace estimated that the brigade now numbered only about 350 men.[2]

Captain Floyd recalled the retreat:

What was left of the division got together during the day and we commenced the retreat up the Appomattox River, the lines in front of Petersburg having been broken and abandoned the night before. A very large wagon train had been sent out from that place and it was almost impossible for us to protect it from falling into the hands of the enemy, who hovered upon our rear. Thus we retreated, fighting sometimes a dozen times in a day. At Amelia Court House we joined General Lee, with the portion of the army that had fallen back from Richmond. We expected to find rations here but were disappointed. The commissary train by some mistake, having been sent on to Richmond, fell into the hands of the enemy. We continued the retreat though nearly starved, having had nothing to eat for several days. At Farmville the enemy dashed into our lines and cut Humphries' Alabama Brigade to pieces. Our brigade was ordered to take their place. We advanced through a piece of timber to the edge of an open field where we halted and corrected our line. The enemy charged us at once in four lines. This was the prettiest cavalry charge that we ever saw. They came in four lines, about 200 yards apart, yelling like demons. As the first line got in range we gave them a volley that emptied many of their saddles. They wheeled right and left and the second line came forward yelling, firing and brandishing their sabres, but a well directed volley from our rifles emptied many more of their saddles and they wheeled right and left and disappeared. The third line advanced just the same, with the same result. When the fourth line dashed forward a counter charge was ordered by General Wallace and this line was "done up" worse than the others, and now the ridiculous spectacle of Confederate infantry charging Yankee cavalry was to be witnessed. We drove them off and then went back and joined our retiring column. We continued to fight and retreat until the morning of the 9th of April, when we were ordered to join General Gordon's charging column at Appomattox Court House. I commanded the brigade skirmishers in this battle and H. E. White, P. S. McLaughlin and J. C. Hogg, the only other men left in Company I for duty, were attached to Company D. We dashed forward and swept everything before us as usual, carrying position after position of the enemy for a mile. Then we were ordered back to the court house and learned that General Lee had surrendered the army. I paroled twenty-two men, but twenty of them were wounded men and officers from the hospitals at Petersburg—myself, Lieutenants Jordan, Moore and Hunter all wounded. Lieutenant Hunter was so severely wounded that he was sent to a Federal hospital.

There was a circumstance in this battle which goes to show the devotion of our young men to the Lost Cause, and for which so many of them gave their young lives: When the brigade was formed in line of battle, 100 men were marked off in the center of the brigade and I was ordered to throw them forward as skirmishers. I gave the simple command to them "as skirmishers deploy forward, double quick, march." They trotted off obliquing right and left, and in less than 160 yards had covered the brigade. I gave them the order to "halt." At the command they deployed five paces apart. The General ordered me to move forward at double quick as the brigade would follow at once. We moved forward as ordered and in less than 300 yards, struck the enemy who was holding a position behind a hedgerow. We halted and exchanged shots with them but they refused to retire. I ordered my men to fix bayonets and charge, which they did, driving the enemy from their position and pursuing them. We had driven them but a few hundred yards when I noticed that the enemy were advancing a regular line of battle and were withdrawing their skirmishers. I ordered my line to halt, but to continue firing while I was waiting for orders from the General, for I had sent a courier back to report.

A young man, who seemed to be not more than 17 years of age, carrying a gun and dressed in the Confederate uniform, approached me from the right and rear of my line and said: "Captain, I want to fight in your line. I know that the circumstances under which I approach you look suspicious, but, sir, I am no skulk. I belong to Gracie's Alabama Brigade and they have surrendered just up to the right in that piece of woods, and while they were stacking arms, I stepped out determined not to surrender but to join and fight with the first troops I saw in action." Just then one of my skirmishers was shot down but a short distance from where we were standing. I told the young man that if he really wanted to fight to take the place of the man who was just shot down. He handed me a card upon which was written: Julius Lewis, Company "E," 13th Regiment, Alabama Volunteers, Gracie's Brigade. "If I am killed or anything serious happens to me, write to Mrs. Mary Lewis, Eufala, Ala.," and hastened to take his position. About this time a courier came dashing up with orders for me to assemble my skirmishers on the right and assist the Holcombe Legion in repulsing a flank movement of the enemy then being organized in a piece of woods on our right. I ordered the line to "assemble on the right group at double quick." When we got to the right Colonel Crawley had already changed the front of his regiment so as to face the enemy. I formed on his left just as the enemy dashed out with glistening bayonets, making the woods resound with their hurrahs. Colonel Crawley ordered our line to fix bayonets and prepare to charge. I also noticed that our line was overlapped about the length of a regiment by the enemy's line, but it was too late to make any change now. Colonel Crawley ordered a counter charge. We dashed forward at the run and as we passed a hedgerow parallel with our line a regiment of Confederates rose up and joined our right. On came the Federals, on pressed the Confederates until it really looked like bayonets would be locked, but when we were almost in reach of each other the Federals faced about and made for the woods from which they had just emerged, pursued by our line, who gave them a parting volley as they entered the woods. I noticed that the Alabama boy was foremost in the charge. We heard the crash of the brigade and the enemy as they went together, but were too busy ourselves to notice the result. When we halted we were surprised to notice that the firing had all ceased, and to see that our line was marching back towards the court house, while the enemy were marching back from whence they came.[3] A staff officer now rode up with orders for us to return to the court house also. When we arrived we learned that General Lee had surrendered the army. The little Alabama man now stepped out from the line and said: "Captain, I must now return to my regiment, as we have all surrendered, and now I want you to do me a favor," at the same time handing me a memorandum book and pencil. "Please write on this page what my conduct has been while under your command." Of course I complied with his request. I have never heard of Julius Lewis since that memorable 9th day of April, 1865, but I often think of him.

Captain Edwards saw the loss at Five Forks as a turning point:

The end had come. Our army had been reduced to a skeleton. We did not have more than one-sixth the number of Grant's army, and perhaps less than that. We were occupying forty miles of defenses. To withdraw this weak line and retreat before a powerful, well-appointed army of two hundred thousand men was a feat of impossible success. But if General Lee's orders had been obeyed and the train load of bacon had been left at Amelia Court House instead of being carried to Richmond, Lee would have joined Johnston with at least half the army that was at Petersburg. Our brigade lost heavily at Five Forks. More than half of the men who went into that battle were killed, wounded or captured. Lieutenant Colonel J. R. Culp, commanding the Seventeenth Regiment, was captured, with half of the small number present for duty. Major J. W. Avery, with the left of the regiment, got away with about half of the men who went into the battle. After the disastrous Battle of the Five Forks was over General Lee continued his retreat, which culminated in the surrender of his army at Appomattox Court House on the 9th of April, 1865.[4] A few officers and men of the Seventeenth South Carolina Volunteers, under the command of Major J. W. Avery, were present at the surrender.[5]

Corporal Robertson recalled the final days of the Twenty-third Regiment:

A day or so before we reached the finality of our struggle, I was informed by a chaplain that we were only marching to a point where General Lee's Army of ragged starving veterans would be surrendered to Grant. Such proved to be the case, and for the life of me I can not see how it could have been otherwise. Wagons by the roadside on fire, men in a starving condition, many without guns, scattered over the face of the country. I managed to keep up with the force that was organized and in line, having use for my gun very often. My dread of the Yankee prisons I guess was the incentive that kept me up to the scratch.

My recollection is that on April 7th our advance arrived at Appomattox. On the first day, our regiment numbered 17 men with guns under the command of a lieutenant. The second day Grant had issued to us nine biscuits and pieces of beef each. When the dinner bell rang, two hundred and fifty reported without arms. In the meantime they had managed to keep out of the way of Yankees and bullets. The third day paroles were given out to those who followed the fortunes of the dying Confederacy to the end, and likewise those who took to the woods before the last gun was fired, all alike commendable in the estimation of the Southern people. All without doubt did the best they could, so charity covers the doings of the weaker ones.

Had a good many visitors from the Federal side inquiring after relatives and old acquaintances. One young man, aid to Sheridan, said he was Southern by birth but living in the North most of his life, espoused their cause. He was hunting his brother. Said brother was found and being true blue declined to shake hands, calling his Yankee brother a traitor who had fought against his own flesh and blood. Some of our men seemed to still be full of fight, declaring to the Yankees that they intended as soon as exchanged to fight them harder than ever before. My belief is that in fact they were in the same fix I was in—all pugnacious qualities knocked sky high.

We surrendered only our flag staff, cutting into pieces the old colors that we had followed through so many storms of shot and shell. . . . The pieces of our old banner were divided as far as they would go. . . . We were formed in lines about two feet apart, victors and vanquished, and we stacked arms. . . . Never did victorious troops behave better, no taunting or harsh talk, they seemed to have a silent regard and respect for the gaunt-faced and ragged veterans in front of them.

Captain Floyd recalled the formal surrender ceremonies:

We stacked arms in front of a Federal line, who honored us by presenting arms as we did so.

Grant chose General Joshua Lawrence Chamberlain of Maine for the honor of receiving the formal surrender of the Army of Northern Virginia on April 12, 1865. As each Confederate unit marched up to stack arms and surrender, Chamberlain had his troops shift their rifles from "order arms" to "carry arms"—the salute of honor. Although this salute was intended to honor his enemy's courage and not his enemy's cause, Chamberlain later received considerable criticism for this action. One Confederate general said to him after the ceremony, "You astonish us by your honorable and generous conduct."[6]

Robert E. Lee issued the following General Order No. 9 to his men:[7]

After four years of arduous service, marked by unsurpassed courage and fortitude, the Army of Northern Virginia has been compelled to yield to overwhelming numbers and resources. I need not tell the brave survivors of so many hard-fought battles, who have remained steadfast to the last, that I have consented to the result from no distrust of them. But, feeling that valor and devotion could accomplish nothing that could compensate for the loss that must have attended the continuance of the contest, I determined to avoid the useless sacrifice of those whose past services have endeared them to their countrymen.

By the terms of the agreement officers and men can return to their homes and remain until exchanged. You will take with you the satisfaction that proceeds from the consciousness of duty faithfully performed; and I earnestly pray that a merciful God will extend to you his blessing and protection.

With an increasing admiration of your constancy and devotion to your country, and a grateful remembrance of your kind and generous considerations for myself, I bid you all an affectionate farewell.

R. E. LEE, General

Captain John Coleman wrote in his diary of going home from Appomattox:

On the evening of April 12th we started home after being paroled. I traded my watch for a horse and rode all the way home in company with Captain Crawford of the York District, making the journey in 12 days and reaching home on the 22nd. Found all well. I soon got rested and became engaged in making a crop for Pappa and my folks. General Johnston's army surrendered about this time and we of course are completely subdued. Our slaves were all declared free. In July, we made a contract with ours to work till the end of the year, giving them one-third of the corn, peas, molasses, and potatoes. I hope the arrangement may prove beneficial to all.

Many of the men who were in prison were not released until months later. Captain John C. Evans described in letters to his wife his final days in prison at Johnson's Island, Ohio:

April 30—A great many here, about 1700 out of 3000, have made application to take the oath to the United States government and be released . . . The South Carolinians generally, are not disposed under the present aspect of affairs to take the oath but prefer to await for further developments. This is my feeling at present, but how soon I may feel compelled to change my mind, I can't tell. I think that since Johnston's surrender of all the forces as far west as Alabama, that our cause is beyond hope, and the necessity for submission is inevitable . . . As soon as I have made up my mind that such is really the case I shall "swallow the Eagle" and come home.

May 12—Out of 2900 officers, all have now applied [to take the oath] except about 60. I held out for a long time but when almost everybody left me I "caved in." I consider our cause as hopeless and the sooner we can get to our families to work for them the better. I don't know how those "Stay at home fighting men" will receive me.[8] I believe though that Annie will welcome me and that is all I care for. There is no telling when we will be released. Every one now seems to be waiting for Andy Johnson's Proclamation which is expected every day.

May 30—I am well with the exception of three boils, two of them now on my right arm. Prison life is not near as hard here as perhaps you imagine although bad enough to make me extremely anxious to get out. The probability is that we will be released before long, but at what particular time we

Dock Owen (wearing medal) and family about 1903
(courtesy of Charles D. Cox)

can't find out. We have been expecting this for the last thirty days, every day. I still hope it will not be long.

June 20—I was calculated to be discharged on Tuesday next. This shall put me behind Godfrey about one week as I will stop in Philadelphia one day. Tell my cute boy William that he shall have a dog knife if one can be found. I will try to bring a pair of shoes for each of the other little girls. God bless them all, they are near my heart. My anxiety for you all increases daily as I don't know how you are provided with food. Oh, I hope that God has been merciful to you as well as he has been to me. [He was finally released on July 1.]

The men of the brigade wandered home from Appomattox and from various Federal prisons by whatever means they could find. Their first priority was to reestablish their civilian lives and to earn a living for their families.[9] In most cases the officers who held the rank of captain or higher carried their military titles into their civilian, and especially into their political, lives. Many of them would soon become leaders in South Carolina politics. Around the turn of the century, some of the veterans would write down what they remembered of the war.

17

THE WAR ENDS FOR GENERAL EVANS

After recovering somewhat from his accident of April 1864, General Evans sought to be restored to command, but Beauregard had no use for him. Evans persisted, and finally in February 1865 the War Department ordered him to report to (of all people) Beauregard, who then commanded the Department of South Carolina, Georgia, and Florida.[1] Beauregard sent him to Joseph E. Johnston's command, noting, "I consider him incompetent to command." Johnston sent Evans back to South Carolina to await orders.[2]

General Evans' brother-in-law, Brigadier General Martin Witherspoon Gary, and his cavalry brigade served as the rear guard as Richmond was abandoned at daylight on April 3.[3] Evans apparently joined Gary and Jefferson Davis' party as it retreated through Danville, Greensboro, and Charlotte and on into South Carolina.[4] The party was in Danville, Virginia, on April 9 when word was received of Lee's surrender, and it immediately set out for Greensboro, North Carolina. Here Davis summoned Generals Johnston and Beauregard to advise him. Both agreed that it was time for peace, and Davis penned a letter to General Sherman asking that hostilities be suspended during negotiations. On April 20, the presidential party continued on to Charlotte. On April 24, in the Phifer house, Davis presided over the last meeting of the full cabinet. On April 26 the party left Charlotte, stopping at the home of Colonel A. B. Springs in Fort Mill. Coincidentally, this was also the date on which General Johnston surrendered his army to General Sherman at the Bennett farmhouse near Raleigh. On April 29 at noon the party stopped in Unionville (now Union), where they were served lunch at the home of General William H. Wallace, the final commander of Evans' now-surrendered brigade.

On May 1 Davis and his party crossed the Saluda River at Puckett's Ferry and stopped for the night at the Gary family home in Cokesbury. General Gary asked and received permission to disband his cavalry because many of his men were from this area and could conveniently return to their homes. It is to be assumed that Generals Gary and Evans remained at Cokesbury, as there is no record of their having continued on with Jefferson Davis and his

Brigadier General Nathan George Evans
(courtesy of Library of Congress)

party. The next day, May 2, 1865, the Davis party moved on to Abbeville, where the final Confederate "Council of War" was held. Later on that same day Jefferson Davis was advised that Federal troops were nearby, and he fled during the night to Georgia, where he was captured by Federal cavalry on May 10, 1865.[5]

Nathan Evans was now unemployed and in ill health. Since each of his first three children—Nathan George Evans Jr., John Gary Evans, and Bernard Bee Evans—were born between 1861 and 1865 at Cokesbury, it is probable that his family had been living at the home of his wife's parents, and it is assumed that this now became his home also. For a time he was involved in the cotton business in Charleston, and then he taught at the Tabernacle School at Cokesbury. This school and the pay were very small, and in December 1867 he accepted a position at a Methodist school in Midway, Alabama.

His fourth child, Mary Martin Evans, was born in Alabama on October 24, 1868.

Nathan George Evans died in Midway, Alabama, on November 23, 1868, and he was buried in the Tabernacle Cemetery at Cokesbury, South Carolina. One source indicated that before he died "he issued a statement saying that he understood the situation, had repented, and was 'trying to serve God.'"[6]

Some time after her husband's death, Victoria Gary Evans moved with her children to Edgefield, South Carolina, to live at Oakley Park, the home of her brother, Martin Witherspoon Gary.[7] "Mart" Gary, as he was called, was a bachelor who lived alone, and some sources say that he bought the large house in order that his widowed sister and her four small children would not be forced to move with their parents into the small Gary family home in Cokesbury.[8]

Nathan George Evans' second son, John Gary Evans, was to play a prominent role in South Carolina politics. He was named for his uncle, Captain John Hillary Gary, who was the next younger brother of his mother.[9] Captain Gary was killed in August 1863 while commanding a company of artillery at Battery Wagner two days after his nephew's birth. John Gary Evans grew up in Edgefield, one of the primary centers of political activity in South Carolina, where he learned Democratic politics from his uncle and guardian. In 1876 "Uncle Mart" and many other Confederate veterans (including William H. Wallace, who became Speaker of the House of Representatives) assisted Wade Hampton in winning the governor's office, thus bringing an end to the Reconstruction Period in South Carolina.[10] Some sources say that the state Democratic campaign of 1876 was planned and coordinated from Martin Gary's Oakley Park Plantation at Edgefield. Martin Gary was elected to the South Carolina Senate in 1876, defeated for United States Senate in 1878, and mentioned in 1880 as a possible candidate for governor. He died in 1881 and is buried in the Tabernacle Cemetery at Cokesbury.[11] Upon his uncle's death, John Gary Evans returned home from Union College in Schenectady, New York, after completing only three years of study. He read law under another uncle, William T. Gary, and established his own law practice in Aiken. His own political career began in 1888, and he soon became a leader within the Ben Tillman faction of the Democratic Party. He served in both the South Carolina House and Senate and was elected the state's youngest governor (at the age of thirty-one) in 1894. In 1895 he presided over the convention that wrote the present constitution for the state of South Carolina.[12]

After the war Lucy Holcombe Pickens also lived near Edgefield, on the Edgewood Plantation.[13] She founded the Maxcy Gregg Chapter of the United

Daughters of the Confederacy and organized the drive to place a monument to the Confederate dead in the Edgefield town square. Lucy died in 1899, and Victoria Gary Evans was serving as president of this UDC chapter in 1900 when the monument was unveiled. In 1924 it was necessary to move the monument when the town square was reconfigured. Helen Sheppard Nicholson, a granddaughter of General William H. Wallace, was the UDC chapter president who presided over moving the monument to its present position.[14] It seems that the ghost of Evans' Brigade has chosen to reside in Edgefield.

APPENDIX I

The Brigade and its Leaders

(from its formation in Charleston on July 17, 1862)

Brigadier General Nathan George Evans (disabled in a buggy accident on April 16, 1864)
Brigadier General William S. Walker (captured at Clay's Farm on May 20, 1864)
Brigadier General Stephen Elliott Jr. (wounded at the Crater on July 30, 1864)
Brigadier General William H. Wallace

The Seventeenth South Carolina Regiment

Colonel John Hugh Means of the Fairfield District (mortally wounded at Second Manassas on August 30, 1862)
Colonel Fitz William McMaster of the Richland District (captured at Fort Stedman on March 25, 1865)

The Eighteenth South Carolina Regiment

Colonel James M. Gadberry of the Union District (killed at Second Manassas on August 30, 1862)
Colonel William H. Wallace of the Union District (appointed brigadier general on September 20, 1864)
Lieutenant Colonel William B. Allison of the York District

The Twenty-second South Carolina Regiment

Colonel Joseph Abney of the Edgefield District (resigned in early 1862)
Colonel Spartan B. Goodlett of the Greenville District (suspended at Kinston in December 1862 and later cashiered)
Lieutenant Colonel James O'Connell of the Pickens District (resigned on January 26, 1864)
Major James H. Rion of the Fairfield District (until April 20, 1864)
Colonel Olin M. Dantzler of the Orangeburg District (killed at Bermuda Hundred on June 2, 1864)

Colonel David G. Fleming of the Spartanburg District (killed at the Battle of the Crater on July 30, 1864)

Colonel William G. Burt of the Edgefield District

The Twenty-third South Carolina Regiment

Colonel Lewis M. Hatch of the Charleston District (reassigned to State Troops in April 1862)

Colonel Henry L. Benbow of the Clarendon District (captured at Five Forks on April 1, 1865)

The Twenty-sixth South Carolina Regiment

(added to the brigade in May 1863)

Colonel Alexander D. Smith of the Marlboro District

The Holcombe Legion Infantry

Colonel Peter Fayssoux Stevens of the Pendleton District (resigned on October 8, 1862)

Lieutenant Colonel William J. Crawley of the Barnwell District (until April 24, 1864)

Colonel Stephen Elliott Jr. of the Beaufort District (appointed brigadier general on May 28, 1864)

Lieutenant Colonel William J. Crawley (severely wounded at Stony Creek on June 28, 1864)

Captain Andrew B. Woodruff of the Spartanburg District (captured at Five Forks on April 1, 1865)

The Macbeth Light Artillery

Captain Robert Boyce of the Union District (died of disease at Wilmington in April 1863)

Captain B. A. Jeter of the Union District

NOTE: The commanding officers of each unit are listed in the order of their service. In each instance, the highest rank attained is shown. Lower ranking officers, who would often lead a unit for a short period when the commanding officer was sick, wounded, or away on leave, are not listed here.

APPENDIX II

District of Origin of Each Company

According to the *Roll of South Carolina Volunteers in the Confederate States Provisional Army* (also known as the "memory rolls") in the South Carolina Archives:

District (Companies)

Abbeville (HF)
Anderson (18D, 22G)
Barnwell (17G, 17H, HD)
Beaufort *
Charleston (23B, 23C, 23D)
Chester (17A, 17D, 23F)
Chesterfield (23A, 26B, 26F)
Clarendon (23I, 26H)
Colleton *
Darlington (18I, 26G)
Edgefield (22A, HH)
Fairfield (17B)
Greenville *
Horry (26A, 26E, 26K)
Georgetown *
Kershaw (23A)
Lancaster (17I, 22E)
Laurens (M)
Lexington (22I)
Marion (23E, 23H, 26C)
Marlboro (23G, 26D)
Newberry (HG, HH)
Orangeburg (22I)
Pickens (22D, 22F, 22H, 22K)
Richland *
Spartanburg (18E, 18F, 18K, 22B, 22C, HA, HB, HC, HE, HI, HK, M)

Sumter (23K)
Union (18A, 18B, 18C, 18F, M)
Williamsburg (26I)
York (17C, 17E, 17F, 17K, 18G, 18H)

Each company is listed in each district that furnished it with twenty or more men.

KEY

Number denotes regiment; letter following denotes company
(26A = Twenty-sixth Regiment, Company A)
H = Holcombe Legion; letter after H denotes company
(HC = Holcombe Legion, Company C)
M = Macbeth Artillery
* = Only a few men from this district served in the brigade

Notes

Chapter One

1. Carlanna Hendrick authored a chapter titled "The Ancient and Honorable Lineage of Governor John Gary Evans," but it was subsequently cut from her University of South Carolina dissertation. This editor is indebted to her for sharing this unpublished chapter. John Gary Evans, General Evans' second son, became governor of South Carolina in 1894. Unless otherwise noted, Hendrick's major source of Evans family history is Evans, *History of Nathaniel Evans of Cat Fish Creek and his Descendants.*
2. The South Carolina Military Academy consisted of two schools. Each student began at The Arsenal Academy in Columbia. Upon completion of one year of study, the student then moved to The Citadel Academy in Charleston.
3. See Tidball, "Getting Through West Point," 68–69. John C. Tidball was a West Point classmate of Evans. He served with distinction in various United States artillery units during the Civil War. After the war he remained in service until his retirement in 1889. He died in 1906, the last survivor of the United States Military Academy class of 1848.
4. See Cullum, *Biographical Register of the Officers and Graduates of the U.S. Military Academy.* Evans is designated as graduate number 1404.
5. See Arnold, *Jeff Davis's Own*, Brackett, *History of the United States Calvary*, Johnson, *A Soldier's Reminiscences in Peace and War*, and Price, *Across the Continent with the Fifth Calvary.*
6. Copies of letters from Robert E. Lee to N. G. Evans during 1856 and 1857 are in the Douglas Southall Freeman Papers at the Virginia Historical Society.
7. See Beverly Daniel Evans IV, "Nathan George Evans: Brigadier General, C.S.A.," 53–59, and also the biographical sketch of General Nathan George Evans in McCrady and Ashe, *Cyclopedia of Eminent and Representative Men of the Carolinas of the Nineteenth Century*, vol. 1, 424–27.
8. Brigadier General Gary commanded the cavalry rearguard as Jefferson Davis fled Richmond. Gary later claimed that during this retreat Davis promised him a promotion to major general. No record of this promotion exists.
9. See note 7, chapter 1.
10. There is some difficulty in tracing Evans' initial state and Confederate appointments. Some of Evans' letters seeking rank and some letters written in his behalf

are in his compiled service records in the National Archives. See also Evans, "Nathan George Evans: Brigadier General C.S.A.," 75–82. A copy of Lee's Special Order 198 sending Major Evans to Manassas Junction to report to Beauregard is in the Douglass Southall Freeman Papers at the Virginia Historical Society.

11. For two eyewitness accounts of this battle, which is also known as the Battle of Bull Run, from opposite sides see Captain James B. Fry, U.S.A. (a member of McDowell's staff), "McDowell's Advance to Bull Run" in Johnson and Buel, *Battles and Leaders*, vol. 1, 167–93, and General G. T. Beauregard, C.S.A., "The First Battle of Bull Run" in Johnson and Buel, *Battles and Leaders*, vol. 1, 196–227. For an excellent account of the role of Evans and his demi-brigade, see "Beauregard Plans a Battle" and "Beauregard's Star at Zenith," chapters 5 and 6 respectively in *Lee's Lieutenants*, vol. 1. For recent accounts of the entire battle, see *Battle at Bull Run* by William C. Davis and *The First Battle of Manassas* by John Hennessy.
12. See Edward Porter Alexander's memoirs, *Fighting for the Confederacy*, 50.
13. Beauregard's report may be found in U.S. War Department, *Official Records*, vol. 2, 484–504. The references to Colonel Evans' conduct (he was promoted on July 26, before Beauregard wrote this report) during the battle are found on pages 489, 490, and 499.
14. Letter dated September 15, 1861, in the Lalla Pelot Papers in the Rare Book, Manuscript, and Special Collections Library at Duke University. James M. Pelot was serving in the Fifth South Carolina Regiment commanded by David R. Jones.
15. For a Federal officer's account, see Lieutenant Colonel Richard B. Irwin, U.S.A., "Ball's Bluff and the Arrest of General Stone," in Johnson and Buel, *Battles and Leaders*, vol. 2, 123–34. For a Confederate officer's account, see Hunter, "Men of Virginia at Ball's Bluff." Also see the monographs by Holien, *Battle at Ball's Bluff*, and Patch, *The Battle of Ball's Bluff*.
16. Evans' official report of the battle related in some detail how he commanded his units throughout the four-day battle. (U.S. War Department, *Official Records*, vol. 5, 348–52.) Beverly Daniel Evans IV devotes an entire chapter of his master's thesis to this battle, describing his great-uncle's hands-on management of the overall strategy and tactics (Evans, "Nathan George Evans: Brigadier General C.S.A.," pages 103–35). R. W. Hunter later recalled that "Colonel Evans, the commander of the whole field, remained at *Fort* Evans, two and a half miles from Edward's Ferry and one and a half miles from Ball's Bluff, during the whole day, watching both points, and directing the general operations. In detaching two-thirds of his command from Gorman's front to reinforce Hunton at the critical juncture he evinced strategic skill and generalship of a high order and added to the fame he had won at First Manassas" (Hunter, "Men of Virginia at Ball's Bluff," 265). Major Lamar Fontaine, a Mississippi officer, said that Evans was present and personally ordered the main charge (McCrady and Ashe, *Cyclopedia of Eminent and Representative Men of the Carolinas*, 487). Haskell stated that Evans was some distance away and either sick or drunk (Haskell, *The Haskell Memoirs*, 11–12).
17. For a detailed account see Burton, *The Siege of Charleston*, 61–119.

18. In a letter to his wife on December 12, 1861, J. E. B. Stuart wrote, "Shanks Evans has gone to South Carolina and is a good riddance. He paid no more attention to orders than to the bite of a fly, and as Field says a reprimand falls on Shanks as harmless as peas on the back of a rhinoceros" (Duncan, ed., *The Letters of Major General James E. B. Stuart*, 27). Captain Blackford of Virginia, who fought under Evans at Manassas and Leesburg, wrote home on December 6, 1861, that he was pleased that General D. H. Hill was relieving Evans: "I do not know where Evans will go. I think the change is a good one as Evans is too indiscreet for a separate command" (Blackford, ed., *Letters From Lee's Army*, 61). Major Thomas J. Goree, an aide to Longstreet, wrote to his wife that "Genl Evans is one of the bravest men I ever saw, and is no doubt a good officer when sober, but he is unfortunately nearly always under the influence of liquor" (Cutrer, ed., *Longstreet's Side: The Civil War Letters of Major Thomas J. Goree*, 51). In contrast, however, the men and officers of the 17th Mississippi Volunteers praised his leadership and insisted that Evans present the "battle flag" to the regiment before he left. One soldier, E. P. Miller wrote home on December 9, 1861, that "I fear that we will never get as good a general as Evans again . . . He goes to his native state, South Carolina, tomorrow. The good wishes of the whole brigade go with him. Both officers and privates, all liked General Evans. We have tried him on the battlefield, and know what he will do" (South Carolina Division of the United Daughters of the Confederacy, *Recollections and Reminiscences*, vol. 2, 264–65).
19. See U.S. War Department, *Official Records*, vol. 6, 334, 344–45, 347, 348, 351. The Seventeenth Regiment would later become a part of Evans' Brigade. The Sixteenth Regiment, from the Greenville District, would become a part of Gist's Brigade. The Third Battalion, also called the Laurens Battalion or James' Battalion, was made up of men from the Laurens and Greenwood Districts. It included only seven companies and never grew to become a full regiment. Throughout most of the war it fought as a unit of Kershaw's Brigade.
20. Lee to Evans, February 15, 1862, in "Letters of the Department of South Carolina, Georgia, and East Florida" in the National Archives, Washington, D.C.

Chapter Two

1. See Records of the Confederate Historian, *Roll of South Carolina Volunteers in the Confederate States Provisional Army*. See also Appendix II: District of Primary Origin of Each Company of Evans' Brigade.
2. This is taken from pages 1 and 2 of the typescript of the "Diary of Samuel (Cosmo) Catawba Lowry." He wrote the first eighteen (typescript) pages of this account from memory after he was wounded at the Second Battle of Manassas and had returned home. He returned to his unit on January 22, 1864, and the diary portion of his account begins on that date. He was killed at the Battle of the Crater about four or five hours into the battle while, as acting captain, he was leading what was left of his company in battle. He was nineteen and one-half years old. His faithful servant, Henry Avery, brought his body back to Yorkville for burial.

3. William H. "Captain Bill" Edwards from Chester County began the war as orderly sergeant of Company A, Seventeenth Regiment S.C.V. He was elected first lieutenant on April 28, 1862, upon the reorganization of the regiment into Confederate service and was appointed captain on September 1, 1862. He led his company throughout most of the war and was a close friend of Colonel McMaster. His account, the only printed history of the Seventeenth Regiment, was written in 1906 at the request of Helen G. McMaster, the daughter of the colonel. Edwards died in 1920.
4. See McCrady, *Heroes of the Old Camden District*, 23–24.
5. See Freeman, *R. E. Lee*, vol. 1, chap. 36, "An Easy Lesson in Combating Sea-Power," for a thorough discussion of the general political and military situation surrounding Lee's appointment.
6. See Freeman, *R. E. Lee*, vol. 2, chap. 3, "Lee and the Conscription Act."
7. The *Roll of the Dead* shows that Captain Holley died on June 18, 1862 on James Island.
8. This is clearly sarcasm. Edwards' low opinion of Evans will become apparent later in his account.
9. Hinson Hyde "Dock" Owen was born in 1835 in the Laurens District. His father was a "botanical and mineral doctor." When he was seventeen his father died, and he worked for three years in the "marble trade" in Columbia. He then accompanied a Virginia slave trader who was taking 109 slaves to Louisiana and Texas, and after the last one was sold in Dallas, Texas, Owen worked for a while in the timber business in Arkansas. After Arkansas seceded, he served in Company F, Ninth Arkansas Regiment, until February 1862. He then came back to South Carolina and joined Company F of the Holcombe Legion "with Captain M. G. Ziegler." He was wounded at Second Manassas but served until the war's end. He had such high respect for Ziegler that he named his next child Etta Ziegler Owen.
10. Letter in the L. M. Hatch Papers in the Southern Historical Collection at the University of North Carolina, Chapel Hill, N.C.
11. Corporal John Forrest Robertson served in Company A of the Twenty-third Regiment until the Mississippi campaign, when he requested a transfer to Company B (the Chicora Rifles) which included many of his friends. He was wounded in the trenches at Petersburg on June 17, 1864, and he was sent home to recover, thus missing the Battle of the Crater. He returned to his regiment in October 1864 and was given the lighter duties of a sergeant thereafter.
12. Joshua Hilary Hudson was born at Chester, South Carolina, in 1832. His father was a tailor, his mother a devout Baptist. He graduated from South Carolina College with honors in 1852. From 1853 until 1857, he taught school and read the law. He began the practice of law in 1857 and served as a state representative from 1858 to 1859. He entered military service as a private in the Twenty-first Regiment then transferred to the Twenty-sixth Regiment, where he served as adjutant, major, and lieutenant colonel. After the war he continued the practice of law, and he served as judge of the Fourth Judicial Circuit from 1878 until 1894. In 1896 and 1897 he presided over the South Carolina Convention of the Baptist Church. In 1903 he received the honorary degree of doctor of letters. He served in the

state senate in 1905 and 1906 and was chosen president of the South Carolina Bar in 1907. Married in 1854, he had fourteen children, and he outlived nearly all of them. See Hemphill, *Men of Mark in South Carolina*, 173–76, and Garlington, *Men of the Time*, 215.

13. This is taken from the second of VIDI's seventeen articles in *The Weekly Union (S.C.) Times*, April 30, 1886.
14. According to Evans, *Confederate Military History*, vol. 5, 10–16, and also Stevens' unpublished "Autobiography." Peter F. Stevens grew up in Pendleton, South Carolina, and graduated first in his class from The Citadel in 1849. After two years as a civil engineer/surveyor for various railroads in central South Carolina, he was appointed professor of mathematics at The Arsenal Academy in Columbia. He later joined the faculty of The Citadel, and he was named superintendent in 1859. After South Carolina seceded, he was directed by Governor Pickens to take a detachment of cadets and man a battery of guns on Morris Island. On January 9, 1861, these cadets fired the first shots of the war at the Federal steamship *Star of the West*, which was attempting to re-supply Fort Sumter. Stevens commanded the "Iron Battery" (designed by his older brother, Clement Hoffman Stevens) during the bombardment of Fort Sumter in April 1861. After his Holcombe Legion was assigned to Evans' Brigade, Stevens was frequently placed in command of the entire brigade because he was the senior colonel. After the Maryland campaign, he felt that he had been diverted from the defense of South Carolina, for which he had volunteered, and he resigned to return to his sacred calling. In his post-war ministry he placed an emphasis upon assisting the former slaves to gain a basic education, and he helped a number of them to enter the ministry.
15. See Chapman, *History of Edgefield County*, 234. For a biographical sketch of the life of Lucy Holcombe Pickens, see Emily L. Bull, "Lucy Pickens: First Lady of the South Carolina Confederacy," *Proceedings of the South Carolina Historical Association*, 1982, 5–18. It should be noted, however, that the reference to a woodcut in *Harper's* magazine showing Lucy reviewing the legion is in error. A woodcut of Mrs. Pickens reviewing the troops at Fort Moultrie did appear in *Leslie's Illustrated Magazine* on February 23, 1861, but the Holcombe Legion was not formed until the following fall. Another reference states that Lucy Pickens' maiden name appeared on the unit's flag above the palmetto tree and that she sold her jewelry and used the proceeds to help to equip the legion (South Carolina Division of the United Daughters of the Confederacy, *Recollections and Reminiscences*, vol. 7, 451–52). According to Fuller, *Confederate Currency and Stamps*, her portrait appeared on one series of the Confederate one-dollar bills and on three series of hundred-dollar bills.
16. There were discussions in December 1861 involving Governor Pickens and Generals Gist, Ripley, and Lee with regard to assigning the Washington Artillery and/or Boyce's Artillery to the Holcombe Legion. See U.S. War Department, *Official Records*, vol. 6, 335–37. Stevens continued to seek an artillery unit, and R. G. Dwight, in a letter to Ellison Capers on June 26, 1862, noted that Stevens had

asked that Henry Capers' Artillery Battery be attached to the Holcombe Legion. Also see U.S. War Department, *Official Records*, series 4, vol. 3, 430.

17. According to James L. Strain, writing in the *Union County News*, on September 6, 1901, the Holcombe Legion cavalry started from Charleston on July 21, 1862, but did not reach Richmond until August 22, a week after the brigade had left by train for Gordonsville.
18. See Fuller, *Confederate Currency and Stamps*, 49. Charles D. Cox, a grandson of Dock Owen, upon reading this account cautioned the editor: "I grew up being told by my older cousins from the Laurens area that one could never know if what Dock Owen was saying was fact or just a story he made up. He was known for making up stories, or possibly stretching facts out of shape, and passing them off as being the absolute truth. My father told me long ago that he never knew when to believe Dock." The account of this event that appeared in *The Charleston Daily Courier* on June 4, 1862, stated that Lucy Holcombe Pickens was not even present but that a letter from her was read to the legion by the adjutant, presumably William Porcher DuBose.
19. William Frank Lominack, Company G of the Holcombe Legion, wrote to his wife from Adams Run on March 6, 1862: "We are satisfied to stay here one month longer if it were not for being under the Command of General Evans, he is a perfect tyrant and there is not one in the Legion that like him. I think that if we cannot get from under his Command no other way the officers and men will unite and vote from under his Command." Colonel Stevens' sister-in-law Annie wrote to her aunt Sarah on May 16, 1862: "I have just had a visit from dear Fayssoux . . . poor child he does not like being under Evans at all and is trying hard to get away but he had an interview with General Pemberton today and it seems impossible for the present . . ." W. H. Faulkner of the Seventeenth Regiment wrote to his cousin, William L. Faulkner, on May 25, 1862: "General Evans said . . . that he would fight them to the last before he would give it [Johns Island] up. I tell you the old fellow is keen for a fight and he is going to have it if there is any chance for it."
20. Chapter 2, titled "War," in Burton, *The Siege of Charleston*, is a very readable account of the Federal capture of Port Royal and the general situation along the South Carolina coast early in the war.
21. J. Anderson Mills of Company K of the Twenty-third Regiment wrote to his brother from Morris Island on June 19, 1862, "We have the Island pretty well fortified now & if we had about a week longer we might make it a perfect Gibralter . . . But as it was on James Island as soon as we get the Island fortified they move us & give some other troops our works to fight behind and make a name."
22. Brennan gives the armament of the fort as one eight-inch Columbiad, two rifled twenty-four-pound pieces, and several eighteen-pound guns, plus a mortar battery in the rear. See Brennan, *Secessionville*, 159. Columbiads were heavy, long-chambered, muzzle-loading, smoothbore artillery pieces. These guns typically had eight, ten, or fifteen-inch bores, weighed nine thousand, fifteen thousand, or fifty thousand pounds, and threw shot weighing 65, 130, or 425 pounds from one to three miles. They were primarily used in seacoast defense and were too large and heavy for portable field use.

23. Colonel Goodlett of the Twenty-second Regiment reported that "In obedience to an order from headquarters I detailed 100 picked men, 10 from each company, to go as a fatigue party about 1 A.M. of the 16th instant to Secessionville." See U.S. War Department, *Official Records*, vol. 14, 97–98. Brennan, *Secessionville*, 170–72, puts their arrival at the fort at about 4:30 A.M.
24. Evans was placed in command of the First Military District, including James Island, on June 14, and he and Hagood immediately made an inspection tour of the island's defenses. See Hagood, *Memoirs of the War of Secession*, 93.
25. After the Ordinance of Secession was passed, a call for one-year troops was issued by the state of South Carolina. The first ten companies that responded to the call for troops came from the Barnwell, Colleton, and Orangeburg Districts, and they were formed into the First Regiment, South Carolina Volunteers, under Colonel Johnson Hagood. This regiment would serve throughout the war as a unit of Hagood's Brigade. Brigadier General Hagood gives a detailed description of the Secessionville Campaign in *Memoirs of the War of Secession*, 83–98.
26. For an interesting and detailed account of this battle, see Brennan, *Secessionville*. A Federal account of this battle in *Papers of the Military Historical Society of Massachusetts* vol. 9, 124–57, cites the incompetence of Brigadier General Henry W. Benham as a primary cause of the Federal defeat. Beauregard would later write, "The truth of the matter is, that the point attacked by Generals Benham and I. I. Stevens near Secessionville was the strongest one of the whole line, which was then unfinished and was designed to be some five miles in length" (in "The Defense of Charleston," in Johnson and Buel, *Battles and Leaders*, vol. 4, 1–23).
27. Lamar evidently recovered from his wounds but died in Charleston of malaria on October 18, 1862.
28. R. E. Seabrook in the *Charleston News and Courier*, as quoted by McLaurin, "The Confederate Chaplain," in *The Life Work of John L. Girardeau*, 109.
29. On June 2, 1862, William Frank Lominack wrote to reassure his mother that ". . . this Legion will not have to go out of this State . . . they will have to keep some troops here, and the Legion is a favorite command of Gov. Pickens." He was wrong.
30. See U.S. War Department, *Official Records*, vol. 14, 586, and also vol. 11, part 3, 644. A word here about the two artillery units listed: Captain W. D. Leake commanded Turner's (Virginia) Light Artillery, which was assigned to Evans' Brigade for only about one month, possibly only for the purpose of moving it to Richmond. However, the Macbeth Artillery fought with Evans' Brigade until early in 1864. According to the *Carolina Spartan* of April 17, 1862, the Macbeth Artillery, commanded by Captain Boyce, ". . . now numbers one hundred and seventy-eight, mostly from Union District, and is named in honor of a worthy citizen of that district . . ." The *Charleston Daily Courier* of May 6, 1863, identified the honoree as Sheriff Robert Macbeth. Boyce died of dysentery on April 19, 1863, in Wilmington, North Carolina, and 1st Lieutenant B. A. Jeter was promoted to command the unit. Some later references refer to the unit as Jeter's Battery. In April 1864, when the brigade left to go north to the Petersburg campaign, the Macbeth Artillery was left in Charleston. It was soon transferred to Asheville, North Carolina, for the remainder of the war.

31. See U.S. War Department, *Official Records*, vol. 11, pt. 3, 675.
32. John Carson of the Holcombe Legion wrote to his mother on June 9, 1862: "Joshua said flee Oh Israel but if he'd been here he would have said fleas Oh Israel. The difficulty in camp is that the fleas won't fly and the flies won't flee."
33. Major Byrd refused to give way for Major Hudson to become the lieutenant colonel of the new regiment. Major Hudson's letter of January 5, 1863, petitioning C.S.A. inspector general Samuel Cooper to resolve this matter, is in Hudson's compiled service records.

Chapter Three

1. Clifford Dowdey provides an extensive overview of the military and political situation at this time in his book, *Lee Takes Command.*
2. Freeman uses these words in his book, *R. E. Lee*, vol. 2, 256.
3. Thomas S. Waring, acting surgeon of the Seventeenth Regiment, wrote to his wife from Camp Mary on August 1, 1862: "Yesterday the Col. informed the mess that he had subscribed for a teacher to instruct the regimental band and had said that the mess would pay for it. All agreed to it immediately. I said nothing, but my name went down. I paid."
4. William Porcher DuBose was born in 1836 in Winnsboro, South Carolina, where he was raised and schooled on the three-thousand-acre, slave-holding plantation called Farmington. He entered The Citadel in January 1852 and graduated at the top of his class in 1855. After a brief period at home, he entered the University of Virginia, from which he received post-graduate certificates in Latin, French, Greek, moral science, mathematics, and natural philosophy. In 1859 he entered the new diocesan seminary in Camden, but before he could complete the program of study, he was asked to join the Holcombe Legion as its adjutant. After two years of hard service, influential friends interceded in his behalf, and DuBose left the legion to be the chaplain of Kershaw's Brigade. After the war Reverend DuBose served Episcopal churches in Winnsboro, Fairfield, and Abbeville. In early 1871 he was almost elected to be the assistant bishop of South Carolina—in his own words, ". . . one of the most fortunate escapes of my life." That summer, he was elected chaplain and professor of moral science by the University of the South. He remained at Sewanee for the remainder of his life and died in 1918.
5. The Battle of Malvern Hill, which took place on July 1, 1862, did not involve Evans' Brigade. Federal troops stayed in the area until July 7 and then began to retreat to Harrison's Landing on the James River for evacuation. Evans' Brigade skirmished with the Federal rearguard in early August.
6. On May 18, 1909, Welborn J. Andrews of Oswego, South Carolina, called together the survivors of his company at the Sumter Courthouse. The result was *Sketch of Company K., 23rd South Carolina Volunteers, In the Civil War, from 1862–1865.* The typesetter misspelled his name as "Welburn" when this booklet was printed.
7. For another account of the Twenty-third Regiment's night in the woods, see Private George R. Jones' recollections in South Carolina Division of the United Daughters of the Confederacy, *Recollections and Reminiscences*, vol. 8, 409–10.
8. U.S. War Department, *Official Records*, vol. 11, pt. 3, 675.

9. See Hennessy, *Return to Bull Run*, 1–31. In chapters 1 through 6 of this work, Hennessy gives a thorough account of the appointment of Pope and of his and Lee's tactics along the Rappahannock during this period. For Pope's account see Pope, "The Second Bull Run Campaign," pt. 4 of *The Military Memoirs of General John Pope*. For a discussion of the July-August campaign from Lee's viewpoint, see Harsh, *Confederate Tide Rising*.
10. Albert Allison James was born in Yorkville, South Carolina, on July 26, 1824. He was educated at Davidson College and at the Theological Seminary in Columbia and became pastor of the Presbyterian church at Fair Forest in Spartanburg County in 1851. After the war he returned to this church and continued to serve it until after the turn of the century. He is also credited with organizing churches at Glenn Springs, Pacolet, Jonesville, Trough Shoals, and Enoree. He died on June 8, 1910. See South Carolina Division of the United Daughters of the Confederacy, *Recollections and Reminiscences*, vol. 2, 499–500.
11. See Hennessy, *Return to Bull Run*, 54–55.
12. Captain William G. Vardell was the quartermaster of the Twenty-third Regiment but was acting brigade quartermaster on many occasions. He was a very religious man who tended to wax philosophical in his letters to his wife. In early 1864 he was promoted to the rank of major and assigned to be the quartermaster of Ripley's Brigade. After the war he became a minister, and he served the Johns Island Presbyterian Church from 1885 until his death in 1897.
13. An article on page 2 of the *Carolina Spartan* newspaper of September 4, 1862, identified the spy as "[a] man named Mason, a resident of Fairfax County, Virginia, but a native of Pennsylvania." It gave the following story, which differs slightly from the accounts of Vardell and Edwards: "The Division commanded by General Longstreet was pushing for a point which it was known that the enemy desired to reach and occupy. As the column was proceeding forward, a courier, pretending to have orders from General Lee, halted each brigade until he reached the last, when Longstreet, observing the movement, desired to know what it meant. He was told that General Lee had ordered the halt, and upon demanding to know the authority for the order from General Lee, was pointed to the courier, who had not time to make his escape. The man was immediately arrested by Longstreet, who frustrated his designs. He was examined and condemned on the spot. Forged orders to both Jackson and Hill were found on his person, those for Longstreet having been delivered, and he acknowledged that he had been acting as a Confederate scout for eleven months, and all that time was a traitor and a spy. He was then condemned and executed in about fifteen minutes." Another source said that the spy had some success in delaying the march. "By the confusion caused by the delay, we lost about an hour, which enabled the Yankees to get most of their wagon train over the road and burn the bridge." (South Carolina Division of the United Daughters of the Confederacy, *Recollections and Reminiscences*, vol. 8, 7.) Owen identified the spy as Charles Mason of Perrysville, Pennsylvania, and indicated that Mason had killed one of Longstreet's couriers on the previous day. Owen put the delay of Longstreet's Division at "nearly three hours." (Owen, *In Camp and Battle with the Washington Artillery*, 101–2.) The "ANONYMOUS"

account in Broadfoot Publishing Company, *Supplement to the Official Records*, pt. 1, vol. 2, 770–72, is actually that of Felix Gregory DeFontaine, the correspondent of the *Charleston Daily Courier* who wrote under the pen name of PERSONNE. See the issue of August 30, 1862.

14. George R. Jones related that "in this affair the first blood was shed in Company I, better known in Clarendon as the Sprott Guards. For this reason the survivors of the Sprott Guards have their annual reunion on the 23rd of August." See South Carolina Division of the United Daughters of the Confederacy, *Recollections and Reminiscences*, vol. 8, 411.
15. See the third of VIDI's seventeen articles in *The Weekly Union (S.C.) Times*, May 14, 1886.
16. William M. Owen indicated that the artillery duel began at sunrise and that, after two hours of heavy fire, the enemy was driven from its forward position on the south side of the river. "The brigades of Gens. Evans and D. R. Jones . . . moved forward to occupy this position. It was found untenable, however, being exposed to a cross-fire of artillery from the other bank. The troops were therefore partially withdrawn . . ." See Owen, *In Camp and Battle with the Washington Artillery*, 103–5. Longstreet wrote: "On August 23d I had quite a spirited artillery combat at Beverly Ford with a force of the enemy that had crossed at the railroad bridge near where I was stationed. The superior position and metal of the Federals gave them an advantage, which they improved by skillful practice. We had more guns, however, and by practice equally clever at length gained the advantage. A little before night the Federals withdrew from the combat." See Longstreet, "Our March Against Pope" in Johnson and Buel, *Battles and Leaders*, vol. 2, 516.
17. They almost lost Stonewall Jackson. Captain Bradford reported in his diary: "While moving on the crest of the hill a solid shot from the enemy's battery passed through the horse of my sergeant, Bob Isbell, who was carrying General Jackson's battle flag . . . The horse fell over perfectly dead; it was between me and the General, its head lapping on the General's horse and its rump on mine, and the ball did not miss the nose of my horse six inches." See Blackford, *Letters from Lee's Army*, 117.
18. This illustration is modified from the original plate. The earthworks shown here were present on March 28, 1862, when this map was drawn. See U.S. War Department, *Official Records*, vol. 12, pt. 1, 413, and vol. 12, pt. 2, 552–53. It is assumed that these fortifications, and perhaps others, were in place on August 23, but no map was drawn of that engagement.
19. Evans reported a total of twenty-seven killed and eighty-two wounded. The brigade was noted for its bravery in this fight. Vardell's letter of August 24, 1862, states that "General Lee, on reviewing the battle field after their retreat said that he regarded it as one of the strongest positions that he had ever seen and thought that they could not have been dislodged by any force." Another observer, Sgt. W. H. Andrews, who was serving nearby in Anderson's Georgia Brigade, wrote on page 58 of his book, *Footprints of a Regiment:* "The Palmetto boys are made of the right material or they could never have retreated in good order under that fire . . .

Glad the Palmetto boys were out of sight when we made our retreat, for we got out the best way we could."

20. Pope related on pages 145 through 147 of *The Military Memoirs of General John Pope* that he planned to "mass my whole force to recross the river by the bridge and fords near Rappahannock Station and Kelly's Ford and to assail the flank and rear of the long column of the enemy slowly moving up the river . . . As it happened, however, a heavy rain set in that night and by morning the river had risen at least eight feet and had become a raging torrent, carrying away one bridge and destroying for some days all the fords below Sulphur Springs. It was no longer practicable to recross the river and make the attack we had prepared for . . ."
21. See Sorrel, *Recollections of a Confederate Staff Officer*, 99–100.
22. See DuBose, *Reminiscences*, 84–85. The Confederate officers' reports of the artillery duel at Rappahannock Station are generally combined with their reports of the Second Battle at Manassas. See U.S. War Department, *Official Records*, vol. 12, pt. 2, 546–73 and 627–40.
23. See Hood, *Advance and Retreat*, 32–33.

Chapter Four

1. Chapter 9, "Bring Out Your Men Gentlemen," in Hennessy's *Return to Bull Run* tells the story of the passage of Longstreet's troops through the lightly defended Thoroughfare Gap. Chapter 10, "A Long and Continuous Roll," gives a complete account of the fight near Groveton on August 28.
2. Hennessy's *Return to Bull Run*, chap. 11, "Pope Finds Jackson—At Last," covers the evening of August 28 and the initial clash of the troops of Pope and Jackson on the morning of the twenty-ninth. Chapter 12, "Siegel's Battle," details the fighting along the unfinished railroad between the troops of Siegel and Jackson (including Maxcy Gregg's South Carolina Brigade) during the late morning.
3. Hennessy's *Return to Bull Run*, chap. 13, "Controversy Comes from the Fringe," tells of the arrival of Hood's Division followed by the remainder of Longstreet's Corps.
4. Chapter 14, "Bloody Afternoon," and chapter 15, "I'll Expect You to Beat Them," in Hennessy's *Return to Bull Run* covers this part of the battle.
5. Chapter 16, "Twilight Clash," in Hennessy's *Return to Bull Run* covers this probing operation, which turned into a considerable fight. Lee and Longstreet conferred later that evening and concluded that they would not attack this heavily defended portion of the Federal line the next morning.
6. Wiley John Floyd was born at Darlington in 1836. When the war came he was third sergeant in the Darlington Guards, a local militia unit. After the surrender of Fort Sumter the militia disbanded, and several new companies were raised by volunteers from the old. John Floyd became first lieutenant of the Darlington Rifles, which became Company I of the Eighteenth Regiment. He would become its captain in 1863. After the war he entered the mercantile and hotel businesses, and he served in the local offices of county commissioner and trial justice and as a state representative.

7. From the fourth of VIDI's seventeen articles in *The Weekly Union (S.C.) Times*, May 28, 1886.
8. Colonel Peter F. Stevens, commanding Evans' Brigade, later reported: "Reaching a wood some mile from our starting point, the right of the brigade passed over the left of a Texas regiment lying down. The enemy's fire now became annoying, and on reaching the edge of the wood it was very severe. The Twenty-third South Carolina, on the left flank, emerged at once and entire; but the skirt of the woods then ran obliquely to my line of battle, so that the Eighteenth and Seventeenth Regiments were gradually uncovered from left to right, while the Holcombe Legion was still in the wood. Upon the appearance of the Twenty-third the enemy's fire was redoubled, and the Eighteenth and Seventeenth, instead of moving straight forward, almost instinctively inclined to the right still to keep under cover. This caused my line to become gradually broken and confused until, when the right flank was finally uncovered, the men of these two regiments were mingled with the Legion some ten or twelve deep. In my efforts to remedy this inclination to the right I had been insensibly carried in the same direction and emerged nearly on the extreme right. Here I found the line halted and staggering under the murderous fire of grape, canister, and musketry which was pouring upon it. Urging them still forward and giving the command to charge, I found it impossible for officers to make themselves be obeyed, owing to the commingling of regiments." See U.S. War Department, *Official Records*, vol. 12, pt. 2, 631.
9. For another recollection of the Twenty-third Regiment at Second Manassas see that of George R. Jones of Company I in South Carolina Division of the United Daughters of the Confederacy, *Recollections and Reminiscences*, vol. 8, 412–18.
10. For the reports of the Confederate officers commanding the brigade and associated units at the Second Battle at Manassas, see U.S. War Department, *Official Records*, vol. 12, pt. 2, 546–73, 604–6, 627–40. The Second Manassas campaign losses for Evans' Brigade are given on page 568 as 133 killed, 593 wounded, and 8 missing. Accurate data for overall losses is very difficult to compile, but overall Confederate losses were about 9,500 of 55,000 men engaged, while the Federal losses were about 14,500 of 77,000 men engaged.
11. Thomas S. Waring wrote home on September 8, 1862, "The Yankee Army made a slight stand near Centreville then retreated rapidly toward Washington. We captured a large amount of stores at Centreville. I have a beautiful amputating case and very pretty set of tooth extracting instruments and a fine pair of blankets."
12. See the *Charleston Daily Courier* for September 23, 1862.
13. Samuel Campbell wrote this letter to his wife Rebecca Wallace Campbell. A typed transcript is in the Special Collections of the Greater Clover Historical Society, Clover, South Carolina. Kidd quotes the letter and reports the "Blind Sam" nickname on pages 39 and 40 of his master's thesis, "A Military History of the Campaigns of the Eighteenth Regiment South Carolina Volunteers During the Civil War."
14. This is quoted from page 574 of D. H. Hill's account, "The Battle at South Mountain, or Boonsboro," in Johnson and Buel, *Battles and Leaders*, vol. 2, 559–81. For an account of this battle from the Federal viewpoint, see the account

of General Jacob D. Cox, "Forcing Fox's Gap and Turner's Gap," Johnson and Buel, *Battles and Leaders*, vol. 2, 583–90.

15. John C. Tidball was cited for gallantry at Sharpsburg. He entered the battle as a brevet major and emerged as a brevet lieutenant colonel. See Miller, *The Photographic History of the Civil War*, vol. 1, 285.
16. Robert E. Lee to Jefferson Davis, September 21, 1862.
17. *Charleston Daily Courier*, October 9, 1862.
18. Willoughby F. Trezevant died on September 24, 1862, at Sharpsburg.
19. From the seventh of VIDI's seventeen articles in *The Weekly Union (S.C.) Times*, July 9, 1886.
20. For Lee's report, see U.S. War Department, *Official Records*, vol. 19, pt. 1, 144–53. For a good overview of this battle, see Freeman, *R. E. Lee*, vol. 2, 378–404.
21. During this period Evans wrote to his wife of his concern that his men would "not be able to stand the winter in this climate clothed as they are," and that his men were "suffering for the want of blankets." He requested that the brigade be transferred to South Carolina, but Lee insisted that Evans and the brigade could not be spared (Evans, "Nathan George Evans: Brigadier General, C.S.A.," 174-76). While Evans showed compassion for his men as a group, he could be stern when he felt a solder was taking advantage of him. Thomas S. Waring, acting surgeon of the Seventeenth Regiment, claimed that he was having problems with his eyes, and when the brigade moved to Kinston in November he requested forty days to go home to recover. Evans refused this request, but Waring went home anyway. McMaster wrote Waring on November 29, warning him that Evans was upset and saying, "I give you this information to put you on your guard." McMaster also stated: "We are . . . getting more and more disgusted every day with our fine General. The sooner he is cashiered will be the better for the Service." On December 12, 1862, Waring wrote to S. P. Moore, surgeon general of the C.S.A. "I have the honor to request that you will grant me a transfer from Genl Evans command to that of Genl Beauregard. My reason for making this request is that during a late illness from which I have not yet recovered, I was treated with so little consideration by Genl Evans, that it would be extremely unpleasant to return to his command. My reason for selecting Genl Beauregard is that, being subject to an inflammatory affliction of the eyes, I am unfit for service in a cold climate during the winter."
22. For the reports of the Confederate officers commanding the brigade and associated units at South Mountain and Sharpsburg, see U.S. War Department, *Official Records*, vol. 19, pt. 1, 929–50. Evans' report begins on page 639. Johnson and Buel, *Battles and Leaders*, vol. 2, 601, cites Maryland Campaign losses for Evans' Brigade as 40 killed, 185 wounded, and 65 missing.

Chapter Five

1. According to Fetzer and Mobray on page 77 of their book, *Unlikely Allies*, the population of prisoners at Fort Delaware Prison increased from 68 to 2,470 as a result of the Sharpsburg Campaign. At this time early in the war, this prison served as a temporary holding facility for prisoners awaiting exchange.

2. This story of DuBose's imprisonment and parole is taken from his "Reminiscences," 98–116. For an account of the practice of paroling and exchanging prisoners of war, see Judge Robert Ould, "The Exchange of Prisoners," in *The Annals of the Civil War Written by Leading Participants North and South*, 32–59.
3. George S. Bernard, author of *War Talks of Confederate Veterans*, was also captured at South Mountain. On pages 29 through 40 of his book, he also relates kind treatment by Federal troops and by a Mr. James Giddings of Frederick County and his family.
4. In his "Reminiscences," 107–8, Reverend DuBose explained his interaction with Dr. Tustin after the war: "After the war and my own ordination, in the rectory of the church in Abbeville, South Carolina, I received a letter from him, then rector of the principal church in Grand Rapids. He recalled our acquaintance and said that he had seen my name on the missionary list in South Carolina and had nominated me, or my mission really, as the recipient of his Sunday School offering for missions, and he enclosed a sum of money. This was repeated some years afterwards, and then Dr. Tustin died. Some years later, after I had removed to Sewanee, I received for the theological department a hundred dollars from an unknown donor, the initials only being signed and no address given. This occurred several times, and I could never make acknowledgment because I never knew the address. Ultimately I found out that it was Mrs. Tustin and in memory of her husband. I then wrote a general acknowledgment referring at the same time to my original acquaintance with her husband. Several years after this, I received a letter from Mrs. Tustin saying that she expected to be in Charleston and Savannah the following winter and wishing that she might meet me. I made an appointment to meet her in Savannah on my return from Florida at the end of the winter. A few days before the time appointed for our meeting, I received notification of Mrs. Tustin's death. A short time after this, I got a letter from a lawyer in Grand Rapids, asking a few technical questions about the name, etc. of our theological department. In the course of the year, Sewanee was the recipient of some thirty thousand dollars, from the will of the late Dr. J. W. Tustin."
5. It was a common practice for South Carolina's prosperous "Low Country" (coastal) families to retreat to the "Upcountry" of South Carolina during the summer months to escape the heat and the coastal diseases such as yellow fever. Summer homes with picturesque names such as Boscobel and Ashtabula and resort hotels such as those at the Williamston Mineral Spring and at Chick Springs and Glenn Springs were common in the Anderson, Pickens, Greenville, and Spartanburg Districts.

Chapter Six

1. Barrett's book, *The Civil War in North Carolina*, is a good general reference. The early Federal coastal victories are chronicled in chapter 3, "Oh, The Horrors of War."
2. In chapter 5, "The Burnside Expedition," in *The Civil War in North Carolina*, Barrett tells of the first Federal land attack on North Carolina.

3. After Burnside was recalled to the peninsula to reinforce McClellan, General John G. Foster was left in charge of the Department of North Carolina. His move on Goldsboro is described in Barrett, "Raids in Eastern North Carolina," chap. 6 in *The Civil War in North Carolina.* See especially pages 131 through 138.
4. See U.S. War Department, *Official Records*, vol. 19, pt. 2, 695, 697, 698.
5. From the eighth of VIDI's seventeen articles in *The Weekly Union (S.C.) Times*, July 23, 1886.
6. In a number of his "Reminiscences of the Macbeth Light Artillery," VIDI makes quite a point of insisting that "The Macbeth" was only "associated" with Evans' Brigade, possibly trying to avoid being tarnished by Evans' reputation. It is true that in major battles, artillery units were often commanded at the division or even army level, but the U.S. War Department's *Official Records* shows clearly that "The Macbeth" was assigned to Evans' Brigade.
7. According to the report of PERSONNE in the *Charleston Daily Courier* of January 5, 1863, the Eighteenth and the Holcombe Legion were originally stationed at Greenville to guard against the approach of enemy forces from this direction. Evans evidently brought the Holcombe Legion to Kinston on Saturday, leaving the Eighteenth Regiment in Greenville. General S. G. French ordered the Eighteenth from Greenville to Goldsboro about mid-day on December 16 but does not indicate in his memoirs when the regiment arrived. See French, *Two Wars*, 152–53.
8. See U.S. War Department, *Official Records*, vol. 18, 106–7.
9. See note 5 in chapter 6.
10. See the *Charleston Daily Courier* for January 10, 1863. PERSONNE wrote a lengthy defense of Evans' tactical skill, courage, and personal behavior in which he stated: "It has been my fortune during the past year to meet General Evans and the officers of his staff frequently. I have seen him in the dawn of morning, in the flush of noon, and at the hour of retirement, before battle, during battle, and after battle, but never on any occasion when it could be said that he was drunk."
11. See note 5 in chapter 6.
12. William E. Wilson of Goodlett's Twenty-second Regiment noted in his diary for December 14: "commensed picket fighting at 9 oclock . . . 12 the firing is pretty constant on the right . . . 22nd is on the left . . . have not fought any yet expecting it every moment . . . the enemy is about to flank us . . . we retreat to the road and up the river . . . take a stand but move on with out firing across the river . . . and then retreat." Goodlett gave a different account in 1864 in his "To the Public" pamphlet: "The forces engaged on Sunday at Kinston had been ordered to fall back by Gen. Evans, and after most of them had crossed, Lieut. Corrie, of Gen Evans' Staff, rode up and said that the General ordered the forces to return to the opposite side, (the side next to the enemy). I believed, from Lieut. Corrie's appearance, actions and conduct, that he was drunk; and, as the order was an unreasonable one, could not think such an order was given. Whereupon I said to Lieut. Corrie, "Go, bring Gen. Evans here, and if he orders me, I will go, be he drunk or sober." He returned, and in a few moments brought Gen. Evans. I was

at once placed in arrest, and the order to recross was immediately countermanded, and our forces retreated in the direction of Goldsboro."

13. PERSONNE wrote this on Christmas Day as a part of his very thorough account of this battle. It was published in the *Charleston Daily Courier* on January 5, 1863. Private Andrews' account had General Evans saying, "Tell Foster—I know him of old—give me two hours to remove the women and children out of town and I will give him hell." W. W. Howe, the correspondent for a New York paper, reported that Evans loaned his own wagon and team to the evacuation efforts. See Howe, *Kinston, Whitehall, and Goldsboro*, 19–20. The Federals, on preparing again to resume action, discovered that "the bird had flown." During the flag of truce, General Evans had succeeded in removing what remained of his command from the town.
14. For Robertson's report of the battle at White Hall, see U.S. War Department, *Official Records*, vol. 18, 121–22. Colonel Stephen D. Pool of the Tenth Regiment (First Artillery) of North Carolina Troops reported this battle in some detail in Clark, *Histories of the Several Regiments and Battalions from North Carolina*, vol. 5, 83–91. He reported the Confederate losses at White Hall as 10 killed and 42 wounded. See also Barrett, *The Civil War in North Carolina*, 144–46; Chapman, *More Terrible Than Victory*, 60–68; French, *Two Wars*, 152–53; and Evans, *Confederate Military History*, vol. 4, 144.
15. According to Smith's official report: "The enemy were driven back from their position on the line of the railroad, but on account of the lateness of the hour, the nature of the ground, and the fact that our artillery, cavalry, and a large portion of the re-enforcements had not yet arrived, it was not advisable to attack their strong second position that evening. During the night the enemy made a hurried retreat to their fortifications and gunboats, moving with such celerity that it was useless to attempt pursuit with any other arm than cavalry, of which at that time, unfortunately, we had none." (U.S. War Department, *Official Records*, vol. 18, 106–12.) Captain Edwards "heard no more of him" because Gustavus W. Smith resigned his commission in February 1863 when six officers who were his junior were promoted over him. See Freeman, *Lee's Lieutenants*, vol. 2, 419–27. Smith served the remainder of the war as a major general in the Georgia Militia.
16. Major General John Foster listed his Federal forces at ten thousand men, forty pieces of artillery, and 640 cavalry. See U.S. War Department, *Official Records*, vol. 18, 53–59. His report complimented Evans' battle strategy before Kinston by saying that the Confederate "position was so well chosen that very little of our artillery could be brought into play." Foster estimated the enemy strength as six thousand men and twenty artillery. Evans reported that his forces included only four of the regiments (the Seventeenth, Twenty-second, and Twenty-third Regiments and the Holcombe Legion) and the Macbeth Artillery of his brigade, and some North Carolina troops (the Sixty-first Regiment, Mallett's Battalion, Bunting's Battery, and Starr's Battery). He reported that his forces totaled 2,014. See U.S. War Department, *Official Records*, vol. 18, 106–19 for Evans' and related reports.
17. First Lieutenant Andrew McConnell, another member of the Seventeenth, referred to this snowball fight as the "Battle of Tull's Field." See South Carolina

Division of the United Daughters of the Confederacy, *Recollections and Reminiscences*, vol. 4, 512–13. David Logan's account of this "battle" was published in the *Yorkville Enquirer* on February 5, 1863.

18. Captain Edwards and the men of the Seventeenth Regiment were very loyal and supportive of their colonel. In early January they contributed over $600 to buy a "very pretty dappled gray" parade horse, which they presented to Colonel McMaster on January 16. See South Carolina Division of the United Daughters of the Confederacy, *Recollections and Reminiscences*, vol. 4, 508–10.

19. The rumors of Evans' drinking during the Battle of Kinston would haunt him for the remainder of his career. Lieutenant David Logan of the Seventeenth Regiment reported in his diary that early on December 14, 1862, "our Genl comes 'powerful for battle' (more whiskey aboard)." See Logan, *A Rising Star of Promise*, 57. In his letter of December 27, 1862, W. Henry Sullivan of the Holcombe Legion wrote: "Any private in the ranks could have carried out things better than Gen. Evans. It was disgraceful the way he acted and sacrificed his men. He was drunk as usual, and it seems that he did not know what he was about. He was not too drunk, however, to keep in a safe place, and he did not show himself once on the battlefield. He kept on this side of the bridge." Lieutenant General Leonidas L. Polk reported in his December 24, 1862, letter to his wife the rumor that Evans was drunk when he ordered the Fifty-first and Fifty-second North Carolina Regiments to attack a strong enemy position at Goldsboro.

20. Colonel F. W. McMaster sometimes turned to pamphlet writing when he felt wronged by another person. In his pamphlet, *Col. McMaster's Rejoinder to Brig. Gen. Evans*, he wrote: "The next day, after the enemy had retreated toward Newbern, a very intelligent Lieutenant of another Regiment was at my camp fire, lamenting the condition of the Brigade, under a man so totally incompetent to manage it, and asked if nothing could be done. I replied that I had determined, before the battle of Kinston, to petition to transfer my Regiment. A joint petition was suggested, and it met the approbation of the officers present. Four Regiments were then closely massed in the woods. As the Colonels of the three other Regiments were absent, the mode adopted as most likely of success, was to procure representatives of each company; so the General, seeing the unanimity of the Brigade, would accede to the petition without hesitation. The petition to be transferred to any Brigadier General, the authorities thought proper, was signed by all the commanders of companies in my Regiment save one, who then had a brother serving with Gen. Evans; then successively by the 22nd, Holcombe Legion, and 23rd; the commanders of the Regiments then present, and 34 commanders of the 40 companies; two officers in other companies approving, but declining as they were from the same district with the General. The petition was forwarded to Gen. Evans on the 20th Dec., and immediately returned with the endorsement, 'The officers will state their reasons for the transfer.' Upon consultation with the commanding officers of the four Regiments, it was proposed to bring charges of cowardice, incompetency, drunkenness, and conduct unbecoming an officer and a gentleman; but I opposed it, on the ground that it would cause delay and ill feeling. We then merely stated that we hoped that the General would

be satisfied with the reason that, 'there was on the part of the officers and men great dissatisfaction with, and want of confidence in, Gen. Evans. The petition was returned the 24th of Dec., and we were surprised that Gen. Evans had, to destroy its effect, dishonorably endorsed it as follows: 'Respectfully forwarded, with the remark that Col. McMaster and Capt. Bancroft are now under charges of misconduct before the enemy.' "The court-martial did not sustain the charges which General Evans brought against McMaster.

21. McMaster's trial was held in Wilmington, North Carolina. It began on March 30, 1863, and ended on April 13, 1863. The decision of the court-martial was dated May 13, 1863. McMaster was judged "not guilty" on all charges except one. The charge of "mutinous conduct" was reduced to "conduct prejudicial to military discipline," and the court levied no sentence, stating that the finding of guilt was sufficient punishment. The official record of this trial has not been preserved, but Colonel McMaster had Lieutenant David J. Logan of the Seventeenth Regiment take down the proceedings and later had them published.
22. Evans' trial was held in Goldsboro between February 9 and 19, 1863. A notice of his acquittal was reported in the *Yorkville Enquirer* on February 25, 1863, and this paper also printed a letter of praise signed by many citizens of Kinston and citing Evans' "skill" and "energetic action" in "checking the advance of an overwhelming force sent to invade this State." About a year later, Evans had the transcript of the court-martial proceedings published, and he appended a number of letters regarding his feud with Colonel McMaster. Also appended was a "To the Public" notice in which Evans argued that his low standing with his troops was because "I was placed in command of Volunteer Regiments . . . which required strict discipline to complete their organization," and because he had to "prefer charges against some who had social position and influence."
23. Goodlett's court-martial took place in Wilmington, North Carolina, beginning on March 7, 1863, but the official record of his trial has not been preserved. After his trial he was sent home on leave to Greenville to await the decision of the court. In May 1864, just before he received word of the verdict of the court, he included what appears to be some of the favorable testimony from the trial in a "To The Public" pamphlet. See also McMaster, *Colonel McMaster's Rejoinder*, 4–5, and Goodlett's compiled service records. Goodlett was cashiered from the service on April 28, 1864.
24. On March 25, 1863, Whiting stated in a letter to Longstreet: "I place little reliance on Evans' Brigade, which certainly is in worse condition than any I have ever seen. It has but 1500 men for duty, a very large number of field officers absent or under arrest, and it requires careful attention and strict discipline." See U.S. War Department, *Official Records*, vol. 18, 943, 945.
25. George R. Jones of Company I of the Twenty-third Regiment wrote a set of ten "Recollections" for *The Manning Times* in 1891. See South Carolina Division of the United Daughters of the Confederacy, *Recollections and Reminiscences*, vol. 8, 409–49.
26. See U.S. War Department, *Official Records*, vol. 14, 900–901.

27. W. L. Faulkner of Company I of the Seventeenth Regiment wrote to his wife on April 27, 1863, "We may stay in our state awhile from the fact that we swaped places with N.C. troops."
28. The "Pound Cake" nickname was a derisive reference to the fact that the Twentieth Regiment had thus far stayed in South Carolina, away from the major battles and close enough to home so that wives and family members could easily bring or send pound cake and other treats. Evans called them "fancy troops."
29. After a lengthy discussion via telegraph with Lee and the War Department of the need to reinforce Vicksburg without abandoning Charleston, Beauregard added the Twenty-sixth Regiment to Evans' Brigade and sent it to Mississippi. See U.S. War Department, *Official Records*, vol. 14, 923–44.
30. William Leonidas Faulkner of the Lancaster District was born in 1825 and was thus somewhat older than most of his comrades. He joined Company I of the Seventeenth Regiment (his cousin, W. H. Faulkner, was a first lieutenant in this unit) on February 15, 1863. He was captured at the Crater and sent to Elmira, N.Y., where he died of typhoid fever on September 17, 1864. He wrote two letters dated May 12, 1863, from Savannah to his wife. These excerpts are taken from both letters.

Chapter Seven

1. Rear Adm. Henry Walke, U.S.N., relates this campaign in "The Western Flotilla at Fort Donelson, Island Number Ten, Fort Pillow, and Memphis" in Johnson and Buel, *Battles and Leaders*, vol. 1, 430–52.
2. Lieutenant Colonel Richard B. Irwin, U.S.V., describes "Military Operations in Louisiana in 1862" in Johnson and Buel, *Battles and Leaders*, vol. 3, 582–84.
3. See note 1 in chapter 7.
4. Bruce Catton gives a good brief overview of this period of the war in the chapter titled "Stalemate, East and West" in *The Civil War*. See particularly pages 121 through 129, 136 through 140, and 146 through 147. General Ulysses S. Grant describes "The Vicksburg Campaign" in detail in Johnson and Buel, *Battles and Leaders*, vol. 3, 493–539.
5. See U.S. War Department, *Official Records*, vol. 14, 923–38. Copies of letters from C.S.A. secretary of war James A. Seddon to local political leaders, to Charleston mayor Charles Macbeth, and to South Carolina governor M. L. Bonham responding to their concerns about the removal of troops from Charleston may be found in U.S. War Department, *Official Records*, vol. 14, 939–42.
6. See South Carolina Division of the United Daughters of the Confederacy, *Recollections and Reminiscences*, vol. 5, 349–50.
7. Silas Pinckney Holbrook Elwell was born in the Sumter District in 1842 near Foreston, which is now in Clarendon County. He joined the Twenty-third Regiment as a color bearer in Charleston in May 1863. The brigade soon left for the Mississippi campaign, where he lost his left arm in the defense of Jackson. After the war he was an enthusiastic member of the United Confederate Veterans. In 1867 he became a minister in the Methodist Episcopal Church South. He was

serving the Bamberg Methodist Church, his eleventh appointment, in 1895 when he wrote his *Recollections of War Times.* He was serving the Spring Street Methodist Church in Charleston when he died in 1900.

8. This notice was published in the May 27, 1863, issue of *The Edgefield Advertiser* under "General News Items": "All absentees from Gen. Evans' Brigade are ordered to meet Capt. McCreedy, of the Holcombe Legion, in Columbia, S.C., on Saturday, the 30th of May. A full pardon for their absence without leave will be granted to all who comply with this order. Those who fail to comply will be pursued, arrested, and punished as deserters." The misspelled name refers to Captain B. H. McCready of Company G of the Holcombe Legion.
9. From the tenth of VIDI's seventeen articles in *The Weekly Union (S.C.) Times*, August 20, 1886.
10. The "twelve-pounder" smoothbore Napoleon was the most popular field artillery piece in both armies.
11. See McMaster, *Col. McMaster's Rejoinder to Brig. Gen. Evans*, 6.
12. Vardell began this letter to his wife at Moody's Farm on Saturday night, June 20, 1863, and finished it on Sunday night.
13. Vardell's letter to his wife from Carraway Farm on June 25, 1863, was very critical of Evans.
14. See Greene, *The Mississippi*, 194.
15. From the eleventh of VIDI's seventeen articles in *The Weekly Union (S.C.) Times*, September 3, 1886.
16. See notes 9 and 15 in chapter 7.
17. U.S. War Department, *Official Records*, vol. 28, pt. 2, 250.
18. William L. Faulkner wrote to his wife from Savannah on August 9, 1863, and from the Isle of Hope on about August 13, 1863.
19. The Macbeth Light Artillery stayed at Forest Station, Mississippi, until August 8 and was then ordered to Mobile, Alabama. See U.S. War Department, *Official Records*, vol. 24, pt. 3, 1048. This account is taken from the eleventh and twelfth of VIDI's seventeen 17 articles in *The Weekly Union (S.C.) Times*, September 3 and 17, 1886.

Chapter Eight

1. Elwell's story was originally published in installments in 1894 and 1895 in *The Southern Christian Advocate*, a publication of the Methodist Episcopal Church South. When friends who were not subscribers pleaded for copies of installments that they had missed, he published the entire account as a small book. This chapter is an abridged version of his account.
2. Leonard Dryman was a private in Company F of the Twenty-second Regiment of South Carolina Volunteers.

Chapter Nine

1. William Grafton Stevenson was only a lieutenant when he wrote this diary. The title "captain" may have been earned later when he served in the Senior Reserves. The editor has corrected his spelling but not his penchant for capitalizing nouns.

2. Throughout his diary, Captain Stevenson encoded her name as "Sallie C." or "S.C.G." However, according to Carl Rust Stevenson, the captain's grandson: "The reference is to Miss Sallie C. Gibson, my grandmother, whom he married after the war. Apparently, at this time he thought her name was 'Greenlow.' When he had passed through Franklin, Alabama, on a troop train after (apparently) campaigning in Mississippi, some girls, among whom was Sallie Catherine Gibson, brought flowers to the troops. He received her bouquet, in which she had left a note signed 'Sallie C. Greenlow.' He corresponded with her under that name. After the war, he returned to Franklin and established her true identity. They became engaged and he returned to South Carolina. Her father, before consenting to the marriage, sent her brother, Allen, to Chester County, South Carolina, to find out what he could about the Stevenson family. Captain Stevenson had not met Allen Gibson. The latter met and became acquainted with the Stevensons under an assumed name. After Allen's departure from South Carolina, Captain Stevenson's sister voiced the belief, judging by the similarity of his features to those of a photograph of Sallie C. Gibson, that Allen was her brother. Captain Stevenson, realizing the truth, thereupon immediately returned to Alabama. Their marriage was the result." This quote is from a footnote to Stevenson, "Diary of William Grafton Stevenson, Captain, C.S.A.," in the *Alabama Historical Quarterly*. After the war, Captain Stevenson and Sallie lived in Notasulga, Alabama. He died in 1910; she lived until 1927.
3. Lieutenant Logan was evidently a friend of William Grafton Stevenson. For a complete and interesting account of Logan's wartime experiences, see Logan, *A Rising Star of Promise*.
4. At least one regiment, the Twenty-second, was still in Savannah according to John R. Aiton's letter of August 30, 1863.
5. "Muster Rolls" were the official bimonthly attendance rolls that were the basis for paying the soldiers. The rolls were written on official forms by the regimental adjutant, and some of the original rolls still survive in the National Archives. As an example, ten rolls (of about nineteen) survive for Company D of the Eighteenth Regiment.
6. See McMaster's letters of September 18 and October 7, 1863, regarding Evans' arrest. In a letter to C.S.A. secretary of war James A. Seddon on November 28, 1863, Evans states that he "was arrested on the 15th of September last and tried by a general court-martial for disobedience of the orders of Brig. Gen. R. S. Ripley, commanding the First Military District. Of which charges and specifications I was informed on the 5th instant, by Col. G. W. C. Lee, aide-de-camp, that I was 'acquitted' and that the proceedings would 'be published in a day or two.'" See U.S. War Department, *Official Records*, vol. 28, pt. 2, 584. Beauregard released Evans from house arrest on January 15, and his response to the War Department on January 26 included this statement:

   "The board of examiners provided for in the act approved October 13, 1862, I did not order, for various reasons, including my inability to appoint at this time 3 officers of suitable rank without serious inconvenience to the service; the delay that hitherto has invariably attended final action on the decisions of all such boards held in the department, and my indisposition to subject an officer who had twice served in battle under my orders in the first year of the war with merit, indeed, distinction, to the humiliation involved by such an examination.

"Knowing, however, that he had become a disturbing element in his brigade, that some of the superior officers in it occupied relations toward him of such fierce personal hostility as to create inextinguishable discord, that the confidence in him of a large number of the officers and men of the brigade had become materially impaired, and that the state of discipline and instruction into which the brigade under his command had fallen was bad, I was forced to be unwilling to intrust the command again to his hands, and accordingly the course I adopted."

For an account of Alfred Roman's inspection of the brigade and the lengthy correspondence among all parties, see U.S. War Department, *Official Records*, vol. 28, pt. 2, 583–90; also vol. 35, pt. 1, 533, 545–46, and 642. On March 11, 1864, the War Department ordered Evans restored to command. On March 16, Beauregard ordered Generals Hill, Gilmer, and Trapier to investigate Evans' case as the War Department had directed; however, there is no record of this board having been convened. See U.S. War Department, *Official Records*, vol. 35, pt. 2, 347, 362.

7. McMaster wrote to his wife from Secessionville on October 20, 1863, that he was now reporting to Colonel Keitt, the senior colonel in that part of the military district. The troop listing of the Department of South Carolina, Georgia, and Florida on November 1, 1863, shows the Seventeenth Regiment in the Seventh Military District, the Twenty-sixth Regiment in the Fifth Military District, and the other four regiments of the brigade in the First Military District. See U.S. War Department, *Official Records*, vol. 28, pt. 2, 467–68.
8. These excerpts are from three of Faulkner's letters dated December 17, 19, and 23, 1863. Nesbit's letter was written on December 20, 1863. See South Carolina Division of the United Daughters of the Confederacy, *Recollections and Reminiscences*, vol. 9, 212–13.
9. Lincoln's Proclamation of Amnesty and Reconstruction was issued on December 8, 1863. It pardoned those who "directly or by implication, participated in the existing rebellion" if they took an oath to the Union. Some persons, primarily military and civil officials, were excepted.
10. J. W. Pursley wrote to his sister on February 16, 1864: "The 17th Regt is gone to green pond. It is out of our Brigade now." At about this time, McMaster wrote to General Samuel Cooper asking that his regiment be transferred out of Evans' Brigade "for the good of the service and upon personal grounds."
11. William H. Nulty addresses the Federal strategy in "Renewed Interest in Florida," chap. 3 in *Confederate Florida*.
12. Federal troops landed at Jacksonville on February 7, 1864, and they marched westward along the Florida Atlantic and Gulf Railway on the next day. The cavalry

preceding the main force entered Baldwin early on February 9, and it was reported that "[b]reakfast in the hotel was paid for by some enterprising Union troopers with Confederate money that was found in the trash in the depot." See Nulty, "Surprise and Success," chap. 4 in *Confederate Florida.*

13. The Battle of Olustee was fought on February 20, 1864, and the Confederate troops involved were mostly from Georgia. For a detailed account see Nulty, "The Battle of Olustee," chap. 5 in *Confederate Florida.*
14. See U.S. War Department, *Official Records*, vol. 35, pt. 1, 622. Joseph Westcoat indicates in his diary that the Eighteenth Regiment arrived in Lake City, Florida, on February 28 and that on March 2 it marched toward Jacksonville and fought the enemy at Cedar Creek, losing eighteen or twenty men. Captain Floyd reported: "On arriving in Charleston, S.C., our regiment was ordered to Florida and arrived just in time to assist in driving Seymore [*sic*] and his army from the field at Olustee. After the enemy were cooped up in Jackson [*sic*] we again returned to Charleston, S.C." Since the Eighteenth could not have arrived in time to fight in the Battle of Olustee, Floyd must have been referring to the later skirmishes as the Federals were pushed back toward Jacksonville.
15. This is taken from the much larger map of southern Georgia and northern Florida shown in this plate.
16. Captain A. L. Evans, the general's brother, challenged McMaster to a duel in a letter dated November 6, 1863. He stated that he was acting to defend the honor of his brother who could not act for himself because he was McMaster's commanding officer. McMaster dismissed A. L. Evans' challenge in a letter dated November 23, 1863. The general then challenged McMaster in a note dated February 1, 1864, and McMaster responded on February 24, 1864. Evans published all of these letters in an appendix to the record of his Goldsboro court-martial. Also see Lawrence Keitt's March 1, 1864, letter to his wife.
17. Evidently the Confederate War Department feared that Federal forces would attack Wilmington from the sea in the hope of cutting Lee's supply lines from the South. Evans' Brigade was one of the units sent to reinforce the Wilmington defenses. On April 14, the C.S.A War Department ordered Beauregard to "[s]end Evans' brigade (five regiments) to Wilmington by railroad immediately. Should any portion be detached beyond Savannah so as to delay the movement, substitute an equal number from the nearest available force." (U.S. War Department, *Official Records*, vol. 35, pt. 2, 425.) A small detachment of men from one regiment was serving in rotation as part of the garrison of Fort Sumter, and it was ordered to follow. The Holcombe Legion was ordered to depart from Savannah and to meet the brigade in Wilmington (U.S. War Department, *Official Records*, vol. 35, pt. 2, 426). The Eighteenth South Carolina was ordered (at least initially) from Florida to Charleston (U.S. War Department, *Official Records*, vol. 35, pt. 2, 427), but General R. S. Ripley, who commanded the First Military District at Charleston and who had recently feuded with Evans, did not want the Eighteenth Regiment in his command (U.S. War Department, *Official Records*, vol. 35, pt. 2, 434–35). The Eighteenth proceeded to Charleston but departed for North Carolina on April 29 (U.S. War Department, *Official Records*, vol. 35, pt. 2, 455). The Macbeth

Artillery, which had always been a part of the brigade, was left in Charleston. It would be transferred to Asheville, North Carolina, for the remainder of the war (U.S. War Department, *Official Records*, vol. 35, pt. 2, 470). According to VIDI, "The Macbeth" was glad to leave Evans' Brigade and glad to get to the mountains (see the eleventh of VIDI's seventeen articles in *The Weekly Union (S.C.) Times*, September 3, 1886).

18. A number of the secondary accounts of this accident refer to Evans falling from his horse, but these accounts are in error.
19. "Cut off the train" refers to uncoupling the train somewhere in the middle. The rear portion of the train stops while the engine proceeds onward with the front cars, unless the engineer notices what has happened. William C. Nesbit, writing to his wife on April 21, 1863, reported that on this occasion, "There was 27 went home from the Barnwell District." See South Carolina Division of the United Daughters of the Confederacy, *Recollections and Reminiscences*, vol. 9, 200–1. W. L. Faulkner, also of Company I of the Seventeenth Regiment, wrote to his wife on April 30, 1863: "There were 34 men from our Regt. jumped off the train and are gone home. Eight of them was from our Company."

Chapter Ten

1. Evidently Beauregard discussed and offered the command of Evans' Brigade to Johnson Hagood, who declined because he thought that it involved only garrison duty in North Carolina (U.S. War Department, *Official Records*, vol. 35, pt. 2, 438). On April 16, Beauregard sent this message to Walker: "Brigadier General Evans met with a serious accident today. He will be laid up about one month. Will you accept temporary command? His brigade en route to North Carolina." (U.S. War Department, *Official Records*, vol. 35, pt. 2, 436.) On April 19, Beauregard ordered Walker's temporary appointment (U.S. War Department, *Official Records*, vol. 35, pt. 2, 443). A temporary appointment of a new leader did not change the name of a brigade.
2. On October 22, 1862, a Federal force of nearly forty-five hundred men from the garrison at Hilton Head had landed near Pocotaligo with orders to destroy the Charleston and Savannah Railroad, particularly its bridges over the nearby rivers. Walker and about five hundred men from miscellaneous commands cleverly utilized the swampy terrain to contain the Federals and to drive them back to their boats after a day of hard fighting. He was promoted to brigadier general following this battle. A description of the Battle of Pocotaligo may be found in Evans, *Confederate Military History*, vol. 5, 101–6. For a sketch of the career of William S. Walker, see Evans, *Confederate Military History*, vol. 11, pt. b, 211–12.
3. J. Warren Pursley of the Eighteenth Regiment wrote letters to his sister on May 1, 1864, and May 15, 1864, describing camp life near Wilmington.
4. On April 20, Dantzler was assigned to command the Twenty-second Regiment, but procedural matters delayed his promotion until April 30. William A. Martin indicated in his April 30, 1864, letter to his wife that Dantzler had initially been sent on temporary assignment but that the men liked him and had petitioned for

him to be permanently assigned as their colonel. Hagood describes Colonel Dantzler as a planter of St. Matthews Parish who "had commenced the war as a lieutenant in the First Carolina (Hagood's); had been elected in the fall of '61 lieutenant-colonel (of Keitt's Twentieth South Carolina), which he had commanded during the greater part of the siege of Charleston with distinguished gallantry and skill; and in consequence he had been recently appointed to the colonelcy of a regiment of Evans' (now Walker's) South Carolina Brigade. This regiment had lately been commanded by Goodlett, who was broken for cowardice, and trained by him was decidedly wanting in dash. It was in an effort to inspire his new command with something of his own spirit of daring that Dantzler threw his life away" (Hagood, *Memoirs of the War of Secession*, 250–51). Hagood was mistaken in one respect—Goodlett had not commanded the Twenty-second since December 1862.

5. William B. Green (Company B, Twenty-second Regiment) wrote to his wife on April 19, 1864, that the regiment was preparing to "go in the morning to Weldon." William A. Martin (Company G, Twenty-second Regiment) wrote letters to his wife on April 25, 1864, and April 30, 1864, noting that the regiment had left Weldon on April 23 and describing the regiment's activities near Kinston. A. H. Lister (Company B, Twenty-second Regiment) wrote his wife on May 9, 1864, that they were camped near Kinston and had attacked New Bern on May 5. Green wrote to his wife from Kinston on May 13, 1864, saying "the troops has been sent from here to Vergina but our Brigade and it is scattered along the Railroad to gard the road and the sercomstance looks favorable that we will remain her for awhile."
6. On May 6, Beauregard ordered five companies of the Holcombe Legion to Weldon and the other five to move further north to defend the Petersburg and Weldon Railroad. (Robertson, *Back Door to Richmond*, 77, 98.) On May 7, M. G. Ziegler reported that the enemy was threatening his unit which was guarding the railroad station and bridge at Stony Creek. He signed his report "Major, Commanding Detachment" and requested, "Please send Lieutenant-Colonel Crawley, who is at Weldon, with the remainder of the regiment to this place and Nottoway railroad bridge." (U.S. War Department, *Official Records*, vol. 51, pt. 2, 901.) Beauregard did send the remainder of the regiment but evidently too late to help Ziegler, because Federal brigadier general August V. Kautz reported capturing Ziegler and fifty men at Stony Creek that afternoon. (Johnson and Buel, *Battles and Leaders*, vol. 4, 534.) See Robertson, "Kautz's First Raid," chap. 7 in *Back Door to Richmond*.
7. Stephen Elliott Jr. was a planter from Parris Island, and he had served in the South Carolina General Assembly. Before the war he was captain of the Beaufort Volunteer Artillery, which took part in the defense of Port Royal in late 1861. It also took part in the Battle at Pocotaligo and continued to defend the Charleston and Savannah Railroad along the South Carolina coast throughout the war. Elliott was responsible for the garrison at Fort Sumter from September 1863 until May 1864. On May 2, 1864, he wrote to his wife, "I was thinking how tired

of the fort I was and wondering how and when I would get out of it when the signal corps stepped up and informed me that I had been appointed Col. of the Holcombe Legion Infantry . . . The Legion has done some excellent fighting and has not had a Col. for some time." In his May 18, 1864, letter to his wife, he reported his high opinion of his new command: "I think that my regiment is comprised of excellent material and tho' shocking in appearance in regard to dress, is full of really fine-looking men and is commanded by officers who appear to understand their duty very well."

8. From the company muster rolls at the end of April.
9. On May 15, Major General W. H. C. Whiting ordered Walker to "move with your brigade to Petersburg at once" (U.S. War Department, *Official Records*, vol. 36, pt. 2, 1010).
10. See Williams, "Return to Virginia," chap. 7 in *P. G. T Beauregard*, and references cited therein.
11. On May 5, before the Siege of Petersburg, Federal forces under General Benjamin F. Butler landed at City Point and nearby at Bermuda Hundred on the James River, about eight miles northeast of Petersburg. Their mission was to destroy the Richmond and Petersburg Railroad and to move on Richmond from the south. William Glenn Robertson gives a detailed report in *Back Door to Richmond.*
12. General William Henry Chase Whiting's actions on this occasion have been the subject of much debate. See Robertson, "The Mystery of Chase Whiting: 16 May 1864," chap. 15 in *Back Door to Richmond.* Also, DuBose of the Holcombe Legion told on pages 116 and 117 of his "Reminiscences" of a chance encounter with Whiting (he referred to him as "General X") praying in a church in Wilmington: "He was undergoing some very deep experiences. His groans and ejaculations evinced the very deepest emotion. I discovered that this was General X, commandant at Wilmington, several of whose staff I several times met, especially one from Charleston . . . It was known that he had been for a long time subject to the curse of drink, but that he was making in the service a heroic fight against the habit . . . There was a well organized plan on the part of the Confederates by which the Butler expedition should have been surrounded and captured. The plan failed and the failure was said afterwards to be due not to the drink, on the part of General X, who did not turn up at the appointed time, but to abstinence from it. I had overheard him in one of his spiritual efforts to overcome that thing." See also Elliott's letter of June 1, 1864.
13. Writing over thirty years later, Floyd forgot that there were only three regiments on his right; the Holcombe Legion had been detached to guard the Petersburg and Weldon Railroad.
14. This was Brigadier General Walker's first time to command the brigade in battle, but he had been with the brigade since about April 25, according to William A. Martin's letter of that date. On April 29 Walker was at Kinston and was placed in command of the Kinston Military District. See U.S. War Department, *Official Records*, vol. 33, 1329.

15. Lieutenant Colonel Hudson is slightly in error here. Upon the capture of General Walker, *Colonel* Elliott, then commanding the Holcombe Legion, was promoted to brigadier general and placed in command of Evans' Brigade. Stephen Elliott's promotion date (May 28, 1864) appears on pages 38 and 39 of the "Roster of General Officers, Heads of Departments, Senators, Representatives, military organizations, etc." which is printed at the end of volume 1 of the *Southern Historical Society Papers* (1876).
16. This probing of Federal strength occurred during the final days of the Bermuda Hundred campaign. See Robertson, "Stalemate," chap. 17 in *Back Door to Richmond.*
17. David Felder Huffman, a grandson of Colonel Dantzler, relates the story of how the colonel's manservant, Caleb Glover, also brought home the body of Colonel L. M. Keitt who was killed nearby at Cold Harbor on June 1 for burial in Lewisville (now St. Matthews) in the Tabernacle Churchyard. Keitt's body was later moved to the West End Cemetery, also in St. Matthews. Caleb Glover lived with the Dantzler family for the remainder of his life, and many years later, the United Daughters of the Confederacy gave him a medal. Shortly after the turn of the century, Mayor Rhett of Charleston received a letter from a Union officer asking if he knew a Dantzler family in South Carolina. The mayor put him in touch with Judge Charles Glover Dantzler of Orangeburg, who was the eldest son of Colonel Dantzler. The Union officer then returned Dantzler's gold watch, uniform insignia, and some letters to him. He had taken these items from a soldier who had stolen them from the wounded Colonel Dantzler.
18. For Beauregard's order naming the battery, see U.S. War Department, *Official Records*, vol. 51, pt. 2, 1010.
19. John Horn gives a good overview of the situation at the beginning of the Siege of Petersburg in "War Comes to the Cockade City" and "The Battle of Old Men and Young Boys," the first two chapters in *The Petersburg Campaign.* Also see Trudeau, "Petersburg is to be and shall be defended," chap. 1 in *The Last Citadel.* Apparently one company of the brigade, Company F of the Twenty-third Regiment, was on duty with Wise's small force defending Petersburg on June 9. See U.S. War Department, *Official Records*, vol. 36, pt. 2, 316, and also Horn, *The Petersburg Campaign*, 41.
20. The dates in this portion of Captain Floyd's account have been corrected by adding one day to each date. For a thorough discussion of the defense of Petersburg before Lee arrived, see Beauregard, "Four Days of Battle at Petersburg" in Johnson and Buel, *Battles and Leaders*, vol. 4, 540–44. Also see Williams, "On the Petersburg Line," chap. 14 in *P. G. T. Beauregard.*
21. For an account of the wartime career of David Jackson Logan, see Logan, *A Rising Star of Promise.*
22. See note 20 in chapter 10.
23. Captain Floyd's statement that the Holcombe Legion, or a part of it, was in the Petersburg line on June 18 is in error. See note 6 in chapter 10. The entire Holcombe Legion was assigned to the First Military District of Virginia under Brigadier General Henry A. Wise on June 10, 1864 (U.S. War Department, *Official*

Records, vol. 36, pt. 3, 890–93). Four companies were assigned to defend the railroad bridge at Stony Creek, four to the Nottoway Bridge, and two to the Rowanty Bridge. Wade Hampton reported that a portion of the Holcombe Legion assisted his cavalry in the skirmishes at Stony Creek and Sappony Church on June 28 and 29 (U.S. War Department, *Official Records*, vol. 40, 807–10). The Holcombe Legion did not rejoin the brigade until October 16.

24. Crawley attempted to return to active duty in late February 1865 but was unable to perform his duties and was transferred to the Invalid Corps (medical release) on March 8. For the reports of the Wilson-Kautz Raid, see U.S. War Department, *Official Records*, vol. 40, pt. 1, 620–33 (Wilson's reports) and 807–10 (Hampton's report). Also see Trudeau, "I have determined to try to envelop Petersburg," chap. 4 in *The Last Citadel*.
25. When Evans arrested McMaster after the Battle of Kinston, he charged him with (among other things) cowardice during the Battle of South Mountain (Boonsboro) and said that McMaster had fled during the heat of battle, hiding behind a large rock on the mountainside. The court found McMaster not guilty of this charge.

Chapter Eleven

1. The construction of the tunnel and the mine was supervised by Lieutenant Colonel Henry Pleasants, a mining engineer who was serving in the Forty-eighth Pennsylvania Volunteer Regiment. His cousin, Henry Pleasants Jr., later wrote an interesting book, *Inferno at Petersburg*, detailing his cousin's part in this project.
2. Blandford Church lies on the next hilltop to the west of the Crater. The small, brown, brick building was built in 1735 as the Episcopal Church for the colonial town of Blandford. By the 1860s the congregation had outgrown the building and had moved into Petersburg. In 1901 the City of Petersburg deeded the building to the Ladies Memorial Association, which restored the building as a Confederate shrine. They secured the services of Louis Comfort Tiffany to design the fifteen stained glass windows, one for each Confederate state, one for Maryland, and one commemorating the Ladies Memorial Association. Around the turn of the century, the State of South Carolina placed an iron tablet on the wall of Blandford Church to honor the men of Elliott's Brigade who lost their lives at the Battle of the Crater. The number of names listed for each regiment are as follows: Seventeenth—43 men; Eighteenth—75 men; Twenty-second—119 men; Twenty-third—24 men; Twenty-sixth—2 men. Total: 263 men. This listing is clearly incomplete.
3. The digging of two Confederate countermines at Pegram's (Elliott's) Salient and one at Colquitt's Salient (about three-fourths of a mile to the north) is described in a series of reports dated July 15–30 in U.S. War Department, *Official Records*, vol. 40, pt. 3, 776–820.
4. The adjutant's statistics are quoted by McMaster in "Elliott's Brigade: How it held the Crater and Saved Petersburg." After the battle the surgeon of the Eighteenth, Dr. Hugh Toland, reported that this regiment lost 101 killed and 62 missing. Toland's letter is quoted in Barnard, *War Talks of Confederate Veterans*, 166–67.

An officer of the Twenty-second, William B. Green, wrote home the day after the battle that three companies and part of a fourth were "all blowen up."

5. Writing forty years later, Captain Floyd wrote "a Battery [Coit's] of Wright's Battalion" when referring to Wright's Battery of Coit's Battalion. He also refers to "Branche's Battery," which all other accounts refer to as Pegram's Battery. The editor has corrected these references in Captain Floyd's account.
6. Colonel Pleasants' report (War Department, *Official Record,s* vol. 40, pt. 1, 556–63) and also Bernard, *War Talks of Confederate Veterans*, 150, give the time of the explosion as 4:44 A.M.
7. After partially recovering, Elliott was placed in command of a brigade on James Island. When Charleston was evacuated, he joined Joseph E. Johnston in North Carolina and was wounded again at the Battle of Bentonville. After Johnston surrendered at Durham, North Carolina, Elliott returned home to Beaufort and was elected to the legislature. He died in March 1866.
8. Elliott's low regard for McMaster has already been noted. When McMaster came to his side, the wounded Elliott said, "Not a word from you . . . If you had obeyed orders, this would have never happened." See Chesnut, *Mary Chesnut's Civil War*, 643.
9. After the Federals gained control of the Mississippi River, they established defensive positions along it. Confederate cavalry under General Nathan Bedford Forrest attacked Fort Pillow, about fifty miles north of Memphis, on April 12, 1864. After a morning of fighting, the Federals refused an opportunity to surrender to Forrest's larger force. During the afternoon Confederate assault that captured the fort, a large number of the Federal colored troops, which comprised about half of the garrison, were killed or wounded. Federal authorities would later refer to this as the "Fort Pillow massacre," although Forrest and General Stephen D. Lee denied this charge. See Johnson and Buel, "The Capture of Fort Pillow," in *Battles and Leaders*, vol. 4, 418–19.
10. General Bushrod Rust Johnson has been criticized for his inaction during this battle. See Cummings, *Yankee Quaker—Confederate General*, 295–301. For Johnson's report, see U.S. War Department, *Official Records*, vol. 40, pt. 1, 787–93.
11. Beaty lists the Sixth, Twelfth, Twenty-sixth, Forty-second, and Sixty-first Virginia Regiments here, but there appear to be some errors. On this day, Brigadier General William Mahone was commanding Anderson's Division of five brigades in the Confederate lines about two miles to the south. When Lee ordered Mahone to send two brigades of reinforcements to the Crater, Mahone chose his old brigade (the Sixth, Twelfth, Sixteenth, Forty-first, and Sixty-first Virginia Regiments) under Colonel David Weisiger and Wright's Brigade (the Third, Twenty-second, Forty-eighth, and Sixty-fourth Georgia Regiments) under Lieutenant Colonel Matthew Hall. Later, just before he led the first charge, Mahone ordered Wilcox's Brigade (the Eighth, Ninth, Tenth, Eleventh, and Fourteenth Alabama Regiments) under Colonel John Sanders to begin moving up.
12. John Cheves Haskell gives his account of the battle in "In Front of Petersburg," chap. 6 in *The Haskell Memoirs*. He is particularly good in his account of the role

of the artillery and also in his discussion of the Confederate brutality toward the Federal colored troops. For another account of the role of artillery in this battle, see Dedmondt, "Sumter had an Artillery Company in the Crater Fight," chap. 14 in *Southern Bronze*.

13. See Featherston, "Battle of the Crater." This story is found on pages 361–62, but Featherston had forgotten the soldier's name. Smith Lipscomb's nephew saw this account and wrote to his uncle.
14. Beaty may be referring to Charner S. Greer, the only survivor of Company A of the Eighteenth Regiment. Greer dug himself out in mid-afternoon, after the battle had ended. Later, Greer was sent home to Union, S.C., to recruit new men for the company, of which he was then made captain. For his account, see South Carolina Division of the United Daughters of the Confederacy, *Recollections and Reminiscences*, vol. 5, 280–81, 443.
15. These data are taken from Cavanaugh and Marvel, "Casualties at the Battle of the Crater," Appendix B in *The Battle of the Crater "The Horrid Pit,"* 128–29.
16. Photos of these and other similar battlefield items may be found in Major William A. Powell, U.S.A., "The Battle of the Petersburg Crater," in Johnson and Buel, *Battles and Leaders*, vol. 4, 545–60.
17. This is not correct. Colonel Wallace's date of rank was August 30, 1862, and Colonel McMaster's date of rank was September 1, 1862. However, since Wallace began the war with the rank of private, while McMaster began as a lieutenant colonel, it could be argued that McMaster was the more experienced officer. General Bushrod Johnson cited three reasons for recommending Wallace's promotion: (1) Elliott's wound would not soon allow his return, (2) "Colonel Wallace is the officer best qualified in the brigade for the position . . . ," and (3) "I believe that the efficiency of the brigade will be improved . . ." Johnson's letter is in Wallace's compiled service records.
18. J. A. F. Coleman wrote in his diary on Sunday, September 25, 1864: "Col. Wallace of the 18th Regt. received appt. of Brig. Gen. of our Brigade. Very agreeable to us all."
19. In *Southern Historical Society Papers* 10 (1882): 122, McMaster stated that Mahone's charge took place "sometime after" ten o'clock. Later (1899) in Dickert (*History of Kershaw's Brigade*, 411), McMaster stated at the end of a three-page discussion titled "Time of Mahone's Charge" that "This would bring Mahone's charge to 9:30 or 9:45."
20. Floyd's letter was dated January 28, 1898, and published in *The (Columbia, S.C.) State* newspaper on January 31, 1898 on pages 1–2.
21. Floyd gives "Altoona" here. He was probably referring to the fall of Atlanta a month later, or possibly to the Battle of Allatoona Pass two months later.
22. McMaster in Dickert, *History of Kershaw's Brigade*, 407–8. This essay was reprinted in *The (Columbia, S.C.) State* newspaper on March 5, 1899. The extensive title given to this front-page article is instructive of the feelings of the day: "ELLIOT'S BRIGADE IN 'THE CRATER' FIGHT. JUSTICE FOR THE SOUTH CAROLINIANS WHO BORE THE BRUNT OF BATTLE AND MADE VICTORY GLORIOUS. A Full Graphic and Authoritative Account,

Showing That South Carolina More Than Virginia is Entitled to the Honors of the Desperate Conflict." McMaster died on September 10, 1899, thus ending his lengthy debate with George Bernard.

Chapter Twelve

1. John Horn lists twenty-two actions in a table, "Major Battles Around Petersburg, 1864–65" on page 33 of *The Petersburg Campaign.* This work gives an overview of the fighting around Petersburg between June 1864 and April 1865.
2. Bruce Catton discusses in broad terms the general military and political situation during the summer and fall of 1864 in the chapter "Total Warfare" in *The Civil War.*
3. U.S. War Department, *Official Records*, vol. 42, pt. 1, 903. Also see McMaster's October 25, 1864, letter to his wife.
4. J. A. F. Coleman puts the legion's losses in the action of November 5–6 at about ninety men killed, wounded, or missing. For Federal reports, see U.S. War Department, *Official Records*, vol. 42, pt. 1, 397; also, vol. 42, pt. 3, 528–61. For Confederate reports, see U.S. War Department, *Official Records*, vol. 42, pt. 1, 909–10 (Bushrod Johnson's report) and 933–34 (William Wallace's report).
5. J. W. Pursley also mentioned desertions in his February 24, 1865, letter to his sister: "Our men is going to the Yanks in perfect droves. Seventeen went from our Brigade last night, but none from the 18th." The accounts of the veterans tend to avoid this topic because it reflects discredit upon their units.
6. Sherman, *Memoirs*, vol. 2, 291–92.
7. For an overview of Lee's strategy and the details of this battle, see Freeman, "Lee Makes His Last Desperate Plan" and "Fort Stedman," chaps. 1 and 2 in *R. E. Lee*, vol. 4. Also see "The Last Attempts at Grand Strategy," chap. 32 in *Lee's Lieutenants*, vol. 3.
8. There was a colonel of the Sixth Regiment named John M. Steedman. However, a photograph caption in Johnson and Buel, *Battles and Leaders*, vol. 4, 586, states that the fort was named for Colonel Griffin A. Stedman of the Eleventh Connecticut, who was mortally wounded in front of Petersburg on August 5, 1864.
9. Humphreys mentions that Brigadier General McLaughlen was captured when he entered Fort Stedman not realizing that it was in Confederate hands. See *The Virginia Campaign of '64 and '65*, 318.
10. McMaster was taken to Fort Delaware Prison, and was paroled on July 24, 1865. After the war, he enjoyed a distinguished career as an attorney and as the owner of the Columbia Granite Quarry. He served in both the South Carolina House and Senate, and was a leader in founding the Columbia public school system. He was a founding trustee of Winthrop College in Columbia (now Winthrop University in Rock Hill, S.C.). McMaster carried his dislike of General Evans over to Evans' son, John Gary Evans, who became governor in 1894. According to Stevens, *Captain Bill*, 69–70, McMaster once referred to the governor as a "miserable wretch" a son of "that miserable scoundrel, Gen. N. G. Evans."
11. General Gordon described this battle in chapter 27 of his *Reminiscences of the Civil War.* For a Federal account see George L. Kilmer, "Gordon's Attack at Fort Stedman," in Johnson and Buel, *Battles and Leaders*, vol. 4, 579–83. Kilmer, of the

Fourteenth New York Heavy Artillery, relates how the Confederates captured this section of the Federal line. During the battle, one of the men of the Fourteenth captured the flag of the Twenty-sixth Regiment, South Carolina Volunteers. According to John Bigham of the South Carolina Confederate Relic Room, this is the only flag of any regiment of the brigade that is known to exist today. For another account of this battle, see John F. Hartranft, Brevet Major General, U.S.V., "The Recapture of Fort Stedman," in Johnson and Buel, *Battles and Leaders*, vol. 4, 584–89.

Chapter Thirteen

1. Beitzell in *Point Lookout Prison Camp for Confederates* indicates that 52,264 Confederate soldiers were taken to this prison and that 2,950 died there. The maximum number of prisoners in residence was 20,110 in April 1865.
2. The compiled service records of Private W. J. Andrews indicate that he was taken prisoner on another occasion and released. His name appears on an Army of the Potomac "Parole of Prisoners of War" list dated October 3, 1862. According to Andrews' booklet, *My War Record*, he was taken prisoner in Frederick City, Maryland, where he had contracted typhoid fever, and was nursed back to health in the home of a Mrs. Mantz.

Chapter Fourteen

1. See John Horn's calculations in the section "Confederate Desertion" on pages 217 and 218 of *The Siege of Petersburg*. See also Power, "The Petersburg-Richmond Front, Winter Quarters, and Hatcher's Run, November 1864–February 1865," chap. 8 in *Lee's Miserables* for a study of the condition and morale of the Army of Northern Virginia during this period.
2. Chris Calkins, the historian at Petersburg National Battlefield, authored a very detailed article, "The Battle of Five Forks: Final Push for the South Side," in *Blue and Gray Magazine* 9 (April 1992): 8–22, 41–52. This account includes very good wartime and modern maps of the area. For other treatments of this battle, see Chamberlain, "Five Forks," chap. 4 in *The Passing of the Armies;* also Horace Porter, Brevet Brigadier General, U.S.A., "Five Forks and the Pursuit of Lee," in Johnson and Buel, *Battles and Leaders*, vol. 4, 708–22.
3. The dates given by John Floyd (March 27, April 1, and April 2) have been corrected to March 29, March 31, and April 1, respectively.
4. See note 3 in chapter 14.
5. See U.S. War Department, *Official Records*, vol. 46, pt. 1, 1286.
6. Chamberlain complimented the fighting abilities of the brigades of Ransom, Wallace, and Wood by saying, ". . . our cavalry kept up sharp attacks upon their right across the works, which by masterly courage and skill they managed to repel, replacing as best they could the great gaps made in their defenses by the withdrawal of so many of Stewart's and Terry's Brigades" (See *The Passing of the Armies*, 109).
7. South Carolina Division of the United Daughters of the Confederacy, *Recollections and Reminiscences*, vol. 8, 111–12.

8. This does not agree with *The Appomattox Roster*, which was published in 1887. It lists one hundred men of the Twenty-third Regiment as having been given paroles at Appomattox Court House on April 9, 1865, and does not include these two names in Company K. Curiously, however, the list includes the name of Private W. J. Andrews, who was in Point Lookout Prison at the time.

Chapter Fifteen

1. This horse would soon be killed under him. See the description of this battle in Marlow, *Matt W. Ransom*, 128–35.
2. See Freeman, *Lee's Lieutenants*, vol. 3, 673–74, for an account of the death of William J. Pegram.
3. For a brief sketch of the life of Joshua Hilary Hudson, see note 12 in chapter 2.

Chapter Sixteen

1. Burke Davis gives an interesting and very readable account of the final days in *To Appomattox: Nine April Days, 1865.*
2. Wallace's report for March 29–April 9 stated: "The strength of the brigade on the 29th of March was about 1,300 aggregate, and the loss about 188. On the 2d of April about 350 men had been reassembled. The losses in the subsequent skirmishes cannot be stated, but were slight." U.S. War Department, *Official Records*, vol. 46, pt. 1, 1291–92.
3. The biographical sketch of William H. Wallace in McCrady and Ashe, *Eminent and Representative Men of the Carolinas of the Nineteenth Century*, vol. 1, 66, noted that ". . . the last firing by infantry of the Army of Northern Virginia was by troops in Gen. Wallace's command." The report of General Bushrod R. Johnson also indicates that the brigade was in action on April 8: "On Saturday, April 8, 1865, we resumed our march at 4 A.M., and marched until about 3 P.M., encamping about one mile from Appomattox Court-House. Under instructions given by the corps commander to Brigadier-General Walker, my division was moved out, under command of Brigadier-General Wallace, about 8 P.M., to Appomattox Court-House, where it remained in line of battle all night, in consequence of a dash made by enemy's cavalry upon that position." U.S. War Department, *Official Records*, vol. 46, pt. 1, 1286–91.
4. For the complete text of General Lee's report to President Davis, see "Lee's Report of the Surrender at Appomattox" in Johnson and Buel, *Battles and Leaders*, vol. 4, 724. This may also be found in U.S. War Department, *Official Records*, vol. 46, pt. 1, 1265–67.
5. In *The Appomattox Roster* on pages 402 through 412 are recorded the names of 631 men of Wallace's Brigade who surrendered with Lee's Army of Northern Virginia. The totals by regiment were: Headquarters—9 men; Seventeenth Regiment —119 men; Eighteenth Regiment—156 men; Twenty-second Regiment—89 men; Twenty-third Regiment—105 men; Twenty-sixth Regiment—121 men; Holcombe Legion—32 men.
6. For Chamberlain's account of the surrender ceremony, see *The Passing of the Armies*, 194–206.

7. See U.S. War Department, *Official Records*, vol. 46, pt. 1, 1267.
8. This issue was apparently a pet peeve of Captain Evans. In his December 3, 1864, letter to his wife he wrote, referring to his children: "Tell them that when the war is over they may carry 20 biscuits to school enough to chunk at all the stayhome children's fathers they pass on the streets."
9. First Lieutenant John Francis Stone, Company D, Eighteenth Regiment, was released from Fort Delaware Prison on June 14, 1865. He had lost his two brothers in the war (George in the Fourth Regiment had died of fever in Farmville, Virginia, in April 1862; Waddy in the Eighteenth Regiment had been mortally wounded in the artillery duel at Rappahannock Station in August 1862). John Francis Stone returned to the family's 350-acre farm in the Anderson District of South Carolina to find that his father, George Stone, had died on June 25, 1865, leaving a wife, three daughters, and two grandchildren for him to support.

Chapter Seventeen

1. U.S. War Department, *Official Records*, vol. 47, pt. 2, 1204.
2. Ibid., 1353.
3. See Clement Sulivane, Captain, C.S.A., "The Fall of Richmond: Part I. The Evacuation" in Johnson and Buel, *Battles and Leaders*, vol. 4, 725–26. This account quotes General Gary as telling the demolition engineers at the Mayo Bridge, "All over, goodbye; blow her to hell," as his rear guard passed over the river. A brief biographical sketch of General Gary in the *Anderson Intelligencer* of May 26, 1914, stated: "When Lee surrendered, Gen. Gary, refusing to hand over his sword to the conquerors, made his way through the lines of the enemy, never accepting pardon or parole. He joined President Davis' party at Greensboro, N.C., and escorted them to Cokesbury, S.C. . . ."
4. See "Gen. Nathan George Evans" in *Cyclopedia of Eminent and Representative Men of the Carolinas*, 427, and Evans, "Nathan George Evans: Brigadier General, C.S.A.," 264.
5. For detailed accounts of the flight of President Davis and his party from Richmond, Virginia, to Washington, Georgia, see Davis, *The Long Surrender*; and Ballard, *A Long Shadow*.
6. See Stevens, *Captain Bill*, 69.
7. Martin Witherspoon Gary was born in 1831 at Cokesbury, South Carolina. He entered South Carolina College in 1850 but was expelled in 1852 for a collegiate prank. He transferred to Harvard College and graduated in 1854. He became a lawyer and was a secessionist member of the General Assembly in 1860–61. As soon as the war began, he organized a company for the Hampton Legion and was given the rank of captain. At the first battle of Manassas, when the three more senior officers were wounded or killed, he commanded the legion, bringing it to the rescue of the demi-brigade of his brother-in-law, Nathan Evans. When the Hampton Legion was reorganized in 1862, Gary was elected lieutenant colonel and placed in command of the eight infantry companies. Gary then fought in

the Pennisula, Second Manassas, Sharpsburg, Fredericksburg, Suffolk, Chickamauga, Knoxville, Petersburg, and Appomattox campaigns. His cavalry brigade was involved in the final defense of Richmond (see note 3 in chapter 17). He claimed that Jefferson Davis told him just before the fall of Richmond that he would be given the rank of major general and given a division to command, but this promotion was never officially completed. When Lee began to negotiate a surrender at Appomattox, Gary left his unit and escaped with a few men through Federal lines. They rode to Greensboro, where they were met by about two hundred of his men who had earlier gone home to procure fresh horses. Gary and his cavalry served as the guard and escort of Jefferson Davis' party until they reached Cokesbury on May 1. After the war, Mart Gary would boast that he had "never surrendered" and that he held the rank of major general at the war's end.

8. South Carolina Division of the United Daughters of the Confederacy, *Recollections and Reminiscences*, vol. 3, 165. The Oakley Park plantation included over one thousand acres when Mart Gary bought it in 1869, but it dwindled in size over time and passed from Martin Gary to Victoria Gary Evans and then to her children. John Gary Evans bought his siblings' shares and owned the property until his death in 1942. He willed the house and the remaining forty acres of land to the Town of Edgefield, with the stipulation that the property was to be used for the benefit of the people. He also specified that the local chapter of the United Daughters of the Confederacy should operate the house as a meeting place and a public museum to the military and political life of Martin W. Gary.
9. South Carolina Division of the United Daughters of the Confederacy, *Recollections and Reminiscences*, vol. 1, 608–9.
10. The Democratic Party's slate of candidates included General Wade Hampton for governor, General William Dunlap Simpson for lieutenant governor, General James Conner for attorney general, and General Johnson Hagood for comptroller general. In addition to nominating these military leaders, the Democratic Party organized their efforts along military lines. See Zuczek, "It was in Every Sense a Military Campaign," chap. 8 in *State of Rebellion.*
11. Tabernacle Cemetery is located just off South Carolina Highway 254 a few miles north of Greenwood, South Carolina. The large monuments of the two generals are impressive.
12. For an overview of his life, see Hendrick's dissertation, "John Gary Evans: A Political Biography."
13. The Edgewood Plantation house, now known as the "Pickens-Sally House," has been moved twice. It is now located on the campus of the University of South Carolina at Aiken.
14. See Emily L. Bull, "Lucy Pickens: First Lady of the South Carolina Confederacy" in *Proceedings of the South Carolina Historical Association*, 1982, 13–15. Also see Agatha Abney Woodson, "The Removal of the Confederate Monument of Edgefield" in South Carolina Division of the United Daughters of the Confederacy, *Recollections and Reminiscences*, vol. 4, 308–9.

BIBLIOGRAPHY

Recollections of the Veterans of the Brigade

Andrews, Welbern J. *My War Record: 1861 to 1865*. Charleston, S.C.: Crescent Printing Company, [1900?]. According to his gravestone, Andrews' correct name was Welborn James Andrews.

Andrews, Welburn J. *Sketch of Company K., 23rd South Carolina Volunteers, In the Civil War, from 1862–1865*. Richmond, Va.: Whittet and Shepperson Printers, n.d. One history of Sumter County indicates that Andrews' compatriot J. Grier White may deserve much of the credit for writing this account. According to his gravestone, Andrews' correct name was Welborn James Andrews.

Beaty, B. Lewis. "The Battle of the Crater." Address given at the meeting of the Horry County Confederate Soldiers' Association, Conway, S.C., July 3, 1903. This address is included as chapter 3 in J. H. Hudson, *Sketches and Reminiscences*, cited below.

DuBose, William Porcher. "Adventures of an Adjutant." *Charleston, S.C., Weekly News*, October 4, 1882. A partial copy is in the archives at the University of the South, Sewanee, Tennessee.

———. "Reminiscences." Typescript compiled by William Haskell DuBose, circa 1911. A copy is in the Southern Historical Collection, Wilson Library, University of North Carolina, Chapel Hill, N.C. At the beginning of the war, DuBose served as adjutant of the Holcombe Legion. He resigned from the legion on November 1, 1863, to become the chaplain of Kershaw's Brigade. After the war he served as a priest in the Episcopal Church in South Carolina until 1871, when he was appointed chaplain and a member of the theology faculty of the University of the South.

Edwards, William H. *A Condensed History of the Seventeenth Regiment S.C.V., C.S.A. From its Organization to the Close of the War*. Columbia, S.C.: R. L. Bryan Company, 1908. The author served as captain of Company A of the Seventeenth Regiment. He wrote this history at the request of Miss Helen G. McMaster, daughter of Colonel F. W. McMaster. A copy is in the collection of the South Caroliniana Library, University of South Carolina, Columbia, S.C.

Elwell, Silas Pinckney Holbrook. *Recollections of War Times: My Experiences in the West.* Bamberg, S.C.: The Bamberg Herald Print, 1895. This was originally printed as a series of articles in *The Southern Christian Advocate* magazine from October 25, 1894, through January 3, 1895.

Floyd, John, and the Committee on History. *History of the Darlington Rifles, Company "I" Eighteenth S.C.V., Late C.S.A. in the War between the States.* Darlington, S.C.: County Messenger Job Print, n.d. The only complete, original copy known is in the collection of the Darlington County Historical Commission. In the opinion of Darlington County historian Horace F. Rudisill, the principal author of this account was John Floyd. None of the other members of the "Committee on History" are known. References to the work cited in this text are attributed to Captain Floyd. John Floyd is referred to in both the first and third person in the original account, but all of the third person references have been changed to the first person in the present work.

Hudson, Joshua Hilary. *Sketches and Reminiscences.* Columbia, S.C.: The State Company, 1903. Hudson was the lieutenant colonel of the Twenty-sixth Regiment. He wrote part of this book in 1885 and part in 1898. It includes a chapter on the Battle of the Crater written by B. L. Beaty in 1903.

James, Albert Allison. "The 18th S.C.V.: Interesting Story of a Gallant Command By the Chaplain." *Yorkville (S.C.) Enquirer,* November 26, 1902. A typescript copy, possibly the original, of this newspaper article is in the South Carolina Department of Archives and History, Columbia, S.C.

Jones, George R. "Recollections." In volume 8 of *Recollections and Reminiscences 1861–1865 through World War I,* 409–49, cited below. Jones served as a private in Company I of the Twenty-third Regiment and later wrote this series of ten recollections.

Lake, George B., in Dickert, *History of Kershaw's Brigade,* pages 412–16, gives a graphic description of his experience and the scenes around the famous "Crater."

Martin, T. B. "Sketch of Prison Life." In volume 10 of *Recollections and Reminiscences 1861–1865 through World War I,* 20–22, cited below. Martin was captain of Company I of the Holcombe Legion. He was captured at Stony Creek on May 7, 1864, and was sent to Fort Delaware prison. He recounts his capture, prison life, and his experience as one of the "immortal six hundred" Confederate prisoners sent from Fort Delaware to various islands near Charleston to serve as shields against Confederate artillery fire.

McLaurin, D. W. "The Confederate Chaplain." Chapter 3 in *The Life Work of John L. Girardeau, D.D., LL.D.,* edited by George A. Blackburn. Columbia, S.C.: The State Company, 1916. The writer was a color bearer of the Twenty-third Regiment S.C.V. along with Silas Elwell.

McMaster, Fitz William. "The Battle of the Crater: July 30, 1864." *Southern Historical Society Papers* 10 (1882): 119–23.

———. "Elliott's Brigade: How It Held the Crater and Saved Petersburg." This address was given before the Confederate Veterans of Camp Hampton, Columbia, S.C., December 5, 1895. It was subsequently printed in *The (Columbia, S.C.) State* newspaper on December 16, 1895, and reprinted in pamphlet format at an unknown date with introductory remarks by Elliott's son, Charles Pinckney Elliott, as a memorial to his father. A copy is in the collection of the South Caroliniana Library, Columbia, S.C.

———. "Elliott's Brigade in 'The Crater Fight.'" Published in *The (Columbia, S.C.) State* newspaper, March 5, 1899, 1–2. This account may also be found in Dickert, *History of Kershaw's Brigade*, cited below.

Owen, Dock. *Campfire Stories and Reminiscences.* Greenwood, S.C.: The Index Publishing Company, n.d. Private Owen served in Company F of the Holcombe Legion. This is a small pamphlet of miscellaneous (mostly tall) tales.

Records of the Confederate Historian. *Roll of South Carolina Volunteers in the Confederate States Provisional Army.* Vols. 3 and 4, n.d. South Carolina Department of Archives and History, Columbia, S.C. Microcopy no. 16, rolls 4 and 5. These rolls were compiled in the 1890s from extant muster rolls and edited from memory by the surviving veterans of each company. The edited rolls were assembled into five large volumes in January 1899 by Colonel John P. Thomas. They are also known as the "memory rolls."

Robertson, John Forrest. "Reminiscences." A 107-page handwritten document in the "Confederate Veteran" papers in the Rare Book, Manuscript, and Special Collections Library at Duke University. Robertson served as a corporal in Companies A and B of the Twenty-third Regiment. A reference to the late Chaplain Girardeau indicates that this account was written after June 23, 1898.

Stevens, Peter Fayssoux. "Autobiography." This small volume of 132 handwritten pages is in the possession of his descendents.

VIDI. "Reminiscences of the Macbeth Light Artillery." *The Weekly Union (S.C.) Times*, April 16, 1886, through November 26, 1886. VIDI was the pen name of the officer, apparently Lieutenant H. F. Scaife, who served in the unit. He wrote this series of seventeen biweekly articles, only twelve of which survive.

Letters, Diaries, and Records of the Veterans of the Brigade

Aiton, John R. Letter dated August 30, 1863, in volume 10 of *Recollections and Reminiscences 1861–1865 through World War I*, 400–401, cited below. Aiton was the first sergeant of Company A of the Twenty-second Regiment.

Alexander, James S. Twenty-three letters to his wife and children—nine in the Special Collections Library, Auburn University, Auburn, Alabama; thirteen in volume 2 of *Recollections and Reminiscences 1861–1865 through World War I*, 455–73, cited below; and one in volume 5 of *Recollections and Reminiscences 1861–1865 through World War I*, 342–44, cited below. Private Alexander served in Company D of the Twenty-second Regiment.

Barkley, George R. and Martin V. Barkley. Ten or more letters (often written jointly) in the Barkley Family Papers in the Southern Historical Collection, Wilson Library, University of North Carolina, Chapel Hill, N.C. These letters were written to another brother and to family in the Anderson District. Both men served as privates in Company D of the Eighteenth Regiment.

Blanton, D. J. Copies of two letters in the United States Army Military History Institute, Carlisle Barracks, Pa. Private Blanton served in Company K of the Twenty-sixth Regiment.

Carson, John Moore. Letters from the Carson Family Papers in the South Caroliniana Library, Columbia, S.C. Private Carson served in Company C of the Holcombe Legion.

Choat, John A., James Vanburen Choat, Stephen M. Choat, and William Choat. Eight letters in volume 8 of *Recollections and Reminiscences 1861–1865 through World War I*, 122–33, cited below. These brothers served in Company E of the Seventeenth Regiment.

Coleman, John Alfred Feister. "Diary: August 3, 1864–Summer 1865." A typescript copy in Special Collections, Woodruff Library, Emory University, Atlanta, Ga. First Lieutenant Coleman served in Company B of the Seventeenth Regiment. He started this diary in order to continue the diary of his friend Lieutenant A. J. McConnell, who had just been killed in the Battle of the Crater.

Dantzler, Olin M. A few letters in the Calhoun County Museum, St. Matthews, S.C. Colonel Dantzler commanded the Twenty-second Regiment in May 1864.

Dean, Edward J. One letter dated May 9, 1864, to Colonel F. W. McMaster in the Fitz William McMaster and Jane McFie McMaster Papers in the South Caroliniana Library, Columbia, S.C. Captain Dean led Company C of the Twenty-second Regiment.

Elliott, Stephen Jr. Approximately twenty letters in the Elliott Family Papers in the South Caroliniana Library, Columbia, S.C. Elliott was the third commander of the brigade.

Evans, Beverly Daniel IV. "Nathan George Evans: Brigadier General, C.S.A." Master's thesis, Duke University, Durham, N.C., 1941. This work contains much quoted material from General Evans' letters, journal, and other papers then in the possession of his son, John Gary Evans of Spartanburg, S.C.

Evans, John C. "War Letters of John Craig Evans." A typescript of twenty-two letters to his wife, in the Georgia Department of Archives and History, Atlanta, Ga. Captain Evans (no relation to General N. G. Evans) led Company A of the Twenty-third Regiment. He wrote these letters between December 3, 1864, and June 16, 1865.

Evans, Nathan George. "Proceedings of a Court of Inquiry, Convened at Goldsboro, North Carolina, February 9, 1863, Pursuant to Special Orders No. 44, Department of North Carolina." This fifty-three page official document contains the record of Evans' court-martial on the charge of drunkenness preferred against him by Colonel Goodlett. Two pages containing a portion of the testimony of Captain Samuel J. Corrie, Evans' aide-de-camp, are missing. Appendices contain transcripts of letters written in late 1863 and early 1864 to Colonel McMaster by Captain A. L. Evans and by General Evans challenging him to duels, as well as McMaster's responses. A "To the Public" statement by General Evans dated January 29, 1864, at Cokesbury, S.C., is included. This document is item 720 on microfilm roll 12 of *Confederate Imprints, 1861–1865*. New Haven, Conn.: Research Publications, 1974.

———. "Records of the Department of South Carolina, Georgia, and Florida." Copies of many of these records from December 1861 through June 1862 are in the Museum of the Confederacy, Richmond, Va.

Faulkner, William H. A typescript copy of his May 25, 1862, letter to W. L. Faulkner in the Faulkner letters at the University of North Carolina, Charlotte, N.C., as noted below. He was a first lieutenant in Company I of the Seventeenth Regiment.

Faulkner, William Leonidas. Letters written to his wife and father in Lancaster, S.C., between March 8, 1863, and July 23, 1864. Photocopies and typescript copies of approximately seventy-five letters are in the Special Collections Library, University of North Carolina, Charlotte, N.C. Many of the original letters are now in the South Caroliniana Library, Columbia, S.C. Faulkner enlisted in February 1863 and was a private in Company I of the Seventeenth Regiment.

Fewell, Alexander Faulkner. *Dear Martha . . . The Confederate War Letters of a South Carolina Soldier.* Edited by Robert Harley Mackintosh Jr. Columbia, S.C.: R. L. Bryan Co., 1976. This book contains seventeen letters written between November 1861 and April 1862, and thirty-nine letters written between September 1864 and January 1865. Fewell served in Company E of the Seventeenth Regiment from its formation until the conscription act was passed in April 1862. He was then allowed to hire a substitute because he was over thirty-five years old. In August 1864, when the older men were called up, he rejoined his company in the trenches at Petersburg and served until the end of the war.

Goodlett, Spartan D. "To the Public." This document is item 2507–3 on microfilm roll 82 of *Confederate Imprints, 1861–1865*. New Haven, Conn.: Research Publications, 1974. This eight-page booklet, dated "Greenville, S.C., May 1864," was written while Goodlett was awaiting the decision of his court-martial.

Green, William B. More than twenty-five letters (April 4, 1864–December 6, 1864) in the William B. Green Papers in the South Caroliniana Library, Columbia, S.C. Green began the war in the Sixteenth Regiment, then served in the reserves, and in April 1864 he joined Company B of the Twenty-second Regiment.

Hatch, Lewis M. The Lewis M. Hatch Papers from 1861 to 1862 in the Southern Historical Collection, Wilson Library, University of North Carolina, Chapel Hill, N.C. He organized the battalion known as Hatch's Coastal Rangers which grew to become the Twenty-third Regiment.

Holley, Turner W. Letters in the Rare Book, Manuscript, and Special Collections Library, Duke University, Durham, N.C. Holley served in the Seventeenth Regiment.

Howe, J. J. Six letters written in 1862 in volume 9 of *Recollections and Reminiscences 1861–1865 through World War I*, 247–53, cited below. Sergeant Howe served in Company G of the Eighteenth Regiment.

Kilpatrick, Robert. Letter of May 17, 1864, in volume 7 of *Recollections and Reminiscences 1861–1865 through World War I*, 415–16, cited below. Private Kilpatrick served in Company D of the Seventeenth Regiment.

———. Letter of December 5, 1863, in volume 5 of *Recollections and Reminiscences 1861–1865 through World War I*, 346, cited below. Dr. Kirkpatrick probably served in the Seventeenth Regiment.

Knight, John W. Four letters in the South Caroliniana Library, Columbia, S.C., and one in the United States Army Military History Institute, Carlisle Barracks, Pa. Sergeant Knight served in Company B of the Twenty-sixth Regiment.

LaMotte, Thomas Jefferson. "Diary." A typescript copy is in the South Caroliniana Library, Columbia, S.C. Private LaMotte served in Company C of the Seventeenth Regiment.

Leak, William C. Photocopies of eleven letters written between May 25, 1864, and January 30, 1865, in the files of the historian at the Petersburg National Battlefield Park, Petersburg, Va. Private Leak served in Company F of the Twenty-second Regiment.

Lipscomb, Smith. Letter in the John Warwick Daniel Papers in the Special Collections Library at the University of Virginia, Charlottesville, Va. He served in Company F of the Eighteenth Regiment. A related letter written after the war by his nephew, W. O. Lipscomb, is also in this collection.

Lister, A. H. Letters in the Lister Family Papers in the South Caroliniana Library, Columbia, S.C. Private Lister served in Company B of the Twenty-second Regiment.

Logan, David Jackson. *A Rising Star of Promise: The Civil War Odyssey of David Jackson Logan, Seventeenth South Carolina Volunteers, 1861–1864*. Edited by Samuel N. Thomas Jr. and Jason H. Silverman. Campbell, Calif: Savas Publishing Company, 1998. Logan's story is told through his personal letters, his diary entries, and the articles he wrote for the *Yorkville (S.C.) Inquirer.*

Lominack, William Frank. "Letters: Confederate Soldier's Memories Kept Alive For 122 Years." *The Newberry (S.C.) Observer and Herald and News*, June 1–22, 1983. Eleven letters were written to his wife and one to his mother. The letters were written between January 1861 and August 1862. Lominack was first sergeant of Company G of the Holcombe Legion and was killed at Second Manassas.

Lowry, Samuel Cosmo "Catawba." "Diary of Samuel Catawba Lowry, Second Lieutenant, Company F, Seventeenth Regiment, South Carolina Volunteers, during the Civil War, 1861–1864." A typescript copy is in the South Caroliniana Library, Columbia, S.C. This diary was converted to typescript by Sumter L. Lowry, chief of the Lowry-Avery Clan, for distribution to each family of the clan. The diary was also was reprinted in *South Carolina Historical Magazine* 79 (July 1978): 182–97.

Martin, William A. Letters in the William A. Martin Papers, in the Rare Book, Manuscript, and Special Collections Library, Duke University, Durham, N.C. Sergeant Martin served in Company G of the Twenty-second Regiment.

McCollough, John DeWitt. Letters in the John DeWitt McCollough Papers in the South Caroliniana Library, Columbia, S.C. He was the chaplain of the Holcombe Legion early in the war.

McConnell, Andrew. "Diary of Lieutenant Andrew McConnell." Reprinted in volume 4 of *Recollections and Reminiscences 1861–1865 through World War I*, 505–18, cited below. This diary covers the period December 5, 1862, to March 3, 1863. McConnell served in Company B of the Seventeenth Regiment and was killed at the Crater.

McMaster, F. W. *Col. McMaster's Rejoinder to Brig. Gen. Evans.* Privately printed, 1864. A copy is in the collection of the South Caroliniana Library, Columbia, S.C. Colonel McMaster wrote this twenty-six–page pamphlet at Green Pond, S.C., in early April 1864.

McMaster, Fitz William. Fitz William McMaster and Jane McFie McMaster Papers in the South Caroliniana Library, Columbia, S.C. This collection includes approximately thirty-five letters written during the war, a personal diary (June 1863–1883), and postwar correspondence with other veterans. He became colonel of the Seventeenth Regiment after the death of Colonel Means at Second Manassas.

Mills, John Anderson. Eight letters in the W. W. Mills Papers in the Winthrop University Archives, Rock Hill, S.C. These letters were written in 1862–63 to his brother at home. Mills was a private in Company K of the Twenty-third Regiment.

Mills, Julius. "Diary of Captain Julius Mills." This diary is in the Winthrop University Archives, Rock Hill, S.C. A portion of this diary is quoted in Lee and Chepesiuk, *South Carolina in the Civil War*, cited below. Mills was the captain of Company F of the Twenty-third Regiment.

Moore, T. J. One letter in volume 1 of *Recollections and Reminiscences 1861–1865 through World War I*, 89–90, cited below. Private Moore served in Company A of the Holcombe Legion.

Nesbit, William C. Nineteen letters to his wife, Nancy W. Nesbit—five in volume 5 of *Recollections and Reminiscences 1861–1865 through World War I*, 347–52, cited below; fourteen in volume 9 of *Recollections and Reminiscences 1861–1865 through World War I*, 200–214, cited below. The transcriber of the second set of letters misspelled the name as "Nisbet." Nesbit served in Company I of the Seventeenth Regiment.

Palmer, P. G. Copy of a letter dated March 30, 1862, describing a raid on Little Edisto Island and included in the John DeWitt McCollough Papers in the South Caroliniana Library, Columbia, S.C. Palmer was the major of the Holcombe Legion infantry.

Patrick, R. C. Two letters in volume 7 of *Recollections and Reminiscences 1861–1865 through World War I*, 416–17, cited below, and two letters in the Lucile Huggin Papers, in the Winthrop University Archives, Rock Hill, S.C. Patrick was a private in Company F of the Eighteenth Regiment.

Porcher, Francis Peyre. Seven letters in the Waring Historical Library at the Medical University of South Carolina, Charleston, S.C. He was the surgeon of the Holcombe Legion early in 1862.

Pursley, J.Warren. Twenty-three letters in the Mary Frances Jane Pursley Papers, in the Rare Book, Manuscript, and Special Collections Library at Duke University, Durham, N.C. Pursley was a first lieutenant in Company G of the Eighteenth Regiment.

Sloan, James F. Papers—mostly receipts, lists, rolls, and soldiers' leave papers —in the South Caroliniana Library, Columbia, S.C. Captain Sloan organized Company B of the Holcombe Legion.

Spence, Hugh Y. Letters in the Barkeley Family Papers in the Southern Historical Collection, Wilson Library, University of North Carolina, Chapel Hill, N.C. Private Spence served in Company D of the Eighteenth Regiment.

Stevens, Peter Fayssoux. Papers. A large collection of the letters (1839–1866) and papers of Colonel Peter Fayssoux Stevens and his family are held by his descendents.

Stevenson, William Grafton. "Diary of William Grafton Stevenson, Captain, C.S.A." *Alabama Historical Quarterly* 23 (1961): 45–72. This diary was transcribed and edited by his grandson, Carl Rush Stevenson. The original diary is in the collection of the Alabama Department of Archives and History, Montgomery, Alabama.

Sullivan, W. Henry. Letters in the Lalla Pelot Papers in the Rare Book, Manuscript, and Special Collections Library at Duke University, Durham, N.C. Sullivan served in Company C of the Holcombe Legion.

Tuck, W. J. "Diary of W. J. Tuck." This diary was published in volume 6 of *Recollections and Reminiscences 1861–1865 through World War I*, 321–23, cited below. The diary covers the period from August 6, 1864, to April 5, 1865. Tuck served in Company C of the Holcombe Legion.

Vardell, William Gildersleeve. Letters in the South Carolina Historical Society, Charleston, S.C. Although Vardell was the quartermaster of the Twenty-third Regiment, he was detailed to Evans' staff as brigade quartermaster from late March until late June 1863.

Waring, Thomas Smith. Papers in the South Caroliniana Library, Columbia, S.C. For an overview of the wartime and postwar life of Dr. Waring, see W. Curtis Worthington Jr., "Confederate Surgeon: The Letters of Thomas Smith Waring, A South Carolina Planter-Physician at War," *Journal of Confederate History* 2, no. 1 (1989): 55–92. Waring was an assistant surgeon in the Seventeenth Regiment.

Wells, Henry DuPlessis. Letters in the Rare Book, Manuscript, and Special Collections Library, Duke University, Durham, N.C. Wells was a first lieutenant in Company I of the Twenty-third Regiment.

Westcoat, Joseph Julius. "Diary, 1863–1865." Typescript copy in the Rare Book, Manuscript, and Special Collections Library, Duke University, Durham, N.C. This soldier of the Eighteenth Regiment writes of the regiment's excursion to Florida, and also of his capture in 1865 and life in the Old Capitol and Fort Delaware Prisons.

Wilson, William E. "Diary 1862–1863." A typescript copy in the Brockman Family Papers in the South Caroliniana Library, Columbia, S.C. Wilson was a corporal in Company C of the Twenty-second Regiment.

Other Primary Sources

Alexander, Edward Porter. *Fighting for the Confederacy: The Personal Recollections of General Edward Porter Alexander.* Edited by Gary W. Gallagher. Chapel Hill: University of North Carolina Press, 1989.

Andrews, William H. *Footprints of a Regiment: A Recollection of the First Georgia Regulars, 1861–1865.* Atlanta: Longstreet Press, 1991. This regiment was assigned to Anderson's Brigade, a companion brigade to Evans' Brigade for much of the war. Andrews wrote this book in the 1890s, basing it upon his war journals.

Beauregard, P. G. T. "Report of General Beauregard of the Battle of Manassas." In *Official Reports of Battles* (published by order of the Confederate Congress at Richmond). New York: Charles B. Richardson, 1863.

Bernard, George S. *War Talks of Confederate Veterans.* Petersburg: Fenn and Owen Publishers, 1892. This is a collection of addresses delivered before the A. P. Hill Camp of Confederate Veterans of Petersburg, Virginia. The address "The Battle of the Crater," delivered by the author on June 24, 1890, runs from pages 149 to 230. Attempting to fix the time of Mahone's first attack is a major theme of Bernard's talk.

Blackford, Charles Minor III, ed. *Letters from Lee's Army.* New York: Charles Scribner's Sons, 1947.

Boykin, Edward M. *The Falling Flag.* New York: R. J. Hale and Son, 1874. Boykin was a member of Company E of the Holcombe Legion Cavalry and later Lieutenant Colonel of the Seventh Regiment of South Carolina Cavalry.

Brackett, Albert G. *History of the United States Cavalry.* Freeport, N.Y.: Books for Libraries Press, 1974. A photographic reprint of the original edition of 1865.

Broadfoot Publishing Company, comp. *South Carolina Confederate Soldiers.* 2 vols. Wilmington, N.C.: Broadfoot Publishing Company, 1998. Volume 1 contains the name roster and volume 2 contains the unit roster. The names in these references are taken from the microfilm reels of the *Consolidated Index to Compiled Service Records of Confederate Soldiers* in the National Archives, Washington, D.C. Officers at the brigade staff level and higher are not included.

———. *Supplement to the Official Records of the Union and Confederate Armies.* 100 vols. Wilmington, N.C.: Broadfoot Publishing Company, 1994–2000. This work includes information left out of *War of the Rebellion: A Compilation of the Official Records of the Union and Confederate Armies,* cited below.

Brock, R. A., ed. *The Appomattox Roster: a list of the paroles of the Army of Northern Virginia, issued at Appomattox Court House on April 9, 1865.* New

York: Antiquarian Press, 1962. A photographic reprint of the original edition of 1887.

Capers, Ellison. Papers in The Citadel Archives and Museum, Charleston, S.C.

Chamberlain, Joshua Lawrence. *The Passing of the Armies.* New York: Bantam Books edition, January 1993. A reprint of the original edition of 1915.

Chesnut, Mary Boykin. *Mary Chesnut's Civil War.* Edited by C. Vann Woodward. New York: Book-of-the-Month-Club, 1994.

Clark, Walter, ed. *Histories of the Several Regiments and Battalions from North Carolina in the Great War 1861–65: Written by Members of the Respective Commands.* 5 vols. Goldsboro, N.C.: State of North Carolina, 1901. In addition to the unit histories, there is an account of the December 1862 Battle at White Hall, North Carolina, which involved Evans' Brigade.

Coit, James C. "Letter to F. W. McMaster on August 2, 1879." *Southern Historical Society Papers* 10 (1882): 123–30.

Dowdey, Clifford, ed. *The Wartime Papers of Robert E. Lee.* Boston: Little, Brown, and Company, 1961.

Dickert, D. Augustus. *History of Kershaw's Brigade.* Dayton, Ohio: Morningside Bookshop, 1973. A photographic reprint of the original edition of 1899. Chapter 33, "In the Trenches Around Petersburg," includes an account of the Battle of the Crater by Colonel F. W. McMaster.

Featherston, John C. "Battle of the Crater." Address given to the veterans of the Forty-eighth Pennsylvania Regiment, Pottsville, Pennsylvania, April 18, 1906. This address was printed in the *Southern Historical Society Papers* 33 (1905): 358–74 and reprinted in booklet form by the Birmingham Public Library in 1987. Captain Featherston served in Wilcox's Alabama Brigade of General Mahone's Division.

French, Samuel G. *Two Wars: An Autobiography.* Nashville: Confederate Veteran, 1901.

Gordon, John B. *Reminiscences of the Civil War.* New York: Scribners, 1903.

Goree, Thomas J. *Longstreet's Aide: The Civil War Letters of Thomas J. Goree.* Edited by Thomas W. Cutrer. Charlottesville: University Press of Virginia, 1955.

Greene, Francis Vinton. *The Mississippi.* New York: Charles Scribner's Sons, 1882.

Guernsey, Alfred H., and Henry M. Alden. *Harper's Pictorial History of the Civil War.* New York: Harper and Brothers, 1866. Images used as illustrations in the present work are taken from the facsimile edition published by The Fairfax Press in 1977. Each is cited as *Harper's Magazine* and the month of original publication is given.

Hagood, Johnson. *Memoirs of the War of Secession.* Columbia, S.C.: The State Company, 1910.

Haskell, John Cheves. *The Haskell Memoirs.* Edited by G. E. Govan and J. W. Livingood. New York: G. P. Putnam's Sons, 1960.

Hood, J. B. *Advance and Retreat: Personal Experiences in the United States and Confederate Armies.* Lincoln: University of Nebraska Press, 1996. A reprint of the original edition of 1880.

Howe, W. W. *Kinston, Whitehall, and Goldsboro (N.C.) Expedition, December 1862.* New York, 1890. Written and privately printed by a correspondent who was with the Federal troops.

Humphreys, Andrew A. *The Virginia Campaign of '64 and '65.* New York: Charles Scribner's Sons, 1883.

Hunter, R. W. "Men of Virginia at Ball's Bluff." *Southern Historical Society Papers* 34 (1906): 254–74.

Johnson, John. *The Defense of Charleston Harbor, Including Fort Sumter and the Adjacent Islands, 1863–1865.* Charleston: Walker, Evans, and Cogswell, 1890.

Johnson, R. V., and C. C. Buel. *Battles and Leaders of the Civil War.* 4 vols. New York: Century Company, 1884–87. This was originally a series of articles written by Federal and Confederate leaders and published in *The Century* magazine between November 1884 and November 1887. These articles were so popular that they were later published in book form. Many reprint editions have since been published.

Johnson, Richard W. *A Soldier's Reminiscences in Peace and War.* Philadelphia: J. B. Lippincott Company, 1886.

Keitt, Laurence. Typescript copies of letters in the Calhoun County Museum, St. Matthews, S.C.

Lee, Robert E. Confidential letters from Lee to Jefferson Davis in the State Library of Virginia, Richmond, Va.

———. Photocopies of letters from Lee to N. G. Evans in the Douglas Southall Freeman Papers in the Virginia Historical Society, Richmond, Va.

Lipscomb, Thomas S. One letter dated May 11, 1862, in the Lipscomb Family Papers in the Southern Historical Collection, Wilson Library, University of North Carolina, Chapel Hill, N.C. Lipscomb was an Alabama soldier who had friends in the Holcombe Legion.

McCrady, Edward. *Heroes of the Old Camden District, S.C.: An Address to the Survivors of Fairfield County.* 1888. A copy of this pamphlet is in the Special Collections Library, University of Virginia, Charlottesville, Va. This pamphlet was reprinted in *Southern Historical Society Papers* 16 (1888): 3–35.

McGuire, Alexander K., ed., *The Annals of the Civil War Written by Leading Participants North and South*. Philadelphia: Philadelphia Weekly Times Publishing Company, 1879. A collection into book form of a series of newspaper articles written by participants in the war. Each chapter is a first-hand account of a battle, unit, or other aspect of the war.

Military Historical Society of Massachusetts. *Papers*. 13 vols. Boston: 1895–1913.

Miller, E. P. One letter in volume 2 of *Recollections and Reminiscences 1861–1865 through World War I*, 263–65, cited below. He served in one of the Mississippi regiments commanded by Evans at Leesburg

Owen, William Miller. *In Camp and Battle with the Washington Artillery of New Orleans*. Baton Rouge: Louisiana State University Press, 1999. This well-known artillery unit served with Lee's Army of Northern Virginia throughout the war. A photographic reprint of the original edition of 1885. This detailed account, written by the battalion adjutant, includes a good description of the artillery duel at Rappahannock Station.

Polk, Leonidas L. Papers in the Southern Historical Collection, Wilson Library, University of North Carolina, Chapel Hill, N.C.

Pope, John. *The Military Memoirs of General John Pope*. Edited by Peter Cozzens and Robert I. Girardi. Chapel Hill: University of North Carolina Press, 1998. Pope wrote these memoirs as a series of articles for the *National Tribune* between 1887 and 1891.

Price, George F. *Across the Continent with the Fifth Cavalry*. New York: D. van Nostrand, 1883. The Second Cavalry, in which Evans served, became the Fifth Cavalry when the United States renumbered its cavalry units on August 3, 1861.

Records of the Confederate Historian: *Roll of the Dead*. South Carolina Department of Archives and History, Columbia, S.C. Microcopy no. 16, roll 2. This listing was compiled by Prof. William J. Rivers between 1864 and 1870 during the time that he served as the historian of Confederate records.

Roman, Alfred. *The Military Operations of General Beauregard in the War Between the States 1861 to 1865*. New York: Harper and Brothers, 1884. Roman served as colonel of the Eighteenth Louisiana Volunteers and then on the staff of General Beauregard.

Sherman, William T. *Memoirs of General William T. Sherman, By Himself*. New York: D. Appleton and Company, 1875.

Simpson, John Hemphill. A typescript of short-entry diaries for 1861, 1862–63, and 1865 in the State Historical Society of Wisconsin, Madison, Wis. Simpson served as a volunteer chaplain of the Sixth South Carolina Regiment, but there are a few references to the Seventeenth and Twenty-third Regiments.

Sorrel, G. Moxley. *Recollections of a Confederate Staff Officer.* New York: The Neale Publishing Company, 1905.

South Carolina Division of the United Daughters of the Confederacy, comp. *Recollections and Reminiscences 1861–1865 through World War I.* vols. 1–10. Columbia: South Carolina Division of the United Daughters of the Confederacy, 1991–2000. Cited as *Recollections and Reminiscences.*

Stuart, J. E. B. *Letters of General J. E. B. Stuart to his Wife—1861.* Edited by Bingham Duncan. Atlanta: Emory University Library, 1943.

Tidball, John C. "Getting Through West Point." Manuscript in the library of the United States Military Academy, West Point, N.Y. A summary overview may be found as "Getting Through West Point: The Cadet Memoirs of John C. Tidball, Class of 1848," edited by James L. Morrison Jr. in *Civil War History* 26 (1980): 304ff.

United States War Department, comp. *Atlas to Accompany the Official Records of the War of the Rebellion.* Washington, D.C., 1891.

———. *War of the Rebellion: A Compilation of the Official Records of the Union and Confederate Armies.* 128 vols. Washington, D.C., 1880–1901. The standard reference, which includes the orders and general information which came down the chain of command, as well as the official reports of the officers to their superiors after troop movements, battles, etc. Cited as *Official Records.* All references are to Series I unless noted. Available on CD-ROM from Guild Press of Indiana.

Secondary Sources

Arnold, James R. *Jeff Davis's Own: Cavalry, Comanches, and the Battle for the Texas Frontier.* New York: John Wiley and Sons, 2000.

Ballard, Michael B. *A Long Shadow: Jefferson Davis and the Final Days of the Confederacy.* Jackson: University Press of Mississippi, 1986.

Barrett, John Gilcrist. *The Civil War in North Carolina.* Chapel Hill: University of North Carolina Press, 1963.

Bearss, Edwin C. *The Siege of Jackson: July 10–17, 1863.* Baltimore: Gateway Press, 1981.

Beitzell, Edwin W. *Point Lookout Prison Camp for Confederates.* Abell, Md.: Privately printed, 1972.

Brennan, Patrick. *Secessionville: Assault on Charleston.* Campbell, Ca.: Savas Publishing Company, 1998.

Burton, E. Milby. *The Siege of Charleston, 1861–1865.* Columbia: University of South Carolina Press, 1970.

Catton, Bruce. *The Civil War.* New York: American Heritage Press, 1960.

Cavanaugh, Michael A., and William Marvel. *The Battle of the Crater "The Horrid Pit."* Lynchburg, Va.: H. E. Howard, 1989.

Chapman, Craig S. *More Terrible Than Victory: North Carolina's Bloody Bethel Regiment.* Washington, D.C.: Brassey's, 1998.

Chapman, John A. *History of Edgefield County, from the Earliest Settlements to 1897.* Newberry, S.C.: Edward H. Aull Publisher and Printer, 1897.

Conrad, James L. "From Glory to Contention: The Sad History of 'Shanks' Evans." *Civil War Times Illustrated* 22 (September 1983): 32–38.

Cox, Charles D. "Tracking the Holcombe Legion (November 1861–April 1865)." Huntsville, Ala., 1997. This unpublished manuscript is unpaged but is organized by month. A copy is in the South Caroliniana Library, Columbia, S.C.

Cullum, George W. *Biographical Register of the Officers and Graduates of the U.S. Military Academy.* Boston: Houghton, Mifflin, 1891.

Cummings, Charles M. *Yankee Quaker—Confederate General: The Curious Career of Bushrod Rust Johnson.* Columbus, Ohio: The General's Books, 1993.

Davis, Burke. *To Appomattox: Nine April Days, 1865.* New York: Rinehart, 1959.

———. *The Long Surrender.* New York: Random House, 1985.

Davis, William C. *Battle at Bull Run: A History of the First Major Campaign of the Civil War.* Baton Rouge: Louisiana State University Press, 1977.

Dedmondt, Glenn. *Southern Bronze: Capt. Garden's (S.C.) Artillery Company during the War Between the States.* Columbia, S.C.: Palmetto Bookworks, 1993.

Dowdey, Clifford. *Lee Takes Command.* New York: Barnes and Noble, 1994. Originally published in 1964 as *The Seven Days: The Emergence of Lee.*

Duncan, Watson B. *Twentieth Century Sketches of the South Carolina Conference, M. E. Church, South.* Columbia, S.C.: The State Company, 1901.

Evans, Clement A., ed. *Confederate Military History.* 12 vols. Atlanta: Confederate Publishing Company, 1899. Volume 5 focuses on South Carolina.

Evans, James Daniel. *History of Nathaniel Evans of Cat Fish Creek and His Descendants.* Williamsburg [Va.?], 1905.

Fetzer, Dale, and Bruce Mowday. *Unlikely Allies: Fort Delaware's Prison Community in the Civil War.* Mechanicsburg, Pa.: Stackpole Books, 2000.

Fiebeger, Gustave Joseph. *Campaigns of the American Civil War: Atlas.* West Point, N.Y.: United States Military Academy Printing Office, 1914. This atlas accompanied a text with the same title.

Freeman, Douglas Southall. *R. E. Lee.* 4 vols. New York: Charles Scribner's Sons, 1935.

———. *Lee's Lieutenants: a study in Command.* 3 vols. New York: Charles Scribner's Sons, 1942–1944.

Fuller, Claud E. *Confederate Currency and Stamps 1861–1865.* Nashville: Parthenon Press, 1949.

Harsh, Joseph L. *Confederate Tide Rising: Robert E. Lee and the Making of Southern Strategy, 1861–1862.* Kent, Ohio: Kent State University Press, 1998.

Harsh, Joseph L. *Taken at the Flood: Robert E. Lee and Confederate Strategy in the Maryland Campaign of 1862.* Kent, Ohio: Kent State University Press, 1999.

Hemphill, J. C. *Men of Mark in South Carolina; Ideals of American Life: A collection of Biographies of Leading Men in the State.* Vols. 1–4. Washington, D.C.: Men of Mark Publishing Company, 1907–1909.

Hendrick, Carlanna L. "The Ancient and Honorable Lineage of Governor John Gary Evans." A chapter written for, but not included in, her doctoral dissertation, "John Gary Evans—A Political Biography," University of South Carolina, 1966.

Hennessy, John J. *The First Battle of Manassas: An End to Innocence, July 18–21, 1861.* Lynchburg, Va.: H. E. Howard, Inc., 1989.

———. *Return to Bull Run: The Campaign and Battle of Second Manassas.* New York: Simon and Schuster, 1993.

Holien, Kim Bernard. *Battle at Ball's Bluff.* Orange, Va.: Moss Publications, 1985.

Horn, John. *The Petersburg Campaign.* Conshohocken, Pa.: Combined Books, 1993.

Howard, William F. *The Battle of Ball's Bluff: The Leesburg Affair—October 21, 1861.* Lynchburg, Va.: H. E. Howard, 1994.

Kidd, Robert Wade. "A Military History of the Campaigns of the Eighteenth Regiment South Carolina Volunteers During the Civil War." Master's thesis, Winthrop University, Rock Hill, S.C., 1997.

Lee, J. Edward, and Ron Chepesiuk, eds. *South Carolina in the Civil War: The Confederate Experience in Letters and Diaries.* Jefferson, N.C.: McFarland and Company, 2000.

Luker, Ralph E. "The Crucible of the Civil War and Reconstruction in the Experience of William Porcher DuBose," *South Carolina Historical Magazine* 83, no. 1 (1982): 50–71.

Marlow, Clayton Charles. *Matt W. Ransom: Confederate General from North Carolina.* Jefferson, N.C.: McFarland and Company, 1996.

McCrady, Edward Jr., and Samuel A. Ashe. *Eminent and Representative Men of the Carolinas of the Nineteenth Century.* Volume 1: *South Carolina.* Madison, Wis.: Bryant and Fuller, 1892.

Miller, Francis Trevelyan, ed. *The Photographic History of the Civil War.* 10 vols. New York: Review of Reviews, 1911.

Nulty, William H. *Confederate Florida.* Tuscaloosa: University of Alabama Press, 1990.

Patch, Joseph Dorst. *The Battle of Ball's Bluff.* Leesburg, Va.: Potomac Press, 1958.

Pleasants, Henry Jr., and George H. Straley. *Inferno at Petersburg*. Philadelphia: Chilton Company, 1961.

Power, J. Tracy. *Lee's Miserables: Life in the Army of Northern Virginia from the Wilderness to Appomattox.* Chapel Hill: University of North Carolina Press, 1997.

Robertson, William G. *Back Door to Richmond: The Bermuda Hundred Campaign, April–June 1864.* Baton Rouge: Louisiana State University Press, 1987.

Stevens, Robert J. *Captain Bill.* Richburg, S.C.: The Chester District Genealogical Society, 1985.

Trudeau, Noah Andre. *The Last Citadel: Petersburg, Virginia, June 1864–April 1865.* Boston: Little, Brown and Company, 1991.

Wilkinson, Warren. *Mother, May You Never See the Sights I Have Seen.* New York: Harper and Row, 1990.

Williams, T. Harry. *P. G. T. Beauregard: Napoleon in Gray.* Baton Rouge: Louisiana State University Press, 1955.

Wilson, Clyde N. *Carolina Cavalier: The Life and Mind of James Johnson Pettigrew.* Athens: University of Georgia Press, 1990.

Wilson, John M. *I Have Looked Death in the Face.* Kingsport, Tenn: Paint Rock Publishing Company, 1996.

Zuczek, Richard. *State of Rebellion: Reconstruction in South Carolina.* Columbia: University of South Carolina Press, 1996.

Index

Grateful acknowledgement is made to the following publishers for permission to publish images in their possession or from previously published sources:

To Charles D. Cox, for use of a photograph of Dock Owen.

To Harold Howard, for permission to reproduce maps by Blake Magner from Mike Cavanaugh, *The Petersburg Campaign: The Battle of the Crater "The Horrid Pit," June 25–August 6, 1864.* Virginia Civil War Battles and Leaders Series (Lynchburg: H. E. Howard), 1989.

To U.S. Army Military History Institute, Carlislie Barracks, Pa., for permission to reproduce a photograph of Col. Henry L. Benbow from the Rod Gragg Collection.

To U.S. Army Military History Institute, Carlislie Barracks, Pa., for permission to reproduce a photograph of Col. John Hugh Means from the Fitzhugh McMaster Collection.

To The Citadel Archives and Museum, Charleston, S.C., for use of a photograph of Peter Fayssoux Stevens.

To Laura N. Vardell, Charleston, S.C., for use of a photograph of William G. Vardell.

To the South Caroliniana Library, University of South Carolina, Columbia, for use of several images.

To the University of the South, Sewanee, Tenn., for use of a photograph of WIlliam Porcher Dubose.

To the Oakley Park Historic Home, Edgefield, S.C., for the portrait of Gen. Nathan G. Evans.

To the Calhoun County Museum, St. Matthews, S.C., for use of a photograph of Olin M. Dantzler and Caleb Glover.

To the Center for Virginia History, Virginia Historical Society, Richmond, Va., for the image of Gen. Nathan G. Evans.

To Celeste Phillips, for use of a photograph of Welborn J. Andrews.

Grateful acknowledgement is made to the following publishers for permission to publish previously unpublished material:

To Susan Vardell Smyth Lindenberger of Blowing Rock, N.C., for the letters of William Gildersleeve Vardell.

To the Rare Book, Manuscript, and Special Collections Library of Duke University (Confederate Veteran Papers), for the excerpts from the manuscript, "Reminiscences," of John Forrest Robertson; and from William A. Martin Papers; from Lalla Pelot Papers; from Mary Frances Jane Pursley Papers.

To the Alabama Department of Archives and History, Montgomery, Ala., for quotations from the diary of William Grafton Stevenson.

To the Southern Historical Collection, Manuscripts Department, University of North Carolina at Chapel Hill, for the Lewis M. Hatch Papers and William Porcher Dubose Reminisces.

To Cynthia Mosely of Spartanburg, S.C., for the manuscripts of Peter Fayssoux Stevens.

To the South Caroliniana Library, Univerisity of South Carolina, for the letters of Stephen Elliott, William L. Faulkner, A. H. Lister, Fitz William McMaster.

To Marie J. Pigott of Fayetteville, N.C., for a letter of D. J. Blanton.

To Special Collections, Robert W. Woodruff Library, Emory University, for excerpts from the diary of John Alfred Feister.

CUMBERLAND MOUNTAINS
TENNESSEE
Abingdon
SMOKY MOUNTAINS
Jefferson
Germantown
Jonesboro
BLUE RIDGE
Wilkesboro
Burnsville
Statesville
GREAT
Morgantown
Salisbury
NORTH
Lincolnton
Asheville
Waynesville
Rutherfordton
Hendersonville
Charlotte
Franklin
Murphy
Spartanburg
Yorkville
Greenville
Clayton
Pickens
Wateree
Lancaster
Chester
Broad R.
GEORGIA
Anderson
Laurensville
Lynchwo
SOUTH
Newberry
Camden
Abbeville
Saluda R.
COLUMBIA
Savannah
Lexington
Congaree R.
Edgefield
CAROL
CHARLESTON HARBOR
SCALE OF MILES
0 1 2 3 4
Orangeburg
Augusta
Windsor
Edisto R.
Silverton
City of Charleston
Mt. Pleasant
Barnwell
Bamberg
R.
CHARLESTON HARBOR
SULLIVAN ISLAND
Fort Moultrie
Walterboro
Fort Johnson
JAMES ISLAND
Fort Sumter
Gillisonville
Gregg's Point
MORRIS ISLAND
Fort Wagner
ATLANTIC OCEAN
Beaufort
Fort Bea
Port Rogal
Fort Walke
FOLLY ISLAND
Savannah
Fort Pulaski